COMPLEX VARIABLE

By

S.C. Sharma

DISCOVERY PUBLISHING HOUSE
NEW DELHI-110002

First Published – 2007

Reprinted – 2024

ISBN: 978-81-8356-208-9

Complex Variable

Published by:

DISCOVERY PUBLISHING HOUSE PVT. LTD.
4383/4B, Ansari Road, Darya Ganj
New Delhi-110 002 (India)
Phone: +91-11-23279245; 23253475; 43596065
Mobile: +91 9811179893 / +91 9871656464
E-mail: discoverypublishinghouse@gmail.com
orderdphbooks@gmail.com
web: www.discoverypublishinggroup.com

Printed at:
Infinity Imaging Systems
Delhi

Preface

The book Complex Variable has been written for the students of degree honours and post-graduate students of various Indian Universities on the subject. The language of this book is simple and easily understandable. The proofs of various theorems and examples have been given with minute details. The numerous solved examples have been given which will help the readers in understanding various concepts easily the book also contains a set of exercises at the end of each topic.

Suggestions for the improvement of the book will be gratefully acknowledge.

Author

CONTENTS

4. Analytic Functions **213**

Complex differentiation, Function of a Complex Variable, Limits and Continuity, Differentiability, Multiple Valued Functions; Branches, Analytic Function, The Necessary and Sufficient Conditions for f(z) to be Analytic, Orthogonal System, Harmonic Function, Determination of the Conjugate Function, Methods of Constructing A Regular Function, Polar Form of Cauchy-Riemann Equations, Derivative of w = f(z) in Polar Form, A Sufficient Condition for Continuity, Differentiability at a Point, Schwarz's and Young's Theorems, Directional Derivatives, Maxima and Minima of Functions of Two Variables, Maxima and Minima Subject to Constraints, Extreme Points of a Function of Three Variables, Lagrange's Method of Undetermined Multipliers, Solved Examples, Exercises.

1

COMPLEX VARIABLE

INTRODUCTION

The extension to the concept of complex numbers from that of real numbers was first necessiated by the solution of algebraical equations. The equations $x^2 + 1 = 0$ and $x^2 - 2x + 3 = 0$, for example, cannot be satisfied by any number in the domain of real numbers. Euler (1707-1783) was first to introduce the symbol i for the square root of -1 with the property, $i^2 = -1$. It was Gauss (1777-1855) who first proved in a satisfactory manner that every algebraic equation with real coefficients has complex roots of the form $a + bi$, the real roots being a particular case of complex numbers for which the coefficient of i is zero. His approach to the concept of complex number was geometrical. Hamilton (1805-1865) also made a great contribution to the development of the theory of complex numbers. His approach was arithmetical.

The concept of complex variable was usefully applied to great variety of problems formerly studied through real functions. Faulty proofs were replaced by more satisfactory ones and a foundation for further progress was thus secured. By means of complex integral calculus it was possible to evaluate a large number of new definite integrals. The theory of differential equations was marvellously developed. The use of complex variable was also made in other sciences. For example, the flow of electricity and the conduction of heat in two dimensions was studied through this medium. As a matter of fact, the application of mathematics to other sciences has made it indispensable to have some knowledge of the theory of analytic functions of a complex variable.

Amongst the great mathematicians who have done immense work towards the development of theory of analytic functions, the name of the French mathematician Cauchy (1789-1857) and the two Germans Riemann (1836-66) and Weierstrass (1815-97) are worth mentioning.

Now assuming the *theory of the aggregates* of real numbers, we proceed to define the complex numbers and the four fundamental algebric operations.

Definition:

A complex number may be defined as an ordered pair of real numbers and may be denoted by the symbol (x, y). If we write z = (x,y), then x is called the real port and y the imaginary part of the complex number z and may be denoted by R (z) and I (z) respectively.

It is clear from the definition that two complex numbers (x, y) and (x', y') are equal if and only if x = x' and y = y'.

We shall denote the set of all complex numbers by the symbol C.

Sum of two complex numbers: The sum of two complex numbers (x,y) and (x', y') is defined by the equality

$$(x, y) + (x', y') = (x + x', y + y').$$

Product of two complex numbers: The product is defined by the equality

$$(x, y) \times (x', y') = (xx' - yy' \; xy' + yx').$$

The symbol i: It is customary to denote the complex number (0, 1) by the symbol i. With this notation

$$i^2 = (0, 1).(0, 1) = (0.0 - 1.1, 0.1 + 1.0) = (-1, 0)$$

so that i may be regarded as the square root of the real number − 1.

Using the symbol i, we may write the complex number (x, y) as x + iy. For, we have

$$\begin{aligned}(x + iy) &= (x, 0) + (0, 1) \,.\, (y, 0)\\ &= (x, 0) + (0.y - 1.0, 0.0 + 1.y)\\ &= (x, 0) + (0, y) = (x + 0, 0 + y) = (x, y).\end{aligned}$$

Remark:

$\because$ $i = \sqrt{1}$ and $i^2 = -1$, we have

$(\sqrt{-1})^2 = (-1).\sqrt{(-1)} = 1$ ...(1)

Again since $\{\sqrt{a}.\sqrt{(-1)}\}^2 = \{\sqrt{a}.\sqrt{-1}\} \times \{\sqrt{a}.\sqrt{-1}\}$

$= (\sqrt{a})^2 \{\sqrt{(-1)}\}^2 = a(-1) = -a$ ...(2)

Hence $\sqrt{-a}$ means the product of $\sqrt{a}$ and $\sqrt{-1}$. Students must note carefully the results (1) and (2). Keeping these results in mind the following computation is correct

$\sqrt{(-a)}.\sqrt{(-b)} = \sqrt{a}.\sqrt{(-1)}.\sqrt{b}.\sqrt{(-1)}$

$= \sqrt{a}.\sqrt{b}.(\sqrt{-1})^2 = -ab$. But the computation

$\sqrt{\{(-a).\sqrt{(-b)}\}} = \sqrt{\{(-a).(\sqrt{b})\}} = \sqrt{(ab)}$ is wrong.

COMPLEX NUMBERS

A complex number is a number which can be written in the form a + ib, where a and b are real numbers and $i = \sqrt{-1}$. It is generally denoted by single letter z. The real number a is called the real part of the complex number z = a + ib and the real number b is called the imaginary part of z.

A complex number is also defined as ordered pair (a, b) of real numbers. Thus, if z if a complex number, then

$z = a + ib = (a, b)$ for some $a, b \in R$.

we can write $z = \text{Re}(z) + i \text{ Im}(z)$

In other words, any order pair of real numbers x, y written as (x, y) is called a *Complex Number*. The equation $x^2 = -1$ has no solution in the set of real numbers because the square of every real number is either positive or zero. Therefore use feel the necessity to extend the system of real numbers. We all know that this defect is remedied by introducing complex numbers.

Definition : A number of the from x + iy, where 1 + j(–1) and x, y are both real numbers, is called a complex number. A complex number is also defined as on ordered pair (x, y) of real number. A complex number x + iy or (x, y) is usually denoted by the symbol z. If we write z = x + iy or (x, y) then x is called the real part and y the imaginary part of the complex number $z = \sqrt{3} + 5i$. We have R(z) = the real part of $z = \sqrt{3}$, and 1(z) = the imaginary part of z = 5.

The complex number a + 0; is simply written as a.

We shall denote the set of all complex number by c.

Equality of Two Complex Numbers

Definition : Two complex numbers

$z_1 = x_1 + iy_1$ or (x_1, y_1) and $z_2 = x_2 + iy_2$ or (x_2, y_2)

are said to be equal if $x_1 = x_2$ and $y_1 = y_2$. Thus, two complex number are equal if and only if the real part of one is equal to the real part of the other and the imaginer part of one is equal to the imaginary part of the other.

ADDITION OF COMPLEX NUMBERS

If zi = $x_1 + iy_1$ or (x_1, y_1) and $z_2 = x_2 + iy_2$ or (x_2, y_2) are any two complex numbers, then the sum of z_1 and z_2 written as $z_1 + z_2$ is defined by

$z_1 + z_2 = (x_1 + iy_1) + (x_2 + iy_2) = (x_1 + x_2) = i(y_1 + y_2)$

or $z_1 + z_2 = (x_1, y_1) + (x_2, y_2) = (x_1 + x_2, y_1 + y_2)$

Thus, $(3 + 51) + (7 - 8i) = (3 + 7) + (5 - 8) = 10 - 3i$.

Properties of the Addition of Complex Numbers

The addition of complex numbers is commutative, associative admits of identity element and every complex number possesses additive inverse.

Set of Complex Numbers

The set of complex numbers is denoted by C, where

$$C = \{z \mid z = a + ib, a, b, \in, R\}$$

or $$C = \{z \mid z = (a, b), ab \in R\}$$

In other words the Cartesian product $R \times R$ Consisting of the ordered pairs of real numbers is called the set of complex numbers

Equality of Two Numbers

Two complex numbers are said to be equal if and only if their real and imaginary parts are separately equal, *i.e.*,

$$a + ib = c + id$$

$$\Leftrightarrow \quad a = c \text{ and } b = d.$$

Negative of a Complex Number

The complex $-z = -a - ib$ is called the negative of the complex number $z = a + ib$ and vice–versa.

Zero Complex Number

The complex number $z = a + ib$, a, b, $\in R$ is said to be zero complex number or zero of C if only $a = O$ and $b = O$.

Conjugate of a Complex Number

Two complex numbers (a, b) and (a, – b) are said to be complex conjugate to each other. In other words, the two complex numbers of the type $a + ib$ and $a — ib$ are said to be complex conjugate to each other. The conjugate of a number $z = a + ib$ is denoted by $z = a - ib = Re(z) - i\, Im(z)$.

Properties of Conjugate

1. $\overline{(\overline{z})} = z$

2. $z + \overline{z} = (a + ib) + (a — ib) = 2a = 2$ Real z or 2 Re z (where real z means the real part of z)

3. $z - \overline{z} = (a + ib) - (a - ib) = 2ib = 2i \times$ Imaginary z or $-2i$ Im z (Where imaginary z or Im z Means the imaginary part of z)

4. $z..\bar{z} = (a + ib)(a - ib) = a^2 + b^2 = \bar{z}.z$

   It may be noted that the conjugate of a real number is the real number it self.

RECIPROCAL OF A COMPLEX NUMBER

Let z = a + ib be a non-zero complex number. Then $\frac{1}{z} = \frac{1}{a+ib}$

$$\Rightarrow \frac{1}{a+ib} \times \frac{a-ib}{a-ib}$$

$$\Rightarrow \frac{a-ib}{a^2 - i^2 - b^2} = \frac{a-ib}{a^2+b^2} = \frac{a}{a^2+b^2} + \frac{i(-b)}{a^2+b^2}$$

Clearly, 1/2 is equal to the multiplicative inverse of z. Also

$$\frac{1}{z} = \frac{a-ib}{a^2+b^2} + i\frac{(-\operatorname{Im}(z))}{|z|^2} = \frac{\bar{z}}{|z|^1}$$

Thus, the multiplicative inverse of a non-zero complex number z is same as its reciprocal and is given by

$$\frac{\operatorname{Re}(z)}{|z|^2} + i\frac{(-\operatorname{Im}(z))}{|z|^2} = \frac{\bar{z}}{|z|^2}$$

LOGARITHM OF COMPLEX NUMBER

In order to find log (x + iy) we write log(x + iy) = a + ib

$$x + iy = e^{a+ib} = e^a [\cos b + i \sin b]$$
$$= e^a [\cos (2k\pi + b) + i \sin (2k\pi + b]$$

$\therefore e^x \cos (2k\pi + b) = x$ and $e^a \sin (2k\pi + b) = y$

Solve for a and b $\therefore e^{2a} = x^2 + y^2$

or $a = 1/2 \ln (x^2 + y^2)$, $\tan (2k\pi + b) = (y/x)$

When k = 0 corresponding values of a and b are referred to as principal values.

METHOD TO FIND $(x + iy)^{a+ib}$

To evaluate $(x + iy)^{a+ib}$ we write

$c + id = (x + iy)^{a+ib}$

$\log (c + id) = (a + ib) \log (x + iy)$

Now evaluate log (x + iy) and then solve

$c + id = e^{(a+ib) \log (x+iy)}$.

MODULUS AND ARGUMENT

The moduls of a complex number $z = a + ib$ is denoted by $| z |$ and is defined as

$$|z| = \sqrt{a^2 + b^2} = \sqrt{\{Re(z)\}^2 + \{Im(z)\}^2}$$

Clearly $| z | \geq 0$ for all $z \in c$.

Argument

If $r \neq O$, the angle θ such that $\theta = \tan^{-1}(y/x)$ is called the argument or amplitude of the complex number $z = x + iy$ and is denoted by $\theta = \arg. z$.

It is important to note that if θ is an argument of z, then $2\pi + \theta$ os also an argument of z as $\cos(2\pi + \theta) = \cos\theta$, $\sin(2\pi + \theta) = \sin\theta$.

In general $2n\pi + \theta$, $n \in N$, is also an argument of z, if θ is it argument. The value of θ which lies between π and $-\pi$ is called the principal value of the argument.

Unimodular Complex Number

A complex number z such that $|z| = 1$ is said to be unimodular complex number since $| z | = 1$ z lies on a circle of radius 1 unit and centre (0, 0) If

$$z = 1 \Rightarrow z = \cos\theta + i\sin\theta$$

$$\Rightarrow 1/z = (\cos\theta + \sin\theta)^{-1} = \cos\theta - i\sin\theta.$$

POLAR REPRESENTATION OF A COMPLEX NUMBER

This representation $z = r(\cos\theta + i\sin\theta)$, where $r = \sqrt{x^2 + y^2}$ and $\theta = \tan^{-1}(y/x)$ is known as the trigonometrical or Polar representation of a complex number z. The non- negative real number $\sqrt{x^2 + y^2}$ called the modulus or absolute value of complex number $z = a + ib$ and is denoted by $| z |$ *i.e.*, $|z| = \sqrt{x^2 + y^2}$ Also $z = x^2 + y^2 = | z | z$

FOUR FUNDAMENTAL OPERATIONS

If $z_1 = a + ib_2$ and $z_2 = c + id$, then

$$z_1 + z_2 = (a + c) + (b + d)i \quad \text{(Addition)}$$

$$z_1 - z_2 = (a - c) + (b - d)i \quad \text{(Subtraction)}$$

$$z_1 z_2 = (ac - bd) + (ad + bc)i \quad \text{(Multiplication)}$$

$$\frac{z_1}{z_2} = \frac{a+bi}{c+di} = \frac{(a+bi)(c+di)}{c^2+d^2} \qquad \text{(Division)}$$

$$= \left[\frac{ac+bd}{c^2+d^2}\right] + \left(\frac{bc=ad}{c^2+c^2}\right) i$$

Important Results

1. $| z | = | -z | = | \bar{z} | = | -\bar{z} |$.
2. $z + \bar{z} = 2 \text{ Re } (z)$.
3. $z - \bar{z} = 2i \ \text{ Im } (z)$.
4. $z. \bar{z} = | z | 2$.
5. $| z_1 + z_2 | \leq | z_1 | + z_2 |$.
6. $| z_1 - z_2 | \geq | z_1 | - z_2 |$.
7. $| z_1 . z_2 | = | z_1 | . z_2 |$.
8. $\left|\frac{z_1}{z_2}\right| = (1z_1 |/ 1z_2|). (z_2 \neq 0)$.
9. $\text{Arg } (z_1 . z_2) = \text{Arg } (z_1) + \text{Arg } (z_2)$
10. $\text{Arg} \left[\frac{z_1}{z_2}\right] = \text{Arg } (z_1) — \text{Arg } (z_2) \ (z_2 \neq 0)$.

DE-MOIVRE'S THEOREM

Definition : If n is an integer, positive or negative, or a rational, number, then the value or one of the value or one or the values of $(\cos \theta + i \sin \theta)$" is $(\cos n \theta + i \sin n \theta)$.

Statement

(i) If n is any integer, then

$(\cos \theta + i \sin \theta)^n = \cos n\theta + i \sin n\theta$.

(ii) If n is a rational number, then the value or one of the values of $(\cos \theta + i \sin \theta)^n$ is $\cos n\theta + i \sin n\theta$.

(iii) If $z = r (\cos \theta + i \sin \theta)$ and n is a positive integer, then

$$z^{1/n} = r^{1/n}\left[\cos\left(\frac{2k\pi + \theta}{n}\right) + i \sin\left(\frac{2k\pi + \theta}{n}\right)\right],$$

where $k = 0, 1, 2, ..., n - 1$.

$\cos \theta + i \sin \theta$ is denoted by cis θ or $e^{i\theta}$.

Thus cis $\theta = e^{i\theta} = \cos \theta + i \sin \theta$.

Note: $|e^{i\theta}| = 1$.

nth Roots of Unity : Let x be a nth root of unity.

Then $x^n = 1 = \cos(2r\pi) + i\sin(2r\pi);\ r \in I$

$\Rightarrow$ $x = [\cos(2r\pi) + i\sin(2r\pi)]^{1/n};\ r \in I$

$= \cos\frac{2r\pi}{n} + i\sin\frac{2r\pi}{n};$

$r = 0, 1, 2, \ldots, n-1$ [De-Moivre's Theorem]

If $\omega = \cos\frac{2\pi}{n} + i\sin\frac{2\pi}{n},$

then nth roots of unity are $1, \omega, \omega^2, \ldots \omega^{n-1}$.

Result : *Sum of nth roots of unity is zero.*

$$1 + \omega + \omega^2 + \ldots + \omega^{n-1} = \frac{1-\omega^n}{1-\omega}$$

$$= \frac{1}{1-\omega}\left[1 - \left\{\cos\left(\frac{2\pi}{n}\right) + i\sin\left(\frac{2\pi}{n}\right)\right\}^n\right]$$

$$= \frac{1}{1-\omega}[1 - \{\cos(2\pi) + i\sin(2\pi)\}]$$ [De-Moivre's Theorem]

$$= \frac{1}{1-\omega}[1 - (1 + i(0)] = 0.$$

Some Results Based on De-moivre's Theorem

1. $(\cos\theta + i\sin\theta)^n = \cos n\theta + i\sin n\theta$.
2. $(\cos\theta + i\sin\theta)^n = \cos n\theta - i\sin n\theta$
3. $(\cos\theta + i\sin\theta)^{-n} = \cos n\theta - i\sin n\theta$.

CUBE ROOTS OF UNITY

The three cube roots of unity are 1, w and w^2, *i.e.*, $x = 1$;

$x = \frac{1+i\sqrt{3}}{2} = w,\ x = \frac{-1-i\sqrt{3}}{2} = w^2$.

Properties of Cube Roots of Unity

(i) $1 + w + w^2 = o$.

(ii) $w^3 = 1$.

(iii) $w^{3n} = 1,\ w^{3+1} = w,\ w^{3n+2} = w^2$

(iv) $a + bw + cw^2 = o \Rightarrow a = b = c$, if a, b, c, are real.

Important Relations in Complex Numbers

(i) $x^2 + y^2 = (x + yi)(x - yi)$

(ii) $x^3 + y^3 = (x + y)(x + wy)(x + w^2y)$.

(iii) $x^3 - y^3 = (x - y)(x - wy)(x - w^2y)$

(iv) $x^2 + y^2 + z^3 - 3xyz = (x + y + y)(x + wy + w^2z)(x + w^2y + wz)$.

(v) $x^2 + y^2 + z^2 - xy - yz - yz - zx = (x + wx + w^2z\ (z + w^2y + wz)$.

(vi) $1 = \cos 0 + i \sin 0$; $w = \cos(2\pi/3) + i \sin(2\pi/3)$

$$w^2 = \cos\left(-\frac{2\pi}{3}\right) + i \sin\left[-\frac{2\pi}{3}\right] = \bar{w}$$

$|w| = |w^2| = 1$.

(vii) $(1 - w + w^2)(1 - w^2 + w^4)(1 - w^4 + w^8)$. –2n factors $= 2^{2n}$

(viii) Euler's theorem : $e^{i\theta} = \cos\theta + i \sin\theta$.

(ix) Exponential representation of z : $z = re^{i\theta}$

(x) nth roots of unity: the n roots are $z = 1$,

$$-e\ i\ (2p/n)\ i \text{ ----- } e\ \frac{i2(N-1)\pi}{n}\ \frac{i2\pi k}{n}$$

$z = e$, $k = 0, 1, 2, \ldots\ (\infty - 1)$

$$\Rightarrow z = \cos\left(\frac{2\pi k}{n}\right) + i \sin\left(\frac{2\pi k}{n}\right), k = 0, 1, 2 \text{ ---- } (n-1)$$

PROPERTIES

Property I.

(i) $|z_1 + z_2|^2 = |z_1|^2 + |z_2|^2 + 2\text{Re}(z_1 \bar{z}_2)$

(ii) $|z_1 - z_2|^2 = |z_1|^2 + |z_2|^2 + 2\text{Re}(z_1 \bar{z}_2)$

(iii) $|z_1 + z_2|^2 + |z_1 - z_2|^2 = 2(|z_1|^2 + |z_2|^2)$.

Property II.

$|z_1 z_2| = |z_1||z_2|$.

In Words : *The absolute value of the product of two complex numbers is equal to the product of the absolute values of the numbers.*

Property III. Triangle Inequality

$|z_1 + z_2| + |z_1| + |z_2|$.

In Words : *The modulus of the sum of two complex numbers cannot be greater than the sum of their moduli.*

Proof:

Let $\quad z_1 = x_1 + iy_1$ and $z_2 = x_2 + iy_2$

so that $\quad |z_1| = \sqrt{x_1^2 + y_1^2}$ and $|z_2| \sqrt{x_2^2 + y_2^2}$.

Now $\quad z_1 + z_2 = (x_1 + iy_1) + (x_2 + iy_2) = (x_1 + y_1) + i(y_1 + y_2)$

so that $\quad |z_1 + z_2| = \sqrt{(x_1 + x_2)^2 + (y_1 + y_2)^2}$.

Now $|z_1 + z_2| \leq |z_1| + |z_2|$ holds true

$\Leftrightarrow \quad \sqrt{(x_1 + x_2)^2 + (y_1 + y_2)^2} \leq \sqrt{x_1^2 + y_1^2} + \sqrt{x_2^2 + y_2^2}$

$\Leftrightarrow (x_1 + x_2)^2 + (y_1 + y_2)^2 \leq (x_1^2 + y_1^2) + (x_2^2 + y_2^2)$

$+ 2\sqrt{x_1^2 + y_1^2}\sqrt{x_2^2 + y_2^2}$ [Squaring]

$\Leftrightarrow 2x_1 x_2 + 2y_1 y_2 \leq + 2\sqrt{x_1^2 + y_1^2}\sqrt{x_2^2 + y_2^2}$

$\Leftrightarrow x_1 x_2 + y_1 y_2 \leq \sqrt{x_1^2 + y_1^2}\sqrt{x_2^2 + y_2^2}$

$\Leftrightarrow (x_1 x_2 + y_1 y_2)^2 \leq (x_1^2 + y_1^2)(x_2^2 + y_2^2)$ [Squaring]

$\Leftrightarrow \quad x_1^2 x_2^2 + y_1^2 y_2^2 + 2x_1x_2y_1y_2 \leq x_1^2 x_2^2 + x_1^2 y_2^2 + x_2^2 y_1^2 + y_1^2 y_2^2$

$\Leftrightarrow \quad 0 \leq x_1^2 y_2^2 + x_2^2 y_1^2 - 2x_1x_2y_1y_2$

$\Leftrightarrow \quad 0 \leq (x_1 y_2 - x_2 y_2)^2$. which is true.

[$\because$ A perfect sq. of a real number is never –ve]

Extension $|z_1 + z_2 + \ldots + x_n| \leq |z_1| - |z_2| + \ldots + |z_n|$.

Property IV.

$$\left|\frac{z_1}{z_2}\right| = \frac{|z_1|}{|z_2|}, \; z_2 \neq 0.$$

In Words : *The absolute value of the quotient of two complex numbers (denominator being non-zero) is equal to the quotient of the absolute values of the numbers.*

Property V.

$$|z_1 - z_2| \geq ||z_1| - |z_2||.$$

In Words : *The modulus of the difference of two complex numbers cannot be less than the modulus of the difference of their moduli.*

Property VI.

$$|z_1 - z_2| \geq |z_1| - |z_2|.$$

In Words : *The modulus of the difference of two complex numbers cannot be less than the difference of their moduli.*

Proof:

Here $\quad z_1 - z_2 = (x_1 + iy_1) - (x_2 + iy_2)$

$= (x_1 - x_2) + i(y_1 - y_2)$

so that $\quad | z_1 - z_2 | = \sqrt{(x_1 - x_2)^2 + (y_1 - y_2)^2}$

Now $| z_1 - z_2 | \geq | z_1 | - | z_2 |$ holds true

$$\Leftrightarrow \sqrt{(x_1 - x_2)^2 + (y_1 - y_2)^2} \geq \sqrt{x_1^2 + y_1^2} - \sqrt{x_2^2 + y_2^2}$$

$$\Leftrightarrow (x_1 - x_2)^2 + (y_1 - y_2)^2 \geq (x_1^2 + y_1^2) + (x_2^2 + y_2^2) - 2\sqrt{x_1^2 + y_1^2}\sqrt{x_2^2 + y_2^2} \quad \text{[Squaring]}$$

$$\Leftrightarrow -2x_1x_2 - 2y_1y_2 \geq -2\sqrt{x_1^2 + y_1^2}\sqrt{x_2^2 + y_2^2}$$

$$\Leftrightarrow x_1x_2 + y_1y_2 \leq \sqrt{x_1^2 + y_1^2}\sqrt{x_2^2 + y_2^2} \quad \text{[Dividing by } -2\text{]}$$

$$\Leftrightarrow (x_1x_2 + y_1y_2)^2 \leq (x_1^2 + y_1^2)(x_2^2 + y_2^2) \quad \text{[Squaring]}$$

$$\Leftrightarrow x_1^2x_2^2 + y_1^2y_2^2 + 2x_1x_2y_1y_2 \leq x_1\,x_2^2 + x_1^2\,y_2^2 + x_2^2\,y_1^2 + y_1^2y_2^2$$

$$\Leftrightarrow 0 \leq x_1^2\,y_2^2 + x_2^2\,y_1^2 - 2x_1x_2y_1y_2$$

$$\Leftrightarrow 0 \leq (x_1\,y_2 - x_2\,y_1)^2, \text{ which is true.}$$

[$\because$ A perfect sq. of a real number is never – ve]

SOLVED EXAMPLES

Example 1:

Determine the region for which

$| z - 1 | + | z + 1 | \leq 4.$

Solution:

Let $\quad z = x + iy$

in the L.H.S. of given inequality, we have

$| z - 1 | + | z + 1 | = | x + iy - 1 | + | x + iy + 1 |$

$= | (x - 1) + iy | + | (x + 1) + iy |$

$$= \sqrt{(x-1)^2 + y^2} + \sqrt{(x+1)^2 + y^2}$$

Thus, $\sqrt{(x-1)^2 + y^2} + \sqrt{(x+1)^2 + y^2} \leq 4$

$\Rightarrow$ $\sqrt{(x+1)^2 + y^2} \leq 4 - \sqrt{(x-1)^2 + y^2}$

Squaring both sides, we have

$$(x+1)^2 + y^2 \leq [4 - \sqrt{(x-1)^2 + y^2}]^2$$

$\Rightarrow$ $(x+1)^2 + y^2 \leq 16 + (x-1)^2 + y^2 - 8\sqrt{(x-1)^2 + y^2}$

$\Rightarrow$ $8\sqrt{(x-1)^2 + y^2} \leq 16 + (x-1)^2 - (x+1)^2$

$\Rightarrow$ $8\sqrt{(x-1)^2 + y^2} \leq 16 - 4x$

$\Rightarrow$ $2\sqrt{(x-1)^2 + y^2} \leq 4 - x$

Squaring both sides, we have

$$4[x-1)^2 + y^2] \leq (4-x)^2$$

$\Rightarrow$ $4x^2 - 8x + 4 + 4y^2 \leq 16 - 8x + x^2$

$\Rightarrow$ $3x^2 + 4y^2 \leq 12$

$\Rightarrow$ $\frac{x^2}{4} + \frac{y^2}{3} \leq 1.$

The equation $\frac{x^2}{4} + \frac{y^2}{3} = 1$ represents an ellipse.

Hence, the relation $\frac{x^2}{4} + \frac{y^2}{3} \leq 1$ represents the region, which is interior and boundary of the ellipse

$$\frac{x^2}{4} + \frac{y^2}{3} = 1.$$

Example 22:

Locate the complex numbers

$z = x + iy$ for which $\log_{1/2} \frac{|z-1|+4}{3|z-1|-2} > 1.$

Solution:

For logarithm to be positive, we must have

$$3\,|z-1|-2>0 \Rightarrow 3\,|z-1|=2$$

$$\Rightarrow \qquad |z-1|>\frac{2}{3} \qquad \ldots(1)$$

By the law of logarithms, $\dfrac{|z-1|+4}{3|z-1|-2}<\dfrac{1}{2}$

$\Rightarrow 2\,|z-1|+8<3\,|z-1|-2$

$\Rightarrow 10<|z-1| \Rightarrow |z-1|>10.$

This does not contradict (1).

Hence, the points z lie in the exterior to the circle with centre (1, 0) and radius 10.

Solution 10:

If 1, ω, ω² be cube roots of unity, prove that $(x-y)(x\omega-y)(x\omega^2-y) = x^3-y^3$.

Solution:

$$\begin{aligned}
\text{L.H.S.} &= (x-y)(x\omega-y)(x\omega^2-y)\\
&= (x-y)[x^2\omega^3 - xy\omega - xy\omega^2 + y^2]\\
&= (x-y).[x^2\omega^3 - (\omega+\omega^2)xy + y^2]\\
&= (x-y).[x^2.\,1 - (-1)xy + y^2)\\
&\qquad\qquad [\because \omega^2 = 1 \text{ and } 1+\omega+\omega^2 = 0]\\
&= (x-y)(x^2+xy+y^2) = x^3-y^3\\
&= \text{R.H.S.}
\end{aligned}$$

Example 30:

Find the tenth roots of unity and show that the product of any two of them is again one of the tenth roots of unity.

Solution:

Since
$$\begin{aligned}
1 &= \cos 0 + i\sin 0\\
&= \cos 2n\pi + i\sin 2n\pi;\ n\in I
\end{aligned}$$

$$\therefore \qquad (1)^{1/10} = (\cos 2n\pi + i\sin 2n\pi)^{1/10}$$

$$= \cos\frac{n\pi}{5} + i\sin\frac{n\pi}{5};\ n = 1, 2, \ldots, 9$$

$$n = 0;\ \cos 0 + i\sin 0 = 1 = r_1$$

$$n = 1;\ \cos\frac{\pi}{5} + \sin\frac{\pi}{5} = r_2$$

$$n = 2;\ \cos\frac{2\pi}{5} + i\sin\frac{2\pi}{5} = r_3$$

....

$$n = 9;\ \cos\frac{9\pi}{5} + i\sin\frac{9\pi}{5} = r_{10}$$

Thus, the tenth roots of unity are obtained by given n = 0, 1, 2, ..., 9.

It can be verified that the product of any two of the above is equal to one of them.

For example, $r_3 . r_8 = \left(\cos\frac{3\pi}{5} + i\sin\frac{3\pi}{5}\right)\left(\cos\frac{8\pi}{5} + i\sin\frac{8\pi}{5}\right)$

$$= \cos\frac{11\pi}{5} + i\sin\frac{11\pi}{5}$$

$$= \cos\left(2\pi + \frac{\pi}{5}\right) + i\sin\left(2\pi + \frac{\pi}{5}\right)$$

$$= \cos\frac{\pi}{5} + i\sin\frac{\pi}{5} = r_2.$$ And so on.

Example 2:

Prove that the complex numbers z_1, z_2 and the origin form an equilateral triangle only, if

$$z_1^2 + z_2^2 - z_1 z_2 = 0.$$

Solution:

Since Δ OAB is equilateral, we have

$$OA = OB = AB$$

$$\Rightarrow \quad \frac{OB}{OA} = \frac{AB}{OB}$$

$$\Rightarrow \quad \left|\frac{z_2 - 0}{z_1 - 0}\right| = \left|\frac{z_2 - z_1}{z_2 - 0}\right|$$

$$\Rightarrow \quad \frac{z_2}{z_1} = \frac{z_2 - z_1}{z_2}$$

$$\Rightarrow \quad z_2^2 = z_1 z_2 - z_1^2$$

$$\Rightarrow \quad z_1^2 + z_2^2 - z_1 z_2 = 0,$$ which is true.

Example 3:

If 1, ω, ω^2 are three cube roots of unity and $x = a + b$, $y = a\omega + b\omega^2$, $z = a\omega^2 + b\omega$, then prove that $x^2 + y^2 + z^2 = 6ab$.

Solution:

We have $x = a + b$, $y = a\omega + b\omega^2$; $z = a\omega^2 + b\omega$.

L.H.S. $= x^2 + y^2 + z^2$

$= (a + b)^2 + (a\omega + b\omega^2)^2 + (a\omega^2 + b\omega)^2$

$= a^2 + b^2 + 2ab + a^2\omega^2 + b^2\omega^4 + 2ab\omega^3 + a^2\omega^4 + b^2\omega^2 + 2ab\omega^3$

$= a^2 + b^2 + 2ab + a^2\omega^2 + b^2\omega + 2ab\,(1) + a^2\omega + b^2\omega^2 + 2ab\,(1)$

$[\because \omega^2 = 1 \text{ and } \omega^4 = \omega^3.\omega = 1.\,\omega = \omega]$

$= a^2(1 + \omega + \omega^2) + b^2(1 + \omega + \omega^2) + 6ab$

$= a^2(0)\, b^2(0) + 6ab \quad [\because 1 + \omega + \omega^2 = 0]$

$= 6ab =$ R.H.S.

Example 4:

Find the real values of x and y if

$\sqrt{x}\,(i + \sqrt{y}) - 15 = i(8 - \sqrt{y})$

Solution:

We have $\sqrt{x}\,(i + \sqrt{y}) - 15 = i\,(8 - \sqrt{y})$

$\Rightarrow \quad i\sqrt{x} + \sqrt{xy} - 15 = 8i - \sqrt{y}\,i$

$\Rightarrow \quad (\sqrt{xy} - 15) + i\,\sqrt{x} = (8 - \sqrt{y})i$

Equating real parts, $\sqrt{xy} - 15 = 0$

$\Rightarrow \quad \sqrt{xy} = 15$ ...(1)

Equating imaginary parts, $\sqrt{x} = 8 - \sqrt{y}$

$\Rightarrow \quad \sqrt{x} + \sqrt{y} = 8$ ...(2)

Squaring (2), $x + y + 2\sqrt{xy} = 64$

$\Rightarrow \quad x + y + 2(15) = 64$ [Using (1)]

$\Rightarrow \quad x + y = 64 - 30 = 34$

$\Rightarrow \quad y = 34 - x$ ...(3)

Squaring (1), $xy = 225$

$\Rightarrow \quad x(34 - x) = 225$ [Using (3)]

$\Rightarrow \quad 34x - x^2 = 225$

$\Rightarrow \quad x^2 - 34x + 225 = 0$

$\Rightarrow \quad (x - 9)\,(x - 25) = 0$

$\Rightarrow \qquad x = 9 \text{ or } 25.$

When $x = 9$, then $y = 34 - 9 = 25$.

When $x = 25$, then $y = 34 - 25 = 9$.

Hence $\left.\begin{matrix} x = 9 \\ y = 25 \end{matrix}\right\}, \quad \left.\begin{matrix} x = 25 \\ y = 9 \end{matrix}\right\}.$

Example 5:

Let z_1, z_2 be any two complex numbers. Then, show that

$$| z_1 + \sqrt{z_1^2 - z_2^2} | + | z_1 - \sqrt{z_1^2 - z_2^2} | = | z_1 + z_2 | + z_1 - z_2 |.$$

Solution:

$$(| z | + \sqrt{z_1^2 - z_2^2} | + | z_1 - \sqrt{z_1^2 - z_2^2} |)^2$$

$$= | z_1 + \sqrt{z_1^2 - z_2^2} |^2 + | z_1 - \sqrt{z_1^2 - z_2^2} |^2$$

$$+ 2 | z_1 + \sqrt{z_1^2 - z_2^2} | | z_1 - \sqrt{z_1^2 - z_2^2} |$$

$$= 2(| z_1 |^2 + | \sqrt{z_1^2 - z_2^2} |^2) + 2 | (z_1 + \sqrt{z_1^2 - z_2^2}) (z_1 - \sqrt{z_1^2 - z_2^2}) |$$

$$= 2(| z_1 |^2 + | z_1^2 - z_2^2 |) + 2 | z_1^2 - (z_1^2 - z_1^2) |$$

$$= 2(| z_1 |^2 + | z_1^2 - z_2^2 |) + 2 | z_2^2 |$$

$$= 2(| z_1 |^2 + | z_2 |^2) + 2 | z_1^2 - z_2^2 |$$

$$= | z_1 + z_2 |^2 + | z_1 - z_2 |^2 + 2 | z_1 + z_2 | | z_1 - z_1 |$$

$$= (| z_1 + z_2 | + | z_1 - z_2 |)^2$$

Hence $| z_1 + \sqrt{z_1^2 - z_2^2} | + | z_1 - \sqrt{z_1^2 - z_2^2} |$

$= | z_1 + z_2 | + | z_1 - z_2 |.$

Example 6:

If 1, ω, ω^2 are three cube roots of unity and $x = a + b$, $y = a\omega + b\omega^2$, $z = a\omega^2 + b\omega$, then prove that $x^2 + y^2 + z^2 = 6ab$.

Solution:

We have $x = a + b$, $y = a\omega + b\omega^2$,

$z = a\omega^2 + b\omega$.

L.H.S. $= x^2 + y^2 + z^2$

$$= (a + b)^2 + (a\omega + b\omega^2)^2 + (a\omega^2 + b\omega)^2$$

$$= a^2 + b^2 + 2ab + a^2\omega^2 + b^2\omega^4 + 2ab\omega^3 + a^2\omega^4 + b^2\omega^2 + 2ab\omega^3$$

$$= a^2 + b^2 + 2ab + a^2\omega^2 + b^2\omega + 2ab\,(1) + a^2\omega + b^2\omega^2 + 2ab\,(1)$$

$$[\because \omega^2 = 1 \text{ and } \omega^4 = \omega^3.\omega = 1.\,\omega = \omega]$$

$$= a^2(1 + \omega + \omega^2) + b^2(1 + \omega + \omega^2) + 6ab$$

$$= a^2(0)\; b^2(0) + 6ab \qquad [\because 1 + \omega + \omega^2 = 0]$$

$$= 6ab = \text{R.H.S.}$$

Example 7:

If z_1, z_2, z_3 are the vertices of an isosceles triangle right angled at the vertex z_2, show that

$$z_1^2 + 2z_2^2 + z_3^2 = 2z_2(z_1 + z_3).$$

Solution:

Let $P(z_1)$, $Q(z_2)$ and $R(z_3)$ be the vertices of the isosceles triangle PQR, right angled at Q.

$$\therefore \quad \angle PQR = \frac{\pi}{2}.$$

$$\text{Thus, } \arg\left(\frac{z_2 - z_1}{z_2 - z_3}\right) = \frac{\pi}{2}.$$

This is possible when the complex number is purely imaginary *i.e.*, its real part must be zero.

$$\text{Now real part of } \left(\frac{z_2 - z_1}{z_2 - z_3}\right) = 0$$

$$\Rightarrow \quad \frac{1}{2}\left[\frac{z_2 - z_1}{z_2 - z_3} + \left(\overline{\frac{z_2 - z_1}{z_2 - z_3}}\right)\right] = 0, \text{ since } \mathrm{Re}(z) = \frac{1}{2}\,(z + \bar{z})$$

$$\Rightarrow \quad \frac{z_2 - z_1}{z_2 - z_3} = \frac{\bar{z}_2 - \bar{z}_1}{\bar{z}_2 - \bar{z}_3} = 0$$

$$\Rightarrow \quad \frac{z_2 - z_1}{z_2 - z_3} = -\frac{\bar{z}_2 - \bar{z}_1}{\bar{z}_2 - \bar{z}_3}$$

$$\Rightarrow \quad \frac{z_2 - z_1}{\bar{z}_2 - \bar{z}_1} = -\frac{z_2 - z_3}{\bar{z}_2 - \bar{z}_3} \qquad \ldots(1)$$

Since the triangle PQR is isosceles *i.e.*, PQ = QR, we have

$| z_2 - z_1 | = | z_2 - z_3 |$

$\Rightarrow | z_2 - z_1 |^2 = | z_2 - z_3 |^2$

$\Rightarrow (z_2 - z_1)(\bar{z}_2 - \bar{z}_1) = (z_2 - z_3)(\bar{z}_2 - \bar{z}_3)$ ...(2)

on using the result $| z |^2 = z\bar{z}$.

Multiplying corresponding sides of (1) and (2), we have

$(z_2 - z_1)^2 = -(z_2 - z_3)^2$

$\Rightarrow z_1^2 + 2z_2^2 + z_3^2 = 2z_2 (z_1 + z_2)$, which is true.

Example 8:

If 1, ω, ω^2 are three cube roots of unity, prove that

$(1 + \omega)(1 + \omega^2)(1 + \omega^4)(1 + \omega^8)$ ... *to 2n factors* = 1.

Solution:

L.H.S. = $(1 + \omega)(1 + \omega^2)(1 + \omega^4)(1 + \omega^8)$ ... to 2n factors.

= $(1 + \omega)(1 + \omega^2)(1 + \omega^3.\omega)(1 + \omega^6.\omega^2)$ ... to 2n factors

= $(1 + \omega)(1 + \omega^2)(1 + \omega)(1 + \omega^2)$ ... to 2n factors

[$\because \omega^3 = \omega^6 = ... = 1$]

= [$(1 + \omega)(1 + \omega)$ ... to n factors]

= [$(1 + \omega^2)(1 + \omega^2)$ ... to n factors] [Note this step]

= $(1 + \omega)^n(1 + \omega^2)^n = (1 + \omega + \omega^2 + \omega^3)^n$

= $(0 + 1)^n$[$\because 1 + \omega + \omega^2 = 0$ and $\omega^3 = 1$]

= 1.

Example 9:

Let the complex numbers z_1, z_2, z_3 be the vertices of an equilateral triangle. Let z_0 be the circumcentre of the triangle, then prove that

$z_1^2 + z_2^2 + z_3^2 = 8z_0^2$.

Solution:

Since Δ ABC is equilateral, we have

AB = BC = CA

$$\Rightarrow \frac{AB}{BC} = \frac{BC}{CA} = 1$$

$$\Rightarrow \left|\frac{z_2 - z_1}{z_3 - z_2}\right| = \left|\frac{z_2 - z_3}{z_3 - z_1}\right| = 1$$

$$\Rightarrow \quad \frac{z_2 - z_1}{z_3 - z_2} = \frac{z_2 - z_3}{z_3 - z_1}$$

$$\Rightarrow \quad (z_2 - z_1)(z_3 - z_1) = (z_3 - z_2)(z_2 - z_3)$$

$$\Rightarrow \quad z_1^2 + z_2^2 + z_3^2 = z_1z_2 + z_2z_3 + z_3z_1 \qquad \ldots(1)$$

Further, since the circumcentre and the centroid of Δ ABC will coincide, we have

$$z_0 = \frac{1}{3}(z_1 + z_2 + z_3)$$

$$\Rightarrow \quad (3z_0)^2 = (z_1 + z_2 + z_3)^2$$

$$\Rightarrow \quad 9z_0^2 = z_1^2 + z_2^2 + z_3^2 + 2(z_1z_2 + z_2z_3 + z_3z_1)$$

$$= 3(z_1^2 + z_2^2 + z_3^2) \qquad [\because \text{ from } (1)]$$

$$\Rightarrow \quad z_1^2 + z_2^2 + z_3^2 = 3z_0^2, \text{ which is true.}$$

Example 10:

(a) If $(a_1 + ib_1)(a_2 + ib_2) \ldots (a_n + ib_n) = A + iB$, show that

(i) $(a_1^2 + b_1^2)(a_2^2 + b_2^2) \ldots (a_n^2 + b_n^2) = A^2 + B^2$.

(ii) $\tan^{-1}\frac{b_1}{a_1} + \tan^{-1}\frac{b_2}{a_2} + \ldots \tan^{-1}\frac{b_n}{a_n} = \tan^{-1}\frac{B}{A}$.

(b) If $\tan(\theta + i\phi) = e^{i\alpha}$, show that

$$\theta = \left(n + \frac{1}{2}\right)\frac{\pi}{2} \text{ and } \phi = \frac{1}{2}\log\tan\left(\frac{\pi}{4} + \frac{\alpha}{2}\right).$$

Solution:

(a) Let

$$\left.\begin{aligned} a_1 + ib_1 &= r_1(\cos\theta_1 + i\sin\theta_1) \\ a_2 + ib_2 &= r_2(\cos\theta_2 + i\sin\theta_2) \\ &\cdots\cdots\cdots\cdots\cdots\cdots \\ a_n + ib_n &= r_n(\cos\theta_n + i\sin\theta_n) \end{aligned}\right\} \qquad \ldots(1)$$

so that $r_1^2 = a_1^2 + b_1^2$, $r_2^2 = a_2^2 + b_2^2$, ...,

$r_n^2 = a_n^2 + b_n^2$

and $\theta_1 = \tan^{-1}\frac{b_1}{a_1}$, $\theta_2 = \tan^{-1}\frac{b_2}{a_2}$, ... $\theta_n = \tan^{-1}\frac{b_n}{a_n}$.

Also let $A + iB = R(\cos\theta + i\sin\theta)$ ...(2)

so that $R^2 = A^2 + B^2$ and $\theta = \tan^{-1}\frac{B}{A}$.

Thus $(\alpha_1 + ib_1)(\alpha_2 + ib_2) \ldots (\alpha_n + ib_n) = A + iB$ becomes :

$r_1(\cos\theta_1 + i\sin\theta_1)\, r_2(\cos\theta_2 + i\sin\theta_2) \ldots$

$r_n(\cos\theta_n + i\sin\theta_n) = R(\cos\theta + i\sin\theta)$ [Using (1) and (2)]

$\Rightarrow \quad r_1 r_2 \ldots r_n[\cos(\theta_1 + \theta_2 + \ldots + \theta_n) + i\sin(\theta_1 + \theta_2 + \ldots + \theta_n)] = R(\cos\theta + i\sin\theta)$

$\Rightarrow \quad r_1 r_2 \ldots r_n = R$ ...(3)

and $\theta_1 + \theta_2 + \ldots + \theta_n = \theta$ ...(4)

(i) $(a_1^2 + b_1^2)(a_2^2 + b_2^2) \ldots (a_n^2 + b_n^2)$
$= r_1^2.r_2^2 \ldots r_n^2 = R^2 = A^2 + B^2$

(ii) $\theta_1 + \theta_2 + \ldots + \theta_n = 0$

$$\Rightarrow \quad \tan^{-1}\frac{b_1}{a_1} + \tan^{-1}\frac{b_2}{a_2}, \ldots + \tan^{-1}\frac{b_n}{a_n} = \tan^{-1}\frac{B}{A}.$$

(b) We have:

$\tan(\theta + i\phi) = e^{i\alpha} = \cos\alpha + i\sin\alpha$ ...(1)

$\therefore \quad \tan(\theta = i\phi) = \cos\alpha = i\sin\alpha$ ...(2)

Now $\tan 2\theta = \tan\,(\overline{\theta + i\phi} + \overline{\theta - i\phi})$

$$= \frac{\tan(\theta + i\phi) + \tan + (\theta - i\phi)}{1 - \tan(\theta + i\phi)\tan(\theta - i\phi)}$$

$$= \frac{(\cos\alpha + i\sin\alpha) + (\cos\alpha - i\sin\alpha)}{1 - (\cos\alpha + i\sin\alpha)(\cos\alpha - i\sin\alpha)}$$

$$= \frac{2\cos\alpha}{1 - (\cos^2\alpha + \sin^2\alpha)} = \frac{2\cos\alpha}{0} = \tan\frac{\pi}{2}$$

$$\therefore \quad 2\theta = n\theta + \frac{\pi}{2}$$

$$\Rightarrow \quad \theta = \left(n + \frac{1}{2}\right)\frac{\pi}{2}$$

And $\tan(2i\phi) = \tan\,(\overline{\theta + i\phi} + \overline{\theta - i\phi})$

$$= \frac{\tan(\theta + i\phi) - \tan + (\theta - i\phi)}{1 + \tan(\theta + i\phi)\tan(\theta - i\phi)}$$

$$= \frac{(\cos\alpha + i\sin\alpha) - (\cos\alpha - i\sin\alpha)}{1 + (\cos\alpha + i\sin\alpha)(\cos\alpha - i\sin\alpha)}$$

$$\Rightarrow \quad i\,\frac{e^{2\phi} - e^{-2\phi}}{e^{2\phi} + e^{-2\phi}} = \frac{2i\sin\alpha}{1 + (\cos^2\alpha + \sin^2\alpha)}$$

$$= \frac{2i\sin\alpha}{1+(\cos^2\alpha+\sin^2\alpha)} = \frac{2i\sin\alpha}{1+1} = i\sin\alpha$$

$$\left[\because \sin 2i\phi = i\left(\frac{e^{2\phi}-e^{-2\phi}}{2}\right), \cos 2u\phi = \frac{e^{2\phi}+e^{-2\phi}}{2}\right]$$

$$\Rightarrow \quad \frac{e^{2\phi}-e^{-2\phi}}{e^{2\phi}+e^{-2\phi}} = \frac{\sin\alpha}{1}$$

By componendo and dividendo,

$$\frac{2e^{2\phi}}{2e^{-2\phi}} = \frac{1+\sin\alpha}{1-\sin\alpha} \frac{\left(\cos\frac{\alpha}{2}+\sin\frac{\alpha}{2}\right)^2}{\left(\cos\frac{\alpha}{2}-\sin\frac{\alpha}{2}\right)^2}$$

$$\Rightarrow \quad e^{4\phi} = \left(\frac{1+\tan\alpha/2}{1-\tan\alpha/2}\right)^2$$

$$\Rightarrow \quad e^{4\phi} = \frac{1+\tan\alpha/2}{1-\tan\alpha/2} = \tan\left(\frac{\pi}{4}+\frac{\alpha}{2}\right)$$

$$\Rightarrow \quad 2\phi = \log\tan\left(\frac{\pi}{4}+\frac{\alpha}{2}\right)$$

$$\Rightarrow \quad \phi = \frac{1}{2}\log\tan\left(\frac{\pi}{4}+\frac{\alpha}{2}\right).$$

Example 11:

If $z = 2+t+i\sqrt{3-t^2}$, where t is real and $t^2 < 3$, show that the modulus of $\frac{z+1}{z-1}$ is independent of t. Also show that the locus of the points z for different values of t is a circle and find its centre and radius.

Solution:

(i) We have : $z = 2+t+i\sqrt{3-t^2}$

$$\therefore \quad \frac{z+1}{z-1} = \frac{3+t+i\sqrt{3-t^2}}{1+t+i\sqrt{3-t^2}}$$

$$\therefore \quad \left|\frac{z+1}{z-1}\right|^2 = \frac{(3+t)^2+(3-t^2)}{(1+t)^2+(3-t^2)} = \frac{12+6t}{4+2t} = 3$$

$\Rightarrow \quad \left|\frac{z+1}{z-1}\right| = \sqrt{3}$, which is independent of t.

(ii) Let $z = x + iy$.

Then $z = 2 + t + i\sqrt{3 - t^2}$

$\Rightarrow \quad x + iy = 2 + t + i\sqrt{3 - t^2}$

$\Rightarrow \quad x = 2 + t \;$ and $\; y = \sqrt{3 - t^2}$

$\Rightarrow \quad x - 2 = 1 \;$ and $\; y = \sqrt{3 - t^2}$

$\Rightarrow (x - 2)^2 = t^2 \;$ and $\; y^2 = 3 - t^2$

$\Rightarrow (x - 2)^2 = 3 - y^2 \Rightarrow (x - 2)^2 + y^2 = (\sqrt{3})^2.$

Hence, locus of points z is a circle with centre 2 + i0 (*i.e.*, (2, 0)) and radius $\sqrt{3}$.

Example 12:

If $x_1, x_2, \ldots, x_n$ are the roots of the equation

$x^n + p_1 x^{n-1} + p_2 x^{n-2} + \ldots + p_{n-1} x + p_n = 0,$

where co-efficients $p_1, p_2, \ldots, p_n$ are real, show that

$$(1 + x_1^2)(1 + x_2^2)(1 + x_3^2) \ldots (1 + x_n^2) = (1 - p_2 + p_4 \ldots)^2 + (p_1 - p_3 + p_5 \ldots)^2.$$

Solution:

Since $x_1, x_2, x_3, \ldots, x_n$ are the roots of the given equation, we have the identity

$$x^n + p_1 x^{n-1} + p_2 x^{n-2} + \ldots + p_{n-1} x + p_n = (x - x_1)(x - x_2)(x - x_3) \ldots (x - x_n)$$

Replacing x by i and –i respectively, we get

$$i^n + p_1 i^{n-1} + p_2 i^{n-2} + \ldots + p_{n-1} i + p_n = (i - x_1)(i - x_2)(i - x_3) \ldots (i - x_n) \qquad \ldots(1)$$

and $$(-i)^n + p_1(-i)^{n-1} + p_2(-i)^{n-2} + \ldots + p_{n-1}(-i) + p_n = (-i - x_1)(-i - x_2)(-i - x_3) \ldots (-i - x_n) \qquad \ldots(2)$$

Now consider L.H.S. of (1). It is

$$i^n\left[1 + p_1 \cdot \frac{1}{i} + p_2 \cdot \frac{1}{i^2} + p_3 \cdot \frac{1}{i^3} + p_4 \cdot \frac{1}{i^4} + \ldots\right]$$

$$= i^n\,[1 - p_1 i - p_2 + p_3 i + p_4 \ldots]$$

$= i^n [(1 - p_2 + p_4 \dots) = i(p_1 - p_3 + \dots)]$ ...(3)

Similarly R.H.S. of (2) becomes

$$(-i)^n\left[1+p_1\left(-\frac{1}{i}\right)+p_2\left(-\frac{1}{i}\right)^2+p_3\left(-\frac{1}{i}\right)^3+p_4\left(-\frac{1}{i}\right)^4+\dots\right]$$

$= (-i)^n [1 + p_1 i - p_2 - p_3 i + p_4 + \dots]$

$= (-1)^n [(1 - p_2 + p_4 \dots) + i(p_1 - p_3 + \dots)]$ ...(4)

Now multiplying (1) and (2) after replacing their L.H. sides by (3) and (4) respectively, we get

$$i^n[(1 - p_2 + p_4 \dots) - i(p_1 - p_2 + \dots)] \times (-i)^n[(1 - p_2 + p_4 \dots) + i(p_1 - p_2 + \dots)]$$

$$= (i - x_1)(i - x_2)(i - x_3) \dots (i - x_n) \times (-i - x_1)(-i - x_2)(-i - x_3) \dots (-i - x_n)$$

$\Rightarrow (-i^2)^n[(1 - p_2 + p_4 \dots)^2 + (p_1 - p_3 + \dots)^2]$

$= (-1)^n[(i - x_1)(i + x_1).(i - x_2)(i + x_2) \dots (i - x_n)(i + x_n)]$

Hence $(1 - p_2 + p_4 \dots)^2 + (p_1 - p_3 + \dots)^2$

$= (-1)^n[(-1 - x_1^2) . (-1 - x_2^2) \dots (-1 - x_n^2)]$

$= (-1)^{2n}[(1 + x_1^2)(1 + x_2^2) \dots (1 + x_n^2)]$

$= (1 + x_1^2)(1 + x_2^2) \dots (1 + x_n)^2.$

Example 13:

Suppose the points $z_1, z_2, \dots, z_n$ all lie on one side of a line drawn through the origin of the complex plane. Prove that the same of the points $\frac{1}{z_1}, \frac{1}{z_2}, \dots, \frac{1}{z_n}$. *Moreover, show that*

$$z_1 + z_2 + \dots + z_n \neq 0, \quad \frac{1}{z_1} + \frac{1}{z_2} + \dots + \frac{1}{z_n} \neq 0.$$

Solution:

The equation of any line passing through the origin is $\bar{a}z + a\bar{z} = 0$.

Since $z_1, z_2, \dots, z_n$ lie in the half-plane $\bar{a}z + a\bar{z} > 0$.

$\therefore \bar{a}z_i + a\bar{z}_i > 0$ for $i = 1, 2, \dots, n$

$$\Rightarrow \quad \bar{a}\left(\frac{z_i\bar{z}_i}{\bar{z}_i}\right) + a\left(\frac{\bar{z}_i\bar{z}_i}{z_i}\right) > 0$$

$$\Rightarrow \quad \bar{a}\left(\frac{|z_i|^2}{\bar{z}_i}\right) + a\left(\frac{|z_i|^2}{z_i}\right) > 0$$

$$\Rightarrow \quad |z_i|^2 \left(\frac{\bar{a}}{z_i} + \frac{a}{z_i}\right) > 0$$

$$\Rightarrow \quad a\left(\frac{1}{z_i}\right) + \bar{a}\left(\frac{1}{z_i}\right) > 0 \text{ for } i = 1, 2, \ldots n \qquad [\because |z_i|^2 > 0]$$

$\Rightarrow \quad \frac{1}{z_1}, \frac{1}{z_2}, \ldots, \frac{1}{z_n}$ lie on one side of the line $\bar{a}z + a\bar{z} = 0$.

Also $\bar{a}z_i + a\bar{z}_i > 0$ for $i = 1, 2, \ldots, n$

$$\Rightarrow \quad \bar{a}\left(\sum_{i=1}^{n} z_i\right) + a\left(\sum_{i=1}^{n} \bar{z}_i\right) > 0$$

$$\Rightarrow \quad \bar{a}\left(\sum_{i=1}^{n} z_i\right) + a\overline{\left(\sum_{i=1}^{n} z_i\right)} > 0$$

$$\Rightarrow \quad \sum_{i=1}^{n} z_i \neq 0.$$

Similarly $\quad \sum_{i=1}^{n} \frac{1}{z_i} \neq 0.$

Example 14:

Show that the triangles whose vertices are z_1, z_2, z_3 and a, b, c are similar if

$$\begin{vmatrix} z_1 & a & 1 \\ z_2 & b & 1 \\ z_3 & c & 1 \end{vmatrix} = 0.$$

Solution:

Let z_1, z_2, z_3 be given by A, B, C respectively and a, b, c be given by D, E, F respectively.

Since Δ ABC and Δ DEF are similar,

$$\therefore \frac{AB}{DE} = \frac{BC}{EF} \text{ and } \angle ABC = \angle DEF = \alpha \text{ (say)}$$

Thus $\quad \alpha = \arg\left(\frac{z_1 - z_2}{z_3 - z_2}\right) = \arg\left(\frac{a - b}{c - b}\right)$

$$\Rightarrow \quad \frac{z_1 - z_2}{z_3 - z_2} = \frac{AB}{BC} (\cos\alpha + i\sin\alpha) \qquad ...(1)$$

and $$\frac{a-b}{c-b} = \frac{DE}{EF} (\cos\alpha + i\sin\alpha) \qquad ...(2)$$

Since $\frac{AB}{DE} = \frac{BC}{EF}$, $\quad \therefore \frac{AB}{BC} = \frac{DE}{EF}$

$\therefore$ From (1) and (2), $\frac{z_1 - z_2}{z_3 - z_2} = \frac{a-b}{c-b}$

$\Rightarrow \quad (c-b)(z_1 - z_2) = (a-b)(z_3 - z_2)$

$\Rightarrow \quad (z_1 - z_2)(c-b) - (a-b)(z_3 - z_2) = 0$

$$\Rightarrow \begin{vmatrix} z_1 - z_2 & a-b \\ z_3 - z_2 & c-b \end{vmatrix} = 0$$

$$\Rightarrow \begin{vmatrix} z_1 - z_2 & a-b & 0 \\ z_2 & b & 1 \\ z_3 - z_2 & c-b & 0 \end{vmatrix} = 0$$

$$\Rightarrow \begin{vmatrix} z_1 & a & 1 \\ z_2 & b & 1 \\ z_3 & c & 1 \end{vmatrix} = 0, \qquad [\text{Operating } R_1 \to R_1 + R_2 \text{ and } R_3 \to R_3 + R_2]$$

which is true.

Example 15:

Prove that $\left(\frac{-1+i\sqrt{3}}{2}\right)^n + \left(\frac{-1-i\sqrt{3}}{2}\right)^n$ *is equal to 2 if n be a multiple of 3 and is equal to – 1 if n any other integer.*

Or

If 1, ω, ω² are the cube roots of unity, prove that $\omega^n + \omega^{2n} = 2$ *or –1 according as n is a multiple of 3 or any other integer.*

Solution:

Three cases arise:

Case I: *When n = 3k, where k is any +ve integer.*

$$\left(\frac{-1+i\sqrt{3}}{2}\right)^n + \left(\frac{-1-i\sqrt{3}}{2}\right)^n = (\omega)^{3k} + (\omega^2)^{3k}$$

$$= (\omega^3)^k + (\omega^3)^{2k}$$

$$= (1)^k + (1)^{2k} \qquad [\because \omega^3 = 1]$$

$$= 1 + 1 = 2.$$

Case II: *When n = 3k + 1, where k is any +ve integer.*

$$\left(\frac{-1 + i\sqrt{3}}{2}\right)^n + \left(\frac{-1 - i\sqrt{3}}{2}\right)^n = (\omega)^{3k+1} + (\omega^2)^{3k+1}$$

$$= (\omega)^{3k}\,\omega + (\omega)^{6k}\,\omega^2$$

$$= (\omega^3)^3\omega + (\omega^3)^{2k}\,\omega^2$$

$$= (1)^k\omega + (1)^{2k}\,\omega^2 \qquad [\because \omega^3 = 1]$$

$$= \omega + \omega^2 = \omega^2 + \omega = -1. \qquad [\because 1 + \omega + \omega^2 = 0]$$

Case III: *When n = 3k + 2, where k is any +ve integer.*

$$\left(\frac{-1 + i\sqrt{3}}{2}\right)^n + \left(\frac{-1 - i\sqrt{3}}{2}\right)^n = (\omega)^{3k+2} + (\omega^2)^{3k+2}$$

$$= (\omega^3)^k\,\omega^2 + (\omega)^{6k}\,\omega^4$$

$$= (\omega^3)^k\omega^2 + (\omega^3)^{2k+1}\,.\,\omega$$

$$= (1)^k(\omega) + (1)^{2k+1}\,(\omega) \qquad [\because \omega^3 = 1]$$

$$= \omega^2 + \omega = -1. \qquad [\because 1 = \omega + \omega^2 = 0]$$

Example 16:

If 1, ω_1, ω_2, ..., ω_{n-1} are the nth roots of unity, then show that $(1 - \omega_1)(1 - \omega_2)(1 - \omega_3) \ldots (1 - \omega_{n-1}) = n$.

Solution:

Since 1, $\omega_1, \omega_2, \ldots, \omega_{n-1}$ are roots of $x^n = 1$,

$$\therefore \quad x^n - 1 = (x - 1)(x - \omega_1)(x - \omega_2) \ldots (x - \omega_{n-1})$$

$$\Rightarrow (x - 1)(x^{n-1} + x^{n-2} + \ldots + x + 1) = (x - 1)(x - \omega_1)(x - \omega_2) \ldots (x - \omega_{n-1})$$

$$\Rightarrow x^{n-1} + x^{n-2} + \ldots + x + 1 = (x - \omega_1)(x - \omega_2) \ldots (x - \omega_{n-1})$$

Putting x = 1, $n = (1 - \omega_1)(1 - \omega_2) \ldots (1 - \omega_{n-1})$, which is true.

Example 17:

Find the least positive integer n for which $\left(\frac{1+i}{1-i}\right)^n = 1.$

Solution:

$$\frac{1+i}{1-i} = \frac{1+i}{1-i} \times \frac{1+i}{1+i} = \frac{(1+i)^2}{1-i^2} = \frac{1+2i+i^2}{1-i^2} = \frac{1+2i-1}{1+1} = \frac{2i}{2} = i$$

$$\therefore \quad \left(\frac{1+i}{1-i}\right)^n = 1 \quad \Rightarrow i^n = 1$$

Hence the least value of $n = 4$. $[\because i^4 = 1]$

Example 18:

If $\dfrac{a+ib}{c+id} = x + iy$, *show that*

$$x^2 + y^2 = \frac{a^2+b^2}{c^2+d^2}.$$

Solution:

We have $x + iy = \dfrac{a+ib}{c+id}$

$$= \frac{a+ib}{c+id} \times \frac{c-id}{c-id}$$

$$= \frac{ac - iad + ibc - i^2bd}{c^2 - (id)^2}$$

$$= \frac{(ac+bd) + i(bc-ad)}{c^2 - d^2} \qquad [\because i^2 = -1]$$

$$= \frac{ac+bd}{c^2+d^2} + i\frac{bc-ad}{c^2+d^2}$$

$$\therefore \quad x = \frac{ac+bd}{c^2+d^2} \text{ and } y = \frac{bc-ad}{c^2+d^2}$$

$$\therefore \quad x^2 + y^2 = \frac{(ac+bd)^2}{(c^2+d^2)^2} + \frac{(bc-ad)^2}{(c^2+d^2)^2}$$

$$= \frac{a^2c^2 + b^2d^2 + 2abcd + b^2c^2 + a^2d^2 - 2abcd}{(c^2+d^2)^2}$$

$$= \frac{(a^2c^2 + b^2d^2) + (b^2d^2 + a^2d^2)}{(c^2+d^2)^2}$$

$$= \frac{c^2(a^2+b^2) + d^2(b^2+a^2)}{(c^2+d^2)^2}$$

$$= \frac{(a^2+b^2)(c^2+d^2)}{(c^2+d^2)^2} = \frac{a^2+b^2}{c^2+d^2}.$$

Example 19:

For what real values of x and y are the numbers $-3 + ix^2y$ and $x^2 + y + 4i$ conjugate complex?

Solution:

The conjugate of $x^2 + y + 4i$ is $x^2 + y - 4i$.

By the question, $x^2 + y - 4i = -3 + ix^2y$

Equating real parts, $x^2 + y = -3$ ...(1)

Equating imag. parts $-4 = x^2y$ ...(2)

From (2), $x^2 = -\frac{4}{y}$ ...(3)

Putting (1) $-\frac{4}{y} + y = -3$

$\Rightarrow$ $-4 + y^2 = -3y$

$\Rightarrow$ $y^2 + 3y - 4 = 0$

$\Rightarrow$ $(y + 4)(y - 1) = 0$

$\Rightarrow$ $y = -4, 1.$

When $y = -4$, then from (3), $x^2 = -\frac{4}{-4} = 1$

$\Rightarrow$ $x = \pm 1$

When $y = 1$, then from (3) $x^2 = -4$

$\Rightarrow$ x is non-real.

Hence $x = 1, y = -4$ and $x = -1, y = -4$.

Example 20:

If the vertices of a triangle ABC represent z_1, z_2, z_3 respectively, show that the orthocentre represents

$$\frac{(a \sec A)z_1 + (b \sec B)z_2 + (c \sec C)z_3}{a \sec A + b \sec B + c \sec C}$$

Solution:

Let $A(z_1)$, $B(z_2)$ and $C(z_3)$ be the vertices of ΔABC. Let AD, BE, CF be the altitudes which meet at H, the orthocentre.

We have $\frac{AD}{AB} = \cos B$

$$\Rightarrow \quad \frac{BD}{c} = \cos B$$

$$\Rightarrow \quad BD = c \cos B$$

and $$\frac{DC}{AC} = \cos C$$

$$\Rightarrow \quad \frac{DC}{b} = \cos C$$

$$\Rightarrow \quad DC = b \cos C.$$

Thus D divides the segment [BC] in the ratio c cos B : b cos C

$\therefore$ D represents $\dfrac{(c\cos B)z_3 + (b\cos C)z_2}{c\cos B + b\cos C}$

i.e., $\dfrac{(b\cos C)z_2 + (a\cos B)z_3}{a}$

In ΔABH, by Sine rule,

$$\frac{AH}{\sin(90° - A)} = \frac{BH}{\sin(90° - B)} = \frac{AB}{\sin(A + B)}$$

$$\Rightarrow \quad \frac{AH}{\cos A} = \frac{BH}{\cos B} = \frac{c}{\sin C} = 2R$$

$\therefore AH = 2R \cos A$ and $BH = 2R \cos B$.

In ΔBDH, $\dfrac{HD}{BH} = \sin(90° - C)$

$$\Rightarrow \quad HD = 2R \cos B \cos C$$

$$\therefore \quad AH : HD = 2R \cos A : 2R \cos B \cos C$$

$$= \cos A : \cos B \cos C$$

$\therefore$ H divides the segment [AD] in the ratio cos A : cos B cos C

$\therefore$ H represents

$$\frac{\cos A\left[\dfrac{(b\cos C)z_2 + (c\cos B)z_3}{a}\right] + (\cos B\cos C)z_1}{\cos A + \cos B\cos C}$$

$$i.e., \quad \frac{(a\cos B\cos C)z_1 + (b\cos C\cos A)z_2 + (c\cos A\cos B)z_3}{a[\cos A + \cos B\cos C]}$$

i.e., $$\frac{(a\cos B\cos C)z_1 + (b\cos C\cos A)z_2 + (c\cos A\cos B)z_3}{a\cos A + a\cos B\cos C}$$

i.e., $$\frac{(a\cos B\cos C)z_1 + (b\cos C\cos A)z_2 + (c\cos A\cos B)z_3}{a\cos B\cos C + (b\cos C + c\cos B)\cos A}$$

i.e., $$\frac{(a\cos B\cos C)z_1 + (b\cos C\cos A)z_2 + (c\cos A\cos B)z_3}{a\cos B\cos C + b\cos C + \cos A + c\cos A\cos B}$$

i.e., $$\frac{(a\sec A)z_1 + (b\sec B)z_2 + (c\sec C)z_3}{a\sec A + b\sec B + c\sec C}$$

[Dividing numerator and denominator by cos A cos B cos C].

Example 21:

Solve the equation $|z| - z = 1 + 2i$, *where* $z = x + iy$.

Solution:

We have $|z| - z = 1 + 2i$

$$\Rightarrow \quad \sqrt{x^2 + y^2} - (x + iy) = 1 + 2i$$

Equating real parts, $\sqrt{x^2 + y^2} - x = 1$ ...(1)

Equating imag. parts, $-y = 2$ ...(2)

From (2), $y = -2$.

Putting in (1) $\sqrt{x^2 + 4} - x = 1$

$$\Rightarrow \quad \sqrt{x^2 + 4} = 1 + z$$

Squaring, $x^2 + 4 = 1 + 2x + x^2$

$$\Rightarrow \quad 4 = 1 + 2x$$

$$\Rightarrow \quad 2x = 3 \Rightarrow x = \frac{3}{2}.$$

Hence the solution is $z = \frac{3}{2} - 2i$.

Example 22:

Evaluate $\dfrac{(-1 + i\sqrt{3})^{15}}{(1 - i)^{20}} + \dfrac{(-1 - i\sqrt{3})^{15}}{(1 + i)^{20}}$.

Solution:

Since $\dfrac{-1+i\sqrt{3}}{2} = \omega$ and $\dfrac{-1-i\sqrt{3}}{2} = \omega^2$.

$\therefore -1 + i\sqrt{3} = 2\omega$ and $-1 + i\sqrt{3} = 2\omega^2$.

$\therefore$ Given expression $= \dfrac{2(\omega)^{15}}{(1-i)^{20}} + \dfrac{2(\omega^2)^{15}}{(1+i)^{20}}$

But$(1 - i)^{20} = ((1 - i)^2)^{10} = (1 + i^2 - 2i)^{10}$

$= (1 - 1 - 2i)^{10} = (-2i)^{10}$

$= 2^{10}i^{10} = 2^{10}(i^2)^5$

$= 2^{10}(-1)^5 = -2^{10}$

and$(1 + i)^{20} = -2^{10}$ (Similarly)

$\therefore$ Given expression $= -\dfrac{1}{2^{10}}[(2\omega)^{15} + (2\omega^2)^{15}]$

$= -\dfrac{1}{2^{10}}[2^{15} + 2^{15}]$ $[\because \omega^{15} = \omega^{30} = 1]$

$= -\dfrac{1}{2^{10}}(2 \,.\, 2^{15}) = -2^6 = -64.$

Example 23:

If $z = \left(\dfrac{\sqrt{3}}{2} + \dfrac{i}{2}\right)^{107} + \left(\dfrac{\sqrt{3}}{2} - \dfrac{i}{2}\right)^{107}$, *then show that* $Im(z) = 0$.

Solution:

We have $z = \left(\dfrac{\sqrt{3}}{2} + \dfrac{i}{2}\right)^{107} + \left(\dfrac{\sqrt{3}}{2} - \dfrac{i}{2}\right)^{107}$

$\therefore \quad \bar{z} = \left(\dfrac{\sqrt{3}}{2} + \dfrac{i}{2}\right)^{107} + \left(\dfrac{\sqrt{3}}{2} - \dfrac{i}{2}\right)^{107} = z$

$\Rightarrow \quad Im(z) = 0.$

Example 24:

Let z_1, z_2, z_3 *be non-real complex numbers and* $z_1 \neq z_2$.

If $\begin{vmatrix} |z_1| & |z_2| & |z_3| \\ |z_2| & |z_3| & |z_1| \\ |z_3| & |z_1| & |z_2| \end{vmatrix} = 0$, *then prove that*

(i) z_1, z_2, z_3 *lie on a circle with centre at the origin.*

(ii) amp. $\left(\frac{z_1}{z_2}\right)$ = amp. $\left(\frac{z_3 - z_1}{z_2 - z_1}\right)^2$.

Solution:

Let $z_1 = r_1 (\cos \alpha_1 + i \sin \alpha_1)$, $z_2 = r_2 (\cos \alpha_2 + i \sin \alpha_2)$ and $z_3 = r_3 (\cos \alpha_3 + i \sin \alpha_3)$.

By the question, $\begin{vmatrix} r_1 & r_2 & r_3 \\ r_2 & r_3 & r_1 \\ r_3 & r_1 & r_2 \end{vmatrix} = 0$

$$\Rightarrow \begin{vmatrix} r_1+r_2+r_3 & r_2 & r_3 \\ r_1+r_2+r_3 & r_3 & r_1 \\ r_1+r_2+r_3 & r_1 & r_2 \end{vmatrix} = 0 \qquad [\text{Operating } C_1 \to C_1 + C_2 + C_3]$$

$$\Rightarrow (r_1+r_2+r_3) \begin{vmatrix} 1 & r_2 & r_3 \\ 1 & r_3 & r_1 \\ 1 & r_1 & r_2 \end{vmatrix} = 0$$

$$\Rightarrow (r_1+r_2+r_3) \begin{vmatrix} 1 & r_2 & r_3 \\ 0 & r_3-r_2 & r_1-r_3 \\ 0 & r_1-r_2 & r_2-r_3 \end{vmatrix} = 0$$

[Operating $R_2 \to R_2 - R_1$ and $R_3 \to R_3 - R_1$]

$\Rightarrow (r_1 + r_2 + r_3) [(r_3 - r_2)(r_2 - r_3) - (r_1 - r_2)(r_1 - r_2)] = 0$

$\Rightarrow - (r_1 + r_2 + r_3)(r_1^2 + r_2^2 + r_3^3 - r_1r_2 - r_2r_3 - r_3r_1) = 0$

$\Rightarrow \frac{1}{2}(r_1 + r_2 + r_3) [(r_1 - r_2)^2 + (r_2 - r_3)^2 + (r_3 - r_1)^2] = 0$

But $r_1 + r_2 + r_3 \neq 0$.[$\because$ r_1, r_2, r_3 are all + ve]

$\therefore r_1 - r_2 = r_2 - r_3 = r_3 - r_1 = 0$

$\Rightarrow \qquad r_1 = r_2 = r_3$

$\Rightarrow z_1, z_2, z_3$ are three complex numbers whose distances from the origin and equal

$\Rightarrow z_1, z_2, z_3$ lie on a circle with centre at the origin.

Let the point representing the complex numbers z_1, z_2, z_3 be A, B, C respectively.

Also amp. $\left(\frac{z_3}{z_2}\right)$ = angle which [CB] makes at the origin and amp. $\left(\frac{z_3 - z_1}{z_2 - z_1}\right)^2 = 2 \text{ amp.} \left(\frac{z_3 - z_1}{z_2 - z_1}\right) = 2 \angle CAB.$

Hence amp. $\left(\frac{z_3}{z_2}\right) = 2 \text{ amp.} \left(\frac{z_3 - z_1}{z_2 - z_1}\right)$

$$= \text{amp.} \left(\frac{z_3 - z_1}{z_2 - z_1}\right)^2.$$

Example 25:

Given $\prod_{k=1}^{n} (P_k + iQ) = R + iS$, *prove that*

$$\sum_{k=1}^{n} \tan^{-1} \frac{Q_k}{P_k} = \tan^{-1} \frac{S}{R} + n\pi.$$

Solution:

Let $P_1 + iQ_1 = r_1(\cos \theta_1 + i \sin \theta_1)$

$$P_2 + iQ_2 = r_2(\cos \theta_2 + i \sin \theta_2)$$

....

$$P_n + iQ_n = r_n(\cos \theta_n + i \sin \theta_n)$$

Also $R + iS = r (\cos \phi + i \sin \phi)$

Now $\prod_{k=1}^{n} (P_k + iQ) = R + iS$

$\Rightarrow$ $r_1 r_2 \ldots r_n [\cos \theta_1 + i \sin \theta_1] [\cos \theta_2 + i \sin \theta_2]$

$$\ldots [\cos \theta_n + i \sin \theta_n] = r (\cos \phi + i \sin \phi)$$

$\Rightarrow$ $r_1 r_2 \ldots r_n [\cos (\theta_1 + \theta_2 + \ldots + \theta_n) + i \sin (\theta_1$

$$+ \theta_2 + \ldots \theta_n)] = r (\cos \phi + i \sin \phi)$$

Comparing, $r_1 r_2 \ldots r_n = r$, $\cos (\theta_1 + \theta_2 + \ldots + \theta_n)$

$$= \cos \phi \text{ and } \sin (\theta_1 + \theta_2 + \ldots + \theta_n) = \sin \phi$$

$$\therefore \frac{\sin(\theta_1 + \theta_2 + \ldots + \theta_n)}{\cos(\theta_1 + \theta_2 + \ldots + \theta_n)} = \frac{\sin\phi}{\cos\phi}$$

$\Rightarrow \tan (\theta_1 + \theta_2 + \ldots + \theta_n) = \tan \phi$

$\Rightarrow \theta_1 + \theta_2 + \ldots + \theta_n = n\pi + \phi.$

But $\theta_1 = \text{amp}\ (P_1 + iQ_1) = \tan^{-1} \dfrac{Q_1}{P_1}$

$\theta_2 = \text{amp}\ (P_2 + iQ_2) = \tan^{-1} \dfrac{Q_2}{P_2}$

....

$\phi = \text{amp}\ (R + S) = \tan^{-1} \dfrac{S}{R}.$

Example 26:

ABCD is a rhombus described in the clockwise direction in the Argand diagram. Suppose that the vertices A, B, C, D are given by z_1, z_2, z_3, z_4 respectively and $\angle CBA = \dfrac{2\pi}{3}$.

Show that $2\sqrt{3}\, z_2 = (\sqrt{3} - i)z_1 + (\sqrt{3} + i)z_3$

and $\quad 2\sqrt{3}\, z_4 = (\sqrt{3} + i)z_1 + (\sqrt{3} - i)z_3.$

Solution:

Given $\angle CBA = \dfrac{2\pi}{3}$

$$\therefore \quad \frac{z_3 - z_2}{z_1 - z_2} = \frac{|z_3 - z_2|}{|z_1 - z_2|}\left[\cos\left(\frac{2\pi}{3}\right) + i\sin\left(\frac{2\pi}{3}\right)\right]$$

$$\Rightarrow \quad \frac{z_3 - z_2}{z_1 - z_2} = -\frac{1}{2} + i\frac{\sqrt{3}}{2}$$

[$\because$ $|z_3 - z_2| = |z_1 - z_2|$ as ABCD is a rhombus]

$$\Rightarrow \quad z_3 - z_2 = \left(-\frac{1}{2} + \frac{i\sqrt{3}}{2}\right)(z_1 - z_2)$$

$$\Rightarrow \quad z_3 + \left(\frac{1}{2} - \frac{i\sqrt{3}}{2}\right)z_1 = \left(\frac{3}{2} - \frac{i\sqrt{3}}{2}\right)z_2$$

$$\Rightarrow \quad \sqrt{3}z_2 = \frac{2}{\sqrt{3} - i}z_3 + \frac{1 - i\sqrt{3}}{\sqrt{3} - i}z_1$$

$$\Rightarrow \quad 2\sqrt{3}\, z_2 = (\sqrt{3} + i)z_3 + \frac{1}{2}(\sqrt{3} + i)(1 - i\sqrt{3})z_1$$

$$= (\sqrt{3} + i)z_3 + \frac{1}{2}(\sqrt{3} + \sqrt{3} + i - 3i)z_1$$

$= (\sqrt{3} + i)z_3 + (\sqrt{3} - i)z_1$ ...(1)

Since the diagonals of a rhombus bisect each other,

$$\therefore \frac{z_1 + z_3}{2} = \frac{z_2 + z_4}{2} \Rightarrow z_1 + z_3 = z_2 + z_4$$

$\Rightarrow \quad z_4 = z_1 + z_3 - z_2$

$\Rightarrow 2\sqrt{3}\, z_4 = 2\sqrt{3}\,(z_1 + z_3) - 2\sqrt{3}\, z_2$

$= 2\sqrt{3}\,(z_1 + z_3) - [(\sqrt{3} + i)z_3 + (\sqrt{3} - i)z_1]$ [Using (1)]

$= (\sqrt{3} + i)z_1 + (\sqrt{3} - i)z_3$ ...(2)

Hence (1) and (2) are the reqd. results.

Example 27:

Show that the circumcentre of the triangle whose vertices are given by the complex numbers z_1, z_2, z_3 is given by

$$z = \frac{\Sigma z_1\bar{z}_2\,(z_2 - z_3)}{\Sigma \bar{z}_1\,(z_2 - z_3)}.$$

Solution:

Let O(z) be the circumcentre of the triangle whose vertices are $A(z_1)$, $B(z_2)$ and $C(z_3)$.

By def., $|z - z_1| = |z - z_2| = |z - z_3|$.

Now $\quad |z - z_1| = |z - z_2|$

$\Rightarrow \quad |z - z_1|^2 = |z - z_2|^2$

$\Rightarrow |z|^2 + |z_1|^2 - \bar{z}z_1 - z\bar{z}_1 = |z|^2 + |z_2|^2 - \bar{z}z_2 - z\bar{z}_2$

$\Rightarrow z(\bar{z}_1 - \bar{z}_2) + \bar{z}(z_1 - z_2) = z_1\bar{z}_1 - z_2\bar{z}_2$ ...(1)

Similarly $|z - z_1| = |z - z_3|$ gives

$z(\bar{z}_1 - \bar{z}_3) + \bar{z}(z_1 - z_3) = z_1\bar{z}_1 - z_3\bar{z}_3$ ...(2)

Multiplying (1) by $z_1 - z_3$ and (2) by $z_1 - z_2$ and subtracting, we get

$z[(\bar{z}_1 - \bar{z}_2)(z_1 - z_2) - (\bar{z}_1 - \bar{z}_3)(z_1 - z_2)]$

$= z_1\bar{z}_1(z_1 - z_3) - z_2\bar{z}_2(z_1 - z_3) - z_1\bar{z}_1(z_1 - z_2) + z_3\bar{z}_3 + (z_1 - z_2)$

$\Rightarrow z[\bar{z}_1(z_2 - z_3) + \bar{z}_2(z_3 - z_1) + \bar{z}_3(z_1 - z_2)]$

$= z_1\bar{z}_1(z_2 - z_3) + z_2\bar{z}_2(z_3 - z_1) + z_3\bar{z}_3(z_1 - z_2)$.

Hence $z = \dfrac{\Sigma z_1\bar{z}_2\,(z_2 - z_3)}{\Sigma \bar{z}_1\,(z_2 - z_3)}$.

Example 28:

Prove that $|z_1 + z_2|^2 + |z_1 - z_2|^2 = 2|z_1|^2 + |z_2|^2$.

Interpret the result geometrically and deduce that

$$|\alpha + \sqrt{\alpha^2 - \beta^2}| + |\alpha - \sqrt{\alpha^2 - \beta^2}| = |\alpha + \beta| + |\alpha - \beta|.$$

where α, β *are complex numbers.*

Solution:

$|z_1 + z_2|^2 + |z_1 - z_2|^2$

$= (z_1 + z_2)\overline{(z_1 + z_2)} + (z_1 - z_2)\overline{(z_1 - z_2)}$

$= (z_1 + z_2)(\bar{z}_1 + \bar{z}_2) + (z_1 - z_2)(\bar{z}_1 - \bar{z}_2)$

$= z_1\bar{z}_1 + z_2\bar{z}_1 + z_1\bar{z}_2 + z_2\bar{z}_2 + z_1\bar{z}_1 - z_2\bar{z}_1 - z_1\bar{z}_2 + z_2\bar{z}_2$

$= 2z_1\bar{z}_2 + 2z_2\bar{z}_2 = 2|z_1|^2 + 2|z_2|^2$ ...(1)

which is true.

Geometrical Interpretation

Let A, B be two points which represent two complex numbers z_1, z_2 respectively in the complex plane. Complete the || gm OACB.

Then $|z_1| = OA$, $|z_2| = OB$,

$|z_1 + z_2| = OC$, $|z_1 - z_2| = AB$.

Thus, the sum of the squares of the diagonals of a parallelogram is equal to the sum of the squares of its sides.

Deduction: Let $z_1 = \alpha + \sqrt{\alpha^2 - \beta^2}$

and $z_2 = \alpha - \sqrt{\alpha^2 - \beta^2}$.

$\therefore$ From (1), $|z_1|^2 + |z_2|^2 = \frac{1}{2}[|z_1 + z_2|^2 + |z_1 - z_2|^2]$

$= \frac{1}{2}[|2\alpha|^2 + |2\sqrt{\alpha^2 - \beta^2}|^2]$

$= 2[|\alpha|^2 + |\alpha^2 - \beta^2|]$ ...(2)

Also $(|z_1| + |z_2|)^2 = |z_1|^2 + |z_2|^2 + 2|z_1||z_2|$

$= 2[|\alpha|^2 + |\alpha^2 - \beta^2|] + 2[\beta^2]$ [Using (2)]

$= |\alpha + \beta|^2 + |\alpha - b|^2 + 2|\alpha^2 - \beta^2|$ [Using (1)]

$= (|\alpha + \beta| + |\alpha - \beta|)^2$

$\Rightarrow | z_1 | + | z_2 | = | \alpha + \beta | + | \alpha - \beta |.$

Hence $| \alpha + \sqrt{\alpha^2 + \beta^2} | + | \alpha - \sqrt{\alpha^2 - \beta^2} | = | \alpha + \beta | + | \alpha - \beta |.$

Example 29:

Find $a \in R$ if atleast one complex number z is to satisfy $|z + 3) = a^2 - 2a + 6$ and $|z - 3\sqrt{3}i| < a^2$ simultaneously.

Solution:

$|z + 3| = a^2 - 2a + 1$ ...(1)

$\Rightarrow$ z lies on a circle whose centre is $(- 3 + i.0)$

and radius is $a^2 - 2a + 6$. Here $a^2 - 2a + 6 > 0$, $\perp a \in R$ (as the roots of the corresponding equation are imaginary)

And$|z - 3\sqrt{3}i| < a^2$ ...(2)

$\Rightarrow$ z lies in the interior of a circle whose centre is $(0 + 3\sqrt{3}i)$ and radius is a^2.

Clearly, atleast one complex would satisfy both the equations if the two circles cut in two real and distinct points or first circle lies entirely inside the second circle.

We know that two circles with centres at c_1 and c_2 and radii being r_1 and r_2 respectively, will never intersect if $c_1c_2 \geq r_1 + r_2$

$\Rightarrow |- 3 - 3\sqrt{3}i| \geq a^2 + a^2 - 2a + 6$

$\Rightarrow 6 \geq 2a^2 - 2a + 6 \Rightarrow a^2 - a \leq 0$

$\Rightarrow a \in [0, 1]$ ...(3)

Hence desired values of a is $R - (-\infty\ 1]$

$= (1, \infty)$.

Example 30:

If 'a' is a complex number such that $|a| = 1$. Find the values of a, so that equation $az^2 + z + 1 = 0$ has one purely imaginary root.

Solution:

$az^2 + z + 1 = 0$ ...(1)

Taking conjugate of both sides, $az^2 + z + 1 = \overline{0}$

$\Rightarrow \bar{a}(\bar{z})^2 + \bar{z} + \bar{1} = 0$

$\bar{a}(\bar{z})^2 + \bar{z} + \bar{1} = 0$

$\bar{a}\ z^2 - z + 1 = 0$ (Since $\bar{z} = -z$ as z is purely imaginary)...(2)

Eliminating z from both the equations.

$[(\bar{a} - a)^2 + 2\ (a + \bar{a}] = 0$

Let a = cos θ + isin θ (since |a| = 1)

So $(-2i \sin \theta)^2 + 2\ (2 \cos \theta) = 0$

$\Rightarrow -4 \sin^2 \theta + 4 \cos \theta = 0$

$\Rightarrow \cos^2 \theta + \cos \theta - 1 = 0$

$\cos \theta = \dfrac{-1 \pm \sqrt{1+4}}{2}$

Only feasible value of cos θ is $\dfrac{\sqrt{5}-1}{2}$

Hence a = cos θ + isin θ, where $\theta = \cos^{-1}\left(\dfrac{\sqrt{5}-1}{2}\right)$.

Example 31:

Find the complex number z with maximum and minimum possible values of |z| satisfying

(i) $z - \dfrac{1}{z} = 1$;

(ii) $\left|z + \dfrac{4}{z}\right| = 3$.

Solution:

(ii) $\left|z + \dfrac{4}{z}\right| = 3 \Rightarrow \left||z| - \dfrac{4}{|z|}\right| \leq 3$

$\Rightarrow -3 \leq |z| - \dfrac{4}{|z|} \leq \Rightarrow 1 \leq |z| \leq 4$

$\Rightarrow |z|_{max} = 4$ and $|z|_{min} = 1$

Let us find out the complex number with maximum value of |z|

$|z| = 4 \Rightarrow z = 4e^{i\alpha}$

$\Rightarrow |4e^{-i\alpha} + e^{i\alpha}| = 3$

$\Rightarrow |4e^{i\alpha} + e^{i\alpha}|^2 = 9$

$\Rightarrow e^{i2\alpha} + e^{i2\alpha} = -2$

$\Rightarrow \cos 2\alpha = -1 \Rightarrow \alpha = \pm \pi/2$

$\Rightarrow z = 4e^{\pm i\pi/2} = \pm 4i$

Similarly, complex number with minimum value of $|z|$ can be obtained.

Example 32:

(i) *If z_1, z_2 are two complex numbers representing consecutive vertices a regular hexagon then find the complex number z_3 representing the vertex adjacent to z_2.*

(ii) *The three points z_1, z_2, z_3 are connected by the relation $az_1 + bz_1 + cz_3 = 0$, where a.b.c are real and $a + b + c = 0$. Prove that the three points are collinear.*

Solution:

(i) Clearly $|z_1 - z_2| = |z_3 - z_2|$ ...(1)

and amp $\dfrac{z_1 - z_2}{z_3 - z_2} = \pm \dfrac{2\pi}{3} = \angle Z_1Z_2Z_3$

(where the point Z_1 represents z_1 etc.)

$$\Rightarrow \frac{z_1 - z_2}{z_3 - z_2} = \frac{|z_1 - z_2|}{|z_3 - z_2|}\left\{\cos\frac{2\pi}{3} + \pm i \sin\frac{2\pi}{3}\right\}$$

$$= \left\{-\frac{1}{2} \pm i\frac{\sqrt{3}}{2}\right\}, \text{ using (1)}$$

$\therefore z_1 - z_2 = a(z_3 - z_2)$,

(where $a = \dfrac{-1 \pm i\sqrt{3}}{2} = \omega, \omega^2$ (and $a^3 = 1$)

or $a^2 (z_1 - z_2) = a^3 (z_3 - z_2) = z_3 - z_2$

or $z_3 = z_2 + a^2 (z_1 - z_2) = a^2z_1 + (1 - a^2)z_2$

$$= \left(-\frac{1}{2} \pm \frac{\sqrt{3}}{2}\right)z_2 + \left(1 - \frac{-1 \pm i\sqrt{3}}{2}\right)z_2$$

$$= -\frac{1}{2}\left(1 \pm i\sqrt{3}\right)z_1 + \frac{1}{2}\left(3 \pm \sqrt{3}\right)z_2$$

Note: If z_1, z_2, z_3 are given to be in anticlock wise sense then amp $\dfrac{z_1 - z_2}{z_3 - z_2} = \dfrac{2\pi}{3}$ will be taken.

Example 33:

(i) *Three points represented by complex numbers a, b, c lie on a circle with centre origin and radius r. The tangents at c cuts the chord joining the points a, b at z. Show that* $z = \dfrac{a^{-1} + b^{-1} - 2c^{-1}}{a^{-1}b^{-1} - c^{-2}}$.

(ii) *Two points represented by complex numbers a, b lie on a circle with centre Q and radius r. The tangents at 'a' and 'b' intersects at z. Find the complex number representing z.*

Solution:

Equation of line AB

$$\frac{z-z}{a-b} = \frac{\bar{z}-\bar{z}}{\bar{a}-\bar{b}} = \frac{\bar{z}-\frac{r^2}{a}}{r^2\left(\frac{1}{a}-\frac{1}{b}\right)}$$

$$\Rightarrow \frac{z-a}{-b} = \frac{\left(a\bar{z}-r^2\right)}{r^2} \Rightarrow \frac{\bar{z}}{r^2} = \left(1-\frac{z-a}{b}\right)\frac{1}{a} \qquad ...(1)$$

Equation of tangent at C(c) is :

$$z\bar{c} + \bar{z}c = 2r^2$$

$$\Rightarrow c\,\frac{\bar{z}}{r^2} = 2 - \frac{z}{c}$$

$$\Rightarrow \frac{\bar{z}}{r^2} = \frac{1}{c}\left(2-\frac{z}{c}\right) \qquad ...(ii)$$

Eliminate $\dfrac{\bar{z}}{r_2}$ from (i) and (ii)

Example 34:

Determine the maximum distance from the origin of co-ordinates to the points z for which $\left|z + \dfrac{1}{z}\right| = 1$.

Solution:

We have $\left|z + \dfrac{1}{z}\right| = 1$

$\Rightarrow \quad z^2 + 1 \mid = \mid z \mid$

Putting $z = r(\cos\theta + i\sin\theta)$, we get

$\mid r^2(\cos\theta + i\sin\theta)^2 + r \mid = r$

$\Rightarrow \mid r^2(\cos 2\theta + i\sin 2\theta) + 1 \mid = r$

$\Rightarrow \mid (r^2\cos 2\theta + 1) + i\, r^2 \sin 2\theta \mid = r$

$\Rightarrow \sqrt{(r^2 \cos 2\theta + 1)^2 + (r^2 \sin 2\theta)^2} = r$

$\Rightarrow (r^2 \cos 2\theta + 1)^2 + r^4 \sin 2\theta = r^2$

$\Rightarrow r^4\cos^2 2\theta + 2r^2 \cos 2\theta + 1 + r^4 \sin^2 2\theta = r^2$

$\Rightarrow r^4 + (2 \cos 2\theta - 1)r^2 + 1 = 0$

$$\therefore r^2 = \frac{(1-2\cos 2\theta) \pm \sqrt{(-2\cos 2\theta+1)^2 - 4}}{2}$$

r^2 is maximum when $-2 \cos 2\theta + 1$ is maximum

i.e., when $\cos 2\theta = -1$

$\therefore$ Max. value of $r^2 = \dfrac{3+\sqrt{5}}{2} = \dfrac{6+2\sqrt{5}}{4}$.

Hence max. value of $r = \dfrac{1}{2}\sqrt{6+2\sqrt{5}}$

$= \dfrac{1}{2}\sqrt{(\sqrt{5}+1)^2} = \dfrac{1}{2}(\sqrt{5}+1)$.

Example 35:

Consider a quadratic equation $az^2 + bz + c = 0$ where a, b, c, are complex numbers. Find the condition that the equation has

(i) one purely imaginary root

(ii) one purely real root

(iii) two purely imaginary roots

(iv) two purely real root

Solution:

(i) Let z_1 (purely imaginary) be a root of the give equation.

$\Rightarrow z_1 = -\bar{z}_1$

and $az_1^2 + bz_1 + c = 0$ ...(1)

$\Rightarrow \overline{az_1^2 + bz_1 + c} = \bar{0}$

$\Rightarrow \overline{az_1^2} + \overline{bz_1} + \bar{c} = 0$

$\Rightarrow \bar{a}\bar{z}_1^2 - \bar{b}z_1 + \bar{c} = 0$ (as $\bar{z}_1 = -z_1$) ...(2)

Now (1) and (2) must have one common root.

$$\Rightarrow \frac{z_1^2}{(b\bar{c}+c\bar{b})} = \frac{z_1}{(c\bar{a}-a\bar{c})} = \frac{1}{-(a\bar{b}+\bar{a}b)}$$

$$\Rightarrow z_1^2 = -\frac{(b\bar{c}+c\bar{b})}{(a\bar{b}+\bar{a}b)} = \frac{(c\bar{a}-a\bar{c})^2}{(a\bar{b}+\bar{a}b)^2}$$

$$\Rightarrow (b\bar{c}+c\bar{b})(a\bar{b}+\bar{a}b)+(c\bar{a}-a\bar{c})^2 = 0$$

(ii) Let z_1 (purely real, be a root of the given equation

$\Rightarrow z_1 = \bar{z}_1$

and $az_1^2\ bz_1 + c = 0$ ...(1)

$\Rightarrow az_1^2 + bz_1 + c = \bar{0}$

$\Rightarrow \overline{az_1^2} + \overline{bz}_1 + \bar{c} = 0$

$\Rightarrow \bar{a}z_1^2 - \bar{b}z_1 + \bar{c} = 0 \quad (\text{as } \bar{z}_1 = -z_1)$ ...(2)

Now (1) and (2) must have one common root.

$$\Rightarrow \frac{z_1^2}{(b\bar{c}-\bar{b}c)} = \frac{z_1}{(a\bar{c}-\bar{a}c)} = \frac{1}{(a\bar{b}-\bar{a}b)}$$

Required condition is

$$\Rightarrow (b\bar{c}-c\bar{b})(a\bar{b}-\bar{a}b)+(c\bar{a}-a\bar{c})^2 = 0$$

(iii) Let z_1 and z_2 be two purely imaginary roots then

$\bar{z}_1 = -z_1, \bar{z}_2 = -z_2$

Now $az^2 + bz + c = 0$ ...(1)

$\Rightarrow az^2 + bz + c = \bar{0}$

$\Rightarrow \overline{az}^2 + \overline{bz} + \bar{c} = 0$

$\Rightarrow \bar{a}z^2 - \bar{b}z + \bar{c} = 0$ ...(2)

Equation (1) and (2) must be identical as their root are same

$$\Rightarrow \frac{a}{a} = -\frac{b}{b} = \frac{c}{c}$$

(iv) Let z_1 and z_2 be two purely real roots then

$$\bar{z}_1 = z_1, \bar{z}_2 = z_2$$

In this case $az^2 + bz + c = 0$ ...(1)

$$\Rightarrow \quad \overline{az^2} + \overline{bz} + \overline{c} = 0$$

$$\Rightarrow \quad \bar{a}z^2 + \bar{b}z + \bar{c} = 0 \quad ...(2)$$

Equation (1) and (2) must be identical, as their root are same

$$\Rightarrow \frac{a}{\bar{a}} = \frac{b}{\bar{b}} = \frac{c}{\bar{c}}.$$

Example 36:

Let z_1, z_2, z_3 three distinct complex numbers satisfying $|z_1 - 1| = |z_2 - 1| = |z_3 - 1|$. Let A, B, and C be the points represented in the Argand plane corresponding to z_1, z_2 and z_3 respectively. Prove that $z_1 + z_2 + z_3 = 3$ if and only of Δ ABC is an equilateral triangle.

Solution:

$|z_1 - 1| = |z_2 - 1| = |z_3 - 1|$

$\Rightarrow$ The point corresponding to 1 (say P) is equidistant from the points A, B and C.

$\Rightarrow$ P is the circumcentre of the ΔABC

Now if $z_1 + z_2 + z_3 = 3$ then the point corresponding to centroid of the ΔABC is $\frac{z_1 + z_2 + z_3}{3} = 1 \Rightarrow$ circumcentre and centroid coincide.

$\Rightarrow$ ΔABC is equilateral

Conversely if ΔABC is equilateral, then centroid is the same as the circumcentre *i.e.*, P. Hence centroid $\frac{z_1 + z_2 + z_3}{3} = 1$

$$\Rightarrow \quad z_1 + z_2 + z_3 = 3.$$

Example 37:

Consider two pairs of non-zero conjugate complex numbers (z_1, z_2) and (z_3, z_4). Find the value of arg

$$\left(\frac{z_1}{z_3}\right) + \arg\left(\frac{z_2}{z_4}\right).$$

Solution:

$$\arg\left(\frac{z_1}{z_3}\right) + \arg\left(\frac{z_2}{z_4}\right) = \arg\left(\frac{z_1 z_2}{z_3 z_4}\right)$$

$$= \arg\left(\frac{|z_1|^2}{|z_3|^2}\right) \quad (\text{as } z_2 = \bar{z}_1 \text{ and } z_4 = \bar{z}_3$$

= 0 (as argument of a positive real number is zero).

Example 38:

If z_1 and z_2 are two complex numbers, then prove that
$|z_1 - z_2|^2 \leq (1 + k)\,|z_1|^2 + (1 + k^{-1})\,|z_2|^2 \;\forall\, k \in R.$

Solution:

$$|(kz_1 + z_2)|^2 \geq 0 \Rightarrow (kz_1 + z_2)\left(k\bar{z}_1 + \bar{z}_2\right) \geq 0$$

$$\Rightarrow \left(z_1 + \frac{z_2}{k}\right)\left(k\bar{z}_1 + \bar{z}_2\right) \geq 0 \text{ as } k > 0$$

$$\Rightarrow k\,|z_1|^2 + \frac{1}{k}\,|z_2|^2 + z_1\bar{z}_2 + \bar{z}_1 z_2 \geq 0$$

$$\Rightarrow (1 + k)\,|z_1)^2 + (1 + k^{-1})\,|z_2)^2 \geq |z_1|^2 + |z_2|^2 - \bar{z}_1 z_2 - \bar{z}_1 z_2$$

$$\Rightarrow (1 + k)\,|z_1|^2 + (1 + k^{-1})\,|z_2|^2 \geq |z_1 - z_2|^2.$$

Example 39:

(i) *If the complex slope of the line joining the points represented by z_1, z_2 in the Argand plane is defined as $\dfrac{z_1 - z_2}{\bar{z}_1 - \bar{z}_2}$, find the condition for perpendicular or two lines with complex slopes; ω_1 and ω_2.*

(ii) *If $x_1 \leq x_2$ and $y_1 \leq y_2$ for complex numbers $z_1 = x_1 + iy_1$ and $z_2 = x_2 + iy_2$ we write $z_1 \leq z_2$. Show that all complex numbers z with $1 \leq z$ we have $\dfrac{1 - z}{1 + z} \leq 0$.*

Solution:

(i) Let $\omega_1 = \dfrac{z_1 - z_2}{\bar{z}_1 - \bar{z}_2}$ and $\omega_2 = \dfrac{z_3 - z_4}{\bar{z}_3 - \bar{z}_4}$

Now $|\omega_2| = \left|\dfrac{z_1 - z_2}{\bar{z}_1 - \bar{z}_2}\right| = \left|\dfrac{z_1 - z_2}{z_1 - z_2}\right| = 1$ $\qquad \left(\text{as } \left|\dfrac{z}{\bar{z}}\right| = 1\right)$

Similarly $|\omega_2| = 1$

Now amp ω_1 = amp $\dfrac{z_1 - z_2}{\bar{z}_1 - \bar{z}_2}$ = amp $\dfrac{z_1 - z_2}{z_1 - z_2}$

= 2 amp $(z_1 - z_2)$ ...(1)

Similarly, amp ω_2 = 2 amp $(z_3 - z_4)$ ...(2)

Now amp $\dfrac{z_1 - z_2}{z_3 - z_4} = \pm\dfrac{\pi}{2}$ because the line segments joining z_1, z_2 and z_3, z_4 are at right angle

From (1) an (2), we get

amp ω_1 = amp ω_2 = 2 {amp($z_1 - z_2$) – amp ($z_3 - z_4$)

$$= 2 \text{ amp} \frac{z_1 - z_2}{z_3 - z_4} = 2\left(\pm\frac{\pi}{2}\right) = \pm\pi$$

$$\Rightarrow \text{amp}\frac{\omega_1}{\omega_2} = \pm\pi \Rightarrow \frac{\omega_1}{\omega_2} = \left|\frac{\omega_1}{\omega_2}\right|$$

{cos (± p) + i sin (± π)} = – 1 = $\omega_1 + \omega_2 = 0$.

(ii) Let z = x + iy the $1 \le z$

$\Rightarrow 1 \le x$ and $0 \le y$

Consider $z' = \dfrac{1-z}{1+z}$

$$\text{Re}(z') = \text{Re}\left(\frac{1-z}{1+z}\right) = \text{Re}\left(\frac{1-x-iy}{1+x+iy}\right)$$

$$= \text{Re}\left(\frac{(1-x-iy)(1+x-iy)}{(1+x)^2 + y^2}\right)$$

$$= \frac{(1-x)(1+x)-y^2}{(1+x)^2+y^2} = \frac{1-x^2-y^2}{(1+x)^2+y^2} \le 0$$

$$\text{Im}(z') = \text{Im}\left(\frac{1-z}{1+z}\right) = \frac{(1-x)(x-y)+(-y)(1+x)}{(1+x)^2+y^2}$$

$$= \frac{-2y}{(1+x)^2+y^2} \le 0$$

Thus, we have $\text{Re}(z') \le 0$ and $\text{Im}(z') \le 0$

$\Rightarrow z' \le 0$.

Example 40:

z_1, z_2, z_3 are three non-zero complex numbers such that z_2 ' z_1, and $a = |z_1|$, $b = |z_2|$,

$c = |z_3|$. *If* $\begin{vmatrix} a & b & c \\ b & c & a \\ c & a & b \end{vmatrix} = 0$, *then show that*

$$arg.\ \frac{z_3}{z_2} = \arg\left(\frac{z_3 - z_1}{z_2 - z_1}\right)^2.$$

Solution:

$$\begin{vmatrix} a & b & c \\ b & c & a \\ c & a & b \end{vmatrix} = (a+b+c)\ (a-b)\ (b-c)\ (c-a) = 0$$

$\Rightarrow a = b = c$ (as $a + b + c \neq 0$)

$\Rightarrow z_1, z_2$ and z_3 lie on a circle with centre at origin

Clearly $\angle BOC = 2\ \angle BAC$

$$\Rightarrow \quad \arg\left(\frac{z_3}{z_2}\right) = 2\arg\left(\frac{z_3 - z_1}{z_2 - z_1}\right) = \arg\left(\frac{z_3 - z_1}{z_2 - z_1}\right)^2.$$

Example 41:

A is represented by the number 6i, B by the number 3, and P by z. If PA = 2PB, then show that the locus of P is the circle $z\bar{z} = (4 + 2i)z + (4 - 2i)\bar{z}$. *Find its radius and the centre.*

Solution:

$A \equiv 6i, \qquad B \equiv 3,\ P \equiv P\ (z)$

$PA = 2PB$

$\Rightarrow |z - 6i| = 2\ |z - 3|$

$\Rightarrow (z - 6i)\ (\bar{z} + 6i) = 4(z - 3)\ (\bar{z} - 3)$

$\Rightarrow z\bar{z} = (4 + 2i)\ z + (4 - 2i)\bar{z}$

Example 42:

Solve the equation $z^7 + 1 = 0$ and hence deduce that

(i) $\cos\frac{\pi}{7}\cos\frac{3\pi}{7}\cos\frac{5\pi}{7} = -\frac{1}{8}$

(ii) $\cos\frac{\pi}{14}\cos\frac{3\pi}{14}\cos\frac{5\pi}{14} = \frac{\sqrt{7}}{8}$

(iii) $\sin\frac{\pi}{14}\sin\frac{3\pi}{14}\sin\frac{5\pi}{14} = \frac{1}{8}$

(iv) $\tan^2\frac{\pi}{14} + \tan^2\frac{3\pi}{14} + \tan^2\frac{5\pi}{14} = 5$

Solution:

$$z^7 + 1 = 0$$

The roots are $-1, \alpha, \alpha^3, \alpha^5, \bar{\alpha}, \bar{\alpha}^3, \bar{\alpha}^5$

Where a = cos $\cos\frac{\pi}{7} + i\sin\frac{3\pi}{7}$

$\alpha^3 = \cos\frac{3\pi}{7} + i\sin\frac{3\pi}{7}$

$\alpha^5 = \cos\frac{5\pi}{7} + i\sin\frac{5\pi}{7}$

Now $z^7 + 1 = (z+1)(z-a)(z-\bar{\alpha})(z-a^3)(z-a^5)(z-\bar{\alpha}^5)$

$$\Rightarrow \frac{z^7+1}{z+1} = \left\{z^2 - (\alpha+\alpha)z + \alpha\bar{\alpha}\right\} \ldots \left\{z^2 - \left(\alpha^5 + \bar{\alpha}^5\right) + \alpha^5\bar{\alpha}^5\right\}$$

$$\Rightarrow (z^6 - z^5 + z^4 - z^3 + z^2 - z + 1)$$

$$= \left(z^2 - 2z\cos\frac{\pi}{7} + 1\right)\left(z^2 - 2z\cos\frac{3\pi}{7} + 1\right)\left(z^2 - 2z\cos\frac{5\pi}{7} + 1\right) \quad \ldots(1)$$

[since $a + \bar{\alpha} = 2\cos\frac{\pi}{7}$, $\alpha\bar{\alpha} = 1$]

$$\Rightarrow \frac{z^6+1}{z^3} - \frac{z^5+z}{z^3} + \frac{z^4+z^2}{z^3} - \frac{z^3}{z^3}$$

$$= \left(\frac{z^2 - 2z\cos\frac{\pi}{7} + 1}{z}\right)\left(\frac{z^2 - 2z\cos\frac{3\pi}{7} + 1}{z}\right)\left(\frac{z^2 - 2z\cos\frac{5\pi}{7} + 1}{z}\right)$$

$$\Rightarrow \left(z_3 + \frac{1}{z^3}\right) - \left(z^2 + \frac{1}{z^2}\right) + \left(z + \frac{1}{z}\right) - 1$$

$$= \left\{\left(z + \frac{1}{z}\right) - 2\cos\frac{\pi}{7}\right\}\left\{\left(z + \frac{1}{z}\right) - 2\cos\frac{3\pi}{7}\right\}\left\{\left(z + \frac{1}{z}\right) - 2\cos\frac{5\pi}{7}\right\}$$

or, $\left(z + \frac{1}{z}\right)^3 - 3\left(z + \frac{1}{z}\right) - \left(z + \frac{1}{z}\right)^2 + 2 + \left(z + \frac{1}{z}\right) - 1$

$$= \left(z + \frac{1}{z} - 2\cos\frac{\pi}{7}\right)\left(z + \frac{1}{z} - 2\cos\frac{3\pi}{7}\right)\left(z + \frac{1}{z} - 2\cos\frac{5\pi}{7}\right)$$

Let $z + \frac{1}{z} = 2x$

We get, $8x^3 - 6x - 4x^2 + 2 + 2x - 1$

$$= 8\left(x - \cos\frac{\pi}{7}\right)\left(x - \cos\frac{3\pi}{7}\right)\left(x - \cos\frac{5\pi}{7}\right)$$

or, $8x^3 - 4x^2 - 4x + 1 = 8\left(x - \cos\frac{\pi}{7}\right)\left(x - \cos\frac{3\pi}{7}\right)\left(x - \cos\frac{5\pi}{7}\right) = 0 \ldots(2)$

$\therefore$ $\cos\frac{\pi}{7}, \cos\frac{3\pi}{7}$ and $\cos\frac{5\pi}{7}$ are the roots of the equation

$$8x^3 - 4x^2 - 4x + 1 = 0$$

$\therefore$ Product of roots $= - -\frac{1}{8}$

$$\therefore \cos\frac{\pi}{7}.\cos\frac{3\pi}{7}.\cos\frac{5\pi}{7} = -\frac{1}{8}.$$

(ii) Putting x = – 1 in (2), we get

$$-8 - 4 + 4 + 1 = -8$$

$$\left(1+\cos\frac{\pi}{7}\right)\left(1+\cos\frac{\pi}{7}\right)\left(1+\cos\frac{3\pi}{7}\right)\left(1+\cos\frac{5\pi}{7}\right)$$

or, $$7 = 8^2\cos^2\frac{\pi}{14}\cos^2\frac{3\pi}{14}\cos^2\frac{5\pi}{14}$$

or $$\cos\frac{\pi}{14}\cos\frac{3\pi}{14}\cos\frac{5\pi}{14} = \pm\frac{\sqrt{7}}{8}$$

since $0 < \frac{\pi}{14}, \frac{3\pi}{14}, \frac{5\pi}{14} < \frac{\pi}{2}$, we reject the –ve sign

$$\therefore \cos\frac{\pi}{14}\cos\frac{3\pi}{14}\cos\frac{5\pi}{14} = \frac{\sqrt{7}}{8}.$$

(iii) Putting x = 1 in (2), we get

$$8 - 4 - 4 + 1 = 8\left(1-\cos\frac{\pi}{7}\right)\left(1-\cos\frac{3\pi}{7}\right)\left(1-\cos\frac{5\pi}{7}\right)$$

or, $$1 = 8^{2\sin^2}\frac{\pi}{14}\sin^2\frac{3\pi}{14}\sin^2\frac{5\pi}{14}$$

$$\sin\frac{\pi}{14}\sin\frac{3\pi}{14}\sin\frac{5\pi}{14} = \pm\frac{\sqrt{1}}{8} = \pm\frac{1}{8}$$

since $0 < \frac{\pi}{14}, \frac{3\pi}{14}, \frac{5\pi}{14} < \frac{\pi}{2}$, we reject the –ve sign

$$\therefore \sin\frac{\pi}{14}\sin\frac{3\pi}{14}\sin\frac{5\pi}{14} = \pm\frac{\sqrt{1}}{8} = \frac{1}{8}$$

(iv) $$\tan\frac{\pi}{14}\tan\frac{3\pi}{14}\tan\frac{5\pi}{14} = \frac{1/8}{\sqrt{7}/8} = \frac{1}{\sqrt{7}}$$

We have (1),

$$\frac{z^7+1}{z+1}=\left(z^2-2z\cos\frac{\pi}{7}+1\right)\left(z^2-2z\cos\frac{3\pi}{7}+1\right)\left(z^2-2z\cos\frac{5\pi}{7}+1\right)$$

Let $\quad z=\dfrac{1+y}{1-y}$

$\therefore \quad z^2-2z\cos$

$$\cos\frac{\pi}{7}+1=\left(\frac{1+y}{1-y}\right)^2-2\left(\frac{1+y}{1-y}\right)\left(\frac{1-\tan^2\frac{\pi}{14}}{1+\tan^2\frac{\pi}{14}}\right)+1 \qquad \text{...(3)}$$

$$=\frac{2\left(1+y^2\right)\left(1+\tan^2\frac{\pi}{14}\right)-2\left(1-y^2\right)\left(1-\tan^2\frac{\pi}{14}\right)}{(1-y)^2\left(1-\tan^2\frac{\pi}{14}\right)}$$

$$=\frac{2\left(2y^2+2\tan^2\frac{\pi}{14}\right)}{(1-y)^2\left(1+\dfrac{\sin^2\frac{\pi}{14}}{\cos^2\frac{\pi}{14}}\right)}=\frac{2^2\cos^2\frac{\pi}{14}}{(1-y)^2}\left(y^2+\tan^2\frac{\pi}{14}\right)$$

$\therefore$ Putting $z=\dfrac{1+y}{1-y}$ in (3), we get $\dfrac{\dfrac{(1+y)^7}{(1-y)^7}-1}{\dfrac{1+y}{1-y}+1}$

$$2^6\cos^2\frac{\pi}{14}\cos^2\frac{3\pi}{14}\cos^2\frac{5\pi}{14}\left(y^2+\tan^2\frac{\pi}{14}\right)$$

$$=\frac{\left(y^2+\tan^2\frac{3\pi}{14}\right)\left(y^2+\tan^2\frac{5\pi}{14}\right)}{(1-y)^6}$$

or, $$\frac{(1+y)^7+(1-y)^7}{2}=2^5\times\frac{7}{64}\left(y^2+\tan^2\frac{\pi}{14}\right)$$

$$\left(y^2-\tan^2\frac{3\pi}{14}\right)\left(y^2+\tan^2\frac{5\pi}{14}\right)$$

$\therefore$ Equating coefficient of y^4 from both sides, we get

$$\frac{1}{2}\left({}^7C_4\right)=7\left(\tan^2\frac{\pi}{14}+\tan^2\frac{3\pi}{14}+\tan^2\frac{5\pi}{14}\right)$$

$$\therefore \tan^2\frac{\pi}{14}+\tan^2\frac{3\pi}{14}+\tan^2\frac{5\pi}{14}=5$$

Example 43:

Consider a 'n' sided regular polygon with origin as it's centre. If z_1 be the complex number representing a vertex A_1, of the polygon, find the complex number associated with the vertex that is adjacent to A_1.

Solution:

Vertex adjacent to A_1 is either A_2 or A_p. Let z_2 and z_1 represent the vertices A_2 and A_n respectively. Considering the rotation about the origin, we get

$$\frac{z_2-0}{z_1-0}=\frac{|z_2|}{|z_1|}e^{i2\pi/n} = e^{i2\pi/n}$$

$\Rightarrow$ $$z_2 = z_1\, e^{2p/n}$$

Similarly,

$$\frac{z_n}{z_1}=e^{-2\pi/n}$$

$\Rightarrow$ $$z_n = z_1 e^{-i2\pi/n}.$$

Example 44:

If $|z_1| = |z_2| = |z_3| = 1$, prove that $|z_1 + z_2 + z_3| = =\left|\frac{1}{z_1}+\frac{1}{z_2}+\frac{1}{z_3}\right|$.

Solution:

We know that $|z| = |\bar{z}|$

$\Rightarrow$ $$|z_1 + z_2 + z_3| = |\bar{z}_1+\bar{z}_2+\bar{z}_3|$$

$$=\frac{\bar{z}_1.z_1}{z_1}+\frac{\bar{z}_2.z_2}{z_2}+\frac{\bar{z}_3.z_3}{z_3}$$

$$=\left|\frac{|z_1|^2}{z_1}+\frac{|z_2|^2}{z_2}+\frac{|z_3|^2}{z_3}\right|$$

$$=\left|\frac{1}{z_1}+\frac{1}{z_2}+\frac{1}{z_3}\right| \qquad (\because |z_1)^2 = |z_2|^2 = |z_3|)^2 = 1)$$

Example 45:

Consider a square ABCD such that z_1, z_2, z_3 and z_4 represent its vertices A, B, C and D respectively. Express 'z_3' and 'z_4' in terms of z_1 and z_2.

Solution:

Consider the rotation of AB about A through an angle π/4, we get

$$\frac{z_3 - z_1}{z_2 - z_1} = \frac{|z_3 - z_1|}{|z_2 - z_1|} e^{i\pi/4}$$

$$= \sqrt{2}\left(\cos\frac{\pi}{4} + i\sin\frac{\pi}{4}\right)$$

$\Rightarrow$ $$z_3 = z_1 + (z_2 - z_1)(1 + i)$$

Similarly, $$\frac{z_4 - z_1}{z_2 - z_1} = \frac{|z_4 - z_1|}{|z_2 - z_1|} e^{i\pi/2} = i$$

$\Rightarrow$ $$z_4 = z_1 + i(z_2 - z_1)$$

Example 46:

Let z_1 and z_2 be the roots of the equation $z^2 + pz + q = 0$, where the coefficients p and q may be complex number. Let A and B represent z_1 and z_2 in the complex plane. If $\angle AOB = a \neq 0$ and OA = OB, where O is the origin, prove that $p^2 = 4\theta\cos^2\left(\frac{\alpha}{2}\right)$.

Solution:

$$z_1 + z_2 = -p \qquad ...(1)$$

and $$z_1 z_2 = q \qquad ...(2)$$

$$z_2 = z_1 e^{i\alpha} \qquad ...(3)$$

Now
$$\begin{aligned} p^2 &= (z_1 + z_2)^2 \\ &= (z_1 + z_1 e^{i\alpha})^2 \\ &= z_1^2(1 + 2e^{i\alpha} + e^{i2\alpha}) \\ &= qe^{-i\alpha}(1 + 2e^{i\alpha} + e^{i2\alpha}) \\ &= q(2 + e^{-i\alpha} + e^{i\alpha}) \\ &= q(2 + 2\cos\alpha) = 4q\cos^2\frac{\alpha}{2} \end{aligned}$$

Example 47:

Consider the complex numbers $A(z_1)$, $B(z_2)$ and $C(z_3)$ as the vertices of a triangle ABC. Let P be the fcot of the altitude from A on BC.

Find the complex number associated with the point P.

Solution:

$$\angle APC = p/2 \Rightarrow \arg\left(\frac{z - z_1}{z_2 - z_3}\right) = \frac{\pi}{2} \text{ or } \frac{\pi}{2}$$

$$\Rightarrow \frac{z-z_1}{z_2-z_3} \text{ is purely imaginary}$$

$$\Rightarrow \frac{z-z_1}{z_2-z_3} + \frac{\bar{z}-\bar{z}_1}{\bar{z}_2-\bar{z}_3} = 0$$

$$\Rightarrow \frac{\bar{z}}{\bar{z}_2-\bar{z}_3} = \frac{\bar{z}_1}{\bar{z}_2-\bar{z}_3} - \frac{z-z_1}{z_2-z_3}$$

Also P(z) is lying on the through B and C.

$$\Rightarrow \frac{z-z_2}{z_2-z_3} = \frac{\bar{z}-\bar{z}_2}{\bar{z}_2-\bar{z}_3}$$

$$\Rightarrow \frac{\bar{z}}{\bar{z}_2-\bar{z}_3} = \frac{\bar{z}_2}{\bar{z}_2-\bar{z}_3} + \frac{z-z_2}{z_2-z_3}$$

$$\frac{z-z_2}{z_2-z_3} + \frac{\bar{z}_2}{\bar{z}_2-\bar{z}_3} = \frac{\bar{z}_1}{\bar{z}_2-\bar{z}_3} - \frac{z-z_1}{z_2-z_3}$$

$$\Rightarrow z = \frac{1}{2}\left(\frac{(\bar{z}_1-\bar{z}_2)(z_2-z_3)}{\bar{z}_2-\bar{z}_3} + z_1 + z_2\right).$$

Example 48:

Complex numbers z_1, z_2, z_3 are the vertices A,B,C respectively of an isosceles right angled triangle with right angle at C. Show that $(z_1-z_2)^2 = 2(z_1 - z_3)(z_3 - z_2)$

Solution:

In the isosceles triangle ABC, AC = BC and BC ⊥ AC. It means that AC is rotated through angle $\pi/2$ to occupy the position BC.

Hence we have $\frac{z_2-z_3}{z_1-z_3} = e^{-i\pi/2} = + i$

$\Rightarrow z_2 - z_3 = + i(z_1 - z_3)$

$\Rightarrow z_2^2 + z_3^2 - 2z_2z_3 = -\left(z_2^2 + z_3^2 - 2z_1z_3\right)$

$\Rightarrow z_1^2 + z_2^2 \; 2z_1z_2 = 2z_1z_3 + 2z_2z_3 - 2z_1z_2 - 2z_3^2 = 2(z_1 - z_3)(z_3 - z_2)$

$\Rightarrow (z_1 - z_2)^2 = 2(z_1 - z_3)(z_3 - z_2).$

Example 49:

If z_1, z_2, z_3 are complex numbers such that $\frac{2}{z_1} = \frac{1}{z_2} + \frac{1}{z_3}$, show that the points represented by z_1, z_2, z_3 lie on a circle passing through the origin.

Solution:

Since $P(z_1)$, $Q(z_2)$, $R(z_3)$ and $S(z_4)$ are concyclic points,
$\Delta PSQ = \angle PRQ$

$$\Rightarrow \arg.\frac{z_2 - z_4}{z_1 - z_4} = \arg\frac{z_2 - z_3}{z_1 - z_3}$$

$$\Rightarrow \arg\left[\left(\frac{z_2 - z_4}{z_1 - z_4}\right)\left(\frac{z_1 - z_3}{z_2 - z_3}\right)\right] = 0$$

$$\Rightarrow \frac{(z_2 - z_4)}{(z_1 - z_4)}\cdot\frac{(z_1 - z_3)}{(z_2 - z_3)} = \text{real} \qquad ...(1)$$

We have $\dfrac{2}{z_1} = \dfrac{1}{z_2} + \dfrac{1}{z_3}$ from which

$$z_3 = \frac{z_1 z_2}{2z_2 - z_1} \qquad ...(2)$$

From (1) and (2), $\dfrac{z_2}{z_1} \times \dfrac{z_1 - \dfrac{z_1 z_2}{2z_2 - z_1}}{z_2 - \dfrac{z_1 z_2}{2z_2 - z_1}} = \text{real}$

$$\Rightarrow \frac{z_2 - z_1}{2(z_2 - z_1)} = \text{real}$$

$\Rightarrow \dfrac{1}{2}$ = real, which is true.

Therefore z_1, z_2, z_3 and the origin are concylic.

Alternative Solution:

$$\frac{2}{z_1} = \frac{1}{z_2} + \frac{1}{z_3}$$

$$\Rightarrow \frac{1}{z_1} - \frac{1}{z_2} = \frac{1}{z_3} - \frac{1}{z_1}$$

$$\Rightarrow \frac{z_2 - z_1}{z_1 z_2} = \frac{z_1 - z_3}{z_1 z_3}$$

$$\Rightarrow \frac{z_2 - z_1}{z_3 - z_1} = -\frac{z_2}{z_3}$$

$$\Rightarrow \arg\left(\frac{z_2 - z_1}{z_3 - z_1}\right) = \arg\left(-\frac{z_2}{z_3}\right) = \pi + \arg\left(\frac{z_2}{z_3}\right)$$

$$\Rightarrow \alpha = \pi - \beta \Rightarrow \alpha + \beta = \pi$$

$\Rightarrow$ points A, B, C, D are concyclic.

Example 50:

Consider the complex numbers $z_1 = 10 + 6i$ and $z_2 = 4 + 2i$. If $\arg\left(\frac{z-z_1}{z-z_2}\right) = \frac{\pi}{4}$, find the centre and radius of the locus of complex number z.

Solution:

Let $O(z_0)$ be the centre of the circle.

We have $\angle AOB = \frac{\pi}{2}.AB = |z_1 - z_2| = |6 + 4i| = \sqrt{52}$

Let $OQ = OB = r$

$\Rightarrow \quad AB = r\sqrt{2}$

$\Rightarrow \quad r = \sqrt{26}$

Also $\quad \frac{z_2 - z_0}{z_1 - z_0} = e^{-ip/2} = -i$

$\Rightarrow \quad z_2 - z_0 = -i(z_1 - z_0)$

$\Rightarrow \quad z_0 = \frac{1}{2}(z_2 - iz_2 + iz_1 + z_1) = 5 - 7i.$

Alternative Solution:

We have $\quad \frac{\pi}{4} = \arg.\frac{z-z}{z-z_2}$

$= \arg(z - z_1) - \arg(z - z_2)$

$\Rightarrow \quad \tan^{-1}1 = \tan^{-1}\frac{y-6}{x-10} - \tan^{-1}\frac{y-2}{x-4}$

$\Rightarrow \quad \tan^{-1} = \tan^{-1}\left[\frac{\frac{y-6}{x-10} - \frac{y-2}{x-4}}{1+\frac{(y-6)(y-2)}{(x-10)(x-4)}}\right]$

$\Rightarrow \quad 1 = \frac{6y - 4x + 4}{x^2 + y^2 - 14x - 8y + 52}$

$\Rightarrow \quad x^2 + y^2 - 10x - 14y + 48 = 0,$

or $\quad (x - 5)^2 + (y - 7)^2 = 26 = \left(\sqrt{26}\right)^2$

or $|x - 5 + i(y - 7)| = \sqrt{26}$

$\Rightarrow$ $|z - 5 - 7i|\ \sqrt{26}$.

Example 50(a):

Construct an equation whose roots are +i, sec(2π/5), sec(4π/5).

Solution:

Let $5\theta = 2np$, $n \in |$

$\Rightarrow \cos 3\theta = \cos 2\theta$

$\Rightarrow 4\cos^3\theta - 2\cos^2\theta - 3\cos\theta + 1 = 0$

Put $\cos\theta = x$, here note that θ may be 0 or $\frac{2\pi}{5}$ or $\frac{4\pi}{5}$ for n = 0, 1, 2 and also if we take n = 3, 4, 5, ..., then the value of $\cos\theta$ will start repeating.

$\Rightarrow 4x^3 - 2x^2 - 3x + 1 = 0$

$\Rightarrow (x - 1)(4x^2 + 2x - 1) = 0$

$\Rightarrow 4x^2 + 2x - 1 = 0$

where $x = \cos\frac{2\pi}{5}, \cos\frac{4\pi}{5}$.

Hence required equation is

$$\left(\frac{4}{x^2} + \frac{2}{x} - 1\right)(x^2 + 1) = 0$$

$\Rightarrow (x^2 - 2x - 4)(x^2 + 1) = 0$

$\Rightarrow x^4 - 2x^3 - 3x^2 - 2x - 4 = 0.$

Example 51:

ABCD is a rhombus. The diagonals AC and BD intersect at the point M and satisfy BD = 2AC. Its points D and M represent the complex numbers 1 + i and 2 – i respectively. Find the complex number represented by A.

Solution:

Let A be (x, y)

It is given that BD = 2AC $\Rightarrow$ MD = 2AM

Also DM is perpendicular to AM

$\Rightarrow (1 - 2)^2 + (1 + 1)^2$

$= 4[(x - 2)^2 + (y + 1)^2]$ ...(1)

and $\frac{y + 1}{x - 2} \cdot \frac{1 + 1}{1 - 2} = -1$

$\Rightarrow$ 2(y + 1) = x − 2

With x − 2 = 2(y + 1), (1) gives $(y + 1)^2$

= 1/4

$\Rightarrow$ y = − 1/2, − 3/2 $\Rightarrow$ x = 3, 1

$\Rightarrow$ A represents z = 3 − i/2,

or 1−3i/2

Alternative Solution:

MD = 2AM and AM $\perp$ DM *i.e.*, AMD = π/2

$$\Rightarrow \quad \frac{z-(2-i)}{(1+i)-(2-i)} = \frac{AM}{MD}.e^{\pm\frac{i\pi}{2}} = \pm\, i/2$$

$$\Rightarrow \quad z-(2-i) = \pm\frac{i}{2}(-1+2i)$$

$$\Rightarrow \quad z = 3-i/2 \text{ or } 1\text{-}3i/2.$$

Example 52:

For every value of c ≥ 0, find all the complex numbers z which satisfy the equation $|z|^2 - 2iz + 2c(1 + i) = 0$

Solution:

If z = x + iy, then the given equation reduces to

$$x^2 + y^2 - 2ix + 2y + 2c + 2ic = 0 \Rightarrow x = c,$$

so that the real part yields $y^2 + 2y + c^2 + 2c = 0$.

$\Rightarrow$ $y \neq R^+$

For real y, $1 - 2c - c^2 \geq 0$

$\Rightarrow$ $c^2 + 2c - 1 \leq 0$.

$\Rightarrow$ $(c + \sqrt{2} + 1)\,[c - (\sqrt{2} - 1)] \leq 0 \leq c \leq \sqrt{2} - 1$.

Hence the solutions $c + \left[-1 \pm \sqrt{1-2c-c^2}\right] i \; 0 \leq c \leq \sqrt{2}-1$.

For c = 0, y = 0, − 2,

so that z = 0, z = − 2i.

Example 53:

Find the complex numbers z which simultaneously satisfy the equations

$$\left|\frac{z-12}{z-8i}\right| = \frac{5}{3}, \left|\frac{z-4}{z-8}\right| = 1.$$

Solution:

Now $$\left|\frac{z-4}{z-8}\right| = 1 \Rightarrow \left|\frac{x-4+iy}{x-8+iy}\right| = 1$$

$\Rightarrow$ $(x-4)^3 + y^2 = (x-8)^2 + y^2$

$\Rightarrow$ $x = 6.$

With $x = 6$, $$\left|\frac{z-12}{z-8i}\right| = \frac{5}{3} \Rightarrow \left|\frac{-6+iy}{6+i(y-8)}\right| = \frac{5}{3}$$

$\Rightarrow$ $9(36 + y^2) = 25[36 + (y-8)^2]$

$\Rightarrow$ $y^2 - 25y + 136 = 0$

$\Rightarrow$ $y = 178.$

Hence, the required numbers are

$$z = 6 + 17i,\ 6 + 8i.$$

Example 54:

Prove that the area of the triangle whose vertices are the points represented by the complex numbers z_1, z_2, z_3 on the Arand diagram is $\sum\left(\frac{(z_2 - z_3)|z_1|^2}{4iz_1}\right)$.

Solution:

$$\text{Area of } \Delta ABC = \frac{1}{2}.AB.CD$$

$$= \frac{1}{2}|z_1 - z_2|CD$$

Equation of AB is $z\bar{a} + \bar{z}a + b =$ where

$$a = i(z_1 - z_1),\ b = \left(\frac{\bar{z}_1 z_2 - z_1\bar{z}_2}{i}\right)$$

$$\Rightarrow CD = \frac{|z_3\bar{a} + \bar{z}_3 a + b|}{2|a|}$$

$$\Rightarrow \text{Required area} = \frac{1}{4|a|}|z_1 - z_2|\,|z_3\bar{a} + \bar{z}_3 a + b|\cdot$$

Example 55:

Find the greatest and the least values of the moduli of complex numbers z satisfying the equation $\left|z - \frac{4}{z}\right| = 2$. *Find also the corresponding complex numbers.*

Solution:

We have $\left||z| - \left|\frac{4}{z}\right|\right| \le \left|z - \frac{4}{z}\right| = 2$

$\Rightarrow \quad -2 \le |z| - \frac{4}{|z|} \le 2$

$\Rightarrow \quad |z|^2 + 2|z| - 4 \ge 0$ or $|z|^2 - 4 \le 0$

$\Rightarrow \quad (|z| + 1)^2 - 5 \ge 0$ or $(|z| - 1)^2 \le 5$

$\Rightarrow \quad (|z| + 1 + \sqrt{5})(|z| + 1 - \sqrt{5}) \ge 0$

or $\quad (|z| - 1 + \sqrt{5})(|z| - 1 - \sqrt{5} \le 0$

$\Rightarrow \quad |z| \le -\sqrt{5} - 1$ or $|z| \ge \sqrt{5} - 1$

or $\quad \sqrt{5} - 1 \le |z| \le \sqrt{5} + 1$

$\Rightarrow$ Greatest value of $|z| = \sqrt{5} + 1$ and least value of $|z| = \sqrt{5} - 1$.

$$|z| = \sqrt{5} + 1 \Rightarrow \frac{4}{|z|} = \sqrt{5} - 1$$

Now, $\frac{4}{z} = \frac{4\bar{z}}{|z|^2} \Rightarrow \frac{4}{z}$ lying in the direction of $\bar{z}$

$$\left|z - \frac{4}{z}\right| = PR = 2 \text{ (given)}$$

We have $OP = \sqrt{5} + 1$ and $OR = \sqrt{5} - 1$

$$\Rightarrow \quad \cos 2\theta = \frac{OP^2 + OR^2 - PR^2}{2OP.OR}$$

$$= \frac{\left(\sqrt{5}+1\right)^2 + \left(\sqrt{5}-1\right)^2}{2(5-1)} = 1$$

$$\Rightarrow \quad 2\theta = 0, 2\pi \Rightarrow Z = \left(\sqrt{5} - 1\right)$$

Similarly for $|z| = \sqrt{5} - 1$

we get $z = \left(\sqrt{5} - 1\right)$

Alternative Solution: In ΔOPQ

$$\cos 2\theta = \frac{OP^2 - OR^2 - PR^2}{2OP.OR} = \frac{|z| - \left|\frac{4}{z}\right|^2 - \left|z - \frac{4}{z}\right|^2}{2|z|.\left|\frac{4}{z}\right|}$$

$$= \frac{r^2 + \frac{16}{r^2} - 2^2}{8} \quad (\text{Let } |z| = r > 0) \quad = \frac{\left(r + \frac{4}{r}\right) - 12}{8}$$

Since $-1 \le \cos 2\theta \le 1$ ...(1)

$$\Rightarrow \qquad -1 \le = \frac{\left(r + \frac{4}{r}\right)^2 - 12}{8}$$

$$\Rightarrow \qquad -8 \le \left(r + \frac{4}{r}\right)^2 - 12 \le 8$$

$$\Rightarrow \qquad \left(r + \frac{4}{r}\right)^2 \ge 4, \text{ which is always true.}$$

And $\left(r + \frac{4}{r}\right)^2 \le 20 \Rightarrow r + \frac{4}{r} \le 2\sqrt{5}$ (as $r > 0$)

$$\Rightarrow \qquad r^2 - 2 2\sqrt{5}\ r + 4 £ 0$$

$$\Rightarrow \qquad \left(r - \sqrt{5} - 1\right)\left(r - \left(\sqrt{5} + 1\right)\right) \le 0$$

$$\Rightarrow \qquad \sqrt{5} - 1 \le r \le \sqrt{5} + 1$$

Hence max. $r = \sqrt{5} + 1$ and min. $r = \sqrt{5} - 1$

and it occurs at the right end of the inequality (1).

Hence $\cos 2\theta = 1 \Rightarrow 2\theta = 0$ or 2π

$$\Rightarrow \qquad \theta = 0 \text{ or } \pi$$

$\Rightarrow$ forr $= \sqrt{5} + 1$, $z = \left(\sqrt{5} + 1\right)$

and forr $= \sqrt{5} - 1$, $z = \pm \left(\sqrt{5} - 1\right)$.

Example 56:

(i) *Prove that* $|2z \cos a + z^2| < 1$, *if* $|z|$ £ 0.41.

(ii) *If* $|z - 3i| < \sqrt{5}$ *then prove that the complex number z also satisfies the inequality* $|i(z + 1) + 1| < 2\sqrt{5}$.

(iii) *Find the complex number z which satisfies the condition* $|z - a + ai| = 1$ *and having the greatest absolute value, where a is a real constant.*

Solution:

(ii) Here i(z + 1) + 1 has to be written as the sum of two complex numbers containing z – 3i because we have to use $|z - 3i| < \sqrt{5}$

$|i(z + 1) + 1| = |i(z - 3i) + i - 2|$ £ $|i(z - 3i)| + |-2 + i)$

(by triangle inequality)

$= |i|\ |z - 3i| + \sqrt{5} < \sqrt{5} + \sqrt{5} = 2\sqrt{5}$

(iii) Letz – a + ai = cos θ + i sin θ

$\Rightarrow\ z = a + \cos\theta + i(\sin\theta - a)$

$$\Rightarrow |z| = \sqrt{2a^2 + 1 + 2\sqrt{2a}\cos\left(\theta + \frac{\pi}{4}\right)}$$

Case I: A > 0, |z| is maximum if θ = – π/4

$\therefore \qquad |z| = \sqrt{2}\ a + 1$

and $\qquad z = \left(\sqrt{2a} + 1\right)\left(\frac{1}{\sqrt{2}} - \frac{i}{\sqrt{2}}\right)$

Case II: A < 0, |a| is maximum if θ = π – π/4 = 3π/4

$$\therefore\ |z| = \left|\sqrt{2a} - 1\right|$$

$$\therefore\ z = \left|\sqrt{2a} - 1\right|\left(-\frac{1}{\sqrt{2}} + \frac{i}{\sqrt{2}}\right).$$

Example 57:

If |z| = 1, then prove that the points represented by $\sqrt{\frac{1+z}{1-z}}$ *lie on one or other of two fixed perpendicular straight lines.*

Solution:

Since |z| = 1. z lies on a unit circle having centre at the origin. arg $\left(\frac{1+z}{1-z}\right) = +\frac{\pi}{2}$ or $+\frac{3\pi}{2}$

$$\Rightarrow \frac{1+z}{1-z} = ke^{i\pi/2} \text{ or } ke^{i3\pi/2}$$

where k is a real parameter and its value depends upon the position of z.

Let $\qquad \alpha = \sqrt{\frac{1+z}{1-z}}$

$\Rightarrow \qquad \alpha = \sqrt{k}\ e^{-i\pi/4}$

or $\quad \sqrt{k}\ e^{i3\pi/4}$

$\Rightarrow$ α lies on one or other of the two perpendicular lines.

Example 58:

If $\alpha = \frac{z-i}{z+i}$, *show that, when z lies above the real axis, α will lie within the unit circle which has centre at the origin. Find the locus of α as z travels on the real axis from* $-\infty$ *to* $+\infty$.

Solution:

From figure, it is clear that $|z - i| < |z - i|$ (as z lies above the real axis).

$$\Rightarrow |a| = \frac{|z-i|}{|z+i|} < 1$$

$\Rightarrow$ α lies within the unit circle which has centre at the origin.

Now if z is travelling one the real axis $\text{Im}(z) = 0$ and $\text{Re}(z)$ varies from $-\infty$ to $+\infty$.

Let $z = x + i0$

$\Rightarrow \alpha = \frac{x-i}{x+i}$ moves on the unit circle which has centre at the origin.

Example 59:

(i) *If the equation $ax^2 + bx + c = 0$, $(0 < a < b < c)$ has non-real complex roots z_1 and z_2, show that $|z_1| > 1$, $|z_2| > 1$.*

(ii) *If z is a complex number and $z^2 + az + b=0$ $(a = 0)$ has roots both of which have unit modulus then prove that $|a| \leq 2$, $|b| = 1$, arg (b) = 2arg(a).*

Solution:

(i) $ax^2 + bx + c = 0$ $(c > b > a > 0)$

As z_1 and z_2 are non real roots of the equation

$$\Rightarrow \qquad z_1 = \bar{z}_2$$

we have $\qquad z_1 z_2 = \frac{c}{a} > 1$

$$\Rightarrow \qquad |z_2|^2 > 1 \Rightarrow |z_2| > 1$$

$$\Rightarrow \qquad |z_2| > 1. \text{ Similarly } |z_1| > 1.$$

Example 60:

Two different non-parallel lines cut the circle $|z| = r$ in points a, b, c and d respectively. Prove that these lines meet in the point z given by

$$z=\frac{a^{-1}+b^{-1}-c^{-1}-d^{-1}}{a^{-1}b^{-1}-c^{-1}d^{-1}}.$$

Solution:

Since P, Q, R are collinear,

$$\begin{vmatrix} z & \bar{z} & 1 \\ c & \bar{c} & 1 \\ d & \bar{d} & 1 \end{vmatrix}=0$$

$$\Rightarrow z\,z(\bar{c}-\bar{d})-\bar{z}\ (c-d)+(c\bar{d}-\bar{c}d)=0 \qquad ...(1)$$

Similarly, $z(\bar{a}-\bar{b})-\bar{z}(a-b)+(a\bar{b}-\bar{a}b)=0$ ...(2)

From {(1) × (a − b)} − {(2) × (c − d)}

$$z[(\bar{c}-\bar{d})\ (a-b)-(\bar{a}-\bar{b})(c-d)]=(a\bar{b}-b\bar{a})(c-d)-(c\bar{d}-\bar{c}d)(a-b)$$

Now $a\bar{a}=r^2 \Rightarrow \bar{a}=\frac{r^2}{a}$,

Similarly $\bar{b}=\frac{r^2}{b},\ \bar{c}=\frac{r^2}{c},\ \bar{d}=\frac{r^2}{d}$ ...(3)

From (3) $z\left[\left(\frac{r^2}{c}-\frac{r^2}{d}\right)(a-b)-\left(\frac{r^2}{a}-\frac{r^2}{b}\right)(c-d)\right]$

$$=\left(\frac{ar^2}{b}-\frac{br^2}{a}\right)(c-d)-\left(\frac{cr^2}{d}-\frac{r^2}{c}d\right)(a-b)$$

$$\Rightarrow z\left[\frac{(d-c)(a-b)}{cd}-\frac{(b-a)(c-d)}{ab}\right]$$

$$=\frac{(a^2-b^2)(c-d)}{ab}-\frac{(c^2-d^2)(a-b)}{cd}$$

$$\Rightarrow z\left[-\frac{1}{cd}+\frac{1}{ab}\right]=\frac{(a+b)}{ab}-\frac{c+d}{cd}$$

$$\Rightarrow z=\frac{a^{-1}+b^{-1}-c^{-1}-d^{-1}}{a^{-1}b^{-1}-c^{-1}d^{-1}}.$$

Example 61:

Plot the region represented by $\frac{\pi}{3} \le \arg\left(\frac{z+1}{z-1}\right) \le \frac{2\pi}{3}$ *in the Argand plane.*

Solution:

Let us take arg $\left(\frac{z+1}{z-1}\right)$ = 2p/3. Clearly z lies on the minor arc of Circle passing through (1, 0) and (–1, 0). Similarly, arg$\left(\frac{z+1}{z-1}\right)$ = p/3 means that 'z' is lying on the major arc of the circle passing through (1, 0) and (–1, 0). Now if we take any point in the region included between the two arcs, say $P_1(z_1)$, we get $\frac{\pi}{3} \le \arg\left(\frac{z+1}{z-1}\right) \le \frac{2\pi}{3}$.

Thus, $\frac{\pi}{3} \le \arg\left(\frac{z+1}{z-1}\right) \le \frac{2\pi}{3}$ represents the shaded region (excluding the points (1, 0) and (–1, 0).

Example 62:

Prove the following inequalities geometrically and analytically:

(a) $\left|\frac{z}{|z|} - 1\right| \le |\arg z|$

(b) $|z-1| \le |z| - 1 + |z|\,|\arg z|$.

Solution:

(a) The quantity $z/|z|$ lies on a unit circle centred at the origin.

It is clear that $\left|\frac{z}{|z|} - 1\right|$ = AP ≤ arc(AP)=a=arg z.

If a is negative, this gives $\left|\frac{z}{|z|} - 1\right| \le |\arg z|$.

To show this analytically, put z = r (cos α + i sin α), where r = |z|. Then

$$\left|\frac{z}{|z|} - 1\right|$$

$$= |(\cos\alpha - 1) + i\sin\alpha|$$
$$= [(\cos\alpha - 1)^2 + \sin^2\alpha]^{1/2}$$
$$= [2(1 - \cos\alpha)]^{1/2}$$

$$= \left(4\sin^2\frac{\alpha}{2}\right)^{1/2} = 2\left|\sin\frac{\alpha}{2}\right|$$

$$\leq 2\left|\frac{\alpha}{2}\right| \quad \therefore |a| = |\arg z|.[\sin\theta \leq \theta \text{ if } \theta \geq 0]$$

(b) Referring to the shown figure and using the result of part (a), we have $(z - 1) = AP \leq QP = ||z| - 1| + |z - |z||$

$$\leq ||z| - 1| + |z| \left|\frac{z}{|z|} - 1\right| \leq ||z| - 1| + |z|\,|\arg z|.$$

Analytically, we can get this result as follows:

$$|z - 1| = |(z - |z|) + (|z| - 1) \leq |z - |z|| + ||z| + 1|$$

$$\Rightarrow |z - 1| \leq ||z| - 1| + |z| \left|\frac{z}{|z|} - 1\right| \leq ||z| - 1| + |z|\,|\arg z|$$

Example 63:

Find the equation of the circle which touches the line $iz + \bar{z} + 1 + i = 0$ and has the lines $(1 - i)z = (1 + i)\bar{z}$ and $(1 + i)z + (1 - i)\bar{z} = 4i$ as its normals.

Solution:

Clearly point of intersection of normals would be the centre of the required circle.

$$(1 - i)z = (1 + i)\bar{z}$$

$$\Rightarrow \qquad \bar{z} = \frac{1-i}{1+i}z$$

$$(1 + i)z + (i - 1)\bar{z} = 4i$$

$$\Rightarrow \qquad \bar{z} = \frac{4i-(1+i)z}{(1-1)}$$

$$\frac{1-i}{1+i}z = \frac{4i-(1+i)z}{(i-1)}$$

$$\Rightarrow (1 - i)(i - 1)z = 4i(1 + i) - (1 + i)^2 z$$

$$\Rightarrow z(1 + i)^2 - (1 - i)^2 = 4i(1 + i)$$

$$\Rightarrow \qquad z(4i) = 4i(1 + i)$$

$$z = (1 + i)$$

Now equation of tangent can be rewritten as,

$$\frac{1}{(1-i)}\left(iz+\bar{z}\right)+1 = 0$$

$\Rightarrow$ $$i(1-i)\,z + (1-i)\,\bar{z} + 2 = 0$$

$\Rightarrow$ $$(i+1)z + (1-i)\bar{z} + 2 = 0$$

Now distance of z = (1 + i) from this line

$$= \frac{|(1+i)(1+i)+(1-i)(1-i)+2|}{2|1-i|} = \frac{1}{\sqrt{2}}$$

Thus the equation of required circle is,

$$|z-(1+i) = \frac{1}{\sqrt{2}}.$$

Example 64:

Consider a triangle formed by the points $A\left(\frac{2}{\sqrt{3}}e^{i\frac{\pi}{2}}\right)$, $B\left(\frac{2}{\sqrt{3}}e^{i\frac{\pi}{6}}\right)$, $C\left(\frac{2}{\sqrt{3}}e^{i\frac{5\pi}{6}}\right)$. *Let P(z) be any point on it's in circle. Prove that*

$AP^2 + BP^2 + CP^2 = 5.$

Solution:

Let $z_1 = \frac{2}{\sqrt{3}}e^{i\frac{\pi}{2}}$, $z_2 = \frac{2}{\sqrt{3}}e^{-i\frac{\pi}{6}}$, $z_3 = \frac{2}{\sqrt{3}}e^{-i\frac{5}{6}}$.

Clearly the points lie on the circle $|z| = \frac{2}{\sqrt{3}}$

If 'l' be the length of side of the ΔABC.

$$AD = |\sin 60^\circ = | \frac{\sqrt{3}}{2}$$

$\Rightarrow$ $$OD = \frac{1}{3}AD = \frac{1\sqrt{3}}{6}$$

Now, $$OA = \frac{2}{3}AD = \frac{2}{3}.\frac{1\sqrt{3}}{2} = \frac{2}{\sqrt{3}}$$

$\Rightarrow$ $$| = 2 \text{ and } OD = \frac{2\sqrt{3}}{6} = \frac{1}{\sqrt{3}}$$

$\Rightarrow$ Equation of in circle is $|z| = \frac{1}{\sqrt{3}}$

Let P(z) be any point on the in circle,

$$\Rightarrow \quad z = \frac{1}{\sqrt{3}}e^{i\pi}$$

Now, $\quad AP^2 = |z - z_1|^2 = |z|^2 + |z_1|^2 - (z\bar{z}_1 + \bar{z}z_1)$

Similarly, $\quad BP^2 = |z|^2 + |z_2|^2 - (z\bar{z}_2 + \bar{z}z_2)$

and $\quad CP^2 = |z|^2 + |z_3|^2 - (z\bar{z}_3 + \bar{z}z_3)$

$AP^2 + BP^2 + CP^2 = 3|z|^2 + |z_1|^2 + |z_2|^2 + |z_3|^2$

$z(\bar{z}_1 + \bar{z}_2 + \bar{z}_3) - \bar{z}(z_1 + z_2 + z_3)$

$= 1 + 3.\frac{4}{3} - z(0) - \bar{z}(0) = 5.$

Example 65:

(i) *Prove that*

$$\left(a_1^2 + b_1^2\right)\left(a_2^2 + b_2^2\right) \ldots \left(a_n^2 + b_n^2\right)$$

can written as the sum of the two squares.

(ii) *Let $x_1, x_2, x_3, \ldots, x_n$ be the roots of the equation $x^n + x^{n-1} + \ldots + x + 1 = 0$ compute the expression*

$$\frac{1}{x_1 - 1} + \frac{1}{x_2 - 1} + \ldots + \frac{1}{x_n - 1}.$$

(iii) *If $|z_1| = |z_2| = \ldots = |z_n| = 1$,*

prove that $|z_1 + z_2 + z_3 + \ldots + z_n|$

$$= \left|\frac{1}{z_1} + \frac{1}{z_2} + \frac{1}{z_3} + \ldots + \frac{1}{z_n}\right|.$$

Solution:

(iii) $\quad |z_r| = 1$ for $r = 1$ to n

$\Rightarrow \quad z_r\bar{z}_r = 1$

$\Rightarrow \quad \bar{z}_r = \frac{1}{z_r}$

Let $\quad a = z_1 + z_2 + \ldots z_n$

$\Rightarrow \bar{\alpha} = \bar{z}_1 + \bar{z}_2 + \ldots + \bar{z}_n = \left(\frac{1}{z_1} + \frac{1}{z_2} + \ldots + \frac{1}{z_n}\right)$ as $|\alpha| = |\bar{\alpha}|$

$\Rightarrow |z_1 + z_2 + \ldots + z_n| = \left|\frac{1}{z_1} + \frac{1}{z_2} + \ldots + \frac{1}{z_n}\right|$

Example 66:

If $iz^3 + z^3 - z + i = 0$, *then show* $|z| = 1$.

Solution:

$iz^3 + z^2 - z + i = 0$

By substituting $z = i$ in the equation, we get $0 = 0$

Hence $z - i$ is a factor of $iz^3 + z^3 - z + i$

$\Rightarrow iz^2 (z - i) (z - i) = 0$

$\Rightarrow (iz^2 - 1) (z - i) = 0$

Either $iz^2 - 1 = 0$ or $z - i = 0$

When $z - i = 0$, $z = i$

$\therefore \quad |z| = |0 + i.1| = \sqrt{0^2 + 1^2} = 1$.

When $iz^2 - 1 = 0$, $z^2 = \dfrac{1}{i} = -i$

$\therefore |z^2| = |0 - 1.i| = \sqrt{0^2 + (-1)^2} = 1$

$\therefore |z^2| = 1$ or $|z| = 1$

$\therefore$ In any case we have $|z| = 1$.

Example 67:

(i) *Let z be a non-real complex number lying on the circle* $|z| = 1$. *then prove that*

$$z = \frac{1 + i \tan\left(\dfrac{\arg z}{2}\right)}{1 - i \tan\left(\dfrac{\arg z}{2}\right)}.$$

(ii) *Find the modulus and the argument of the complex number* z_1, *where* $z_1 = z^2 - z$ *and* $z = \cos\theta + i \sin\theta$.

(iii) *If* z_1 *and* z_2 *are complex numbers, prove that*

$|z_1 + z_2|^2 + |z_1|^2 + |z_2|^2$

if and only if $z_1 \bar{z}_2$ *is purely imaginary.*

Solution:

(i) Since z lies on $|z| = 1$

$z = \cos\alpha + i \sin\alpha$, $\alpha = \arg(z)$

$$= \frac{\cos^2\frac{\alpha}{2} - \sin^2\frac{\alpha}{2} + 2i\sin\frac{\alpha}{2}\cos\frac{\alpha}{2}}{\cos^2\frac{\alpha}{2} + \sin^2\frac{\alpha}{2}}$$

$$= \frac{\left(\cos\frac{\alpha}{2} + i\sin\frac{\alpha}{2}\right)^2}{\left(\cos\frac{\alpha}{2} - i\sin\frac{\alpha}{2}\right)\left(\cos\frac{\alpha}{2} + i\sin\frac{\alpha}{2}\right)}$$

$$= \frac{\cos\frac{\alpha}{2} + i\sin\frac{\alpha}{2}}{\cos\frac{\alpha}{2} - i\sin\frac{\alpha}{2}} = \frac{1 + i\tan\frac{\alpha}{2}}{1 - i\tan\frac{\alpha}{2}} = \frac{1 + i\tan\left(\frac{\arg z}{2}\right)}{1 - i\tan\left(\frac{\arg z}{2}\right)}$$

(ii) $z_1 = z^2 - z = (z - 1)$

$\Rightarrow |z_1| = |z|\,|z - 1|$ and $\arg(z_1) = \arg(z) + \arg(z - 1)$

$$z = e^{i\theta} \Rightarrow z - 1 = e^{i\theta} - 1 = 2i\sin\frac{\theta}{2}e^{i\theta/2}$$

$\Rightarrow |z_1| = 2\,|\sin\theta/2|$

and $\arg(z_1) = \theta + \arg\left(2i\sin\frac{\theta}{2}e^{i\theta/2}\right) = \theta + \left(\frac{\pi}{2} + \frac{\theta}{2}\right) = \frac{1}{2}(\pi + 3\theta)$

(if $z \neq 1$)

If $z = 1$, $|z_1| = 1$ and $\arg(z_1|$ will not be defined.

Example 68:

(i) *Show that the triangle whose vertices are z_1, z_2, z_3 and a.b.c. are*

similarly, if $\begin{vmatrix} z_1 & a & 1 \\ z_2 & b & 1 \\ z_3 & c & 1 \end{vmatrix} = 0$.

(ii) *If a, b, c and u, v, w are the complex numbers representing the vertices of two triangles such that $c = (1 - r)\,a + rb$, $w = (1 - r)\,u + rv$, where r is non real complex then prove that the triangles are similar.*

Solution:

(i) The triangle are similar, therefore

$$\frac{z_1 - z_2}{z_3 - z_2} = \frac{a - b}{c - b}$$

$$\Leftrightarrow \begin{vmatrix} z_1 - z_2 & a-b \\ z_3 - z_2 & c-b \end{vmatrix} = 0$$

$$\Leftrightarrow \begin{vmatrix} z_1 - z_2 & a-b & 0 \\ z_2 & b & 1 \\ z_3 - z_2 & c-b & 0 \end{vmatrix} = 0 \Leftrightarrow \begin{vmatrix} z_1 & a & 1 \\ z_2 & b & 1 \\ z_3 & c & 1 \end{vmatrix} = 0$$

(ii) $c = (1 - r)\, a + rb,\ \omega = (1 - r)\, u + rv$

$\Rightarrow$ $c\text{-}a = r\,(b - a),\ \omega\text{-}u = r(v - u)$

$$\Rightarrow r = \frac{c-a}{b-a},\ r = \frac{\omega - u}{v-u}$$

$$\Rightarrow \frac{c-a}{b-a} = \frac{\omega-u}{v-u} \Rightarrow \frac{|c-a|}{|b-a|} = \frac{|\omega-u|}{|v-u|}$$

and $\arg\left(\dfrac{c-a}{b-a}\right) = \arg\left(\dfrac{\omega-u}{v-u}\right)$

Hence, given triangles would be similar.

Example 69:

Locate the complex number $z = x + iy$ for which

(i) $\log_{1/2} |z - 2|\ \log_{1/2} |z|$

(ii) $\log \log_{1/\sqrt{3}} \dfrac{|z|^2 - z + 1}{2 + |z|} > -2$

(iii) $\log_{14}\left(13 + |z^2 - 4i|\right) + \log_{196} \dfrac{1}{\left(13 + |z^2 + 4i\right)^2} = 0$

(iv) $\log_{1/2} \dfrac{|z-1| + 4}{3|z-1| - 2} > 1$

(v) $\log_{\cos\frac{\pi}{6}} \dfrac{|z-2| + 5}{4|z-2| - 4} < 2$

(vi) $\log_{\sec\frac{\pi}{4}} \dfrac{|z|^2 + |z| + 4}{2|z| - 1} > 2$.

Solution:

$$\log_{\frac{\sqrt{3}}{2}} \frac{|z-2|+5}{4|z-2|-4} < \log_{\frac{\sqrt{3}}{2}} \left(\frac{\sqrt{3}}{2}\right)^2$$

so $\frac{|z-2|+5}{4|z-2|-4} > \frac{3}{4}$ $\left(\text{since base } \frac{\sqrt{3}}{2} < 1\right)$

Also for the logarithmic to be defined

$4|z-2| - 4 > 0$, *i.e.*, $|z-2| > 1$

when $|z-2| > 1$, $\frac{|z-2|+5}{4|z-2|-4} > \frac{3}{4}$

gives $4(|z-2| + 5) > 3.4(|z-2| - 1)$

or $|z-2| + 5 > 3|z-2| - 3$

or $8 > 2|z-2|$

$\Rightarrow |z-2| < 4$

$\Rightarrow$ z is such that $1 < |z-2| < 4$

Hence, the region for z in the Argand plane is as shown being by the shaded area. This the area shaded between two circles with a common centre z = 2 and radii 1 and 4.

COMMUTATIVITY OF ADDITION IN C

We have $z_1 + z_2 = z_2 + z_1$ where z_1 and z_2 are any complex numbers.

Associativity of Addition in C : We have $(z_1 + z_2) + z_3 = z_1 + (z_2 + z_3)$, for all complex numbers z_1, z_2 and z_3. The complex number (0, 0) or 0 + i0 is additive identity, since of every complex number (x, y), we have

$(x, y) + (0, 0) = (x + 0, y + 0) = (0, 0) + (x, y)$

The complex number (0, 0) is called the zero complex number and is simply written as 0.

A complex number x – iy is said to be a non-zero complex number if at least one of x and y is not zero.

The complex number (– x, – y) is the additive inverse of the complex number (x, y) since (x, y) + (– x, – y) = (x – x, y – y) = (0, 0) = the additive identity and also (– x, – y) + (x, y) = (0, 0). The complex number (– x, – y) is called the negative of the complex number (x, y) and denote (– x, – y) by – (x, y),. Thus if z = (x, y), then – 2 = – (x, y) = (– x, – y).

Cancellation Low for Addition in C

If z_1, z_2, z_3 are any complex numbers, the $z_1 + z_3 = z_2 + z_3 = 7z_1 = 2_2$.

Multiplication of Complex Numbers : If $z_1 = x_1 + iy_1$ or (x_1, y_1) and $z_2 = x_2 + iy_2$ or $(x_2 - y_2)$ are any two complex numbers, then the product of z_1 and z_2 written as z_1z_2 is defined by

$$z_1z_2 = (x_1 + iy_1)(x_2 + iy_2)$$
$$= (x_1x_2 - y_1y_2) + i(x_1y_2 + y_1x_2)$$

or $$= z_1z_2 = (x_1, y_1)(x_2, y_2)$$
$$= (x_1x_2 - y_1y_2, x_1x_2 + y_1x_2).$$

Thus, $(3 + 5i)(7 + 6i) = (3 \times 7 - 5 \times 6) + (3 \times 6 + 5 \times 7)i$
$$= -9 + 53i,$$

or using the notation of ordered pairs, we have

$(3, 5)(7, 6) = (3 \times 7 - 5 \times 6, 3 \times 6 + 5 \times 7) = (-9, 53).$

Properties of the Multiplication of Complex Numbers : The multiplication of complex number is commutative, associative, admits of identity element and every non-zero complex number possesses multiplicative inverse.

Commutativity of Multiplication in C

We have $z_1z_2 = z_2, z_1$, for all complex numbers z_1 and z_2.

Associativity of Multiplication in C : We have $(z_1z_2)z_3 = z_1(z_1z_3)$, for all complex numbers z_1,z_2 and z_3.

The complex number (1, 0) or 1 + i0 or simply 1 is the multiplication identity since of for ever complex number (x, y), we have

$(x, y)(1, 0) = (x.1 - y.0, x.0 + y.1) = (x, y) = (1, 0)(x, y).$

MULTIPLICATION INVERSE

The complex number (x, y) is called the multiplicative inverse of the complex number (a, b) if

$$(x, y)(a, b) = (1, 0) \text{ or simply } 1.$$

We have $(x, y)(a, b) = (1, 0)$

$\Rightarrow$ $(xa - yb, xb + ya) = (1, 0)$

$\Rightarrow$ $xa - yb = 1$ and $xb + ya = 0$

The equations $xa - yb = 1$ and $xb + ya = 0$ give

$$x = \frac{a}{a^2 + b^2}, y = -\frac{b}{a^2 - b^2}$$

Provided $a^2 - b^2 \neq 0$ which implies that a and bare not both zero *i.e.*, (a, b) is a non-zero complex number.

Thus every non-zero complex number possesses multiplicative inverse and the multiplicative inverse and the multiplication inverse of the complex number $(a, b) \neq (0, 0)$ is the complex number.

$$\left[\frac{a}{a^2+b^2}, \frac{-b}{a^2+b^2}\right]$$

If z is a non-zero complex number, the multiplicative inverse of z is denoted by 1/z or z^{-1}.

Cancellation low for multiplication in C. If z_1, z_2, z_3 are complex numbers and $z_3 \neq 0$, then $z_1 z_3 = z_2 z_3 \Rightarrow z_1 = z_2$. Multiplication distributes addition in C. We have $z_1(z_2 + z_3) = z_1 z_2 + z_1 z_3$, for all complex numbers z_1,z_2 and z_3.

DIFFERENCE OF TWO COMPLEX NUMBERS

If z_1 and z_2 are two complex numbers, we define $z_1 - z_2 = z_1 + (-z_2)$.

Thus if $z_1 = (x_1, y_1)$ and $z_2 = (x_2, y_2)$ then

$z_1 - z_2 = z_1 + (-z_2) = (x_1, y_1) + (-x_2, -y_2) = (x_1 - x_2 y_1 - y_2)$.

DIVISION INC

Definition : A complex number (a, b) is said to be divisible by a complex number (c, d) if there exists a complex number (x, y) such that.

$$(x, y)\,(c, d) = (a, b)$$

we have $\quad (x, y)\,(c, d) = (a, b)$

$\Rightarrow \quad (xc - yd, xd + yc) = (a, b)$

$\Rightarrow \quad xc - yd = a$ and $xd + yc = b$.

The equations $xc - yd = a$ and $xd + yc = b$ give

$$x = \frac{ad + bd}{c^2 + d^2}, \; y = \frac{bc - ad}{c^2 + d^2}$$

Provided $c^2 + d^2 \neq 0$ which implies that c and d are not both zero.

Thus division, except by (0, 0) is always possible in the set of complex numbers. If z_1 and z_2 are two complex numbers such that $z_2 \neq 0$ then the quotient of the complex numbers z_1 and z_2 is defined by the relation.

$$\frac{z_1}{z_2} = z_1 . \frac{1}{z_2} = z_1(z_2) - 1.$$

MODULUS OF A COMPLEX NUMBER

If $z = x + iy$ is any complex number then the non-negative real number $v(x^2 + y^2)$ is called the modulus of the complex number z and is denoted by $|z|$. Thus, if $z = x + iy$, then $|z|$ *i.e.*, modulus of $z = v(x^2 + y^2)$. Obviously

$|z| = 0$ if and only if $x = 0$ and $x = 0$ *i.e.*, if and only if $z = 0$. Also it can be easily seen that far any complex number z, $|z| \geq R(z)$ and $|z| \geq (z)$.

Remember that far all real values of θ, we have

$|\cos\theta + i \sin\theta| = v(\cos^2\theta + \sin^2\theta) =|$.

Thus, the complex number $\cos\theta + i\sin\theta$ has always its modulus equal to 1 and is called uni-modular complex number.

If z_1 and z_2 are any two complex numbers, then

$$|z_1 z_2| = |z_1|\,|z_2|.$$

If z_1 is any complex number and z_2 is any non-zero complex number, then

$$\left|\frac{z_1}{z_2}\right| = \frac{|z_1|}{|z_2|}.$$

CONJUGATE OF A COMPLEX NUMBER

If $z = x + iy$ is any complex number, then the complex number $x - iy$ is called the conjugate of the complex number z and is written as $\bar{z}$. Thus

if $\qquad z = 3 + 4i$, then $\bar{z} = 3 - 4i$

Obviously $\qquad |z| = |\bar{z}|$.

The following results are obvious and should be remembered.

(i) Two complex numbers are equal if and only if their conjugates are equal *i.e.*,

$$z_1 = z_2 \text{ if and only if } \bar{z}_1 = \bar{z}_2$$

(ii) $\qquad \overline{(\bar{z})} = z$.

(iii) We have $\overline{z_1 + z_2} = \bar{z}_1 + \bar{z}_2$, $\overline{z_1 - z_2} = \bar{z}_1 - \bar{z}_2$, $\overline{z_1 z_2} = \bar{z}_1\,\bar{z}_2$ and

$$\overline{\left[\frac{z_1}{z_2}\right]} = \frac{\bar{z}_1}{\bar{z}_2}. \text{ Provided } z_2 \neq 0.$$

(iv) If $z = x + iy$, then

$$z + \bar{z} = (x + iy) + (x - iy) = 2x = 2R(z).$$

(v) A complex numbers $z = x + iy$ is purely imaginary if and only if $z + \bar{z} = 0$.

(vi) If $z = x + iy$, then $z - \bar{z} = x + iy - (x - iy) = 2iy = 2i(z)$.

(vii) A complex number is purely real if and only if $z - \overline{z} = 0$.

(viii) If z = x + iy

then $z\overline{z}$ = (x + iy) (x – iy) = $x^2 + y^2$

$$= \left\{\sqrt{x^2 + y^2}\right\}^2 = |z|^2.$$

Thus, the product of two conjugate complex numbers which is always 7, 0 *i.e.* which is never negative.

MODULUS-ARGUMENT FORM OR ROLAR STANDARD FORM

Every non-zero complex number x + iy can always be put in the form r(cos θ i sin θ) where r and θ are both real numbers.

Let x + iy = r(cos θ + ir sin θ)

The equating real and every part we have

$$x = r \cos \theta \qquad ...(1)$$

$$y = r \sin \theta \qquad ...(2)$$

Squaring and adding (1) and (2) we get

$$x^2 + y^2 = r^2$$

$$\text{or } r = \pm \sqrt{x^2 + y^2}$$

$$r = |z|$$

r is called as the modulus of the complex number z. Then from (i) and (ii) we have

$$\text{cosec} = \frac{x}{\sqrt{x^2 + y^2}}$$

and $$\sin \theta = \frac{y}{\sqrt{x^2 + y^2}} \qquad ...(3)$$

If z is a non-zero complex number then there exist values of θ which satisfies the equation (3) simultaneously.

Any value of θ satisfying the equation (3) is called an argument or amplitude of the complex number and we write θ = arg z or 8 amp z.

Argument of a complex number is not unique since. If θ be a value of the argument, so also is 2nπ + θ where n is any integer.

The value of argument which satisfies the inequating $-\pi \leq \theta \leq \pi$ is called the principal value of the argument.

GEOMETRICAL APPLICATIONS OF COMPLEX NUMBERS

Theorem 1:

Formula for Distance Between Two Points : *If two complex numbers z_1 and z_2 be represented by the points A and B on the Argand Plane, then the distance AB = $|z_2 - z_1| = |z_1 - z_2|$.*

Proof:

Let $z_1 = x_1 + iy_1$ and $z_2 = x_2 + iy_2$. Then, these numbers on the Argand diagram are represented by the points $A(x_1,y_1)$ and $B(x_2,y_2)$ respectively.

We have, $z_2 - z_1 = (x_2 + iy_2) - (x_1 + iy_1)$

$$= (x_2 - x_1) + i\,(y_2 - y_1).$$

$$\therefore \qquad |z_2 - z_1) = \sqrt{(x_2 - x_1)^2 + (y_2 - y_1)^2}$$

$$= \text{distance AB.} \qquad \text{[From Co-ordinate Geometry]}$$

Hence, $\qquad AB = |z_2 - z_1| = |z_1 - z_2|$.

Theorem 2:

If two complex numbers z_1 and z_2 are represented by the points A and B on the Argand plane, then the affix of the point dividing AB internally in the ratio $m_1 : m_2$ is the complex number $\left(\dfrac{m_1z_2 + m_2z_1}{m_1 + m_2}\right)$.

Proof:

Let $z_1 = x_1 + iy_1$ and $z_2 = x_2 + iy_2$.

Then, these numbers on the Argand diagram are represented by the points A (x_1, y_1) and B (x_2, y_2) respectively.

From co-ordinate geometry, the co-ordinates of the point P dividing AB internally in the ratio $m_1 : m_2$ are

$$\left(\frac{m_1x_2 + m_2x_1}{m_1 + m_2}, \frac{m_1y_2 + m_2y_1}{m_1 + m_2}\right).$$

Hence, the affix of the point P

= the complex number representing the point P

$$= \left(\frac{m_1x_2 + m_2x_1}{m_1 + m_2}\right) + i\left(\frac{m_1y_2 + m_2y_1}{m_1 + m_2}\right)$$

$$= \frac{m_1(x_2 + iy_2) + m_2(x_1 + iy_1)}{m_1 + m_2} = \frac{m_1z_2 + m_2z_1}{m_1 + m_2}.$$

Corollary 1:

The affix of the middle point of z_1, z_2 is $\frac{1}{2}(z_1 + z_2)$.

Corollary 2:

If z_1, $z_2 z_3$ be the affixes of the vertices of a triangle, then the centroid of the triangle has the affix $\frac{1}{3}(z_1 + z_2 + z_3)$.

Corollary 3:

Point dividing a line segment in the ratio $\lambda : 1$, $l \neq -1$.

Let $z_1 = x_1 + iy_1$, $z_2 = x_2 + iy_2$ be the affixes of the points A and B respectively in the Argand plane.

If λ be a real number $\neq -1$, then there is a unique point C on AB such that

$$AC : CB = \lambda : 1.$$

The coordinates of C are given by

$$\left(\frac{x_1 + \lambda x_2}{1 + \lambda}, \frac{y_1 + \lambda y_2}{1 + \lambda}\right).$$

The affix of C is therefore $\dfrac{z_1 + \lambda z_2}{1 + \lambda}$.

EQUATION OF A STRAIGHT LINE IN THE COMPLEX PLANE

The *equation of a straight line* passing through a point of affix a in the complex plane can be put in the form

$$z = a + bt$$

where b is a non-zero complex number and the parameter t runs through all real values. It is easy to see that the two equations

$$z = a + bt \text{ and } z = a' + b't$$

represent the same line if and only if a' – a and b' are real multiples of b. The *lines are parallel* if b' is a real multiple of b and they are *equally directed* if b' is a positive multiple of b. We can identify the direction of a directed line by arg b. If α is the *angle between the lines* $z = a + bt$ and $z = a' + b't$, then

$$\alpha = \arg\left(\frac{b'}{b}\right).$$

Note that it depends on the order in which the lines occur. It follows that the *lines are perpendicular if* $\frac{b'}{b}$ is purely imaginary.

The directed line z = a + bt determines a *right half plane* consisting of all points z such that

$$I\left(\frac{z-a}{b}\right) < 0$$

and a *left half plane* consisting of all points z with

$$I\left(\frac{z-a}{b}\right) > 0.$$

Theorem 1:

The equation of any straight line passing through the origin and making an angle α with the real axis is $z = re^{i\alpha}$, where r is any real parameter.

Proof:

Let z = x + iy be any point on the straight line passing through the origin and making an angle α with the real axis. Then

$$x = r\cos\alpha,\ y = r\sin\alpha, \text{ where r is any real number.}$$

$$\therefore \quad x + iy = r\cos\alpha + ir\sin\alpha = r(\cos\alpha + i\sin\alpha)$$

or $$z = re^{i\alpha}.$$

Hence, the equation of the required straight line is $z = re^{i\alpha}$, where r is a real parameter.

Theorem 2:

The equation of any straight line passing through the point z_1 and making an angle α with the real axis is $z = z_1 + re^{i\alpha}$, where r is any real parameter.

Proof:

Let $z_1 = x_1 + iy_1$.

Let z = x + iy be any point on the straight line passing through the point z_1 and making an angle α with the real axis. Then

$x - x_1 = r\cos\alpha$, $y - y_1 = r\sin\alpha$, where r is any real number.

$\therefore \quad (x - x_1) + i(y - y_1) = r\cos\alpha + ir\sin\alpha$

or $(x + iy) - (x_1 + iy_1) = r(\cos\alpha + i\sin\alpha)$

or $\quad z - z_1 = re^{i\alpha}$

or $z = z_1 + re^{i\alpha}$.

Hence, the equation of the required straight line is $z = z_1 + re^{i\alpha}$, where r is a real parameter.

Theorem 3:

The equation of the straight line joining the points z_1 and z_2 is $z = tz_1 + (1 - t)z_2$, *where t is a real parameter.*

Proof:

Let z be the affix of any point on the straight line joining the points z_1 and z_2.

Suppose the point z divides the join of z_1 and z_2 in the ratio $\lambda : 1$, where λ is any real number not equal to -1.

We have $z = \dfrac{z_1 + \lambda z_2}{1+\lambda}$ or $z = \left(\dfrac{1}{1+\lambda}\right)z_1 + \left(\dfrac{\lambda}{1+\lambda}\right)z_2$. ...(1)

Put $\dfrac{1}{1+\lambda} = t$. Then $1 - t = 1 - \dfrac{1}{1+\lambda} = \dfrac{1}{1+\lambda}$.

$\therefore$ the equation (1) becomes $z = tz_1 + (1 - t)z_2$.

Hence, the equation of the straight line joining the points z_1 and z_2 is $z = tz_1 + (1 - t)z_2$, where t is a real parameter.

Remark:

The above equation is the equation of the straight line joining the points z_1 and z_2 in ***Parametric Form.***

Theorem 4:

The equation of the straight line joining the origin to the point z_1 is $z = tz_1$, where t is a real parameter.

Proof:

Let z be the affix of any point on the straight line joining the origin to the point z_1.

Suppose the point z divides the join of the point z_1 and the origin in the ratio $\lambda : 1$, where λ is any real number not equal to -1.

We have $z = \dfrac{1.z_1 + \lambda .0}{1+\lambda} = \left(\dfrac{1}{1+\lambda}\right)z_1$. ...(1)

Put $\dfrac{1}{1+\lambda} = t$.

Then the equation (1) becomes $z = tz_1$.

Hence, the equation of the straight line joining the origin to the point z_1 is $z = tz_1$, where t is a real parameter.

SOLVED EXAMPLES

Example 1:

Show that the equation of the circle having centre z_0 and radius r is

$$z\bar{z} - z_0\bar{z} - \bar{z}_0 z + z_0\bar{z}_0 - r^2 = 0.$$

Solution :

The equation of the circle whose centre is the point z_0 and whose radius is r is

$$|z - z_0| = r.$$

We have $|z - z_0| = r$

$\Leftrightarrow \quad |z - z_0|^2 = r^2$

$\Leftrightarrow (z - z_0)\overline{(z - z_0)} = r^2 \qquad [\because z\bar{z} = |z|^2]$

$\Leftrightarrow (z - z_0)(\bar{z} - \bar{z}_0) = r^2$

$\Leftrightarrow z\bar{z} - z_0\bar{z} - \bar{z}_0 z + z_0\bar{z}_0 - r^2 = 0.$

Hence, the required equation o the circle is

$z\bar{z} - z_0\bar{z} - \bar{z}_0 z + z_0\bar{z}_0 - r^2 = 0.$

Example 2:

Find the moduli and arguments of the following complex numbers.

(i) $\left(\dfrac{2+i}{3-i}\right)^2$

(ii) $\dfrac{2+i}{4i+(1+i)^2}.$

Solution:

(i) We have

$$\left(\frac{2+i}{3-i}\right)^2 = \frac{3+4i}{8-6i} = \frac{(3+4i)(8+6i)}{(8-6i)(8+6i)} = \frac{50i}{100} = \frac{1}{2}i.$$

Let $\frac{1}{2}i = r(\cos\theta + i\sin\theta)$.

Then 0 r $\cos\theta$, $\frac{1}{2} = r\sin\theta$.

Squaring and adding these relations, we get

$r^2 = \frac{1}{4}$ so that $r = \frac{1}{2}$.

Putting $r = \frac{1}{2}$, we have $\cos\theta = 0$, $\sin\theta = 1$.

The value of θ lying between $-\pi$ and π which satisfies both these equations is $\pi/2$.

$$\therefore \left|\left(\frac{2+i}{3-i}\right)^2\right| = r = \frac{1}{2}$$

and the principal value of $\arg\left(\frac{2+i}{3-i}\right)^2 = \frac{\pi}{2}$.

(ii) $\frac{2+i}{4i+(1+i)^2} = \frac{2+i}{6i} = \frac{1}{6} - \frac{1}{3}i$.

Let $\frac{1}{6} - \frac{1}{3}i = r(\cos\theta + i\sin\theta)$.

Then $\frac{1}{6} = r\cos\theta$, $-\frac{1}{3} = r\sin\theta$.

Squaring and adding these relations, we get

$r^2 = \frac{1}{36} + \frac{1}{9} = \frac{5}{36}$ so that $r = \frac{\sqrt{5}}{6}$.

Dividing, we get $\tan\theta = -2 \Rightarrow \theta = -\tan^{-1} 2$.

Hence required modulus $= r = \frac{\sqrt{5}}{6}$

and argument $= \theta = -\tan^{-1} 2$.

Example 3:

Show that the triangle whose vertices are the points represented by the complex numbers z_1, z_2, z_3 on the Argand diagram is equivalent if and only if

$$\frac{1}{z_2 - z_3} + \frac{1}{z_3 - z_1} + \frac{1}{z_1 - z_2} = 0$$

i.e., if and only if $z_1^2 + z_2^2 + z_3^2 = z_1z_2 + z_2z_3 + z_3z_1$.

Solution:

Let the vertices A, B, C of a ΔABC be represented by the complex numbers z_1, z_2, z_3 respectively. Then

$$BC = |z_2 - z_3|,\ CA = |z_3 - z_1|,\ AB = |z_1 - z_2|.$$

Suppose $z_2 - z_3 = \alpha$, $z_3 - z_1 = \beta$, $z_1 - z_2 = \gamma$.

Then $\quad \alpha + \beta + \gamma = 0.$ ...(1)

$\therefore \quad \alpha + \beta + \gamma = 0$ or $\bar{\alpha} + \bar{\beta} + \bar{\gamma} = 0$. ...(2)

'Only if' part : Let the ΔABC be equilateral.

Then $\quad BC = CA = AB$

or $\quad |z_2 - z_3| = |z_3 - z_1| = |z_1 - z_2|$

or $\quad |\alpha| = |\beta| = |\gamma|$ or $|\alpha|^2 = |\beta|^2 = |\gamma|^2$

or $\quad \alpha\bar{\alpha} = \beta\bar{\beta} = \gamma\bar{\gamma} = k$, (say). ...(3)

From (3), $\bar{\alpha} = k/\alpha$, $\bar{\beta} = k/\beta$, $\gamma = k/\gamma$. Putting these values in (2), we have

$k/\alpha + k/\beta + k/\gamma = 0$ or $1/\alpha + 1/\beta + 1/\gamma = 0$

or
$$\frac{1}{z_2 - z_3} + \frac{1}{z_3 - z_1} + \frac{1}{z_1 + z_2} = 0. \quad ...(4)$$

or
$$\frac{z_2 - z_1}{(z_2 - z_3)(z_3 - z_1)} + \frac{1}{z_1 - z_2} = 0$$

or $\quad (z_2 - z_1)(z_1 - z_2) + (z_2 - z_3)(z_3 - z_1) = 0$

or $\quad z_1^2 + z_2^2 + z_3^2 - z_1z_2 - z_2z_3 - z_3z_1 = 0.$ ...(4')

Thus, (4) or (4') is the necessary condition for the triangle to be equilateral.

If part : Conversely let the condition (4') or (4) hold. Then we have to prove that the triangle is equilateral.

From (4), we have

$$1/\alpha + 1/\beta + 1/\gamma = 0 \qquad [\because z_2 - z_3 = \alpha, \text{ etc.}]$$

or
$$\beta\gamma + \alpha(-\alpha) = 0 \qquad [\because \alpha + \beta + \gamma = 0]$$

or
$$\alpha^2 = \beta\gamma. \quad ...(5)$$

$\therefore$
$$\overline{(\alpha_2)} = \overline{(\beta\gamma)} \text{ or } (\bar{\alpha})^2 = \bar{\beta}\,\bar{\gamma}. \quad ...(6)$$

Multiplying (5) and (6), we get

$$\alpha^2(\overline{\alpha^2}) = (\beta\gamma)(\bar{\beta}\bar{\gamma}) \text{ or } (\alpha\bar{\alpha})^2 = (\beta\bar{\beta})(\gamma\bar{\gamma})$$

or
$$(\alpha\bar{\alpha})^3 = (\alpha\bar{\alpha})(\beta\bar{\beta})(\gamma\bar{\gamma}). \quad ...(7)$$

Similarly $(\beta\bar{\beta})^3 = (\alpha\bar{\alpha})(\beta\bar{\beta})(\gamma\bar{\gamma}) = (\gamma\bar{\gamma})^3$. ...(8)

From (7) and (8), we have

$$(\alpha\overline{\alpha})^3 = (\beta\overline{\beta})^3 = (\gamma\overline{\gamma})^3$$

$\Rightarrow$ $\alpha\overline{\alpha} = \beta\overline{\beta} = \gamma\overline{\gamma} \Rightarrow |\alpha|^2 = |\beta|^2 = |\gamma|^2$

$\Rightarrow$ $|z_2 - z_3|^2 = |z_3 - z_1|^2 = |z_1 - z_2|^2$

$\Rightarrow$ $|z_2 - z_3| = |z_3 - z_1| = |z_1 - z_2|$

$\Rightarrow$ BC = A = AB

$\Rightarrow$ the ΔABC is equilateral.

Hence if the condition (4) or (4') is satisfied, the triangle is equilateral.

$\therefore$ the triangle is equilateral if and only if the condition (4) or (4') is satisfied.

Example 4:

Express $-1 - \sqrt{-3}$ in the polar form.

Solution:

Here $-1 - \sqrt{-3} = -1 - \sqrt{\{3(-1)\}} = -1 - i\sqrt{3}$.

Equating real and imaginary parts, we have

$-1 = r\cos\theta$ ...(1)

and $-\sqrt{3} = r\sin\theta$. ...(2)

Squaring and adding (1) and (2), we have

$r^2 = 1 + 3 = 4$ so that $r = 2$.

Dividing (2) by (1), we have $\tan\theta = \sqrt{3}$. This gives $\theta = -2\pi/3$, choosing the value of θ lying between $-\pi$ and π for which both $\cos\theta$ and $\sin\theta$ are negative.

$\therefore -1 - \sqrt{(-3)} = 2[\cos(-2\pi/3) + i\sin(-2\pi/3)]$

or $-1 - \sqrt{(-3)} = 2[\cos(2\pi/3) - i\sin(2\pi/3)]$.

Example 5:

Show that the representative points of the complex numbers i, –2 – 5i, 1 + 4i and 3 + 10i are collinear.

Solution:

Let the representative points of the complex numbers i, – 2 – 5i, 1 + 4i and 3 + 10i be A, B, C and D respectively. Then the cartesian coordinates of these points are

A(0, 1), B(– 2, – 5), C (1, 4) and D (3, 10).

The equation of the line AB is

$$y - 1 = \frac{-5-1}{-2-0}(x - 0) \text{ i.e., } y - 1 = 3x$$

i.e., $y - 3x = 1.$

Substituting the coordinates of C *i.e.,* (1, 4) in (1), we have $4 - 3 = 1$, which is satisfied. Therefore C(1, 4) lies on the line AB.

Again substituting the coordinates of D *i.e.,* (3, 10) in (1), we have $10 - 9 = 1$, which is also satisfied.

Therefore, D (3, 10) also lies on the line AB.

Hence, the four points A, B, C and D are collinear.

Example 6:

Show that arg z + arg $\bar{z}$ = $2n\pi$, where n is any integer.

Solution:

Let $z = x + iy$, then $\bar{z} = x - iy$, where x, y are real.

We have

$$\arg z + \arg \bar{z} = \arg(z\bar{z}) = \arg\{(x + iy)(x - iy)\}$$
$$= \arg(x^2 + y^2).$$

Now $x^2 + y^2$ is a positive real number, say a. Since a is a positive real number, therefore the representative point of a in the Argand plane will lie on the positive side of the real axis. So the principal value of arg a is 0 and the general value is $2n\pi$, where n is any integer.

Hence $\arg z + \arg \bar{z} = 2n\pi$.

Example 7:

Express $\frac{1 + 7i}{(2-i)^2}$ *in the modulus amplitude form.*

Solution:

Here $$\frac{1 + 7i}{(2 - i)^2} = \frac{1 + 7i}{4 - 4i + i^2} = \frac{1 + 7i}{3 - 4i}, \qquad (\because i^2 = -1)$$

$$= \frac{(1 + 7i)(3 + 4i)}{(3 - 4i)(3 + 4i)} = \frac{3 + 4i + 21i + 28i^2}{9 - 16i^2}$$

$$= \frac{-25 + 25i}{25} = -1 + i.$$

Now let $-1 + i = r(\cos\theta + i\sin\theta)$.

Equating real and imaginary parts, we have

$$-1 = r\cos\theta \qquad \text{...(1)}$$

and $$1 = r\sin\theta. \qquad \text{...(2)}$$

Squaring (1) and (2) and adding, we have

$$r^2 = 1 + 1 = 2.$$

$\therefore$ $$r = \sqrt{2}.$$

Now, putting $r = \sqrt{2}$ in (1) and (2), we have

$\cos\theta = 1/\sqrt{2}$ and $\sin\theta = 1/\sqrt{2}$, giving $\theta = 3\pi/4$.

Hence, $$\frac{1+7i}{(2-i)^2} = \sqrt{2}\left(\cos\frac{3\pi}{4} + i\sin\frac{3\pi}{4}\right).$$

Example 8:

Express $\dfrac{2+3i}{4+5i}$ *in the form* $x + iy$.

Solution:

Multiplying the numerator and the denominator of the given fraction by the conjugate complex of the denominator, we have

$$\frac{2+3i}{4+5i} = \frac{(2+3i)(4-5i)}{(4+5i)(4-5i)} = \frac{8-10i+12i-15i^2}{16-25i^2}$$

$$= \frac{23+2i}{16+25} = \frac{23+2i}{41} = \frac{23}{41} + \frac{2}{41}i. \qquad [\because i^2 = -1]$$

$\therefore$ the real part $x = 23/41$ and the imaginary part $y = 2/41$.

Example 9:

Express $1 - i$ *in the modulus amplitude form.*

Solution:

Equating real and imaginary parts, we have

$$r\cos\theta = 1 \qquad \text{...(1)}$$

and $$r\sin\theta = -1. \qquad \text{...(2)}$$

Squaring and adding (1) and (2), we have

$$r^2 = 1 + 1 = 2.$$

$\therefore \qquad r = +\sqrt{2}$.

Substituting the value of r in (1) and (2), we have

$\cos\theta = 1/\sqrt{2}$ and $\sin\theta = -1/\sqrt{2}$.

These give $\theta = -\pi/4$.

Hence, $1 - i = \sqrt{2}\,\{\cos(-\pi/4) + i\sin(-\pi/4)\}$.

Example 10:

Find the equation of the straight line in the complex plane passing through the origin and making an angle π/3 with the real axis.

Solution:

We know that the equation of the straight line passing through the origin and making an angle α with the real axis is

$z = re^{i\alpha}$, where is a real parameter.

Hence, the equation of the required straight line is

$$z = re^{i\pi/3} = r\left(\cos\frac{\pi}{3} + i\sin\frac{\pi}{3}\right) = r\left(\frac{1}{2} + i\frac{\sqrt{3}}{2}\right),$$ where r is a real parameter.

The above equation is also equivalent to $z = t\left(1 + i\sqrt{3}\right)$, where t is a real parameter.

Example 11:

If P, Q, R are points of affix z_1, z_2, $z_1 + z_2$ respectively, show that OPRQ is a parallelogram.

Solution:

Let $\qquad z_1 = x_1 + iy_1,\ z_2 = x_2 + iy_2$, so that

$$z_1 + z_2 = (x_1 + x_2) + i\,(y_1 + y_2).$$

Thus, the coordinates of O, P, Q, R are (0, 0), (x_1, y_1), (x_2, y_2) and $(x_1 + x_2, y_1 + y_2)$ respectively.

Now, the mid-point of PQ is $\left(\frac{x_1 + x_2}{2}, \frac{y_1 + y_2}{2}\right)$

and the mid-point of OR is also

$$\left(\frac{0 + x_1 + x_2}{2}, \frac{0 + y_1 + y_2}{2}\right), \text{ i.e., } \left(\frac{x_1 + x_2}{2}, \frac{y_1 + y_2}{2}\right).$$

Hence OPRQ is a parallelogram.

Example 12:

Find the equation of the circle whose radius is 5 and whose centre is the point $-2 + 3i$.

Solution:

We know that the equation of the circle whose centre is the point z_0 and whose radius is R is

$$|z - z_0| = R.$$

Hence, the equation of the required circle is

$$|z - (-2 + 3i)| = 5 \text{ i.e. } |z + 2 - 3i| = 5.$$

Example 13:

Show that the equation of a straight line in the Argand plane can be put in the form $z\bar{b} + b\bar{z} = c$, where b is a non-zero complex constant and c is real.

Solution:

Let z_1, z_2 be two given points, say A, B on the Argand plane. Let z be any point, say P, on the line AB. Then we have

$$\arg\frac{z-z_1}{z_1-z_2} = 0 \text{ or } \pi$$

so that $\frac{z-z_1}{z_1-z_2}$ is purely real *i.e.*, I.P. of $\frac{z-z_1}{z_1-z_2} = 0$

$$\text{or} \left(\frac{z-z_1}{z_1-z_2}\right) - \overline{\left(\frac{z-z_1}{z_1-z_2}\right)} = 0$$

$$\text{or} (z-z_1)(\overline{z_1}-\overline{z_2}) - (\bar{z}-\overline{z_1})(z_1-z_2) = 0$$

$$\text{or } z(\overline{z_1}-\overline{z_2}) - \bar{z}(z_1-z_2) + (z_1\overline{z_2}-\overline{z_1}z_2) = 0. \qquad ...(1)$$

Since $\overline{z_1}z_2$ is conjugate of $z_1\overline{z_1}$ hence the number $z_1\overline{z_1} - \overline{z_1}z_2$ is purely imaginary.

Let $z_1\overline{z_1} - \overline{z_1}z_2$. ...(2)

Multiplying (1) by i, we get

$$zi(\overline{z_1}-\overline{z_2}) - \bar{z}i(z_1-z_2) + i(z_1\overline{z_2}-\overline{z_1}z_2) = 0$$

or $zi\left(\overline{z_1}-\overline{z_2}\right)-\bar{z}i\left(z_1-z_2\right)-c=0$, using (2).

Now let $i(z_2 - z_1) = b$ then $i\left(\overline{z_1}-\overline{z_2}\right)=\bar{b}$.

Hence the equation takes the form

$$z\bar{b}+\bar{z}b=c.$$

Example 14:

Show that the equation of a circle described on the line segment joining z_1 and z_2 as diameter is

$$(z-z_1)\left(\bar{z}-\overline{z_2}\right)+(z-z_2)\left(\bar{z}-\overline{z_1}\right)=0.$$

Let z be the affix of any point P on the circle described on the line segment joining z_1 and z_2 as diameter. We then have

$$\arg\frac{z-z_1}{z-z_2}=\frac{\pi}{2} \text{ or } -\frac{\pi}{2}$$

so that $\dfrac{z-z_1}{z-z_2}$ is purely imaginary.

$$\therefore \quad \frac{z-z_1}{z-z_2}+\frac{\bar{z}-\bar{z}_1}{\bar{z}-\bar{z}_1}=0$$

$$\text{or } (z-z_1)(\bar{z}-\bar{z}_2)+(z-z_2)(\bar{z}-\bar{z}_1)=0.$$

which is the equation of the locus of the point z *i.e.*, the equation of the circle described on the line segment joining z_1 and z_2 as diameter.

Example 15:

Find the equation of the straight line in the complex plane passing through the points $-1+3i$ and $5+4i$.

Solution:

We know that the equation of the straight line joining the points z_1 and z_2 is

$z = tz_1 + (1 - t)z_2$, where t is a real parameter.

Hence, the equation of the required straight line is

$z = t(-1 + 3i) + (1 - t)(5 + 4i)$, where t is a real parameter.

Example 16:

A variable complex number $z = x + iy$ is such that the argument of the

fraction $\frac{z-1}{z+1}$ *is always equal to* $\frac{1}{4}\pi$.

Show that the locus of the point z is the circle $x^2 + y^2 - 2y = 1$.

Solution:

We have

$$\frac{z-1}{z+1} = \frac{(x+iy)-1}{(x+iy)+1} = \frac{(x-1)+iy}{(x+1)+iy} \qquad [\because z = x + iy]$$

$$= \frac{[(x-1)+iy][(x+1)-iy]}{[(x+1)+iy][(x+1)-iy]},$$

multiplying the Nr and the Dr by the conjugate of the Dr

$$= \frac{[(x^2-1)+y^2] + iy[(x+1)-(x-1)]}{(x+1)^2+y^2} = \frac{(x^2+y^2-1)+2y_i}{(x+i)^2+y^2}$$

$$= \frac{x^2+y^2-1}{(x+1)^2+y^2} + i\frac{2y}{(x+1)^2+y^2} = r(\cos\theta + i\sin\theta), \text{ say.}$$

$\therefore$ equating real and imaginary parts, we have

$$\frac{x^2+y^2-1}{(x+1)^2+y^2} = r\cos\theta$$

and

$$\frac{2y}{(x+1)^2+y^2} = r\sin\theta$$

Dividing these, we get

$$\tan\theta = 2y/(x^2+y^2-1).$$

But as given, $\theta = \arg[(z-1)/(z+1)]$ is always equal to $\frac{1}{4}\pi$.

$$\therefore \qquad \frac{2y}{x^2+y^2-1} = \tan\theta = \tan\frac{1}{4}\pi = 1$$

or

$$2y = x^2 + y^2 - 1, \text{ or } x^2 + y^2 - 2y = 1.$$

Example 17:

If z_1, z_2, z_3 *are the vertices of an isosceles triangle, right angled at the vertex* z_2, *prove that*

$$z_1^2 + 2z_2^2 + z_3^2 = 2z_2(z_1 + z_3).$$

Solution:

Let the complex numbers z_1, z_2, z_3 represent the points A, B, C respectively in the Argand diagram.

Since $\angle ABC = 90°$, we have

$$\arg\frac{z_2 - z_2}{z_3 - z_3} = \frac{\pi}{2} \text{ or } -\frac{\pi}{2},$$

so that $\dfrac{z_2 - z_1}{z_2 - z_3}$ is purely imaginary.

Now, if a complex number $z = x + iy$ is purely imaginary *i.e.*, $x = 0$ then $z + \overline{z} = 0$.

$$\therefore \quad \frac{z_2 - z_1}{z_2 - z_3} + \frac{\overline{z}_2 - \overline{z}_1}{z_2 - z_3} = 0$$

$$\text{or} \quad \frac{z_2 - z_1}{z_2 - z_3} = -\frac{\overline{z}_2 - \overline{z}_1}{\overline{z}_2 - \overline{z}_3} \qquad ...(1)$$

Again BA = BC

so that $|z_2 - z_1| = |z_2 - z_3|$

or $|z_2 - z_1|^2 = |z_2 - z_3|^2$

or $(z_2 - z_1)(\overline{z}_2 - \overline{z}_1) = (z_2 - z_3)(\overline{z}_2 - \overline{z}_3)$. ...(2)

Multiplying (1) and (2), we get

$$\frac{(z_2 - z_1)^2(\overline{z}_2 - \overline{z}_1)}{(z_2 - z_3)} = -(\overline{z}_2 - \overline{z}_1)(z_2 - z_3)$$

$$\text{or} \quad \left[(z_2 - z_1)^2 + (z_2 - z_3)^2\right](\overline{z}_2 - \overline{z}_1) = 0$$

$$\text{or} \quad (z_2 - z_1)^2 + (z_2 - z_3)^2 = 0 \quad [\because z_2 \neq z_1 \Rightarrow \overline{z}_2 \neq \overline{z}_1]$$

$$\text{or} \quad z_1^2 + 2z_2^2 + z_3^2 = 2z_2(z_1 + z_3).$$

Example 18:

Prove that

$$\left|\frac{z_1 - z_2}{1 - \overline{z}_1 z_2}\right| < 1 \text{ if } |z_1| < 1 \text{ and } |z_2| < 1.$$

Solution:

The inequality $\left|\dfrac{z_1 - z_2}{1 - \overline{z}_1 z_2}\right| < 1$ will hold good if

$$|z_1 - z_2| < |1 - \bar{z}_1 z_2|$$

or $$|z_1 - z_2|^2 < |1 + \bar{z}_1 z_2|^2$$

or $$(z_1 - z_2)\,\overline{(z_1 - z_2)} < (1 - \bar{z}_1 z_2)\,\overline{(1 - \bar{z}_1 z_2)}$$

$[\because |z|^2 = z\bar{z}]$

or $$(z_1 - z_2)(\bar{z}_1 - \bar{z}_2) < (1 - \bar{z}_1 z_2)(1 - z_1 \bar{z}_2)$$

or $$z_1\bar{z}_1 - z_1\bar{z}_2 - z_2\bar{z}_1 + z_2\bar{z}_2 < 1 - z_1\bar{z}_2 - \bar{z}_1 z_2 + z\bar{z}_1\ z_2\bar{z}_2$$

$$|z_1|^2 + |z_2|^2 < 1 + |z_1|^2\ |z_2|^2$$

or $$|z_1|^2 + |z_2|^2 - 1 - |z_1|^2\ |z_2|^2 < 0$$

or $$(|z_1|^2 - 1)\ (1 - |z_2|^2) < 0. \quad ...(1)$$

Now, the inequality (1) will hold if $|z_1| < 1$ and $|z_2| < 1$.

Hence, $\left|\dfrac{z_1 - z_2}{1 - \bar{z}_1 z_2}\right| < 1$ if $|z_1| < 1$ and $|z_2| < 1$.

Example 19:

Find the radius and centre of the circle

$$\left|\frac{z-i}{z+i}\right| = 5.$$

Solution:

We have $$\left|\frac{z-i}{z+i}\right| = 5. \quad ...(1)$$

$\therefore$ $$|z - i| = 5|z + i| \quad \left[\because \left|\frac{z_1}{z_2}\right| = \frac{|z_1|}{|z_2|}\right]$$

or $$|x + iy - i| = 5|x + iy + i| \quad [\because z = x + iy]$$

or $$|x + i\,(y - 1)|^2 = 25|x + i(y + 1)|^2$$

or $$x^2 + (y - 1)^2 = 25[x^2 + (y + 1)^2]$$

or $$x^2 + y^2 - 2y + 1 = 25[x^2 + y^2 + 2y + 1]$$

or $$24(x^2 + y^2) + 52y + 24 = 0$$

or $$x^2 + y^2 + (13/6)y + 1 = 0, \quad ...(2)$$

which is the equation of a circle.

Hence the locus of the points on the Argand plane which satisfy the condition (1) is a circle.

The coordinates of the centre of the circle (1) are $\left(0, -\frac{13}{12}\right)$ and its radius is

$$\sqrt{\left[0^2 + \left(-\frac{13}{2}\right)^2 - 1\right]} \text{ i.e., } \sqrt{\left(\frac{25}{144}\right)} \text{ i.e., } \frac{5}{12}.$$

Hence, the centre of the given circle is the point whose affix is

$$z = 0 + (-13/12)i$$

i.e., $(-13/12)\,i$

and its radius is 5/12.

Example 20:

Show that the equation of a circle in the Argand plane can be put in the form

$$z\bar{z} + b\bar{z} + \bar{b}z + c = 0,$$

where c is a real and b a complex constant.

Solution:

Let r be the radius and α the affix of the centre of the circle, say the point C. Let z be the affix of any point P on the circle. Then we have

$$|z - \alpha| = CP = r$$

or $|z - \alpha|^2 = r^2$

or $(z - \alpha)\overline{(z-\alpha)} = r^2$ or $(z - \alpha)(\bar{z} - \bar{\alpha}) = r^2$

or $z\bar{z} - \alpha\bar{z} - z\bar{\alpha} + \alpha\bar{\alpha} - r^2 = 0$, which is of the form

$$z\bar{z} + b\bar{z} + \bar{b}z + c = 0,$$

where c is real, since $\alpha\bar{\alpha} - r^2$ is real, and b is complex.

Remark:

The affix α of the centre of the circle $z\bar{z} + b\bar{z} + \bar{b}z + c = 0$ *is given by* $\alpha = -b$ *and the radius r is given by* $\alpha\bar{\alpha} - r^2 = c$.

We have $\alpha\bar{\alpha} - r^2 = c \Rightarrow r^2 = \alpha\bar{\alpha} - c = (-b)\overline{(-b)} - c = |-b|^2 - c = |b|^2 - c$

Hence, the centre of the circle $z\bar{z} + b\bar{z} + c = 0$ is the point $-b$ and its radius is $\sqrt{(b\bar{b} - c)}$ *i.e.,* $\sqrt{(|b|^2 - c)}$.

Example 21:

The vertices of a triangle are represented in Argand diagram by the complex numbers z_1, z_2, z_3. Interpret the modulus and argument of $\frac{z_2 - z_1}{z_3 - z_1}$ in terms of the sides and angles of the triangle.

Solution:

Let the points $z = z_1$, $z = z_2$, $z = z_3$ be A, B, C respectively in the Argand plane.

Then, $z_1 = \vec{OA}$, $z_2 = \vec{OB}$, $z_3 = \vec{OC}$, where O is the origin.

We have $z_2 - z_1 = \vec{OB} - \vec{OA} = \vec{AB}$ and $z_3 - z_1 = \vec{OC} - \vec{OA} = \vec{AC}$.

Now, $AB = |z_2 - z_1|$ and $AC = |z_3 - z_1|$.

$$\therefore \quad \frac{AB}{AC} = \frac{|z_2 - z_1|}{|z_3 - z_1|} = \left|\frac{z_2 - z_1}{z_3 - z_1}\right|.$$

Again $\arg(z_2 - z_1)$ is the angle which AB makes with the positive direction of x-axis and $\arg(z_3 - z_1)$ is the angle which AC makes with the positive direction of x-axis.

$\therefore$ angle between the lines AB and AC *i.e.*, $\angle BAC$

$$= \arg(z_2 - z_1) - \arg(z_3 - z_1)$$

$$= \arg[(z_2 - z_1)/(z_3 - z_1)].$$

Hence, $\left|\frac{z_2 - z_1}{z_3 - z_1}\right| = \frac{AB}{AC}$ and $\arg\frac{z_2 - z_1}{z_3 - z_1} = \angle BAC$.

Example 22:

Prove that the area of the triangle whose vertices are the points represented by the complex numbers z_1, z_2, z_3 on the Argand diagram is

$\Sigma[(z_2 - z_3)\,|z_1|^2/4iz_1]$.

Solution:

Let $z_1 = x_1 + iy_1$, $z_2 = x_2 + iy_2$, $z_3 = x_3 + iy_3$, so that the coordinates of the vertices of the given triangle are (x_1, y_1), (x_2, y_2) and (x_3, y_3).

Now the required area of the triangle

$$= \frac{1}{2}\begin{vmatrix} x_1 & y_1 & 1 \\ x_2 & y_2 & 1 \\ x_3 & y_3 & 1 \end{vmatrix} = \frac{1}{2i}\begin{vmatrix} x_1 & iy_1 & 1 \\ x_2 & iy_2 & 1 \\ x_3 & iy_3 & 1 \end{vmatrix}$$

$$= \frac{1}{2i}\begin{vmatrix} x_1 & x_1+iy_1 & 1 \\ x_2 & x_2+iy_2 & 1 \\ x_3 & x_3+iy_3 & 1 \end{vmatrix}, C_2+C_1$$

$$= \frac{1}{2i}\begin{vmatrix} x_1 & z_1 & 1 \\ x_2 & z_2 & 1 \\ x_3 & x_3 & 1 \end{vmatrix}$$

$$= \frac{1}{2i}\Sigma\left[x_1(z_2 - z_3)\right], \text{ expanding the determinant along the first column}$$

$$= \frac{1}{2i}\Sigma\left[\frac{1}{2}(z_1+\bar{z}_1)\,(z_2-z_3)\right]$$

$$\left[\because z_1 + \bar{z}_1 = (x_1 + iy_1) + (x_1 - iy_1) = 2x_1\right]$$

$$= \frac{1}{4i}\Sigma\, z_1(z_2 - z_3) + \frac{1}{4i}\Sigma\bar{z}_1(z_2 - z_3)$$

$$= \frac{1}{4i}(0) + \frac{1}{4i}\,\Sigma\left[\frac{z_1\,\bar{z}_1}{z_1}(z_2 - z_3)\right] \qquad \left[\because \Sigma\, z_1(z_2 - z_3) = 0\right]$$

$$= \Sigma\left[\frac{(z_2 - z_3)\,|z_1|^2}{4iz_1}\right]. \qquad \left[\because z_1\,\bar{z}_1 = |z_1|^2\right]$$

EXPONENTIAL, TRIGONOMETRIC AND HYPERBOLIC FUNCTIONS OF A COMPLEX VARIABLE (SEPARATION INTO REAL AND IMAGINARY PARTS)

The Exponential Function of a Complex Variable

We know that if x is any real number, then

$$e^x = 1 + \frac{x}{1!} + \frac{x^2}{2!} + \frac{x^3}{3!} + \ \ldots \text{ ad.infi.}$$

We shall take motivation from this expansion of e^x as a power series in x, to define the exponential function e^z of a complex variable $z = x + iy$, where x and y are real. Thus we define

$$e^z = 1 + \frac{z}{1!} + \frac{z^2}{2!} + \frac{z^3}{3!} + \ \ldots \text{ ad.infi.} \qquad \ldots(1)$$

It can be shown by D' Alembert's Ratio Test, that the power series (1) is absolutely convergent for all values of the complex variable z. If we denote the nth term of the series (1) by u_n, we have

$$\lim_{n\to\infty}\left|\frac{u_{n+1}}{u_n}\right| = \lim_{n\to\infty}\left|\frac{z_n}{n!}\cdot\frac{(n-1)!}{z^{n-1}}\right| = \lim_{n\to\infty}\frac{|z|}{n} = 0,$$

which is < 1. Therefore, the series (1) is absolutely convergent and hence convergent for all values of the complex variable z. Thus, the sum of the series (1) exists for all z and this justifies our definition of e^z given in (1). Hence for the complex variable z, we define e^z as the sum of the power series (1).

The other ways to denote e^z are E(z) and exp(z). Either of these symbols is read as 'exponential z.'

Putting z = 0 on both sides of (1), we see that $e^0 = 1$.

Remark:

It should be noted that when z is complex, e^z is only a symbol used to represent the sum of the series on the R.H.S. of (1). It does not mean that

$$e^z = \left(1+\frac{1}{1!}+\frac{1}{2!}+\frac{1}{3!}+\ldots+\infty\right)^z.$$

Index Law for the Exponential Functions

To prove that $e^{z_1}.e^{z_2} = e^{z_1+z_2}$

i.e., $E(z_1).E(z_2) = E(z_1 + z_2)$.

Proof:

If z_1 and z_2 be two complex numbers, then by the definition of E (z), we have

$$E(z_1) = 1+\frac{z_1}{1!}+\frac{z_1^2}{2!}+\frac{z_1^3}{3!}+\ldots+\frac{z_1^n}{n!}+\ldots\infty \qquad \ldots(1)$$

$$\text{and } E(z_2) = 1+\frac{z_2}{1!}+\frac{z_2^2}{2!}+\frac{z_2^3}{3!}+\ldots+\frac{z_2^n}{n!}+\ldots\infty \qquad \ldots(2)$$

Since the series (1) and (2) are absolutely convergent, therefore by Cauchy's theorem on multiplication of absolutely convergent series, we have

$$E(z_1).E(z_2)$$

$$= \left(1+\frac{z_1}{1!}+\frac{z_1^2}{2!}+\ldots+\frac{z_1^n}{n!}+\ldots\right).\left(1+\frac{z_2}{1!}+\frac{z_2^2}{2!}+\ldots+\frac{z_2^n}{n!}+\ldots\right)$$

$$= 1+\frac{1}{1!}(z_1-z_2)+\left(\frac{z_1^2}{2!}+\frac{z_1z_2}{1!}+\frac{z_2^2}{2!}\right)+\ldots$$

$$+\left(\frac{z_1^n}{n!}+\frac{z_1^{n-1}}{(n-1)!}\cdot\frac{z_2}{1!}+\frac{z_1^{n-2}}{(n-2)}\cdot\frac{z_2^2}{2!}+\ldots+\frac{z_2^n}{n!}\right)+\ldots$$

$$= 1 + \frac{1}{1!}(z_1 + z_2) + \frac{1}{2!}(z_1^2 + 2z_1z_2 + z_2^2) + \ldots$$

$$+ \frac{1}{n!}\left[z_1^n + nz_1^{n-1}z_2 + \frac{n(n-1)}{2!}z_1^{n-2}z_2^2 + \ldots + z_2^n\right] + \ldots$$

$$= 1 + \frac{(z_1 + z_2)}{1!} + \frac{(z_1 + z_2)^2}{2!} + \ldots + \frac{(z_1 + z_2)^n}{n!} + \ldots$$

$= E(z_1 + z_2)$, by def. of $E(z)$.

The above result may also be written as

$$\exp(z_1).\exp(z_2) = \exp(z_1 + z_2).$$

Deductions:

(i) If $z_1, z_2, \ldots, z_n$ be n complex numbers, then from the above law, we see by induction that

$$E(z_1).E(z_2) \ldots E(z_n) = E(z_1 + z_2 + \ldots + z_n).$$

If we put $z_1 + z_2 = \ldots = z_n = z$ (say), we have

$$[E(z)]^n = E(nz), \text{ n being a positive integer.}$$

This result may also be written as

$$[e^z]^n = e^{nz} \text{ or } [\exp(z)]^n = \exp(nz).$$

(ii) If z be any complex number, then

$$e^z.e^{-z} = e^{z-z} = e^0 = 1.$$

From this result, it follows that $e^z \neq 0$ for all z.

For if there were such a value of z, then since e^{-z} would exist for this value of z, we would have $0 = 1$, which is absurd.

TRIGONOMETRICAL FUNCTIONS OR CIRCULAR FUNCTIONS OF A COMPLEX VARIABLE

We know that if x is any real number, then

$$\cos x = 1 - \frac{x^2}{2!} + \frac{x^4}{4!} - \ldots + (-1)^n \frac{x^{2n}}{(2n)!} + \ldots \text{ad.inf.}$$

$$\text{and} \quad \sin x = x - \frac{x^3}{3!} + \frac{x^5}{5!} - \ldots + (-1)^n \frac{x^{2n+1}}{(2n+1)!} + \ldots \text{ ad.inf.}$$

We shall take motivation from these expansions of cos x and sin x as power series in x, to define cos z and sin z, when z is a complex number.

So,if $z = x + iy$ is a complex variable, we define

$$\cos z = 1 - \frac{z^2}{2!} + \frac{z^4}{4!} - \ldots + (-1)^n \frac{z^{2n}}{(2n)!} + \ldots \text{ad.inf.}$$

and $$\sin z = z - \frac{z^3}{3!} + \frac{z^5}{5!} - \ldots + (-1)^n \frac{z^{2n+1}}{(2n+1)} + \ldots \text{ ad.inf.}$$

Our definitions are sensible because both the series used to define cos z and sin z are absolutely convergent for all z.

Replacing z by –z in the above definitions, we find that

$$\cos(-z) = \cos z, \text{ and } \sin(-z) = -\sin z.$$

The other circular functions for a complex variable are defined in the same way as those for a real variable. Thus we define

$$\tan z = \frac{\sin z}{\cos z}, \cot z = \frac{\cos z}{\sin a}, \sec z = \frac{1}{\cos z} \text{ and } \operatorname{cosec} z = \frac{1}{\sin z}.$$

Remark:

For a complex variable $z = x + iy$, we have defined e^z, cos z, sin z etc. in such a way that if we take

$$z = x + i0 = x \text{ (i.e., real)},$$

then these definitions give results which are in sound agreement with those for a real variable.

Euler's Theorem

If θ be real or complex, we have $e^{i\theta} = \cos\theta + i\sin\theta$.

Proof:

If z is any complex number, then by definition of e^z, we have

$$e^z = 1 + \frac{z}{1!} + \frac{z^2}{2!} + \frac{z^2}{3!} + \ldots$$

Replacing z by $i\theta$, we have

$$e^{i\theta} = 1 + \frac{i\theta}{1!} + \frac{(i\theta)^2}{2!} + \frac{(i\theta)^3}{3!} + \frac{(i\theta)^4}{4!} + \ldots$$

$$= \left(1 - \frac{\theta^2}{2!} + \frac{\theta^4}{4!} - \ldots\right) + i\left(\theta - \frac{\theta^3}{3!} + \frac{\theta^5}{5!} - \ldots\right)$$

$= \cos\theta + i\sin\theta$, by definitions of $\cos\theta$ and $\sin\theta$.

Thus, $e^{i\theta} = \cos\theta + i\sin\theta$. ...(1)

This result is known as *Euler's theorem.*

Replacing θ by $-\theta$ in (1), we get

$$e^{-i\theta} = \cos(-\theta) + i\sin(-\theta)$$

or $$e^{-i\theta} = \cos\theta - i\sin\theta. \qquad ...(2)$$

From (1) and (2) on addition and subtraction, we get

$$e^{i\theta} + e^{-i\theta} = 2\cos\theta,$$

and $$e^{i\theta} - e^{i\theta} = 2i\sin\theta.$$

$\therefore$ $$\cos\theta = \frac{e^{i\theta} + e^{-i\theta}}{2} \text{ and}$$

$$\sin\theta = \frac{e^{i\theta} - e^{-i\theta}}{2i}. \qquad ...(3)$$

These results are known as *Euler's exponential values* of cos θ and sin θ.

From exponential values of cos θ and sin θ, we see that

$$\tan\theta = \frac{\sin\theta}{\cos\theta} = \frac{e^{i\theta} - e^{-i\theta}}{i\left(e^{i\theta} + e^{-i\theta}\right)}, \cot\theta = i\frac{e^{i\theta} + e^{-i\theta}}{e^{i\theta} - e^{-i\theta}}, \text{ etc.}$$

Putting θ = 0 in the formulae (3), we get

$$\cos 0 = \frac{1}{2}\left(e^0 + e^0\right) = \frac{1}{2}(1+1) = \frac{1}{2}.2 = 1, \text{ and } \sin 0 = 0.$$

PERIODICITY OF FUNCTIONS

Theorem:

(a) *Prove that e^z is a periodic function, where z is a complex quantity.*

If $$z = x + iy, \text{ then}$$

$$e^z = e^{x+iy} = e^x.e^{iy}$$

$$= e^x(\cos y + i\sin y), \text{ by Euler's Theorem}$$

$$= e^x[\cos(2n\pi + y) + i\sin(2n\pi + y)], \text{ where n is any integer}$$

$$= e^x.e^i(2n\pi + y) = e^{x+iy} + 2n\pi i = e^{z+2n\pi i}.$$

Hence, e^z is a periodic function of period $2\pi i$.

(b) *Prove that sin z, cos z, tan z etc., are periodic functions, where z is a complex quantity.*

Proof:

We have

$$\cos(z + 2n\pi) = \cos z\cos 2n\pi - \sin z\sin 2n\pi$$

$$= \cos z, \text{ n being any integer}$$

$$\sin (z + 2n\pi) = \sin z \cos 2n\pi + \cos z \sin 2n\pi$$

$$= \sin z, \text{ n being any integer}$$

$$\text{and } \tan (z + n\pi) = \frac{\sin (z + n\pi)}{\cos (z + n\pi)}$$

$$= \frac{\sin z \cos n\pi + \cos z \sin n\pi}{\cos z \cos n\pi - \sin z \sin n\pi}$$

$$= \tan z, \text{ n being any integer.}$$

From these we conclude that cos z and sin z are periodic functions of period 2π and tan z is a periodic function of period π.

DE-MOIVRE'S THEOREM FOR COMPLEX ARGUMENT

We have already mentioned De Moivre's Theorem for real values of θ. Now we extend that theorem for complex values of θ. We have

$$(e^{i\theta})^n = e^{in\theta}, \text{ whether } \theta \text{ be real or complex.}$$

$$\therefore \quad (\cos \theta + i \sin \theta)^n = \cos n\theta + i \sin n\theta, \text{ by Euler's theorem.}$$

This shows that De-Moivre's Theorem is true whether θ be real or complex.

SOME STANDARD TRIGONOMETRICAL RESULTS FOR COMPLEX ARGUMENTS

Since our trigonometric functions of a complex variable are generalizations of trigonometric functions of a real variable, therefore most of our results for trigonometric functions of a real variable also hold good for trigonometric functions of a complex variable.

Theorem:

To prove that for all values of x, y, real or complex, the following are true:

(i) $\cos^2 x + \sin^2 x = 1$,

(ii) $\cos (-x) = \cos x$,

(iii) $\cos 2x = \cos^2 x - \sin^2 x$,

(iv) $\sin 3x = 3 \sin x - 4 \sin^3 x$,

(v) $\cos 3x = 4 \cos^3 x - 3 \cos x$,

(vi) $\sin x + \sin y = 2 \sin \frac{1}{2} (x + y) \cos \frac{1}{2} (x - y)$,

(vii) $\cos x - \cos y = 2 \sin \frac{1}{2} (x + y) \sin \frac{1}{2} (y - x)$

(viii) $\sin (x \pm y) = \sin x \cos y \pm \cos x \sin y,$

(ix) $\cos (x \pm y) = \cos x \cos y \pm \sin x \sin y.$

Proof:

(i) To prove that $\cos^2 x + \sin^2 x = 1.$

$$\text{L.H.S.} = \cos^2 x - \sin^2 x$$

$$= \left\{\frac{e^{ix} + e^{-ix}}{2}\right\}^2 + \left\{\frac{e^{ix} - e^{-ix}}{2i}\right\}^2$$

$$= \frac{1}{4}\left[\left(e^{ix} + e^{-ix}\right)^2 - \left(e^{ix} - e^{-ix}\right)^2\right] \quad [\because i^2 = -1]$$

$$= \frac{1}{4}[(e^{2ix} + e^{-2ix} + 2e^{ix}.e^{ix}) - (e^{2ix} + e^{-2ix} - 2e^{ix}.e^{-ix})]$$

$$= \frac{1}{4}[4e^{ix}.e^{-ix}] = e^{ix - ix} = e^0 = 1 = \text{R.H.S.}$$

Alter. We have $\cos^2 x + \sin^2 x = (\cos x + i \sin x)(\cos x - i \sin x)$

(ii) To prove that $\cos (-x) = \cos x.$

$$\text{L.H.S.} = \cos (-x) = \frac{e^{i(-x)} + e^{-i(-x)}}{2}$$

$$= \frac{e^{-ix} + e^{ix}}{2} = \frac{e^{ix} + e^{-ix}}{2} = \cos x = \text{R.H.S.}$$

(iii) To prove that $\cos 2x = \cos 2x - \cos^2 x - \sin^2 x.$

$$\text{R.H.S.} = \cos^2 x - \sin^2 x$$

$$= \left\{\frac{e^{ix} + e^{-ix}}{2}\right\}^2 - \left\{\frac{e^{ix} - e^{-ix}}{2i}\right\}^2,$$

by Euler's exponential values of cos x and sin x

$$= \frac{1}{4}[(e^{ix} + e^{-ix})^2 + (e^{ix} - e^{-ix})^2] \quad [\because i^2 = -1]$$

$$= \frac{1}{4}[(e^{2ix} + e^{-2ix} + 2e^{ix}.e^{-ix}) + (e^{2ix} + e^{-2ix} - 2e^{ix}.e^{-ix})]$$

$$= \frac{1}{4}[2(e^{2ix} + e^{-2ix})] = \frac{1}{2}(e^{2ix} + e^{-2ix})$$

$$= \frac{1}{2}[e^{i(2x)} + e^{-i(2x)}] = \cos 2x = \text{L.H.S.}$$

(iv) To prove that sin 3x = 3 sin x − 4 sin³ x.

$$\text{L.H.S.} = \sin 3x = \frac{e^{i(3x)} - e^{-(3x)}}{2i} = \frac{e^{3ix} - e^{-3ix}}{2i}$$

$$= \frac{\left(e^{ix}\right)^3 - \left(e^{-ix}\right)^3}{2i} = \frac{\left(e^{ix} - e^{-ix}\right)^3 + 3e^{ix}.e^{-ix}\left(e^{ix} - e^{-ix}\right)}{2i}$$

$$[\because a^3 - b^3 = (a - b^3 = (a - b)^3 + 3ab\ (a - b)]$$

$$= \frac{1}{2i}[(2i \sin x)^3 = 3.e^0.(2i \sin x)] \quad \left[\because \sin x = \frac{e^{ix} - e^{-ix}}{2i}\right]$$

$$= \frac{1}{2i}\left[8i^3 \sin^3 x + 6i \sin x\right] = \frac{1}{2i}\left[2i\left(-4 \sin^3 x + \sin x\right)\right]$$

$$= -4 \sin^3 x + 3 \sin x = 3 \sin x - 4 \sin^3 x = \text{R.H.S.}$$

(v) To prove that cos 3x = 4 cos³x − 3 cos x.

$$\text{L.H.S.} = \frac{1}{2} \cos 3x = \frac{1}{2}\left[e^{i(3x)} + e^{-i(3x)}\right] = \frac{1}{2}\left[\left(e^{ix}\right)^3 + \left(e^{-ix}\right)^3\right]$$

$$= \frac{1}{2}[(e^{ix} + e^{-ix})^3 - 3e^{ix}.e^{-ix}(e^{ix} + e^{-ix})]$$

$$[\because a^3 + b^3 = (a + b)^3 - 3ab\ (a + b)]$$

$$= \frac{1}{2}[(2 \cos x)^3 - 3.e^0.(2 \cos x] \qquad \left[\because \cos x = \frac{1}{2}\left(e^{ix} + e^{-ix}\right)\right]$$

$$= \frac{1}{2}[8 \cos^3 x - 6 \cos x] = 4 \cos^3 x - 3 \cos x = \text{R.H.S.}$$

(iv) To prove that

$$\sin x + \sin y = 2 \sin \frac{1}{2}(x - y).$$

$$\text{L.H.S.} = \sin x + \sin y$$

$$= \frac{e^{ix} - e^{-ix}}{2i} + \frac{e^{iy} - e^{-iy}}{2i} = \frac{1}{2i}\left[\left(e^{ix} - e^{-ix}\right) + \left(e^{iy} - e^{-iy}\right)\right]$$

$$= (1/2i)\ [\{e^{i[(x + y)/2 + (x - y)/2]} - e^{-i[(x + y)/2 + (x - y)/2]}$$

$$+ \{e^{i[(x + y)/2 - (x - y)/2]} - e^{-i[(x + y)/2 - (x - y)/2]}\}]$$

$$= (1/2i)\ [\{e^{i[(x + y)/2 + (x - y)/2]} + e^{i[(x + y)/2 - (x - y)/2]}$$

$$- \{e^{-i[x + y)/2 + (x - y)/2]} + e^{-i[(x + y)/2 - (x - y)/2]}\}]$$

$$= (1/2i)\ [e^{i(x + y)/2}\ \{e^{i(x - y)/2} + e^{-i(x - y)/2}\}$$

$$-e^{-i(x+y)/2}\ \{e^{-i(x-y)/2} + e^{i(x-y)/2}\}\ ]$$

$$= \frac{1}{2i}\left[2\cos\left\{\frac{x-y}{2}\right\}\right].\left[2i\sin\left\{\frac{x+y}{2}\right\}\right]$$

$$= 2\sin\frac{1}{2}(x+y)\cos\frac{1}{2}(x-y) = \text{R.H.S.}$$

(vii) To prove that

$$\cos x - \cos y = 2\sin\frac{1}{2}(x+y).\sin\frac{1}{2}(y-x).$$

$$\text{R.H.S.} = 2\sin\frac{1}{2}(x+y).\frac{1}{2}(y-x)$$

$$= 2\left[\frac{e^{i(x+y)/2} - e^{-i(x+y)/2}}{2i}\right]\left[\frac{e^{i(y-x)/2} - e^{-i(y-x)/2}}{2i}\right]$$

$$= -\frac{1}{2}[e^{i(x+y+y-x)/2} - e^{i(x+y-y+x)/2} - e^{-i(x+y-y+x)/2} + e^{-i(x+y+y-x)/2}]$$

(simply by multiplication)

$$= -\frac{1}{2}\left[e^{iy} - e^{ix} - e^{-ix} + e^{-iy}\right] = \frac{1}{2}\left(e^{ix} + e^{-ix}\right) - \frac{1}{2}\left(e^{iy} + e^{-iy}\right)$$

$= \cos x - \cos y = \text{L.H.S.}$

(viii) To prove that $\sin(x+y) = \sin x \cos y + \cos x \sin y$.

$$\text{R.H.S.} = \frac{e^{ix} - e^{-ix}}{2i} \times \frac{e^{iy} + e^{-iy}}{2} + \frac{e^{ix} + e^{-ix}}{2} \times \frac{e^{iy} - e^{-iy}}{2i}$$

$$= (1/4i)\,[\{e^{i(x+y)} + e^{i(x-y)} - e^{-i(x-y)} - e^{-i(x+y)}\}$$
$$+ \{e^{i(x+y)} - e^{i(x-y)} + e^{-i(x-y)} - e^{-i(x+y)}\}]$$

$$= \frac{1}{4i}\left[2e^{i(x+y)} - 2e^{-i(x+y)}\right] = \frac{e^{i(x+y)} - e^{-i(x+y)}}{2i}$$

$= \sin(x+y) = \text{L.H.S.}$

Similarly, $\sin(x-y) = \sin x \cos y - \cos x \sin y$.

$\therefore \sin(x \pm y) = \sin x \cos y \pm \cos x \sin y$.

(ix) To prove that $\cos(x \pm y) = \cos x \cos y \pm \sin x \sin y$.

We have $\cos x \cos y + \sin x \sin y$

$$= \frac{e^{ix} + e^{-ix}}{2}.\frac{e^{iy} + e^{-iy}}{2} + \frac{e^{ix} - e^{-ix}}{2i}.\frac{e^{iy} - e^{-iy}}{2i}$$

$$= \frac{1}{4}[e^{i(x+y)} + e^{i(x-y)} + e^{-i(x-y)} + e^{-i(x+y)}]$$

$$-\frac{1}{4}[e^{i(x+y)} - e^{i(x-y)} - e^{-i(x-y)} + e^{-i(x+y)}] \qquad [\because i^2 = -1]$$

$$= \frac{1}{4}\left[2e^{i(x-y)} + 2e^{-i(x-y)}\right] = \frac{1}{2}\left[e^{i(x-y)} + e^{-i(x-y)}\right] = \cos(x-y)$$

Similarly we can prove that

$$\cos x \cos y - \sin x \sin y = \cos(x + y).$$

$$\therefore \qquad \cos(x \pm y) = \cos x \cos y \mp \sin x \sin y.$$

Remark:

If u and v are any complex numbers, we can easily prove that

$2 \sin u \cos v = \sin(u + v) + \sin(u - v)$, $2 \cos u \sin v = \sin(u + v) - \sin(u - v)$

$2 \cos u \cos v = \cos(u + v) + \cos(u - v)$, $2 \sin u \sin v = \cos(u - v) - \cos(u + v)$.

Example 1:

Show that $\exp(\pm i\pi/2) = \pm i$.

Solution:

Since $\exp(\pm i\theta) = \cos\theta \pm i \sin\theta$, we have

$\exp(\pm i\,\pi/2) = \cos \pi/2 \pm i \sin \pi/2 = 0 \pm i.1 = \pm i$.

Example 2:

Prove that

$(\sin(\alpha - \theta) + e^{-\alpha i} \sin\theta)^n = \sin^{n-1}\alpha\,\{\sin(\alpha - n\theta) + e^{-\alpha i} \sin n\theta\}$.

Solution:

L.H.S. $= \{\sin\alpha\cos\theta - \cos\alpha\sin\theta + (\cos\alpha - i\sin\alpha)\sin\theta\}^n$

$= \{\sin\alpha\cos\theta - i\sin\alpha\sin\theta\}^n = \sin^n\alpha\,(\cos\theta - i\sin\theta)^n$

$= \sin^n\alpha\,(\cos n\theta - i\sin n\theta)$, by De-Moivre's Theorem

and

R.H.S. $= \sin^{n-1}\alpha\,\{\sin(\alpha - n\theta) + e^{-\alpha i}\sin n\theta\}$

$= \sin^{n-1}\alpha\,\{\sin\alpha\cos n\theta - \cos\alpha\sin n\theta + (\cos\alpha - i\sin\alpha)\sin n\theta\}$

$= \sin^{n-1}\alpha\,\{\sin\alpha\cos n\theta - i\sin\alpha\sin n\theta\}$

$= \sin^{n-1}\alpha\,.\,\sin\alpha\,.\,(\cos n\theta - i\sin n\theta)$

$= \sin^n\alpha\,(\cos n\theta - i\sin n\theta)$.

$\therefore$ L.H.S. = R.H.S.

HYPERBOLIC FUNCTIONS

Definition : For all values of x, real or complex, the quantity $\frac{e^x + e^{-x}}{2}$ is called the *hyperbolic cosine* of x and is written as *cosh x*. Similarly, the quantity $\frac{e^x - e^{-x}}{2}$ is called the *hyperbolic sine* of x and is written as *sinh x* (read as sin x). Thus we define

$$\mathbf{sinh\ x = \frac{e^{-x} - e^{-x}}{2}\ \text{and}\ cosh\ x = \frac{e^x + e^{-x}}{2}.}$$

The hyperbolic tangent, contangent, secant and cosecant are obtained from hyperbolic cosine and sine just as circular tangent, cotangent, secant and cosecant are obtained from circular cosine and sine. Thus

$$\tan x = \frac{\sinh x}{\cosh x} = \frac{\left(e^x - e^{-x}\right)/2}{\left(e^x + e^{-x}\right)/2} = \frac{e^x - e^{-x}}{e^x + e^{-x}}$$

$$\coth x = \frac{\cosh x}{\sinh x} = \frac{\left(e^x + e^{-x}\right)/2}{\left(e^x - e^{-x}\right)/2} = \frac{e^x + e^{-x}}{e^x - e^{-x}}$$

$$\sec h = \frac{1}{\cosh x} = \frac{1}{\left(e^x + e^{-x}\right)/2} = \frac{2}{e^x + e^{-x}}$$

$$\text{and cosech } x = \frac{1}{\sin x} = \frac{1}{\left(e^x - e^{-x}\right)/2} = \frac{2}{e^x - e^{-x}}.$$

RELATIONS BETWEEN HYPERBOLIC AND CIRCULAR FUNCTIONS

The hyperbolic functions can be expressed in terms of circular functions as follows :

We have

$$\sin(ix) = \frac{e^{i(ix)} - e^{-i(ix)}}{2i} = \frac{e^{i^2x} - e^{-i^2x}}{2i} = \frac{e^{-x} - e^x}{2i}$$

$$= i.\frac{e^{-x} - e^x}{2i^2} = i.\frac{e^x - e^{-x}}{2}, \qquad [\because i^2 = -1]$$

$$= i \sinh x.$$

From this relation sin (ix) = i sinh x,

we have $\sinh x = \frac{1}{i}\sin(ix) = \frac{i}{i^2}\sin(ix) = -i\sin(ix)$

Similarly

$$\cos ix = \frac{e^{i(ix)} + e^{-i(ix)}}{2} = \frac{e^{i^2x} + e^{-i^2x}}{2} = \frac{e^{-x} + e^{x}}{2} = \frac{e^{x} + e^{-x}}{2}$$

$$= \cosh x.$$

Now,

$$\tan(ix) = \frac{\sin(ix)}{\cos(ix)} = \frac{i \sinh x}{\cosh x} = i \tanh x,$$

$$\cot(ix) = \frac{1}{\tan(ix)} = \frac{1}{i \tanh x} = \frac{-i}{\tanh x} = -i \coth x,$$

$$\sec(ix) = \frac{1}{\cos(ix)} = \frac{1}{\cosh x} = \operatorname{sech} x,$$

and $$\operatorname{cosec}(ix) = \frac{1}{\sin(ix)} = \frac{1}{i \sinh x} = \frac{-i}{\sinh x} = -i \operatorname{cosech} x.$$

Similarly we can prove that

$\sinh(ix) = i \sin x$; $\cosh(ix) = \cos x$;

$\tanh(ix) = i \tan x$ and $\coth(ix) = -i \cot x$, etc.

PROPERTIES OF HYPERBOLIC FUNCTIONS

Formulae involving hyperbolic functions can be easily deduced with the help of the above relations. A list of some such formulae is given below.

(a) $\sinh 0 = 0$, $\cosh 0 = 1$, $\tanh 0 = 0$.

(b) $\cosh^2 x - \sinh^2 x = 1$

(c) $\sinh 2x = 2 \sinh x \cosh x$

(d) $\cosh 2x = \cosh^2 x + \sinh^2 x = 1 + 2 \sinh^2 x = 2 \cosh^2 x - 1$

(e) $\operatorname{sech}^2 x = 1 - \tanh^2 x$

(f) $\tanh 2x = 2 \tanh x/(1 + \tanh^2 x)$

(g) (i) $\sinh(x + y) = \sinh x \cosh y + \cosh x \sinh y$,

(ii) $\cosh(x + y) = \cosh x \cosh y + \sinh x \sinh y$.

(h) $e^x = \cosh x + \sinh x$ and $e^{-x} = \cosh x - \sinh x$.

(i) $\sinh 3x = 3 \sinh x + 4 \sinh^3 x$

(j) $\cosh 3x = 4 \cosh^3 x - 3 \cosh x$

(k) $$\tanh 3x = \frac{3 \tanh x + \tanh^3 x}{1 + 3 \tanh^2 x}.$$

Proof:

(a) sinh 0 = 0, cosh 0 = 1, tanh 0 = 0.

By definition,

$$\sinh x = \frac{1}{2}\left(e^{x} - e^{-x}\right) \text{ and } \cosh x = \frac{1}{2}\left(e^{x} + e^{-x}\right)$$

$$\therefore \quad \sinh 0 = \frac{1}{2}\left(e^{0} - e^{-0}\right) = \frac{1}{2}(1-1) = 0 \qquad [\because e^{0} = e^{-0} = 1]$$

$$\text{and} \quad \cosh 0 = \frac{1}{2}\left(e^{0} + e^{-0}\right) = \frac{1}{2}(1+1) = \frac{1}{2}.2 = 1.$$

$$\text{Also} \quad \tanh 0 = \frac{\sinh 0}{\cosh 0} = \frac{0}{1} = 0.$$

(b) $\cosh^2 x - \sinh^2 x = 1$.

$$\text{We have } \cosh^2 x - \sinh^2 x = \left(\frac{e^{x} + e^{-x}}{2}\right)^2 - \left(\frac{e^{x} - e^{-x}}{2}\right)^2$$

$$= \frac{1}{4}\left(e^{2x} + 2 + e^{-2x}\right) - \frac{1}{4}\left(e^{2x} - 2 + e^{-2x}\right) = \frac{1}{2} + \frac{1}{2} = 1.$$

(c) sinh 2x = 2 sinh x cosh x.

L.H.S. = sinh 2x = 1/i) sin (2ix)

= (1/i) 2 sin (ix) cos (ix) = (1/i) 2.(i sinh x).(cosh x)

= 2 sinh x cosh x = R.H.S.

(d) $\cosh 2x = \cosh^2 x + \sinh^2 x = 1 + 2\sinh^2 x = 2\cosh^2 x - 1$.

We have cosh 2x = cos (2ix) = cos 2 (ix)

$= \cos^2 (ix) - \sin^2 (ix) = \cosh^2 x - i^2 \sinh^2 x$

$= \cosh^2 x + \sinh^2 x$ ...(1)

$= 1 + \sinh^2 x + \sinh^2 x = 1 + 2\sinh^2 x$ ...(2)

Also $\cosh 2x = \cosh^2 x + \sinh^2 x = \cosh^2 x + (\cosh^2 x - 1)$

$= 2\cosh^2 x - 1.$ ...(3)

(e) $\text{sech}^2 x = 1 - \tanh^2 x$.

We have $\cosh^2 x - \sinh^2 x = 1$, by property (b).

Dividing by $\cosh^2 x$, we get $1 - \tanh^2 x = \text{sech}^2 x$.

Similarly, $\coth^2 x - 1 = \text{cosech}^2 x$.

(f) $\tanh 2x = 2 \tanh x/1(1 + \tanh^2 x)$.

We have i tanh 2x = tan (2ix).

$\therefore$ tanh 2x = (1/i) tan (2ix) = (1/i) tan 2 (ix)

$$= \frac{1}{i}.\frac{2 \tan ix}{\left(1 - \tan^2 ix\right)} = \frac{1}{i}.\frac{2i \tanh x}{\left(1 - i^2 \tanh^2 x\right)}$$

Similarly, we find

$$\textbf{sinh 2x} = \frac{2 \tanh x}{1 - \tanh^2 x} \text{ and } \cosh 2x = \frac{1 + \tanh^2 x}{1 - \tanh^2 x}.$$

(g) (i) *sinh (x + y) = sinh x cosh y + cosh x sinh y.*

$$\text{R.H.S.} = \frac{1}{2}\left(e^x - e^{-x}\right).\frac{1}{2}\left(e^y + e^{-y}\right) + \frac{1}{2}\left(e^x + e^{-x}\right).\frac{1}{2}\left(e^y - e^{-y}\right)$$

$$= \frac{1}{4}[e^{x+y} + e^{x-y} - e^{-(x-y)} - e^{-(x+y)} + e^{x+y} - e^{x-y} + e^{-(x-y)} - e^{-(x+y)}]$$

$$= \frac{1}{4}[2e^{(x+y)} - 2e^{-(x+y)}] = \frac{1}{2}[e^{(x+y)} - e^{-(x+y)}]$$

= sinh (x + y) = L.H.S.

(ii) *cosh (x + y) = cosh x cosh y + sinh x sinh y.*

L.H.S. = cosh (x + y) = cos i (x + y) = cos (ix + iy)

= cos (ix) cos (iy) – sin (ix) sin (iy)

= cosh x cosh y – i sinh x.i sinh y

= cosh x cosh y – i^2 sinh x sinh y

= cosh x cosh y + sinh x sinh y = R.H.S.

(h) *e^x = cosh x + sinh x and e^{-x} = cosh x – sinh x.*

We have cosh x = $\frac{1}{2}(e^x + e^{-x})$; sinh x = $\frac{1}{2}(e^x - e^{-x})$.

Adding, we get

$$\cosh x + \sinh x = \frac{1}{2}(e^x + e^{-x} + e^x - e^{-x}) = \frac{1}{2}.2e^x = e^x$$

and subtracting, we get

$$\cosh x - \sinh x = \frac{1}{2}(e^x + e^{-x} - e^x + e^{-x})$$

$$= \frac{1}{2}.2e^{-x} = e^{-x}.$$

(i) *sinh 3x = 3 sinh x + 4 sinh³ x.*

L.H.S. $= \sinh 3x = (1/i) \sin (3ix) = (1/i) \sin 3 (ix)$

$= (1/i) [3 \sin (ix) - 4 \sin^3 (ix)]$

$= (1/i) [3 (i \sinh x) - 4 (i \sinh x)^3]$

$[\because \sin (ix) = i \sinh x]$

$= (1/i) [3i \sinh x + 4i \sinh^3 x]$ $[\because i^2 = -1; i^3 = -i]$

$= 3 \sinh x + 4 \sinh^3 x =$ R.H.S.

(j) $\cosh 3x = 4 \cosh^3 x - 3 \cosh x.$

L.H.S. $= \cosh 3x = \cos (3ix) = \cos 3 (ix)$

$= 4 \cos^3 (ix) - 3 \cos (ix)$

$= 4 \cosh^3 x - 3 \cosh x.$ $[\because \cos (ix) = \cosh x]$

(k) $\tanh 3x = (3 \tanh x + \tan^3 x)/(1 + 3 \tanh^2 x).$

L.H.S. $= \tanh 3x = (1/i) \tan (3ix)$

$$= \left(\frac{1}{i}\right)\left[\frac{3 \tan (ix) - \tan^3 (ix)}{1 - 3 \tan^2 (ix)}\right]$$

$$= \frac{1}{i}\left[\frac{3i \tanh x - i^3 \tanh^3 x}{1 - 3i^2 \tanh^2 x}\right] \qquad [\because \tan (ix) = i \tanh x]$$

$$= \frac{1}{i}\left[\frac{3i \tanh x + i \tanh^3 x}{1 + 3 \tanh^2 x}\right] = \frac{3 \tanh x + \tanh^3 x}{1 + 3 \tanh^2 x}$$

EXPANSIONS IN SERIES FOR SINH X AND COSH X

We have $\sinh x = \frac{1}{2} [e^x - e^{-x}]$

$$= \frac{1}{2}\left[\left(1 + x + \frac{x^2}{2!} + \frac{x^3}{3!} + \ldots\right) - \left(1 - x + \frac{x^2}{2!} - \frac{x^3}{3!} + \ldots\right)\right]$$

$$= \frac{1}{2}\left[2x + \frac{2x^3}{3!} + \frac{2x^5}{5!} + \ldots\right] = x + \frac{x^3}{3!} + \frac{x^5}{5!} + \ldots \text{ad.inf.}$$

Thus $\mathbf{\sinh x = x + \frac{x^3}{3!} + \frac{x^5}{5!} + \ldots ad.inf.}$

Also $\cosh x = \frac{1}{2}\left[e^x + e^{-x}\right]$

$$= \frac{1}{2}\left[\left(1 + x + \frac{x^2}{2i} + \frac{x^3}{3!} + ...\right) + \left(1 - x + \frac{x^2}{2!} - \frac{x^3}{3!} + ...\right)\right]$$

$$= \frac{1}{2}\left[2x + \frac{2x^2}{2!} + \frac{2x^4}{4!} + ...\right] = 1 + \frac{x^2}{2!} + \frac{x^4}{4!} + ...\text{ad.inf.}$$

Thus, $\mathbf{\cosh x = 1 + \frac{x^2}{2!} + \frac{x^4}{4!} + ...ad.inf.}$

Remark:

The students should note that to change a formula for the circular functions into a formula for the hyperbolic functions, we must replace cosx by cosh x and sin x by i sinh x i.e., we must write $\cosh^2 x$ for $\cos^2 x$ and $-\sinh^2 x$ for $\sin^2 x$ etc.

CURVES IN THE ARGAND PLANE

We know that the equations of the type x = x(t), y = y(t), where t is the parameter, give the parametric representation of a curve in the plane. Using the complex variable z, these equations can be written as a single equations.

$z = z(t) = x(t) + iy(t)$ where $z = x + iy$.

Definitions : (a) *In the Argand plane, a continuous complex valued function z(t) = x(t) + iy (t), where x(t) and y(t) are real values continuous functions of a real variable t, defined in the range $\alpha \le t \le \beta$ where $\alpha < \beta$ is called a continuous arc or a curve.* We call $z(\alpha)$ and $z(\beta)$ the end points of the curve, $z(\alpha)$ is the initial point and $z(\beta)$ the terminal point of the curve. If $z(\alpha) = z(\beta)$ *i.e.*, if the initial and terminal points of a curve coincide, the curve is said to be a *closed curve.*

A point z_1 is a multiple point of the curve if the equation $z_1 = x(t) = iy(t)$ is satisfied by more than one value of t in the given range. In particular the multiple point is called a double point if the above equation is satisfied by two values of t in the given range.

(b) A curve $z(t) = x(t) + iy(t)$, $\alpha \le t \le \beta$ is called a *Jordan arc* or a *simple curve* if $t_1 \ne t_2$ implies $z(t_1) \ne z(t_2)$ *i.e.*, z(t) is one-one. A Jordan arc is a curve without multiple points.

(c) A closed curve given by $z(t) = x(t) + iy(t)$, $\alpha \le t \le \beta$, is called simple if $t_1 > t_2$ and $z(t_1) = z(t_2)$ imply $t_1 = \alpha$ and $t_2 = \beta$.

We usually refer to such curves as *simple closed Jordan curves.*

Example :

The circle $z = \cos t + i \sin t$, $0 \le t \le 2\pi$ is a simple closed Jordan curve since the values of z(t) coincide only at the end points $t = 0$ and $t = 2\pi$.

The Jordan Curve Theorem : The theorem states that a *simple clised Jordan curve divides the Argand plane into two open domains which have the curve as common boundary.*

Of these two domains one is bounded and it is called the *interior domain;* the other is unbounded and is called the *exterior domain.* For example, the circle $|z| = r$ divides the Argand plane into two open domains given by $|z| < r$ and $|z| > r$. Out of these $|z| < r$ is bounded and is the interior of the circle $|z| = r$; the other $|z| > r$ is unbounded and is the exterior of the circle, $|z| = r$. The circle is the common boundary of the two domains.

FUNCTIONS OF A COMPLEX VARIABLE

If certain rules be given by means of which it is possible to find one or more complex numbers w for every value of z in a certain domain D, w is said to be a function of z defined on the domain D and we write w = f(z).

Since $z = x + iy$, $f(z)$ will be of the form $u + iv$ where u and v are function of two real variables x and y. Thus, we can write $w = u(x, y) + iv(x, y)$, x, y are real.

Single Valued and Multiple Valued Functions : If w takes only one value for each value of z in the region D, w is said to be a *uniform* or *single valued function* of z. If there correspond two or more values of w for some or all values of z in the region D, w is called *multiple valued function* of z.

Neighbourhood of a Point

A neighbourhood of a point z_0 in the Argand plane is the set of all points z such that $|z - z_0| < \delta$, and δ is an arbitrary small positive number. The number δ is called the radius of this neighbourhood.

Deleted Neighbourhood : If from a neighbourhood of a point z_0, the point z_0, the point z_0 itself is deleted or excluded, we get a *deleted neighbourhood* of z_0.

Periods of Hyperbolic Functions

By Euler's Theorem, we know that

$$e^{2n\pi i} = \cos 2n\pi + i \sin 2n\pi = 1 + i.0 = 1, \text{ n being any integer}$$

and $e^{-2n\pi i} = \cos 2n\pi - i \sin 2n\pi = 1 - i.0 = 1.$

$$\therefore \quad \sinh(x + 2n\pi i) = \frac{1}{2}[e^{x + 2n\pi i} - e^{-(x + 2n\pi i)}], \text{ by definition}$$

$$= \frac{1}{2}[e^x e^{2n\pi i} - e^{-x} e^{-2n\pi i}]$$

$$= \frac{1}{2}[e^x - e^{-x}]$$

$[\because\ e^{\pm 2n\pi i} = 1$, n being any integer]

$$= \sinh x.$$

Also, $\cosh(x + 2n\pi i) = \frac{1}{2}[e^{x + 2n\pi i} + e^{-(x + 2n\pi i)}]$ [By definition]

$$= \frac{1}{2}[e^x.e^{2n\pi i} + e^{-x}.e^{-2n\pi i}]$$

$$= \frac{1}{2}[e^x + e^{-x}] \qquad [\because\ e^{\pm 2n\pi i} = 1]$$

$$= \cosh x.$$

It follows that sinh x are periodic functions and both have a period $2\pi i$.

Hence hyperbolic functions differ from circular functions in having no real period. Their periods are imaginary.

Again, $\tanh(x + n\pi i) = \dfrac{\sinh(x + n\pi i)}{\cosh(x + n\pi i)}$

$$= \frac{\frac{1}{2}\left[e^{(x+n+n\pi i)} - e^{-(x+n\pi i)}\right]}{\frac{1}{2}\left[e^{(x+n\pi i)} + e^{-(x+n\pi i)}\right]}$$

$$= \frac{e^{npi}\left[e^x - e^{-x}.e^{-2n\pi i}\right]}{e^{n\pi i}\left[e^x + e^{-x}.e^{-2n\pi i}\right]}$$

$$= \frac{\left[e^x - e^{-x}\right]}{\left[e^x + e^{-x}\right]} \qquad [\because\ e^{-2n\pi i} = 1]$$

$$= \frac{\sin x}{\cosh x} = \tanh x.$$

Thus, $\tanh(x + n\pi i) = \tanh x$,

i.e., tanh x is a periodic function with period πi.

Therefore sinh x and cosh x are periodic functions of period $2\pi i$ and tanh x is a periodic function of period πi.

Remark:

Note that the hyperbolic functions have imaginary periods while the circular functions have real periods.

Example 1:

Show that $\cos(\alpha + i\beta) + i \sin(\alpha + i\beta) = e^{-b}(\cos\alpha + i \sin\alpha)$.

Solution:

The L.H.S. = $\cos\alpha \cos i\beta - \sin\alpha \sin i\beta + i \sin\alpha \cos i\beta + i \cos\alpha \sin i\beta$

$= \cos\alpha (\cos i\beta + i \sin i\beta) + i \sin\alpha (\cos i\beta + i \sin i\beta)$

$= (\cos i\beta + i \sin\beta)(\cos\alpha + i \sin\alpha)$

$= (\cosh\beta - \sinh\beta)(\cos\alpha + i \sin\alpha)$

$[\because \cos i\beta = \cosh\beta, \sin i\beta = i \sinh\beta]$

$= e^{-\beta}(\cos\alpha + i \sin\alpha) = \text{R.H.S.}$

Example 2:

Show that

$$\sinh(x + y) \cosh(x - y) = \frac{1}{2}(\sinh 2x + \sinh 2y).$$

Solution:

The L.H.S. = $\sinh(x + y).\cosh(x - y)$

$$= \frac{1}{2}\left[e^{(x+y)} - e^{-(x+y)}\right].\frac{1}{2}\left[e^{(x+y)} + e^{-(x-y)}\right]$$

$$= \frac{1}{4}\left[e^{2x} + e^{2y} - e^{-2y} - e^{-2x}\right]$$

$$= \frac{1}{2}.\left[\frac{1}{2}\left(e^{2x} - e^{-2x}\right) + \frac{1}{2}\left(e^{2y} - e^{-2y}\right)\right]$$

$$= \frac{1}{2}\left[\sinh 2x + \sinh 2y\right] = \text{R.H.S.}$$

Example 3:

If $\tan\theta = \tanh x \cot y$ *and* $\tan\phi = \tanh x \tan y$, *show that*

$$\frac{\sin 2\theta}{\sin 2\phi} = \frac{\cosh 2x + \cos 2y}{\cosh 2x - \cos 2y}.$$

Solution:

L.H.S

$$= \frac{\sin 2\theta}{\sin 2\phi} = \frac{2\tan\theta/\left(1 + \tan^2\theta\right)}{2\tan\phi/\left(1 + \tan^2\phi\right)}$$

$$= \frac{\tan\theta}{1+\tan^2\theta} \times \frac{1+\tan^2\phi}{\tan\phi} = \frac{\tan\theta}{\tan\phi}.\frac{1+\tan^2\phi}{1+\tan^2\theta}$$

$$= \frac{\tanh x \cot y}{\tanh x \tan y} \times \frac{1+\tanh^2 x \tan^2 y}{1+\tanh^2 x \cot^2 y},$$

putting the given values of $\tan\theta$ and $\tan\phi$

$$= \frac{\cos^2 y}{\sin^2 y}.\frac{\cosh^2 x \cos^2 y + \sinh^2 x \sin^2 y}{\cosh^2 x \cos^2 y}.\frac{\cosh^2 x \sin^2 y}{\cosh^2 x \sinh^2 x \cos^2 y}$$

$$= \frac{\cosh^2 x \cos^2 y + \sinh^2 x \sin^2 y}{\cosh^2 x \sin^2 y + \sinh^2 x \cos^2 y}$$

$$= \frac{\left(2\cosh^2 x\right)\left(2\cos^2 y\right) + \left(2\sinh^2 x\right)\left(2\sin^2 y\right)}{\left(2\cosh^2 x\right)\left(2\sin^2 y\right) + \left(2\sinh^2 x\right)\left(2\cos^2 y\right)}$$

$$= \frac{(1+\cosh 2x)(1+\cos 2y) + (\cosh 2x - 1)(1-\cos 2y)}{(1+\cosh 2x)(1-\cos 2y) + (\cosh 2x - 1)(1+\cos 2y)}$$

$[\because 2\cosh^2 x = 1 + \cosh 2x;\ 2\sinh^2 x = \cosh 2x - 1]$

$$= \frac{2(\cosh 2x + \cos 2y)}{2(\cosh 2x - \cos 2y)} = \frac{\cosh 2x + \cos 2y}{\cosh 2x - \cos 2y} = \text{R.H.S.}$$

Example 4:

If $\cosh\alpha = \sec\theta$, prove that $\tanh^2\frac{1}{2}\alpha = \tan^2\frac{1}{2}\theta$.

Solution:

We have $\cosh\alpha = \sec\theta$.

$$\therefore \quad \frac{\cosh\alpha}{1} = \frac{1}{\cos\theta}$$

Applying Componendo and Dividendo, we get

$$\frac{\cosh\alpha - 1}{\cosh\alpha + 1} = \frac{1-\cos\theta}{1+\cos\theta}$$

or

$$\frac{2\sinh^2\frac{1}{2}\alpha}{2\cosh^2\frac{1}{2}\alpha} = \frac{2\sin^2\frac{1}{2}\theta}{2\cos^2\frac{1}{2}\theta}$$

or $$\tanh^2 \frac{1}{2}\alpha = \tan^2 \frac{1}{2}\theta.$$

Note: The Componendo and Dividendo is that if

$$\frac{a}{b} = \frac{c}{d}, \text{ then } \frac{a-b}{a+b} = \frac{c-d}{c+d}.$$

SEPARATION INTO REAL AND IMAGINARY PARTS

By separation or resolving into real and imaginary parts, we mean to put a complex quantity in the form x + iy where x and y are real quantities.

When we are given a fraction to separate into real and imaginary parts whose numerator and denominator are both complex functions, we multiply the numerator and denominator by the conjugate of the denominator and thus make the denominator real

The conjugate complex is obtained by putting –i for i,

i.e., x + iy

and x – iy are conjugate complex quantities.

Now, we shall separate the functions e^z, sin z, cos z, tan z, etc. into real and imaginary parts.

(i) *To separate e^z into real and imaginary parts.*

We have $e^z = e^{x+iy} = e^x e^{iy}$

$= e^x(\cos y + i \sin y)$ [By Euler's Theorem]

$= e^x \cos y + ie^x \sin y,$

which is of the form a + ib, where a and b are real.

(ii) *To separate sin z into real and imaginary parts.*

We have $\sin z = \sin(x + iy)$

$= \sin x \cos(iy) + \cos x \sin(iy)$

$= \sin x \cosh y + i \cos x \sinh y.$

$[\because \cos(iy) = \cosh y, \sin(iy) = i \sinh y]$

(iii) *To separate cos z into real and imaginary parts.*

We have $\cos z = \cos(x + iy)$

$= \cos x \cos(iy) - \sin x \sin(iy)$

$= \cos x \cosh y - i \sin x \sin y.$

(iv) *To separate tan z into real and imaginary parts.*

We have

$$\tan z = \frac{\sin z}{\cos z} = \frac{\sin(x+iy)}{\cos(x+iy)}$$

$$= \frac{\sin(x+iy)}{\cos(x+iy)} \times \frac{2\cos(x-iy)}{2\cos(x-iy)}$$

$$= \frac{2\sin(x+iy)\cos(x-iy)}{2\cos(x+iy)\cos(x-iy)}$$

$$= \frac{\sin[(x+iy)+(x-iy)] + \sin[(x+iy)-(x-iy)]}{\cos[(x+iy)+(x-iy)] + \cos[(x+iy)-(x-iy)]}$$

$$= \frac{\sin 2x + \sin(2iy)}{\cos 2x + \cos(2iy)}$$

$$= \frac{\sin 2x + i\sinh 2y}{\cos 2x + \cosh 2y} \qquad [\because \sin(i\theta) = i\sinh\theta, \cos(i\theta) = \cosh\theta]$$

$$= \left(\frac{\sin 2x}{\cos 2x + \cosh 2y}\right) + i\left(\frac{\sinh 2y}{\cos 2x + \cosh 2y}\right).$$

(v) *to separate sinh z into real and imaginary parts.*

We have $\sinh z = \sinh(x + iy)$

$$= \frac{1}{i}\sin[i(x+iy)] \qquad [\because \sin(i\theta) = i\sinh\theta]$$

$$= \frac{1}{i^2}\sin(ix + i^2 y)$$

$$= -i\sin(ix - y) \quad [\because i^2 = -1]$$

$$= -i[\sin(ix)\cos y - \cos(ix)\sin y]$$

$$= -i[i\sinh x\cos y - \cosh x\sin y]$$

$$= -i^2\sinh x\cos y + i\cosh x\sin y$$

$$= \sinh x\cos y + i\cosh x\sin y.$$

(vi) *To separate tanh z into real and imaginary parts.*

We have $\tanh z = \dfrac{\sinh z}{\cosh z} = \dfrac{\sinh(x+iy)}{\cosh(x+iy)}$

$$= \frac{1}{i}\left[\frac{\sin i(x+iy)}{\cos i(x+iy)}\right] \qquad [\because \sin(i\theta) = i\sinh\theta,\ \cos(i\theta) = \cosh\theta]$$

$$= \frac{1}{i}\frac{\sin(ix-y)}{\cos(ix-y)} \qquad [\because i^2 = -1]$$

$$= -\frac{1}{i}\frac{\sin(y-ix)}{\cos(y-ix)} \qquad [\because \cos(-x) = \cos x,\ \sin(-x) = -\sin x]$$

$$= -\frac{i\,2\sin(y-ix)\cos(y+ix)}{i^2\,2\cos(y-ix)\cos(y+ix)}$$ [Multiplying the Nr. and the Dr. by cos (y + ix) which is the conjugate complex of cos (y – ix)]

$$= i\frac{\sin[(y-ix)+(y+ix)] + \sin[(y-ix)-(y+ix)]}{\cos[(y-ix)+(y+ix)] + \cos[(y-ix)-(y+ix)]}$$

[∵ 2 sin A cos B = sin (A + B) + sin (A – B) and 2 cos A cos B = cos (A + B) + cos (A – B)]

$$= i\frac{\sin 2y + \sin(-2ix)}{\cos 2y + \cos(-2ix)} = i\frac{\sin 2y - \sin(2ix)}{\cos 2y + \cos(2ix)}$$

$$= i\frac{\sin 2y - i\sinh 2x}{\cos 2y + \cosh 2x} = \frac{i\sin 2y - i^2\sinh 2x}{\cos 2y + \cosh 2x}$$

$$= \frac{\sinh 2x + i\sin 2y}{\cos 2y + \cosh 2x}$$

$$= \frac{\sinh 2x}{\cosh 2x + \cos 2y} + i\frac{\sin 2y}{\cosh 2x + \cos 2y}.$$

(vii) *To separate sech z into real and imaginary parts.*

We have $\operatorname{sech} z = \frac{1}{\cosh z} = \frac{1}{\cosh(x+iy)}$

$$= \frac{1}{\cos i(x+iy)} = \frac{1}{\cos(ix-y)} = \frac{1}{\cos(y-ix)}$$

$$= \frac{2\cos(y+ix)}{2\cos(y+ix)\cos(y-ix)}$$

$$= 2.\frac{\cos y\cos(ix) - \sin y\sin(ix)}{\cos[(y+ix)+(y-ix)] + \cos[(y+ix)-(y-ix)]}$$

$$= 2.\frac{\cos y \cosh x - i \sin y \sinh x}{\cos 2y + \cos(2ix)}$$

$$= \frac{2 \cos y \cosh x}{\cosh 2x + \cos 2y} - i\frac{2 \sin y \sinh x}{\cosh 2x + \cos 2y}.$$

Example 1:

Resolve $e^{\sin(x + iy)}$ into real and imaginary parts.

Solution:

We have $e^{\sin(x + iy)}$

$= e^{\sin x \cos (iy) + \cos x \sin (iy)}$

$= e^{\sin x \cosh y + i \cos x \sinh y}$

$= e^{\sin x \cosh y}.e^{i \cos x \sinh y}$

$= e^{\sin x \cosh y} [\cos (\cos x \sinh y) + i \sin (\cos x \sinh y)],$

$[\because e^{i\theta} = \cos \theta + i \sin \theta]$

which is of the form a + ib

Example 2:

If $\sin (\theta + i\phi) = \cos \alpha + i \sin \alpha$, then prove that

$$\cos^2 \theta = \sinh^2 \phi = \pm \sin \alpha.$$

Solution:

We have $\sin (\theta + i\phi) = \cos \alpha + i \sin \alpha$

or $\sin \theta \cosh \phi + i \cos \theta \sinh \phi = \cos \alpha + i \sin \alpha.$

Equating real and imaginary parts, we have

$$\sin \theta \cosh \phi = \cos \alpha \quad ...(1)$$

$$\cos \theta \sinh \phi = \sin \alpha. \quad ...(2)$$

First, we shall eliminate ϕ between (1) and (2).

We have $\cosh^2 \phi - \sinh^2 \phi = 1.$

$$\therefore \quad \frac{\cos^2 \alpha}{\sin^2 \theta} - \frac{\sin^2 \alpha}{\cos^2 \theta} = 1$$

or $$\frac{\cos^2 \alpha \cos^2 \theta - \sin^2 \alpha \sin^2 \theta}{\sin^2 \theta \cos^2 \theta} = 1$$

or$\cos^2 \alpha \cos^2 \theta - \sin2 \alpha \sin^2 \theta = \sin^2 \theta \cos^2 \theta$

or$\cos^2 \theta\ (1 - \sin^2 \alpha) - \sin^2 \alpha\ (1 - \cos^2 \theta) = \cos^2 \theta\ (1 - \cos^2 \theta)$

[changing all the terms to cos θ and sin α]

or$\cos^2 \theta - \cos^2 \theta \sin^2 \alpha - \sin^2 \alpha + \sin^2 \alpha \cos^2 \theta = \cos^2 \theta - \cos^4 \theta$

or $\cos^4 \theta = \sin^2 \alpha$.

$\therefore \cos^2 \theta = \pm \sin \alpha$.

Now, we shall eliminate θ between (1) and (2).

We have $\sin^2 \theta + \cos^2 \theta = 1$.

Therefore from (1) and (2), we have

$$\frac{\cos^2 \alpha}{\cosh^2 \phi} + \frac{\sin^2 \alpha}{\sinh^2 \phi} = 1$$

or$\cos^2 \alpha \sinh^2 \phi + \cosh^2 \sin^2 \alpha = \cosh^2 \phi \sinh^2 \phi$

or$\sinh^2 \phi\ (1 - \sin^2 \alpha) + \sin^2 \alpha\ (1 + \sinh^2 \phi) = (1 + \sinh^2 \phi) \sinh^2 \phi$

[changing all the terms to sinh φ and sin α]

or $\sinh^2 \phi - \sinh^2 \phi \sin^2 \alpha + \sin^2 \alpha + \sinh^2 \phi \sin^2 \alpha = \sinh^2 \phi + \sinh^4 \phi$

or $\sinh^4 \phi = \sin^2 \alpha$.

$\therefore \sinh^2 \phi = \pm \sin \alpha$

Thus, $\cos^2 \theta = \sinh^2 \phi = \pm \sin \alpha$.

Example 3:

If $\sin(\theta + i\phi) = r\ (\cos \alpha + i \sin \theta)$, *prove that*

$\rho^2 = \frac{1}{2}\,[\cosh 2f - \cos 2\theta]$ *and* $\tan \alpha = \tanh \phi \cot \theta$.

Solution:

We have $\sin\ (\theta + i\phi) = \rho \cos \alpha + i\rho \sin$

or$\sin \theta \cosh \phi + i \cos \theta \sinh \phi = \rho \cos \alpha + i\rho \sin \alpha$

$\therefore\ \sin \theta \cosh \phi = \rho \cos \alpha$ ...(1)

and $\cos \theta \sinh \phi = \rho \sin \alpha$. ...(2)

Squaring (1) and (2) and adding, we get

$\rho^2 = \sin^2 \theta \cosh^2 \phi + \cos^2 \theta \sinh^2 \phi$.

$\therefore\ 2\rho^2 = 2 \sin^2 \theta \cosh^2 \phi + 2 \cos^2 \theta \sinh^2 \phi$

$= (1 - \cos 2\theta) \cosh^2 \phi + (1 + \cos 2\theta) \sinh^2 \phi$, changing to double angles

$= (\cosh^2 \phi + \sinh^2 \phi) - \cos 2\theta\ (\cosh^2 \phi - \sinh^2 \phi)$

$= \cosh 2\phi - \cos 2\theta$. $[\because \cosh^2 \phi + \sinh^2 \phi = \cosh 2\phi]$

$$\therefore\ \rho^2 = \frac{1}{2}(\cosh 2\phi - \cos 2\theta).$$

Again, dividing (2) by (1), we get

$$\frac{\cos\theta \sinh\phi}{\sin\theta \cosh\phi} = \frac{\sin\alpha}{\cos\alpha} \text{ or } \tan\alpha = \tanh\phi \cot\theta.$$

Example 4:

Split into real and imaginary parts $e^{i\theta}/(1 - ke^{i\phi})$.

Solution:

We have $\dfrac{e^{i\theta}}{1-ke^{i\phi}} = \dfrac{e^{i\theta}\left(1-ke^{-i\phi}\right)}{\left(1-ke^{i\phi}\right)\left(1-ke^{-i\phi}\right)}$

multiplying the Nr. and Dr. by the conjugate complex of the Dr.

[Note that $1 - ke^{i\phi} = 1 - k(\cos\phi + i\sin\phi) = 1 - \cos\phi - ik\sin\phi$ so that its conjugate complex is

$1 - k\cos\phi + ik\sin\phi$ *i.e.*, $1 - k(\cos\phi - i\sin\phi)$ *i.e.*, $1 - ke^{-i\phi}$]

$$= \frac{e^{i\theta} - k e^{i(\theta-\phi)}}{1-k\left(e^{i\phi} + e^{-i\phi}\right) + k^2 e^{i\phi}.e^{-i\phi}}$$

$$= \frac{(\cos\theta + i\sin\theta) - k\left[\cos(\theta-\phi) + i\sin(\theta-\phi)\right]}{1-2k\cos\phi + k^2}$$

$$= \left(\frac{\cos\theta - k\cos(\theta-\phi)}{1-2k\cos\phi + k^2}\right) + i\left(\frac{\sin\theta - k\sin(\theta-\phi)}{1-2k\cos\phi + k^2}\right).$$

Example 5:

If $\tan(\theta + i\phi) = \tan\alpha + i\sec\alpha$, then prove that

$$e^{2\phi} = \pm \cot\frac{1}{2}\alpha \text{ and } 2\theta = n\pi + \frac{1}{2}\pi + \alpha$$

Solution:

We have $\tan(\theta + i\phi) = \tan\alpha + i\sec\alpha$,

So thattan $(\theta - i\phi) = \tan\alpha - i\sec\alpha$.

Nowtan $2\theta = \tan[(\theta + i\phi) + (\theta - i\phi)]$

$$= \frac{\tan(\theta + i\phi) + \tan(\theta - i\phi)}{1 - \tan(\theta + i\phi)\tan(\theta - i\phi)}$$

$$= \frac{(\tan\alpha + i\sec\alpha) + (\tan\alpha - i\sec\alpha)}{1-(\tan\alpha + i\sec\alpha)(\tan\alpha - i\sec\alpha)} = \frac{2\tan\alpha}{1-(\tan^2\alpha + \sec^2\alpha)}$$

$$= \frac{2\tan\alpha}{-2\tan^2\alpha} = -\frac{1}{\tan\alpha} = -\cot\alpha.$$

Thus $\tan 2\theta = -\cot\alpha = \tan\left(\frac{1}{2}\pi + \alpha\right)$.

$$\therefore \qquad 2\theta + \frac{1}{2}\pi + \alpha. \text{ (principal value)}$$

or
$$2\theta = n\pi + \frac{1}{2}\pi + \alpha \text{ (general value)}$$

Again, $\tan 2i\phi = \tan[(\theta + i\phi) - (\theta - i\phi)]$

$$= \frac{\tan(\theta + i\phi) - \tan(\theta - i\phi)}{1 + \tan(\theta + i\phi)\tan(\theta - i\phi)}$$

$$= \frac{(\tan\alpha + i\sec\alpha) - (\tan\alpha - i\sec\alpha)}{1 + (\tan^2\alpha + \sec^2\alpha)} = \frac{2i\sec\alpha}{2\sec^2\alpha} = i\cos\alpha$$

$$\therefore \qquad i\tanh 2\phi = i\cos\alpha, \text{ or } \tanh 2\phi = \cos\alpha$$

or
$$\frac{e^{2\phi} - e^{-2\phi}}{e^{2\phi} + e^{-2\phi}} = \frac{\cos\alpha}{1}$$

Applying Componendo and Dividendo, we have

$$\frac{2e^{2\phi}}{2e^{-2\phi}} = \frac{1 + \cos\alpha}{1 - \cos\alpha}$$

or
$$e^{4\phi} = \frac{2\cos^2\frac{1}{2}\alpha}{2\sin^2\frac{1}{2}\alpha} = \cot^2\frac{1}{2}\alpha$$

$$\therefore \qquad e^{2\phi} = \pm\cot\frac{1}{2}\alpha.$$

Example 6:

Separate $\frac{\cos(x + iy)}{(x + iy) + 1}$ *into real and imaginary parts.*

Solution:

We have

$$\frac{\cos(x+iy)}{(x+iy)+1} = \frac{\cos(x+iy)}{(x+1)+iy} = \frac{\cos(x+iy)\{(x+1)-iy\}}{\{(x+1)+iy\}\{(x+1)-iy\}},$$

multiplying the Nr. and the Dr. by the conjugate complex of the Dr.

$$= \frac{[\cos x \cos(iy) - \sin x \sin(iy)][(x+1)-iy]}{(x+1)^2 + i^2y^2}$$

$$= \frac{(\cos x \cosh y - i \sin x \sinh y)[(x+1)-iy)]}{(x+1)^2 + y^2}$$

$$= \frac{[(x+1)\cos x \cosh y - y \sin x \sinh y] - i[(x+1)\sin x \sinh y + y \cos x \cosh y]}{(x+1)^2 + y^2}$$

$= a - ib$, where

$a = [(x + 1) \cos x \cosh y - y \sin x \sinh y]/\{(x + 1)^2 + y^2\}$

and $b = [(x + 1) \sin x \sinh y + y \cos x \cosh y]/\{(x + 1)^2 + y^2\}$.

Example 7:

If $E\left(\dfrac{x-a+iy}{x+a+iy}\right) = P + iQ$, *find P and Q.*

Solution:

Let $\dfrac{x-a+iy}{x+a+iy} = p + iq$.

Then $p + iq = \dfrac{\{(x-a)+iy\}\{(x+a)-iy\}}{\{(x+a)+iy\}\{(x+a)-iy)\}}$

multiplying the Nr. and the Dr. by the conjugate complex of the Dr.

$$= \frac{(x^2-a^2) - i^2y^2 + i\{y(x+a) - y(x-a)\}}{(x+a)^2 - i^2y^2}$$

$$= \frac{(x^2-a^2) - i^2y^2 + i\{y(x+a) - y(x-a)\}}{(x+a)^2 - i^2y^2}$$

$$= \frac{(x^2+y^2-a^2) + 2iya}{(x+a)^2 + y^2}.$$

Equating real and imaginary parts, we have

$$p = \frac{x^2 + y^2 - a^2}{(x + a)^2 + y^2} \text{ and } q = \frac{2ay}{(x + a)^2 + y^2}$$

Again, $P + iQ = E\left(\frac{x - a + iy}{x + a + iy}\right) = e^{p+iq}$

$$= e^p . e^{iq} = e^p (\cos q + i \sin q).$$

Equating real and imaginary parts, we have

$$P = e^p \cos q \text{ and } Q = e^p \sin q,$$

where $p = \frac{x^2 + y^2 - a^2}{(x + a)^2 + y^2}$ and $q = \frac{2ay}{(x + a)^2 + y^2}$.

Example 8:

Resolve $\sin^2 (x + iy)$ into real and imaginary parts.

Solution:

We have

$$\sin^2(x + iy) = \frac{1}{2}\left[2 \sin^2(x + iy)\right]$$

$$= \frac{1}{2}\left[1 - \cos 2(x + iy)\right] \qquad [\because 2 \sin^2 \theta = 1 - \cos 2\theta]$$

$$= \frac{1}{2}\left[1 - \cos (2x + 2iy)\right]$$

$$= \frac{1}{2}\left[1 - \{\cos 2x \cos (2iy) - \sin 2x \sin (2iy)\}\right]$$

$$= \frac{1}{2}\left[1 - \cos 2x \cosh 2y + i \sin 2x \sinh 2y\right]$$

$$= \frac{1}{2}(1 - \cos 2x \cosh 2y) + i\frac{1}{2}(\sin 2x \sinh 2y).$$

EXERCISES

1. Find real numbers A and B, if $A + iB = \frac{3 - 2i}{7 + 4i}$.

   Ans. $A = \frac{1}{5}, B = -\frac{2}{5}$.

2. Find real numbers A and B, if $A + iB = \frac{1}{(1 - 2i)(2 + 3i)}$.

Ans. $A = \frac{8}{65}, B = \frac{1}{65}$.

3. Find the value of the principal arguments of :

(i) x,

(ii) – x,

(iii) iy,

(iv) – iy, where x > 0, y > 0.

Ans. (i) 0, (ii) π, (iii) $\frac{1}{2}\pi$, (iv) $-\frac{1}{2}\pi$.

4. Find the moduli and arguments of the following complex numbers:

(i) $\frac{1-i}{1+i}$,

(ii) $\frac{1+2i}{1-(1-i)^2}$,

(iii) $\frac{3-i}{2+i} + \frac{3+i}{2-i}$.

Ans. (i) Modulus 1, argument $-\frac{\pi}{2}$;

(ii) Modulus 1, argument 0;

(iii) Modulus 2, argument 0.

5. Find the moduli and arguments of the following complex numbers :

(i) $\left(\frac{2+i}{3-i}\right)^2$, (ii) $\frac{2+i}{4i+(1+i)^2}$.

Ans. (i) Modulus $\frac{1}{2}$, argument $\frac{\pi}{2}$;

(ii) Modulus $\frac{\sqrt{5}}{6}$, argument $(-\tan^{-1} 2)$.

6. Show that the representative points of the complex number 6i, 2 + 2i, – 1 + 8i and 6 – 6i are collinear.

7. Show that the representative points of the complex numbers 1 + i, 2 + i, + 2 + 3i, 1 + 3i form a rectangle.

8. Show that the triangle whose vertices are the points –1, 1 and $i\sqrt{3}$, in the Argand plane is equilateral.

9. If P, Q, R are points of affix z_1, z_2, $z_1 + z_2$ respectively, show that OPRQ is a parallelogram.

10. If z_1 and z_2 are two complex numbers, prove that

$$|z_1 + z_2|^2 = |z_1|^2 + |z_2|^2,$$

if and only if, $z\bar{z}_2$ is purely imaginary.

11. Prove that the centroid of the triangle whose vertices are z_1, z_2, z_3 is $\dfrac{z_1 + z_2 + z_3}{3}$.

12. If $x + iy = \dfrac{3}{2 + \cos\theta + i\sin\theta}$, prove that $(x - 1)(x - 3) + y^2 = 0$.

13. Find the equation of the straight line in the complex plane passing through the origin and making an angle $\pi/4$ with the real axis.

Ans. $z = t(1 + i)$, where t is a real parameter.

14. Find the equation of the straight line in the complex plane passing through the points $2 + 7i$ and $3 - 6i$.

Ans. $z = t(2 + 7i) + (1 - t)(3 - 6i)$, where t is a real parameter.

15. Find the equation of the circle whose radius is 3 and whose centre is the point $5 + 4i$.

Ans. $|z - 5 - 4i| = 3$.

16. If $\left|\dfrac{z-1}{z+1}\right| = 2$, prove that the locus of z on the Argand plane is a circle, whose centre has the affix $(-5/3, 0)$ and whose radius is $4/3$.

17. Find the radius and centre of the circle :

$$z\bar{z} - (2 + 3i)z - (2 - 3i)\bar{z} + 9 = 0.$$

Ans. Radius, 2, centre $2 - 3i$.

18. Find the locus of the points z satisfying the condition

$$\arg\frac{z-1}{z+1} = \frac{\pi}{3}.$$

Ans. $x^2 + y^2 - \left(2/\sqrt{3}\right)y - 1 = 0$.

19. Find the locus of the variable point z in the Argand plane, when

$$\arg\left(\frac{z-1}{z+1}\right) = \frac{\pi}{2}.$$

Ans. The circle $x^2 + y^2 = 1$.

20. Find the locus of the variable point z in the Argand plane, when $|z - 2| = 2\,|z + 2|$.

    Ans. The circle $3x^2 + 3y^2 + 20x + 12 = 0$.

21. Let $z_1 = 10 + 6i$ and $z_2 = 4 + 6i$. If z is any complex number such that the argument of $\frac{z - z_1}{z - z_2}$ is $\frac{\pi}{4}$, then prove that $|z - 7 - 9i| = 3\sqrt{2}$.

22. Show that the two lines joining the points z = a, z = b and z = c, z = d are perpendicular if $\arg\left(\frac{a-b}{c-d}\right) = \pm\frac{\pi}{2}$ *i.e.*, if the complex number $\frac{a-b}{c-d}$ is purely imaginary.

23. Find the locus of the points z satisfying the condition $\left|\frac{z-i}{z+i}\right| \geq 2$.

    Ans. The interior and boundary of the circle $3x^2 + 3y^2 + 10y + 3 = 0$.

24. Find the locus of the points z satisfying the condition $|z - 1| \geq 2$.

    Ans. The boundary and outside of the circle $(x - 1)^2 + y^2 = 4$.

25. Find the locus of the points z satisfying the condition

    $$\left|\frac{z-1}{z+1}\right| \leq 2.$$

    Ans. The exterior and boundary of the circle $3x^2 + 3y^2 + 10x + 3 = 0$.

26. Show that the area of the triangle on the Argand plane formed by the complex numbers z, iz and z + iz is $\frac{1}{2}|z|^2$.

27. Prove that $\left|\frac{z-1}{z+1}\right|$ = constant and amp $\left(\frac{z-1}{z+1}\right)$ = constant are orthogonal circles.

28. If $\frac{z-i}{z+i}$ is wholly imaginary, show that the locus of z is a circle whose centre is the point $\frac{1}{2}(-1 + i)$ and radius is $1/\sqrt{2}$.

29. Show that the points representing the complex numbers 5 + 3i, 1 + 3i, 2 – 2i and 6 – i on the Argand plane are the vertices of a square. Also find the equation of its circumscribed circle in complex notation.

Ans. $\left|z - \left(\frac{3}{2} + \frac{1}{2}i\right)\right| = \frac{\sqrt{34}}{2}$

30. A represents the number 6i, B the number 3 and P some number z. If P moves so that PA = 2PB, show that

$z\bar{z} = (4 + 2i)\, z + (4 - 2i)\, \bar{z}$.

Ans. Radius $2\sqrt{5}$ and centre the point 4 – 2i.

Show also that the locus of P is a circle. Find its radius and centre.

31. Locate the points representing the complex numbers z on the Argand plane for which

(i) $|z| < 3$;

(ii) $|z| \geq 2$;

(iii) $|z - 3| = 2$;

(iv) $|z + i| < 5$;

(v) $|i - 1 - 2z| > 9$;

(vi) $|z + i| = |z - 3|$;

(vii) $3 \leq |z + i| \leq 4$;

(viii) $|z| - 4 = |z - i| - |z + 5i| = 0$;

(ix) $|z - 2|^2 + |z + 2|^2 = 16$;

(x) $|z - 1| = |z - 3| = |z - i|$.

Ans. (i) All the points lying within the circle (excluding the boundary of the circle) whose centre is origin and radius 3.

(ii) All the points which lie outside or on the circle whose centre is origin and radius 2.

(iii) All points which lie on the boundary of the circle whose centre is the point (3, 0) and whose radius 2.

(iv) All the points which lie in the circle (excluding the boundary of the circle) whose centre is the point (0, – 1) and whose radius is 5.

(v) All the points which lie outside the circle whose centre is the point $\left(-\frac{1}{2}, \frac{1}{2}\right)$ and whose radius is $\frac{9}{2}$.

(vi) All the points which lie on the straight line $3x + y - 4 = 0$.

(vii) All the points which lie in the region bounded by two concentric circles (the boundaries of the circles are also included) whose common centre is the point (0, –1) and whose radii are 3 and 4.

(viii) The points $z = 2\left(\sqrt{3} - i\right)$ and $z = -2\left(\sqrt{3} + i\right)$.

(ix) All the points which lie on the circle whose centre is origin and radius 2.

(x) The point $z = 2 + 2i$.

32. Show that the triangles whose vertices are z_1, z_2, z_3 and z_1', z_2', z_3' are directly similar if $\begin{vmatrix} z_1 & z_1' & 1 \\ z_2 & z_2' & 1 \\ z_3 & z_3' & 1 \end{vmatrix} = 0$

33. Among the complex numbers z which satisfy the condition $|z - 25i| \le 15$, find the numbers having the least positive argument.

    Ans. The only complex number $z = 12 + 16i$.

34. Show that the triangles whose vertices are z_1, z_2, z_3 and z_1', z_2', z_3' are equilateral if

    $(z_1 - z_2)(z_1' - z_2') = (z_2 - z_3)(z_2' + z_3') = (z_3 - z_1)(z_3' - z_1')$.

35. Complex numbers z_1, z_2, z_3 are the vertices A, B, C respectively of an isosceles right angled triangle with right angle at C. Show that

    $(z_1 - z_2)^2 = 2(z_1 - z_3)(z_3 - z_2)$.

36. Let the complex numbers z_1, z_2 and z_3 be the vertices of an equilateral triangle. Let z_0 be the circumcentre of the triangle. Prove that

    $z_1^2 + z_2^2 + z_3^2 = 3z_0^2$.

37. Show that in the Argand plane the equation of the straight line bisecting at right angles the line segment joining the points $3 - 5i$ and $2 + 7i$ is

    $|z - 3 + 5i| = |z - 2 - 7i|$.

38. In the Argand plane find the equation of the straight line passing through the origin and the middle point of the line segment joining the points $2 + 8i$ and $4 - 6i$.

    Ans. $z = t(3 + i)$, where t is a real parameter.

39. Prove that $\sin(\alpha + n\theta) - e^{i\alpha} \sin n\theta = e^{-in\theta} \sin \alpha$.

40. Prove that $\{\sin(\alpha + \theta) - e^{i\alpha} \sin \theta\}^n = \sin^n \alpha \, e^{-n\theta i}$.

41. Show that $\dfrac{1+\tanh x}{1-\tanh x} = \cosh 2x + \sinh 2x.$

42. Show that $\tanh (x + y) = \dfrac{\tanh x + \tanh y}{1 + \tanh x \tanh y}.$

43. Show that

(i) $\sinh x + \sinh y = 2 \sinh \frac{1}{2}(x + y) \cosh \frac{1}{2}(x - y)$

(ii) $\cosh x - \cosh y = 2 \sinh \frac{1}{2}(x + y) \sinh \frac{1}{2}(x - y).$

44. If $a = \log \tan\left(\frac{\pi}{4} + \frac{\theta}{2}\right)$, prove that

(i) $\tan\frac{\alpha}{2} = \tan\frac{\theta}{2}$;

(ii) $\cos \theta \cosh a = 1$;

(iii) $\sinh a = \tan \theta$;

(iv) $\tanh a = \sin \theta$;

(v) If $\alpha = \theta + a_3\theta^3 + a_5\theta^5 + \ldots$, show that $\theta = \alpha - a_3\alpha^3 + a_5\alpha^5 \ \ldots$

45. Resolve into real and imaginary parts:

(i) $\sin (\alpha \pm i\beta)$

(ii) $\cos (\alpha \pm i\beta))$

(iii) $\cot (\alpha - i\beta)$

(iv) $\sec (\alpha + i\beta)$

(v) $\text{cosec} (\alpha + i\beta)$

(vi) $\cosh (\alpha + i\beta)$

(vii) $\coth (\alpha + i\beta)$.

Ans. (i) $\sin \alpha \cosh \beta \pm i \cos \alpha \sinh \beta$.

(ii) $\cos \alpha \cosh \beta \mp i \sin \alpha \sinh \beta$.

(iii) $\left(\dfrac{\sin 2\alpha}{\cosh 2\beta - \cos 2\alpha}\right) - i\left(\dfrac{\sinh 2\beta}{\cosh 2\beta - \cos 2\alpha}\right).$

(iv) $\left(\dfrac{2 \cos \alpha \cosh \beta}{\cos 2\alpha + \cosh 2\beta}\right) + i\left(\dfrac{2 \sin \alpha \sinh \beta}{\cos 2\alpha + \cosh 2\beta}\right).$

(v) $\left(\dfrac{2 \sin \alpha \cosh \beta}{\cosh 2\beta - \cos 2\alpha}\right) + i\left(\dfrac{2 \cos \alpha \sinh \beta}{\cosh 2\beta - \cos 2\alpha}\right).$

(vi) $\cos\alpha\cos\beta + i\sin\alpha\sin\beta$.

(vii) $\left(\dfrac{\sin 2\alpha}{\cosh 2\alpha - \cos 2\beta}\right) - i\left(\dfrac{\sinh 2\beta}{\cosh 2\alpha - \cos 2\beta}\right)$.

46. Resolve $e^{\cosh(x \pm iy)}$ into real and imaginary parts.

Ans. $e^{\cosh x \cos y}[\cos(\sinh x \sin y) \pm i \sin(\sinh x \sin y)]$.

47. Resolve $e^{\sinh(x + iy)}$ into real and imaginary parts.

Ans. $e^{\sinh x \cos y}[\cos(\cosh x \sin y) + i \sin(\cosh x \sin y)]$.

48. If $\sin(\alpha + i\beta) = x + iy$, prove that

(i) $x \operatorname{cosec}^2\alpha - y^2 \sec^2\alpha = 1$

(ii) $x^2 \operatorname{sech}^2\beta + y^2 \operatorname{cosech}^2\beta = 1$.

49. If $\cosh u = \sec\theta$, show that $u = \log \tan\left(\dfrac{\pi}{4} + \dfrac{\theta}{2}\right)$ and $\tanh^2\dfrac{u}{2} = \tan^2\dfrac{\theta}{2}$.

50. If $A + iB = C\tan(x - iy)$, then prove that $\tan 2x = \dfrac{2CA}{C^2 - A^2 - B^2}$.

51. If $\cos^{-1}(x + iy) = A + iB$, prove that

(i) $x^2 \operatorname{sech}^2 B + y^2 \operatorname{cosech}^2 B = 1$

(ii) $x^2 \sec^2 A - y^2 \operatorname{cosec}^2 A = 1$.

52. If $\tan(\theta + i\phi) = \sin(x + iy)$, then prove that $\coth y \sinh 2\phi = \cot x \sin 2\theta$.

53. If $\tanh(\alpha + i\beta) = \sin(x + iy)$, prove that $\sinh 2\alpha \operatorname{cosec} 2\beta = \tan x \coth y$.

54. If $u + iv \cot(x + iy)$, show that $v = -\dfrac{\sin 2y}{\cosh 2y - \cos 2x}$.

55. If $\cos(u + iv) = x + iy$, prove that

$(1 + x)^2 + y^2 = (\cosh v + \cos u)^2$

and $(1 - x)^2 + y^2 = (\cosh v - \cos u)^2$, where x, y, u, v are all real.

56. If $\cosh(x + iy) = p + iq$, where x, y, p and q are real, show that

$$\frac{p^2}{\cos^2 y} - \frac{q^2}{\sin^2 y} = 1.$$

57. If $\sin(x + iy)\sin(\theta + i\phi) = 1$, show that

(i) $\tanh^2 y \cosh^2\phi = \cos^2\theta$;

(ii) $\tanh^2 \phi \cosh^2 y = \cos^2 x$.

58. If $\cos(\theta + i\phi)\cos(\alpha + i\beta) = 1$, prove that

$\tanh^2 \phi \cosh^2 \beta = \sin^2 \alpha$ and $\tanh^2 \beta \cosh^2 \phi = \sin^2 \theta$.

59. If $x = 2\cos\alpha \cosh\beta$ and $y = 2\sin\alpha \sinh\beta$, prove that

(a) $\sec(\alpha + i\beta) + \sec(\alpha - i\beta) = \dfrac{4x}{x^2 + y^2}$,

(b) $\sec(\alpha + i\beta) - \sec(\alpha - i\beta) = \dfrac{4iy}{x^2 + y^2}$.

60. If α, β be the imaginary cube roots of unity, prove that

$$\alpha e^{\alpha x} + \beta e^{\beta x} = -e^{-x/2}\left[\sqrt{3}\sin\frac{\sqrt{3}}{2}x + \cos\frac{\sqrt{3}}{2}x\right].$$

61. Show that $\dfrac{\sin(\alpha + i\beta)}{\sin(\alpha - i\beta)} + \dfrac{\sin(\alpha - i\beta)}{\sin(a + i\beta)} = 2.\dfrac{2 - \left(e^{2\beta} + e^{-2\beta}\right)\cos 2\alpha}{4\sin^2 a + \left(e^{\beta} - e^{-\beta}\right)^2}$

62. Put $(a + be^{i\theta})^n$ in the form $A + iB$.

Ans. $r^n(\cos n\phi + i\sin n\phi)$, where $r = \sqrt{\left(a^2 + b^2 + 2ab\cos\theta\right)}$

and $\tan\phi = \dfrac{b\sin\theta}{a + b\cos\theta}$.

63. If $\tan(\alpha + i\beta) = x + iy$, prove that

(i) $x^2 + y^2 + 2x\cot 2\alpha = 1$;

(ii) $x^2 + y^2 - 2y\coth 2\beta + 1 = 0$;

(iii) $x\coth 2\alpha + y\coth 2\beta = 1$.

64. If $\tan(\theta + i\phi) = \cos\alpha + i\sin\alpha$, prove that

$$\theta = \frac{n\pi}{2} + \frac{\pi}{4} \text{ and } \phi = \frac{1}{2}\log\tan\left(\frac{\pi}{4} + \frac{\alpha}{2}\right).$$

65. If $\tan(\alpha + i\beta) = i$, where α and β are real, then prove that α is indeterminate and β is infinite.

66. If $\sin(\theta + i\phi) = \tan\alpha + i\sec\alpha$, then prove that

$\cos 2\theta \cosh 2\phi = 3$.

67. If $\cos(x + iy) = \cos\alpha + i\sin\alpha$, prove that

(i) $\cosh 2y + \cos 2x = 2$

(ii) $\sin^4 x = \sin^2 \alpha$

(iii) $\sinh^4 y = \sin^2 \alpha$.

68. If $\cos(\theta + i\phi) = r(\cos\alpha + i\sin\alpha)$, then prove that

$$\phi = \frac{1}{2}\log\frac{\sin(\theta-\alpha)}{\sin(\theta+\alpha)}.$$

69. Complex numbers z_1, z_2, z_3 are the vertices A, B, C respectively of an isosceles right angled triangle with right angle at C. Show that $(z_1 - z_2)^2 = 2(z_1 - z_3)(z_3 - z_2)$.

70. Let the complex numbers z_1, z_2 and z_3 be the vertices of an equilateral triangle. Let z_0 be the circumcentre of the triangle. Prove that $z_1^2 + z_2^2 + z_3^2 = 3z_0^2$.

71. Let $z_1 = 10 + 6i$ and $z_2 = 4 + 6i$. If z is any complex number such that the argument of $\frac{z-z_1}{z-z_2}$ is $\frac{\pi}{4}$, then prove that $|z-7-9i| = 3\sqrt{2}$.

2

LIMITS, CONTINUITY AND FUNCTIONS

INTRODUCTION OF LIMITS

Let f(z) be any function of the complex variable z defined in a bounded and closed domain D. Then l is said to be the limit of f(z) as z approaches a along any path in D if for any arbitrarily chosen positive number ε, however small but not zero, there exists a corresponding number δ greater than zero such that +|f(z) – l| < ε, for all values of z for which 0 < |z – a| < δ.

In symbols, we write $\lim\limits_{z \to a} f(z) = l$.

Definition of Limit

A function f(x) is said to tend to the limit A as x tends to a, if corresponding to any arbitrary chosen positive number ε, however small (but not zero), there exists a positive number δ, such that

$$|f(x) - A| < \varepsilon,$$

for all values of x for which $0 < |x - a| < \delta$.

We write it as $\lim\limits_{x \to a} f(x) = A$.

Right Hand Limit

A function f(x) is said to tend to the limit A as x → a from the right, if corresponding to any arbitrary chosen +ive number ε, however small (but not zero), there exists a +ive number δ, such that

$$|f(x) - A| < \varepsilon,$$

for all values of x for which $0 < x - a < \delta$.

The limit of f(x) as x → a from the right is called the *right hand limit* of f(x) and is denoted by $\lim\limits_{x \to a+0} f(x)$

or by f(a + 0).

We calculate f(a + 0) by evaluating $\lim_{h\to 0} f(a+h)$, where h is +ive and sufficiently small.

Left Hand Limit: A function f(x) is said to tend to the limit A as $x \to a$ from the left, if corresponding to any arbitrary chosen +ive number ε, however small (but not zero), there exists a +ive number δ, such that

$$|f(x) - A| < \varepsilon,$$

for all values of x for which $0 < a - x < \delta$.

The limit of f(x) as $x \to a$ from the left is called the *left hand limit* of f(x) and is denoted by $\lim_{x\to a-0} f(x)$ or by f(a + 0).

We calculate f(a − 0) by evaluating $\lim_{h\to 0} f(a-h)$, where h is +ive and sufficiently small.

From the definition it is clear that the limit of f(x) as $x \to a$ has no necessary connection with the value of the function at a except that when the function is continuous at x = a. The two are equals; even in the case of such functions the limit is distinct in idea from the value.

Note 1: $\lim_{x\to a} f_1(x)$ exists only if, limit on the left = limit on the right.

Note 2: If $f(x) \to A$ and $f_2(x) \to B$, as $x \to a$, where A and B are both finite, we have

(i) $\lim_{x\to a} \{f_1(x) \pm f_2(x)\} = A \pm B$,

(ii) $\lim_{x\to a} \{f_1(x) \,.\, f_2(x)\} = A \,.\, B$,

(iii) $\lim_{x\to a} \left\{\frac{f_1(x)}{f_2(x)}\right\} = \frac{A}{B}$, provided $B \neq 0$,

(iv) $\lim_{x\to a} cf(x) = cA$ where c is constant.

LIMIT OF INEQUALITIES

It $\phi(x) + A$ and $\psi(x) \to B$ as $x \to a$ and if

$$\phi(x) < \psi(x),\ x \neq u$$

Then $A \leq B$

Since $\phi(x) < \psi(x)$ for all values of a an which the limit depend one would naturally expect that A < B. But it is also possible that A may be equal to B. Let $\phi(x) = 1 + x^2$. and $\psi(x) = 1 + 2u^2$. We have $\lim_{x\to a} \phi(x) = 1$, $\lim_{x\to a} \psi(x) = 1$. Also if $x \neq 0$ we have $\phi(x) < \psi(x)$ for all values of x on which the limit depend.

Example 1:

The limit of a sum is equal to the sum of the limits.

Solution:

Let $\lim_{x \to a} f_1(x) = A$ and $\lim_{x \to a} f_2(x) = B$.

Let ε be any arbitrary chosen positive number.

We can choose δ_1, δ_2 such that

$$|f_1(x) - A| < \frac{1}{2}\varepsilon, \text{ when } 0 < |x - a| < \delta_1,$$

and $$|f_2(x) - B| < \frac{1}{2}\varepsilon, \text{ when } 0 < |x - a| < \delta_2,$$

Let δ be any positive number smaller than both δ_1 and δ_2. Then

$|f_1(x) - A| < \frac{1}{2}\varepsilon$ and $|f_2(x) - B| < \frac{1}{2}\varepsilon$, for $0 < |x - a| < \delta$

Now from algebra, we have

$|\{f_1(x) + f_2(x)\} - (A + B)| = |\{f_1(x) - A\} + f_2(x)\} - B)\}|$

$\leq |\{f_1(x) - A| + |f_2(x)\} - B)\}| < \frac{\varepsilon}{2} + \frac{\varepsilon}{2}$ *i.e.*, $< \varepsilon$

$\therefore \lim_{x \to a} \{f_1(x) + f_2(x)\} = A + B$.

Example 2:

The limit of a product is equal to the product of the limits.

Solution:

Let $\lim_{x \to a} f_1(x) = A$ and $\lim_{x \to a} f_2(x) = B$.

Let $A \neq 0$ and $B \neq 0$

Again let, $f_1(x)f_2(x) - AB$

$= [f_1(x) - A]\,[f_2(x)\} - B] + A\,[f_2(x) - B] + B[f_1(x) - A]$.

$\therefore$ by algebra, we have $|f_1(x) - f|\,f_2(x) - AB|$

$\leq |f_1(x) - A|\,.\,|f_2(x) - B)| + |A|\,.\,|f_2(x) - B| + |B|\,f_1(x) - A|$

Now, $\lim_{x \to a} f_1(x) = A$ and $\lim_{x \to a} f_2(x) = B$. Therefore, for a given ε we can take δ such that

$|f_1(x) - A| < \frac{\varepsilon}{3|B|}$ and $|f_2(x) - B| < \frac{\varepsilon}{3|A|}$, when $0 < |x - a| < \delta$. Then

$$|f_1(x)f_2(x) - AB| < \frac{\varepsilon}{3} \cdot \frac{\varepsilon}{3|A||B|} + \frac{\varepsilon}{3} + \frac{\varepsilon}{3}.$$

Since only small values of ε need by considered, we can take ε such that $\frac{\varepsilon}{3|A||B|} < 1$. Then

$$|f_1(x)f_2(x) - AB| < \frac{\varepsilon}{3} + \frac{\varepsilon}{3} + \frac{\varepsilon}{3} \text{ i.e, } < \varepsilon, \text{ when } 0 < |x - a| < \delta.$$

Hence $\lim_{x \to a} \{f_1(x) \,.\, f_2(x)\} = AB$.

CONTINUITY

Definition: *A function f(x) defined for x = a is said to be continuous at x = a if*

(i) f(a) i.e., the value of f(x) at x = a is a definite number.

(ii) the limit of the function f(x) as x → a exists and is equal to the value of f(x) at x = a.

Otherwise the function is *discontinuous* at x = a.

A function is said to be continuous in an interval (a, b) if it is continuous at every point of that interval.

In other words, a function f(z) of a complex variable z defined in the closed and bounded domain D is said to be continuous at $a \in D$ if and only if for any arbitrarily chosen positive number ε, however small but not zero, there exists a corresponding number $\delta > 0$ such that

$$|f(z) - f(a)| < e \text{ whenever } |z - a| < \delta.$$

It follows from the definitions of limit and continuity that f(z) is continuous at z = a iff $\lim_{z \to a} f(z) = f(a)$.

We say that f(z) is a continuous function in a domain D if it is continuous at every $z \in D$.

We can easily show that $f(z) = u(x, y) + iv(x, y)$ is a continuous function of z iff u and v are continuous functions of x and y.

Uniform Continuity : *A function f(z) defined in a domain D is said to be uniformly continuous in D if given $\varepsilon > 0$, there a $\delta > 0$ such that $|f(z_1) - f(z_2)| < \varepsilon$ whenever $|z_1 - z_2| < \delta$, where z_1 and z_2 are points in D.*

It should be noted carefully that uniform continuity is a property associated with a domain and not with a single point of it.

If f(z) is uniformly continuous in a domain D, it is continuous in D.

A function which is continuous in a closed and bounded domain D is uniformly continuous in D, whereas a function continuous in an open domain D' may fail to be uniformly continuous in the domain D'.

Arithmetical Definition of Continuity: *A function f(x) is said to be continuous at x = a, if for any arbitrarily chosen positive number ε, however small (but not zero), we can find a corresponding number δ such that*

$$|f(x) - f(a)| < \varepsilon$$

for all values of x for which $|x - a| < \delta$.

This definition, as given by Cauchy, is known as Cauchy's definition of continuity.

Remark:

One comparing the definitions of limit and continuity, we find that a function f(x) is continuous at x = a if

$$\lim_{x \to a} f(x) = f(a).$$

Thus f(x) is continuous at x = a if we have L.H.L. = R.H.L. = f(a); otherwise it is discontinuous at x = a.

DIFFERENTIABILITY

Definition: *A function f(x) is said to be differentiable at x = a if both*

$$\lim_{h \to 0} \frac{f(a+h) - f(a)}{h}, h > 0$$

and

$$\lim_{h \to 0} \frac{f(a-h) - f(a)}{-h}, \text{ (L.H.L. = R.H.L.)}$$

exist and have a common value (finite or infinite). This common value is called the *derivative* of f(x) at the point x = a and is denoted by f'(a). Another name for derivative is known as differential co-efficient.

Progressive and Regressive Derivatives

Progressive derivative or *the right hand differential coefficient of* f(x) at x = a is given by

$$\lim_{h \to 0} \frac{f(a+h) - f(a)}{h}, h > 0.$$

It is denoted by Rf'(a).

Regressive derivative or *the left hand differential coefficient* of f(x) at x = a is given by

$$\lim_{h\to 0} \frac{f(a-h)-f(a)}{-h}, h>0.$$

It is denoted by Lf'(a).

A function f(x) is said to be differentiable at x = a if both Rf'(a) and Lf '(a) exist and are equal; otherwise it is said to be not differential.

Theorem:

Continuity is necessary but not a sufficient condition for the existence of a finite derivative.

Proof:

Let f(x) have a finite derivative f'(a) at x = a. Then

$$\lim_{h\to 0} \frac{f(a+h)-f(a)}{h} = f'(a). \qquad ...(1)$$

Now $f(a + h) - f(a) = \dfrac{f(a-h)-f(a)}{h} \times h,\ h \neq 0.$

Taking limit of both sides when $h \to 0$, we get

$$\lim_{h\to 0} \left[f(a+h)-f(a)\right] = \lim_{h\to 0} \frac{f(a+h)-f(a)}{h} \times \lim_{h\to 0} h$$

$= f'(a) \times 0,$ [from (1)]

$= 0$, since f'(a) is finite.

Now, $\lim_{h\to 0}$ [f(a + h) – f (a)] = 0

$\Rightarrow$ $\lim_{h\to 0}$ f(a + h) = f(a). ...(2)

From the condition (2) we see that f(x) is necessarily continuous at x = a. Thus continuity is a necessary condition for the existence of a finite derivative.

In order to show that continuity is not a sufficient condition for differentiability, we should give an example of a function which is continuous at a point but is not differentiable at that point.

In other words, the mode of definitions of continuity is the same both in case of the function of the real and complex variables therefore definition of differentiability of a complex function is identical with that of the real function.

Let f(z) be a function of a complex variable z defined in a domain D. Then f(z) is said to be differentiable at a point z_0 of D iff

$$\lim_{\Delta z \to 0} \frac{f(z_0 + \Delta z) - f(z_0)}{\Delta z} \text{ or } \lim_{z \to z_0} \frac{f(z) - f(z_0)}{z - z_0}$$

exist finitely and this limit, if it exists finitely, *is called the differential coefficient or derivative* of f with respect to z at $z = z_0$.

It is denoted by $f'(z_0)$ or by $Df(z_0)$.

If the value of the above limit as $z \to z_0$ is not unique *i.e.*, if the limit depends upon and Δz, we say that the derivative of f(z) at $z = z_0$ does not exist or the function f(z) is non-differentiable at $z = z_0$.

Hence, if we have to show that f(z) is non-differentiable, we should try different paths for Δz. Convenient paths for Δz are along real and imaginary axes *i.e.*, we can take Δz either wholly real or wholly imaginary.

Note : Since the derivative of a complex function has been defined in the same manner as the derivative of a function of a single real variable, therefore, all the rules of Differential Calculus remain the same when applied to complex functions.

Theorem 1:

Continuity is a necessary but not a sufficient condition for the existence of a finite derivative.

Proof:

Let f(z) be differentiable at z_0. Then,

$\lim_{z \to z_0} \frac{f(z) - f(z_0)}{z - z_0}$ exists and equals $f'(z_0)$. Now we can write

$$f(z) - f(z_0) = (z - z_0) \frac{f(z) - f(z_0)}{z - z_0}, \text{ if } z \neq z_0.$$

Taking limit of both sides as $z \to z_0$, we get

$$\lim_{z \to z_0} [f(z) - f(z_0)] = \lim_{z \to z_0} \left[(z - z_0) \frac{\{f(z) 0 f(z_0)\}}{z - z_0} \right]$$

$$= \lim_{z \to z_0} (z - z_0) \lim_{z \to z_0} \frac{f(z) - f(z_0)}{z - z_0}$$

$= f'(z_0).0 = 0,$

so that $\lim_{z \to z_0} f(z) = f(z_0)$.

Hence, f(z) is continuous at z_0. Thus continuity is a necessary condition for differentiability but it is not a sufficient condition for the existence of a finite derivative.

The following example illustrates this fact :

Let $f(z) = |z|^2$, where $z = x + iy$.

This function is continuous at every point because $x^2 + y^2$ is continuous at all points.

Now,
$$f'(a) = \lim_{\Delta z \to 0} \frac{f(a + \Delta z) - f(a)}{\Delta z}$$
$$= \lim_{\Delta z \to 0} \frac{|a + \Delta z|^2 - |a|^2}{\Delta z}$$
$$= \lim_{\Delta z \to 0} \frac{(a + \Delta z)(\bar{a} + \Delta \bar{z}) - a\bar{a}}{\Delta z}$$
$$= \lim_{\Delta z \to 0} \left[\frac{a\Delta \bar{z} + a\Delta z + \Delta z \Delta \bar{z}}{\Delta z}\right]$$
$$= \lim_{\Delta z \to 0} \left[a\frac{\Delta \bar{z}}{\Delta z} + \bar{a} + \Delta \bar{z}\right]$$
$$= \lim_{\Delta z \to 0} \left[a\frac{\Delta \bar{z}}{\Delta z} + \bar{a}\right]. \qquad [\because \Delta \bar{z} \to 0 \text{ as } \Delta z \to 0]$$

$\because$ at $a = 0$, we have $\bar{a} = 0$, therefore $f'(a) = 0$.

Again at $a \neq 0$, let $\Delta z = r(\cos \phi + i \sin \phi)$.

Then $\Delta \bar{z} = r(\cos \phi - i \sin \phi)$.

$$\therefore \frac{\Delta \bar{z}}{\Delta z} = \frac{\cos \phi - i \sin \phi}{\cos \phi + i \sin \phi} = \cos 2\phi - i \sin 2\phi,$$

which does not tend to a unique limit as $\Delta z \to 0$ since this limit depends upon arg Δz.

Thus, f(z) is not differentiable for any non-zero value of z, though it is continuous everywhere.

Theorem 2:

Rules of Differentiation : *If f(z) and g(z) are analytic functions in a domain D, then their sum, product and quotient {provided g(z) ≠ 0} are also analytic and we have* *(i)* $\frac{d}{dz}[f(z) \pm g(z)] = \frac{d}{dz}f(z) \pm \frac{d}{dz}g(z)$

(ii) $\frac{d}{dz}[cf(z)] = c\frac{d}{dz}f(z)$

(iii) $\frac{d}{dz}[f(z)\,g(z)] = f(z)\frac{d}{dz}g(z) + g(z)\frac{d}{dz}f(z)$

(iv) $\frac{d}{dz}[f(z)/g(z)] = \frac{\left[\frac{d}{dz}f(z)\right].g(z) - \left[\frac{d}{dz}g(z)\right].f(z)}{[g(z)]^2}$, $[g(z) \neq 0]$

(v) *If* $f(z) = F[g(z)]$, *then* $\frac{d}{dz}f(z) = F'[g(z)]\,g'(z)$.

Proof:

The proofs of (i) to (iv) are easy and left as an exercise.

We prove the chain rule given in (v).

We first assume that for some point z in D, $g'(z) \neq 0$. Then by the definition of derivative, we conclude that

$$\left|\frac{g(z) - g(z_1)}{z - z_1}\right| > c > 0$$

for some positive constant c provided z_1 is a point of D sufficiently close to z. It follows that $g(z) - g(z_1) \neq 0$ for $z \neq z_1$ and we have

$$\frac{f(z) - f(z_1)}{z - z_1} = \frac{F[g(z)] - F[g(z_1)]}{g(z) - g(z_1)} \cdot \frac{g(z) - g(z_1)}{z - z_1}.$$

Proceeding to the limits as $z \to z_1$, we obtain

$f'(z) = F'[g(z)]g'(z)$.

The proof of this formula for case $g'(z) = 0$ is left is an exercise.

CONSTANT

It is a quantity which during any set of mathematical operations, retains the same value. The constant are generally denoted by earlier letter a, b, c, . . . , or by numbers 1, 2, 3, ...

VARIABLE

It is a quantity which during any set of mathematical operation, does not retain the same value but is capable of assuming different value. The variable are generally denoted by the last letters of the alphabet *i.e.*, u, v, w, x, y, z etc., the variable are of following kinds:

(a) *Continuous and Discrete Variables :* If a variable can take all values from one given numbers to another, then it is called a continuous variable, but if it cannot take all values from one given number to another, then it is called a discontinuous or discrete variable.

(b) *Independent Variable :* The variable which may take up any arbitrary value that may be assigned to it is called an independent variables.

(c) *Dependent Variable :* This is an variable which assumes its value in consequence of some second variable or a system of variables taking up any set of arbitrary value that may be assigned to them.

FUNCTIONS

If x is a variable then a symbol which has one definite value for every value which x can have, is called 0 function of x.

Notation : A function of x is generally denoted by a single letter y. More generally it is denoted by symbols like f(x), F(x), $\phi(x)$, $\psi(x)$, $f_1(x_2)$, $f_2(x)$ etc. If a is any particular value of x, the value of the function f(x) obtained by putting x = a in it, is called the functional value of f(x) and is denoted by f(a).

A function of x is generally written as

$$y = f(x)$$

Here x and y are called the related variable because the variation of y depends upon the variation of x.

To be more clear about variation, consider the function.

$$y = x^2 + 2x + 6 \qquad \text{...(1)}$$

For different values of x, y (or the expression $x^2 + 2x + 6$) assumes different values as shown below:

x	1	2	3	4	5
y	9	14	21	20	41

Here y is a dependent variable and x is the independent variable.

If y = f(x) = c *i.e.* the value of function always remain 'c', whatever by the x, then such a function is called 0 constant function.

TYPES OF FUNCTIONS

(i) *Algebraic Functions:* A function consisting a finites number of term involving powers and roots of the variable x and the four basic mathematical operations (addition, subtraction, multiplication and division) is called an algebraic function. For example:

$2x^3 + 5x^2 + 6x + 1$, $(x + 8)^7$, $\frac{x}{(x^2 - 1)}$ etc. are all algebraic functions.

(ii) *Transcendental Functions:* The functions which are not algebraic are called transcendental functions. These functions include:

(a) Trigonometric function such as

$\sin x, \cos x, \tan x,$ etc.

(b) Inverse trigonometric functions such as

$\sin^{-1} x, \cos^{-1} x, \cot^{-1} x,$ etc.

(c) Logarithmic functions such as

$\log_e x \; \log_a x \; \log\left(\sqrt{x} + \frac{1}{\sqrt{x}}\right)$ etc.

(d) Exponential functions such as

$e^x, a^x, e^{\tan x}, x^{\cos x}, x^x$ etc.

(e) In commensurable power functions of x as

$x^6, a^{\sqrt{7}}, x^{5/2},$ etc.

(iii) *Explicit Functions:* A function which is directly expressed in terms of the independent variable, is called an explicit function.

For example in $y = x^2$, or $y = e^x + 2\cos x$, y is an explicit function of x.

(iv) *Implicit Functions:* A function in which the variable x and y both occur together in an equation, but y cannot be directly expressed in terms of x, then y is called and implicit functions of x.

For example $2 + x^4 + 6x^2y^2 + 4xy + y^2 = 0$ is a implicit function of x. The implicit functions are usually denoted by $f(x, y) = 0$.

(v) *Even or Odd Functions:* If a functions does not change its sign when the sign of its independent variable is changed, then it is said, to be on even functions such as x^6, cos x, etc., are even functions of x because if we put (–x) in place of x, their signs are unchanged. But if a function changed its sign when the sign of its variable is changed, then it is called an odd function such as x^7, sin x, cot x etc., are odd function because their signs are changed if we put (–x) in place of x in these.

(vi) *Periodic Functions:* If $f(x + T) = f(x)$, where T is a constant then f(x) is called a periodic function of x with period T. For example $\sin(2\pi + x) = \sin x$, and hence sin x is a periodic functions with period 2π.

(vii) *Single-Valued and Many-Valued Functions:* The function is a single-valued function when to every value of the independent variable there corresponds only one value of the function, otherwise it is a many-valued function. An implicit function is often a many-valued function.

CONTINUITY OF ELEMENTARY FUNCTION

The student as supposed to be familiar with the elementary functions and to know that:

(i) x^n is continuous for all values of x when n is positive.

(ii) x^n is continuous for all values of x except x = 0 when n is negative. For when n is negative and equal to –m say, where m iis positive we can write x^n as $\frac{1}{x^m}$ and as $x \to 0$ $\frac{1}{x^m}$ either does not tends to a limit or $\to \infty$.

(iii) sin x and cos x are continuous for all values of x.

(iv) tan x is continuous for all values of x except $\pm\frac{\pi}{2}, \pm\frac{3\pi}{2}, \pm\frac{5\pi}{2}$ etc. as $x \to \frac{\pi}{2}$ from the right $\tan x \to -\infty$ as $x \to \frac{\pi}{2}$ from the left $\tan x \to +\infty$. Thus, $\lim_{x\to\pi/2} \tan x$ does not exist.

(v) Similarly, statement can be made for cot x, sec x and cosec x.

(vi) $\sin^{-1}x$ and $\cos^{-1}x$ are not real for value of x out side the domain [– 1, 1] similarly, $\sec^{-1} x$ and $\text{cosec}^{-1} x$ are not real for values of x between + and.

(vii) All the inverse circular function are continuous at every point with in the domain in which they are real.

(viii) Log x is continuous for all values of $x > 0$. For values of $x < 0$ the function is not real and we shall not consider these values as x tends to zero from the right log x tends to $-\infty$.

CONTINUITY OF SUM, PRODUCIS etc.

(i) The sum of two continuous function is continuous.

(ii) The product of two continuous function is continuous.

(iii) The quotient of two continuous function is a continuous function except for value of x which make the denominator zero.

SOLVED EXAMPLES

Example 1:

A function is defined by

$f(x) = -x^2$ *if* $x \le 0$

$= 5x - 4$ *if* $0 < x < 1$

$= 4x^2 - 3x$ *if* $1 < x < 2$

$= 3x + 4$ *if* $x \ge 2.$

Examine f for continuity at x = 0, 1, 2. Also discuss the kind of discontinuity if axis.

Solution:

At x = 0

$$\lim_{x\to 0} - f(x) = \lim_{x\to 0} \left(-x^2\right) = 0$$

$$\lim_{x\to 0} + f(x) = \lim_{x\to 0} (5x - 4) = -4$$

Also f(0) = 0

Thus, $\lim_{x\to 0} + f(x) \pm f(0)$ and so f has a does continuity of the first and from the right at x = 0

At x = 1

$$\lim_{x\to 1} - f(x) = \lim(5x - 4) = 1$$

$$\lim_{x\to 1} + f(x) = \lim_{x\to 1}\left(4x^2 - 3x\right) = 1$$

Also f(1) = 5 × 1 − 4 = 1

Thus, $1 \lim_{x\to 1-} f(x) = \lim_{x\to 1+} f(x)$ and so f(x) is continuous let $x \le 1$

At x = 2

$$\lim_{x\to 2-} f(x) = \lim_{x\to 2} (4x^2 - 3x) = 4 \times 4 - 3 \times 2 = 10$$

$\lim_{x\to 2+} f(x) = \lim_{x\to 2} (34 + 4) = 10$

Thus, $\lim_{x\to 2-} f(x) = \lim_{x\to 2+} f(x) = f(2)$

and so f(x) is continuous at x = 2.

Example 2:

Test the following function for continuity

$f(x) = x \cos (1/x)$ for x ' 0; $f(0) = 0$ at $x = 0$.

Solution:

We have

$$f(0+0) = \lim_{h\to 0} f(0+h) = \lim_{h\to 0} f(h) = \lim_{h\to 0} h\cos\frac{1}{h} = 0.$$

Againf$(0 - 0) = \lim_{h\to 0} f(0 - h) = \lim_{h\to 0} f(-h) = \lim_{h\to 0} -h\cos\left(\frac{-1}{h}\right) = 0.$

Also f(0) = 0. Thus f(0 + 0) = f(0 – 0) = f(0). Therefore f(x) is continuous at x = 0.

Example 3:

If a function f is continuous at x = a and if y is a function continuous at f(a) show that the function got is continuous at x = a.

Solution:

If f: R = R and g: R → R then the product or composite of t and g. Written as fog: R → R is defined as

(fog) (x) = f[g(x)] for all x ∀ R.

Similarly (gof) (x) = g[f(x)] for all x ∀ R. Since g is continuous at f(a), so for any $\varepsilon > 0$. There exist some $\delta_1 > 0$, such that

$|g[f(x)] - g(fog)] < \varepsilon$ when

$|f(x) - f(a)| < \delta_1$ ...(1)

Since f is continuous at a fog $\delta_1 > 0$ there exist some $\delta > 0$ such that

$|f(x) - f(a)| < \delta$ when $|x - a| < \delta$ ...(2)

fron (1) and (2) we obtain

$|g(f(x)) - g(f(a))| < \varepsilon$, when $|x - a| < \delta$

$|(g\,of)(x) - (gof)(a)| < \varepsilon$ when $|x - a| < \delta$

If follows that gof is continuous at x = a.

Let y = [x] or E(x) denotes the integral part of x. Prove that this function is discontinuous where x has an integral value. Also draw the graph.

Solution:

From the definition of E(x), we have

$$E(x) = n - 1 \text{ for } n - 1 \le x < n,$$

$$E(x) = n \text{ for } n \le x < n + 1,$$

$$E(x) = n + 1 \text{ for } n + 1 \le x < n + 2,$$

also so on where n is an integer.

We consider x = n. Then E(n) = n, E(n – 0) = n – 1 and E(n + 0) = n.

Since E(n + 0) ≠ E(n – 0), the function E(x) is discontinuous at x = n *i.e.*, when x has an integral value. Evidently it is continuous for all other values of x.

To draw the graph, we put

n = ..., – 4, – 3, – 2, – 1, 0, 1, 2, 3, 4, ..., so that

$y = -4$, when $-4 \le x < -3$

$y = -3$, when $-3 \le x < -2$

$y = -2$, when $-2 \le x < -1$

$y = -1$, when $-1 \le x < 0$

$y = 0$, when $0 \le x < 1$

$y = 1$ when $1 \le x < 2$

$y = 2$, when $2 \le x < 3$

$y = 3$, when $3 \le x < 4$

$y = 4$, when $4 \le x < 5$ and so on.

The graph is shown by thick lines.

Example 4:

The function for continuity

$f(x) = 2^{1/x}$, *when* $x \ne 0$; $f(0) = 0$ *at* $x = 0$.

Solution:

We have

$$f(0 + 0) = \lim_{h\to 0} f(0 + h) = \lim_{h\to 0} f(h) = \lim_{h\to 0} 2^{1/h} = \infty.$$

$$\text{Again } f(0 - 0) = \lim_{h\to 0} f(0 - h) = \lim_{h\to 0} f(-h) = \lim_{h\to 0} 2^{1/h} = 2^{-\infty} = 0.$$

Since f(0 + 0) ≠ f(0 – 0), the function f(x) is discontinuous at x = 0.

Note: A function f(x) is said to have an *infinite discontinuity* at a point x = a, if one or both of the limits f(a + 0) and f(a – 0) are infinite.

Test the function for continuity

Example 5:

$$f(x) = \frac{1}{1-e^{-1/x}};\ x = 0;\ f(0) = 0 \text{ at } x = 0.$$

Solution:

We have

$$f(0+0) = \lim_{h\to 0} f(0+h) = \lim_{h\to 0} f(h)$$

$$= \lim_{h\to 0}\frac{1}{1-e^{-1/h}}$$

$$= \frac{1}{e^{-\infty}} = \frac{1}{1-0} = 1.$$

Again

$$f(0-0) = \lim_{h\to 0} f(0-h) = \lim_{h\to 0} f(-h) = \lim_{h\to 0}\frac{1}{1-e^{1/h}}$$

$$= \frac{1}{1-e^{\infty}} = \frac{1}{1-\infty} = 0.$$

Since f(0 + 0) ≠ f(0 – 0), the function f(x) is discontinuous at x = 0.

Example 6:

Test the following functions for continuity:

f(x) = x^3 *at x = 2.*

Solution:

We have f(2) = 2^3 = 8;

$$f(2 + 0) = \lim_{h\to 0} f(2+h) = \lim_{h\to 0} (2+h)^3 = 2^3 = 8;$$

$$\text{and} f(2 - 0) = \lim_{h\to 0} f(2 - h) = \lim_{h\to 0} (2 - h)^3 = 2^3 = 8.$$

Since f(2) = f(2 + 0) = f(2 – 0), therefore f(x) is continuous at x = 2.

Example 7:

If f(x) - x $\tan^{-1}\left(\frac{1}{x}\right)$ *when x ≠ 0 and f(0) = 0 show that f is continuous but not deriable for x = 0.*

Solution:

$$\lim_{x\to 0} f(x) = \lim_{x\to 0} x \tan^{-1}\left(\frac{1}{x}\right) = 0\left(-\frac{\pi}{2}\right) = 0$$

$$\lim_{x\to 0} f(x) = \lim_{x\to 0}+ x \tan^{-1}\left(\frac{1}{x}\right) = 0\left(\frac{1}{2}\pi\right) = 0$$

Also f(0) = 0 Hence f is continuous at x = 0

$$\text{Now } Lf'(0) = \lim_{x\to 0}- \frac{x\tan^{-1}\left(\frac{1}{x}\right) - 0}{x-0} = \lim_{x\to 0}- \tan^{-1}\left(\frac{1}{x}\right) = \frac{-\pi}{2}$$

$$Rf'(0) = \lim_{x\to 0}+ \tan^{-1}\left(\frac{1}{x}\right) = \frac{\pi}{2}$$

$\therefore$ Lf'(0) $\neq$ Rf'(0)

Hence f is not deriable at x = 0.

Example 8:

Show that f(x) = $(x^2 - 1)/(x - 1)$ is continuous for all values of x except x = 1.

How may this function be defined to make it continuous at x = 1?

Solution:

At first we have to test continuity of f(x) at x = a where a ± 1 f(a) = $\frac{a^2-1}{a-1}$ = a definite real number because a − 1 $\neq$ 0;

$$\text{We have R.H.L.} = f(a+0) = \lim_{h\to 0} f(a+h) = \lim_{h\to 0} \frac{(a+h)^2-1}{a+h-1} = \frac{a^2-1}{a-1};$$

$$\text{L.H.L.} \ f(a-0) = \lim_{h\to 0} f(a-h) = \lim_{h\to 0} \frac{(a-h)^2-1}{a-h-1} = \frac{a^2-1}{a-1}.$$

L.H.L. = R.H.L.

Thus f(a + 0) = f(a − 0) = f(a). Therefore, f(x) is continuous at x = a where a $\neq$ 1.

From the formula definiting f(x), we have f(1) = $\frac{1-1}{1-1} = \frac{0}{0}$ which is meaningless. Thus f(x) has no definite value at x = 1. Therefore, f(x) is not continuous at x = 1. To make f(x) continuous at x = 1, we shall find $\lim_{x\to 1} f(x)$.

We have

$$f(1+0) = \lim_{h\to 0} f(1+h) = \lim_{h\to 0} \frac{(1+h)^2 - 1}{1+h-1} = \lim_{h\to 0} \frac{2h+h^2}{h}$$

$$= \lim_{h\to 0} \frac{h(2+h)}{h} = \lim_{h\to 0}(2+h) = 2;$$

and

$$f(1-0) = \lim_{h\to 0} f(1-h) = \lim_{h\to 0} \frac{(1-h)^2 - 1}{1-h-1}$$

$$= \lim_{h\to 0} \frac{-2h+h^2}{-h}$$

$$= \lim_{h\to 0} (2-h) = 2.$$

Thus, $\lim_{x\to 1} f(x)$ = 2. So if we take $f(x) = \frac{(x^2-1)}{(x-1)}$ when $x \neq 1$ and $f(x) = 2$ when $x = 1$, it will become continuous at $x = 1$.

Example 9:

Define continuity of function at a point and in an interval. Discuss the continuity of

$f(x) = 2,\ x \le 0;\ f(x) = 3x + 2,\ 0 < x \le 1;\ f(x) = x/(x - 1),\ 1 < x$ at $x = 0$ and at $x = 1$.

Solution:

See definition of continuity.

(i) To test f(x) for continuity at x = 0. We have

$$f(0) = 2;\ \text{R.H.L.} = f(0+0) = \lim_{h\to 0} f(0+h)$$

$$= \lim_{h\to 0} f(h) = \lim_{h\to 0}(3h+2) = 2$$

$$\text{L.H.L.} = f(0-0) = \lim_{h\to 0} f(0-h) = \lim_{h\to 0} f(-h)$$

$$= \lim_{h\to 0} (2) = 2.$$

Since L.H.L. = R.H.L. = f(0) = 2, the function is continuous at x = 0.

(ii) To test f(x) for continuity at x = 1. We have

$$f(1) = 3.1 + 2 = 5.$$

$$\text{R.H.L.} = f(1+0) = \lim_{h\to 0} f(1+h)$$

$$= \lim_{h\to 0} \frac{1+h}{(1+h)-1} = \lim_{h\to 0} \frac{1+h}{h} = \infty,$$

L.H.L. $= f(1-0) = \lim_{h\to 0} f(1-h)$

$= \lim_{h\to 0} [3(1-h)+2] = \lim_{h\to 0} [5-3h] = 5.$

Since R.H.L. $\neq$ L.H.L. the function is not continuous at $x = 1$.

Example 10:

Show that the function $f(x) = |x|$ is continuous at $x = 0$, but not differentiable at $x = 0$, where $|x|$ means the numerical value of x.

Solution:

To test the continuity of $f(x)$ at $x = 0$.

We have $f(0) = |x| = 0$;

R.H.L. $f(0+h) = \lim_{h\to 0} f(0+h) = \lim_{h\to 0} f(h) = \lim_{h\to 0} |h|$

L.H.L. $f(0-0) = \lim_{h\to 0} f(0-h) = \lim_{h\to 0} f(-h) = \lim_{h\to 0} |-h|$

$= \lim_{h\to 0} h = 0$

L.H.L. = R.H.L.

Since $f(0+0) = f(0-0) = f(0)$, therefore $f(x)$ is continuous at $x = 0$.

To test the differentiability of f(x) at x = 0.

We have $Rf'(0) = \lim_{h\to 0} \frac{f(0+h)-f(0)}{h}$, where h is +ive and sufficiently small

$$= \lim_{h\to 0} \frac{f(h)-f(0)}{h} = \lim_{h\to 0} \frac{|h|-|0|}{h} = \lim_{h\to 0} \frac{h}{h}$$

$$= \lim_{h\to 0} 1 = 1;$$

and $Lf'(0) = \lim_{h\to 0} \frac{f(0-h)-f(0)}{-h}$.h being +ive and sufficiently small

$$= \lim_{h\to 0} \frac{f(-h)-f(0)}{-h} = \lim_{h\to 0} \frac{|-h|-|0|}{-h} = \lim_{h\to 0} \frac{h-0}{-h}$$

$$= \lim_{h\to 0} (-1)$$

$$= -1.$$

Since Rf′(0) ≠ Lf′(0), therefore the function f(x) is not differentiable at x = 0.

Example 11:

Test two function for continuity

f(x) = x sin (1/x), x ≠ 0 and f(0) = 0 at x = 0.

Solution:

We have

$$f(0+0) = \lim_{h\to 0} f(0+h) = \lim_{h\to 0} f(h) = \lim_{h\to 0} h \sin\frac{1}{h} = 0.$$

Again $f(0-0) = \lim_{h\to 0} \lim_{h\to 0} f(0-h) = \lim_{h\to 0} f(-h)$

$$= \lim_{h\to 0}(-h)\sin\left(-\frac{1}{h}\right) = 0.$$

Also f(0) = 0. Thus f(0 + 0) = f(0 – 0) = f(0). Therefore f(x) is continuous at x = 0.

Note: If we are given that f(0) = 2, the above function becomes discontinuous at x = 0.

Example 12:

Give ∈ – δ definition of continuity of a function f at a point use this definition to show that if f is continuous at c, then so |B| |f| is the converse true 3 justify.

Solution:

A function f is said to be continuous at a point c_1 if for any ∈ > 0 three exist some δ > 0 such that

$|f(x) - f(c)| < \in$ when $|x - c| < \delta$ ...(1)

Now we show that if f is continuous at c then |f| is continuous at c.

We know

$||x| - |f|| \le |x - y|$ for all x, y ∈ R

$||f(x)| - |f(c)|| \le |f(x) - f(c)|$ ...(2)

from equation (1) and (2) we get

$\therefore |f(x) - |f(c)| < \in$ when $|x - c| < \delta$

Hence |f| is continuous at c

However, the converse is not true *i.e.* If |t| is continuous at a point.

Then f may not be continuous at that point

Let $f(x) = \begin{cases} \dfrac{|x|}{x} & \text{if } x \neq 0 \\ 1 & \text{if } x = 0 \end{cases}$

We have $\lim_{x\to 0} f(x) = \lim_{x\to 0} \frac{-x}{x} = -1$

$\lim_{x\to 0} f(x) = \lim_{x\to 0} \frac{x}{n} = 1$

$f(0) = 1$

Hence f is discontinuous at x = 0

We have [| f | (x) = 1 ∀ x ∈ n]

i.e., | f | is a constant function and so | f | is continuous at ever point of R including x = 0

Example 13:

Discuss the points of discontinuity of the function given by:

$$f(x) = \begin{cases} -x, & \text{for } x \le 0 \\ x, & \text{for } 0 < x \le 1 \\ 2-x, & \text{for } 1 < x \le 2 \\ 1, & \text{for } x > 2 \end{cases}$$

Solution:

Here we shall test f(x) for continuity at the points x = 0, 1 and 2. Obviously at all other points the function is continuous.

(i) Continuity at x = 0. We have f(0) = 0, because f(x) = – x for x = 0.

L.H.L. of f(0) as x → 0 *i.e.*,

$f(0-0) = \lim_{h\to 0} f(0-h)\, f(-h) = \lim_{h\to 0}[-(-h)]$, [∵ f(x) = –x or x < 0]

$= \lim_{h\to 0}(h) = 0$;

R.H.L. of f(x) as x → 0 *i.e.*,

$f(0+0) = \lim_{h\to 0} f(0+h) = \lim_{h\to 0} f(h) = \lim_{h\to 0} h$,

[∵ f(x) = x for 0 < x ≤ 1]

= 0.

R.H.L. = L.H.L.

Thus, f(0 – 0) = f(0 + 0) = f(0) and so f(x) is continuous at x = 0.

(ii) Continuity at x = 1. We have f(1) = 1, because f(x) = x for 0 < x ≤ 1.

Now L.H.L. of f(x) as $x \to 1$ *i.e.*,

$f(1-0) = \lim_{h\to 0} f(1-h) = \lim_{h\to 0} (1-h)$,

[$\because f(x) = x$ for $0 < x \le 1$]

$= 1$;

and R.H.L. $f(1+0) = \lim_{h\to 0} f(1+h) = \lim_{h\to 0} [2-(1+h)]$,

[$\because f(x) = 2 - x$ for $0 < x \le 2$]

$\lim_{h\to 0} (1-h) = 1$.

L.H.L. = R.H.L.

Since $f(1-0) = f(1+0) = f(1)$, therefore f(x) is continuous at $x = 1$.

(iii) Continuity at x = 2. We have $f(2) = 2 - 2 = 0$, because f(x) 2 – x, for $1 < x \le 2$.

L.H.L. of f(x) as $x \to 2$ *i.e.*,

$f(2-0) = \lim_{h\to 0} f(2-h) = \lim_{h\to 0} [2-(2-h)]$,

[$\because f(x) = 2 - x$, for $1 < x \le 2$]

$= \lim_{h\to 0} (h) = 0$;

and R.H.L. $= f(2+0) = \lim_{h\to 0} f(2+h) = \lim_{h\to 0} (1)$,

$= 1$

[$\because f(x) = 1$ for $x > 2$]

L.H.L. = R.H.L.

Since $f(2+0) \neq f(2-0)$, the function f(x) is discontinuous at $x = 2$.

Example 14:

Discuss the continuity of the function f(x) at $x = \frac{1}{2}$ *where* $f(x) = x$, $0 \le x < \frac{1}{2}$; $f(x) = 1$, $x = \frac{1}{2}$; $f(x) = 1 - x$, $\frac{1}{2} < x \le 1$.

Solution:

We have $f(x) = 1$, when $x = \frac{1}{2}$.

Now R.H.L. $= \lim_{h\to 0} f\left(\frac{1}{2} + h\right)$, where h is +ive and sufficiently small

$= \lim_{h \to 0}\left[1-\left(\frac{1}{2}+h\right)\right],$ $\left[\because f(x)=1-x \text{ when } \frac{1}{2}<x\le 1\right]$

$= \lim_{h \to 0}\left(\frac{1}{2}-h\right)=\frac{1}{2},$

L.H.L. $= \lim_{h \to 0} f\left(\frac{1}{2}-h\right),$ $\left[\because f(x)=x \text{ when } 0\le x<\frac{1}{2}\right]$

Since R.H.L. = L.H.L. ≠ the value of f(x) at $x=\frac{1}{2}$, therefore the function is discontinuous at $x=\frac{1}{2}$.

Example 15:

Define continuity of a function f(x) at x = a. Discuss the continuity of the function f(x) defined as:

f(0) = 0; f9x) = 1 – x, 0 < x < 1; f(1) = 1;

f(x) = 2 – x, 1 < x < 2; f(2) = 0

at the points x = 0, 1, 2,.

Solution:

For definition of continuity

(i) To test f(x) for continuity at x = 0. We have f(0) = 0.

Now $f(0+0) = \lim_{h \to 0} f(1+h) = \lim_{h \to 0} f(h) = \lim_{h \to 0} (1-h)$

$[\because f(x) = 1 - x \text{ for } 0 < x < 1]$

= 1.

As f(0 + 0) ≠ f(0), therefore f(x) is discontinuous at x = 0.

(ii) To test f(x) for continuity at x = 1. We have f(1) = 1.

Now $f(1-0) = \lim_{h \to 0} f(1-h) = \lim_{h \to 0} [1-(1-h)]$

$[\because f(x) = 1 - x \text{ for } 0 < x < 1]$

= 0,

and $f(1+0) = \lim_{h \to 0} f(1+h) = \lim_{h \to 0} [2-(1+h)],$

$[\because f(x) = 2 - x, \text{ for } 1 < x < 2]$

= 1.

∵ f(1 – 0) ≠ f(1 + 0), therefore f(x) is discontinuous at x = 1.

(iii) To test f(x) for continuity at x = 2. We have f(2) = 0.

Now, $f(2-0) = \lim_{h \to 0} f(2-h) = \lim_{h \to 0} [2-(2-h)]$,

[$\because$ f(x) = 2 – x for 1 < x < 2]

= 0.

Since f(2) = f(2 – 0), f(x) is continuous at x = 2.

Note that here f(x) is not defined for x < 2. So the question of finding f(2 + 0) does not arise. Here f(x) will be continuous at x = 2 if f(2) = f(2 – 0).

Example 16:

Determine the continuity of the function f(x) defined as follows:

$$f(0)=0;\ f(x)=\frac{1}{2}-x,\ 0<x<\frac{1}{2};\ f\left(\frac{1}{2}\right)=0;$$

$$f(x) = 4x^2 - 1,\ \frac{1}{2} < x < 3/4;\ f(x) = 1 - x^2,\ 3/4 \le x \le 1.$$

Solution:

The function is continuous at x = 0, 3/4.

Example 17:

A function f(x) is defined as follows:

$$f(x) = \begin{cases} \left(x^2/a\right) - a, & \text{when} \quad x < 0 \\ 0, & \text{when} \quad x = a \\ a - \left(a^2/x\right), & \text{when} \quad x > 0 \end{cases}$$

Prove that the function f(x) is continuous at x = a.

Solution:

We have f(a) = 0.

Also the right hand limit of f(x) at x = a *i.e.*,

$$f(a+0) = \lim_{h \to 0} f(a+h) = \lim_{h \to 0}\left[a - \frac{a^2}{(a+h)}\right],$$

[$\because$ f(x) = a – (a^2/x) for x > a]

= a – (a^2/a) = a – a = 0;

and the left hand limit of f(x) at x = a *i.e.*,

$$f(a-0) = \lim_{h \to 0} f(a-h) = \lim_{h \to 0}\left[\frac{(a-h)^2}{a} - a\right],$$

$[\because f(x) = (x^2/a) - a \text{ for } x < a]$

$= (a^2/a) - a = a - a = 0.$

$\because f(a + 0) = f(a - 0) = f(a)$, therefore f(x) is continuous at x = a.

Example 18:

Give $\in - \delta$ definition of continuity of a function f at a point and use two definition to show that if f is continuous at c then so is | f | is the converse true? Justify.

Solution:

A function f is said to be continuous at a point c. If for any $\in > 0$. There exist some $\delta > 0$ such that

$|f(x) - f(c)| < \in$ when $|x - c| < \delta$ ...(1)

Now we show that if f is continuous at c then |f| f is continuous at c

We know $||x| - |y|| \leq |x - y|$, for all $x, y \in R$

$\therefore ||f(x)| - f(c)|| \leq f(x) - f(c)|$ ...(2)

from (1) and (2) we get

$||f(x) - |f(c)|| < \in$ when $|x - c| < \delta$

Hence δ is continuous at c

However, the converse is not true *i.e.*, if |f| is continuous at a point. Then f may not be continuous at that point

$$\text{Let } f(x) = \begin{cases} \dfrac{|x|}{x} & \text{if } x \neq 0 \\ 1 & \text{if } x = 0 \end{cases}$$

$$\text{we have } \lim_{x\to 0-} f(x) = \lim_{x\to 0} \frac{-x}{x} = -1$$

$$\lim_{x\to 0+} f(x) = \lim_{x\to 0} \frac{x}{x} = 1$$

$$f(0) = 1$$

Hence f is continuous at x = 0

We have $(|f|)(x) = 1 \ \forall x \in R$

i.e. | f | is a constant function and so | f | is continuous at every point of R including x = 0.

Example 19:

Examine the function

$f(x) = (x - a) \sin \{1/(x - a)\}$, when $x \neq a$ and $f(a) = 0$ for continuity at $x = a$.

Solution:

We have R.H.L. = f(a + 0) = $\lim_{h\to 0}$ f(a + h)

$= \lim_{h\to 0} (a + h - a) \sin \{1/(a + h - a)\} = \lim_{h\to 0} h \sin (1/h) = 0.$

Again

L.H.L. $= f(a - 0) = \lim_{h\to 0} f(a - h)$

$= \lim_{h\to 0} (a - h - a) \sin \{1/(a - h - a)\}$

$= \lim_{h\to 0} - h \sin (- 1/h) = 0.$

Also f(a) = 0. Thus, f(a + 0) = f(a – 0) = f(a). Therefore f(x) is continuous at x = a.

Example 20:

Investigate the points of continuity and discontinuity of the following function:

$$f(x) = \frac{1}{x-a} \, cosec\left(\frac{1}{x-a}\right), \; x \neq a;$$

$$f(x) = 0, \qquad x = a.$$

Solution:

We have L.H.L. $f(a + 0) = \lim_{h\to 0} f(a+h)$

$$= \lim_{h\to 0} \frac{1}{a+h-a} \text{cosec}\left(\frac{1}{a+h-a}\right) = \lim_{h\to 0} \frac{1}{h \sin(1/h)}$$

$= + \infty$, since h sin (1/h) → 0 as h → 0.

Again,

$$\text{R.H.L.} = f(a - 0) = \lim_{h\to 0} f(a-h) = \lim_{h\to 0} \frac{1}{a-h-a} \text{cosec}\left(\frac{1}{a-h-a}\right)$$

$$= \lim_{h\to 0} -\frac{1}{h} \cdot \frac{1}{\sin\{-(1/h)\}} = \lim_{h\to 0} \frac{1}{h \sin(1/h)}$$

$= + \infty$, since h sin (1/h) → 0 as h → 0.

Also as given f(a) = 0.

Since f(a + 0) = f(a – 0) → f(a), the function f(x) is discontinuous at x = a, having an infinite discontinuity of second kind.

Example 21:

Examine the function defined below for continuity at x = 0:

$$f(x)=\frac{\sin^2 ax}{x^2} \text{ for } x \neq 0,\ f(x) = 1 \text{ for } x = 0.$$

Solution:

We have f(0) = 1;

$$\text{R.H.L.} = f(0+0) = \lim_{h\to 0} f(0+h) = \lim_{h\to 0} f(h) = \lim_{h\to 0} \frac{\sin^2 ah}{h^2}$$

$$= \lim_{h\to 0}\left(\frac{\sin ah}{ah}\right)^2 . a^2 = 1.a^2 = a^2;$$

$$\text{and L.H.L. } f(0-0) = \lim_{h\to 0} f(0-h) = \lim_{h\to 0} f(-h) = \lim_{h\to 0} \frac{\sin^2(-ah)}{(-h)^2}$$

$$= \lim_{h\to 0} \frac{\sin^2 ah}{h^2} = a^2 .$$

Now f(x) is continuous at x = 0 if and only if

$$f(0) = f(0 + 0) = f(0 - 0).$$

Therefore f(x) is discontinuous at x = 0 unless a = ± 1.

Example 22:

Discuss the continuity at x = 0, 1, 2 of function f(x) defined as follows:

$f(x) = -x^2$ for $x \leq 0$, $f(x) = 5x - 4$ for $0 < x \leq 1$.

$f(x) = 4x^2 - 3x$ for $1 < x < 2$ and $f(x) = 3x + 4$ for $x \geq 2$.

Solution:

(i) Continuity at x = 0. We have $f(0) = -0^2 = 0$;

We have

$$\text{L.H.L.} = f(0-0) = \lim_{h\to 0} f(0-h) = \lim_{h\to 0} f(-h) = \lim_{h\to 0} -(-h)^2$$

$$= \lim_{h\to 0} -h^2 = 0 ;$$

$$\text{and R.H.L. } f(0+0) = \lim_{h\to 0} f(0+h) = \lim_{h\to 0} f(h) = \lim_{h\to 0} (5h-4). \quad [\because 0 < h < 1]$$

$$= 4.$$

Since R.H.L. ≠ L.H.L.

⇒ f(0 + 0) ≠ f(0 − 0), the function f(x) is discontinuous at x = 0.

(ii) Continuity at x = 1. We have f(1) = 5 × 1 – 4 = 1;

R.H.L = $f(1+0) = \lim_{h\to 0} f(1+h) = \lim_{h\to 0} [4(1+h)^2 - 3(1+h)]$,

$[\because 1 < 1+h < 2]$

$= \lim_{h\to 0} [4h^2 + 5h + 1] = 1$;

and L.H.L. $f(1-0) = \lim_{h\to 0} f(1-h) = \lim_{h\to 0} [5(1-h) - 4]$,

$[\because 0 \le 1-h < 1]$

$= \lim_{h\to 0} (1 - 5h) = 1$.

Thus, f(1 + 0) = f(1 – 0) = f(1). Therefore f(x) is continuous at x = 1.

(iii) Continuity at x = 2. We have f(2) = 3 × 2 + 4 = 10;

L.H.L. = $f(2-0) = \lim_{h\to 0} f(2-h) = \lim_{h\to 0} [4(2-h)^2 - 3(2-h)]$;

$[\because 1 < 2-h < 2]$

$= \lim_{h\to 0} [4h^2 - 13h + 10] = 10$;

and R.H.L.= $f(2+0) = \lim_{h\to 0} f(2+h) = \lim_{h\to 0} [3(2+h) + 4]$

$= \lim_{h\to 0} (3h + 10) = 10$

f(2) = f(2 – 0) = f(2 + 0) therefore f(x) continuous at x = 2.

Example 23:

Let $f(x) = x\dfrac{e^{1/x} - e^{-1/x}}{e^{1/x} + e^{-1/x}}$, $x \ne 0$; $f(0) = 0$.

Show that f(x) is continuous but not derivable at x = 0.

Solution:

We have f(0) = 0;

R.H.L. = $f(0+0) = \lim_{h\to 0} f(0+h) = \lim_{h\to 0} f(h)$

$= \lim_{h\to 0} h\dfrac{e^{1/h} - e^{-1/h}}{e^{1/h} + e^{-1/h}} = \lim_{h\to 0} h\dfrac{1 - e^{-2h}}{1 + e^{-2h}}$, dividing Nr. and Dr. by $e^{1/h}$

$= 0 \times \dfrac{1-0}{1+0} = 0 \times 1 = 0$;

andL.H.L. $f(0-0) = \lim_{h\to 0} f(0-h) = \lim_{h\to 0} f(-h)$

$= \lim_{h\to 0} -h.\dfrac{e^{-1/h} - e^{1/h}}{e^{-1/h} + e^{1/h}}$

$$= \lim_{h\to 0} -h\frac{e^{-2/h}-1}{e^{-2/h}+1} = 0\times\frac{0-1}{0+1} = 0.$$

R.H.L. = L.H.L.

$\Rightarrow$ f(0 + 0) = f(0 − 0) = f(0), the function is continuous at x = 0

Now to test f(x) for differentiability at x = 0, e have

$$Rf'(0) = \lim_{h\to 0}\frac{f(0+h)-f(0)}{h} = \lim_{h\to 0}\frac{f(h)-f(0)}{h}$$

$$= \lim_{h\to 0}\left[h\frac{e^{1/h}-e^{-1/h}}{e^{1/h}-e^{-1/h}}-0\right]/h = \lim_{h\to 0}\frac{1-e^{-2/h}}{1+e^{-2/h}} = \frac{1-0}{1+0} = 1,$$

and $$Lf'(0) = \lim_{h\to 0}\frac{f(0-h)-f(0)}{-h} = \lim_{h\to 0}\frac{f(-h)-f(0)}{-h}$$

$$= \lim_{h\to 0}\left[(-h).\frac{e^{-1/h}-e^{1/h}}{e^{-1/h}+e^{1/h}}-0\right]/(-h)$$

$$= \lim_{h\to 0}\frac{e^{-2/h}-1}{e^{-2/h}+1} = \frac{0-1}{0+1} = -1.$$

Since Rf '(0) ≠ Lf '(0), the function is not differentiable at x = 0.

Example 24:

Consider the function f(x) = x – [x], where x is a positive variable, and [x] denotes the integral part of x and show that it is discontinuous for all integral values of x, and continuous for all others. Draw the graph.

Solution:

From the definition of the function f(x), we have

$$f(x) = x - (n-1) \qquad \text{for } n-1 < x < n,$$

$$f(x) = 0 \qquad \text{for } x = n,$$

$$f(x) = x - n \qquad \text{for } n < x < n+1$$

and so on, where n is an integer.

We shall test the function f(x) for continuity at x = n. We have f(n) = 0;

$$f(n+0) = \lim_{h\to 0} f(n+h) = \lim_{h\to 0}\left[(n+h)-n\right] = \lim_{h\to 0} h = 0,$$

$$[\because n < n+h < n+1]$$

and L.H.L. = $$f(n-0) = \lim_{h\to 0} f(n-h) = \lim_{h\to 0}\left[(n-h)-(n-1)\right],$$

$$[\because n-1 < n-h < n]$$

$$= \lim_{h\to 0}(1-h) = 1.$$

Since $f(n+0) \neq f(n-0)$, the function $f(x)$ is discontinuous at $x = n$. Thus, $f(x)$ is discontinuous for all integral values of x. It is obviously continuous for all other values of x.

Since x is a positive variable, putting n = 1, 2, 3, 4, 5, ..., we observe that the graph of f(x) consists of the following:

$$\begin{array}{rl} y = x \text{ when } 0 < x < 1, & y = 0 \text{ when } x = 1 \\ y = x - 1 \text{ when } 1 < x < 2, & y = 0 \text{ when } x = 2 \\ y = x - 2 \text{ when } 2 < x < 3, & y = 0 \text{ when } x = 3 \\ y = x - 3 \text{ when } 3 < x < 4, & y = 0 \text{ when } x = 4 \end{array}$$

and so on.

The graph of the function thus obtained is shown by thick lines from $x = 0$ to $x = 4$.

Example 25:

If $f(x) = \dfrac{xe^{1/x}}{1+e^{1/x}}$ *for* $x \neq 0$ *and* $f(0) = 0$, *show that* $f(x)$ *is continuous at* $x = 0$, *but* $f'(0)$ *does not exist.*

Solution:

Here $f(0) = 0$. Also right hand limit *i.e.*,

R.H.L. $f(0+0) = \lim_{h\to 0} f(0+h) = \lim_{h\to 0} f(h)$

$$= \lim_{h\to 0} \frac{he^{1/h}}{1+e^{1/h}} = \lim_{h\to 0} \frac{h}{e^{-1/h}+1} \text{ (Note)} = \frac{0}{0+1} = 0,$$

and L.H.L. $f(0-0) = \lim_{h\to 0} f(0-h) = \lim_{h\to 0} f(-h)$

$$= \lim_{h\to 0}\left[\frac{-he^{-1/h}}{1+e^{-1/h}}\right] = \frac{0}{1+0} = 0.$$

Since $f(0+0) = f(0-0) = f(0)$, the function is continuous at $x = 0$.

Now we have to the derivative of $f(x)$ at $x = 0$.

We have,

$$Rf'(0) = \lim_{h\to 0} \frac{f(0+h)-f(0)}{h} = \lim_{h\to 0} \frac{f(h)-f(0)}{h}$$

$$= \lim_{h\to 0}\frac{\left(\dfrac{he^{1/h}}{1+e^{1/h}}\right)}{h} = \lim_{h\to 0}\frac{e^{1/h}}{1+e^{1/h}} = \lim_{h\to 0}\frac{1}{e^{1/h}+1}$$

$$= \frac{1}{0+1} = 0$$

and $Lf'(0) = \lim_{h\to 0} = \dfrac{f(0-h)-f(0)}{-h} = \lim_{h\to 0}\dfrac{f(-h)-f(0)}{-h}$

$$= \lim_{h\to 0}\frac{\dfrac{-he^{-1/h}}{1+e^{-1/h}}}{-h} = \lim_{h\to 0}\frac{e^{-1/h}}{1+e^{-1/h}} = \frac{0}{1+0} = 0\cdot$$

Since $Rf'(0) \neq Lf'(0)$, the derivative of f(x) at x = 0 does not exist.

Example 26:

Let $f(x) = \dfrac{x^2}{1+x^2} + \dfrac{x^2}{(1+x^2)^2} + \dfrac{x^2}{(1+x^2)^3} + \dfrac{x^2}{(1+x^2)^4} = \ldots\infty.$

Is f(x) continuous at the origin? Give reasons for your answer.

Solution:

Here the function f(x) forms an infinite G.P whose first terms a is $\dfrac{x^2}{1+x^2}$ and common ratio r is $\dfrac{1}{1+x^2}$ which is less than one when $x \neq 0$.

$$\therefore f(x) = \frac{a}{1-r} = \frac{x^2/(1+x^2)}{1-1/(1+x^2)} = \frac{x^2/(1+x^2)}{x^2/(1+x^2)} = 1, \qquad \text{provided } x \neq 0.$$

Thus, f(x) = 1 for $x \neq 0$ and f(x) = 0 for x = 0.

We have

$$f(0+0) = \lim_{h\to 0} f(0+h) = \lim_{h\to 0} f(h) = \lim_{h\to 0} 1 = 1.$$

Thus $f(0+0) \neq f(0)$ and so f(x) is not continuous at x = 0.

Example 27:

A function f(x) is defined as follows:

$f(x) = 0 \quad for \quad x = 0$

$\phi(x) = \dfrac{1}{2} - x \; for \qquad\qquad 0 < x < \dfrac{1}{2}$

$$\phi(x) = \frac{1}{2} \text{ for } \qquad x = \frac{1}{2}$$

$$\phi(x) = \frac{3}{2} - x \text{ for } \qquad \frac{1}{2} < x < 1$$

$$\phi(x) = 1 \text{ for } \qquad x = 1.$$

Find the points of discontinuity. Also draw the graph of the function.

Solution:

We shall test the function for continuity at $x = 0, \frac{1}{2}$ and 1.

(i) For $x = 0$, we have $\phi(0) = 0$, $\phi(0+0) = \lim_{h \to 0} \phi(0+h)$

$= \lim_{h \to 0} \phi(h) = \lim_{h \to 0} \left(\frac{1}{2} - h\right) = \frac{1}{2}$. Since $\phi(0) \neq \phi(0+0)$, the function $\phi(0)$ is discontinuous at $x = 0$.

(ii) For $x = \frac{1}{2}$, we have $\phi\left(\frac{1}{2}\right) = \frac{1}{2}$, $\phi\left(\frac{1}{2} - 0\right) = \lim_{h \to 0} \phi\left(\frac{1}{2} - h\right)$

$= \lim_{h \to 0} \left[\frac{1}{2} - \left(\frac{1}{2} - h\right)\right]$, $\left(\text{Note that } 0 < \frac{1}{2} - h < \frac{1}{2}\right)$

$= \lim_{h \to 0} h = 0$.

Since $\phi\left(\frac{1}{2} - 0\right) \neq \phi\left(\frac{1}{2}\right)$, the function $\phi(x)$ is discontinuous at $x = \frac{1}{2}$.

(iii) For $x = 1$, we have $\phi(1) = 1$, $\phi(1-0) = \lim_{h \to 0} \phi(1-h)$

$= \lim_{h \to 0} [3/2 - (1-h)]$, $\qquad \left[\text{Note that } \frac{1}{2} < 1 - h < 1\right]$

$= \lim_{h \to 0} \left(\frac{1}{2} + h\right) = \frac{1}{2}$.

Since $\phi(1) \neq \phi(1-0)$, the function $\phi(x)$ is discontinuous at $x = 1$.

Hence the function $\phi(x)$ has three points of discontinuity at $x = 0, \frac{1}{2}$ and 1.

The graph of the function consists of the point (0, 0); the segment of the line $y = \frac{1}{2}, 0 < x < \frac{1}{2}$;

the point $\left(\frac{1}{2}, \frac{1}{2}\right)$; the segment of the line

$y = (3/2) - x, \frac{1}{2} < x < 1$; and the point (1, 1).

Thus, the graph is as shown in the figure. From the graph we observe that the function is discontinuous at x = 0, $\frac{1}{2}$ and 1.

Example 28:

If f(x) = – x for x ≤ 0 and f(x) = + x for x ≥ 0, prove that f(x) is continuous but not differentiable at x = 0.

Solution:

(i) **To test f(x) for continuity at x = 0.** We have f(0) = 0; f(0 + 0)

$= \lim_{h\to 0} f(0+h) = \lim_{h\to 0} f(h) = \lim_{h\to 0} -(-h) = \lim_{h\to 0} h = 0$.

Since f(0 + 0) = f(0 – 0) = f(0), the function f(x) is continuous at x = 0.

(ii) **To test f(x) for differentiability at x = 0.**

We have $Rf'(0) = \lim_{h\to 0} \frac{f(0+h)-f(0)}{h} = \lim_{h\to 0} \frac{f(h)-f(0)}{h}$

$= \lim_{h\to 0} \frac{h-0}{h} = \lim_{h\to 0} 1 = 1$.

Again $Lf'(0) = \lim_{h\to 0} \frac{f(0-h)-f(0)}{-h} = \lim_{h\to 0} \frac{f(-h)-f(0)}{-h}$

$= \lim_{h\to 0} \frac{-(-h)-0}{-h} = \lim_{h\to 0} \frac{h}{-h} = \lim_{h\to 0} -1 = 1$.

Since Lf '(0) ≠ Lf '(0) the function f(x) is not differentiable at x = 0.

Example 29:

Discuss the continuity of the function f(x) defined as follows:

f(x) = x^2 for x < – 2, f(x) = 4 for – 2 ≤ x ≤ 2, f(x) = x^2 for x > 2.

Solution:

We shall test f(x) for continuity only at the points x = – 2 and 2. It is obviously continuous at all other points.

(i) **Continuity of f(x) at x = – 2.** We have f(– 2) = 4;

$f(-2+0) = \lim_{h\to 0} f(-2+h) = \lim_{h\to 0} 4 = 4$;

$f(-2-0) = \lim_{h\to 0} f(-2-h) = \lim_{h\to 0} (-2-h)^2$ [∵ – 2 – h < – 2]

= 4.

Thus f(– 2 + 0) = f(– 2 – 0) = f(– 2). Therefore f(x) is continuous at x = – 2.

(ii) Continuity of f(x) at x = 2. We have f(2) = 4;

$$f(2+0)=\lim_{h\to 0} f(2+h)=\lim_{h\to 0}(2+h)^2=4.$$

and $f(2-0)=\lim_{h\to 0} f(2-h)=\lim_{h\to 0}(2-h)^2=4=4.$

Thus, f(x) is also continuous at x = 2.

Example 30:

Discuss the continuity and differentiability of the function f(x) defined as follows:

f(x) = 1 for – ∞ < x 0, f(x) = 1 + sin x for 0 ≤ x < π/2,

$$f(x) = 2 + \left(x-\frac{\pi}{2}\right)^2 \text{ for } \frac{\pi}{2} \le x < \infty.$$

Solution:

We shall test f(x) for continuity and differentiability at x = 0 and π/2. It is obviously continuous as well as differentiable at all other points.

(i) *Continuity and differentiability of f(x) at x = 0.* We have

f(0) = 1 + sin 0 = 1; f(0 + 0) = $\lim_{h\to 0} f(0+h)$

$= \lim_{h\to 0} f(h)=\lim_{h\to 0}(1+\sin h)=1$; and

$f(0-0)=\lim_{h\to 0} f(0-h)$

$= \lim_{h\to 0} f(-h)=\lim_{h\to 0} 1=1.$ Thus, f(0) = f(0 + 0) = f(0 – 0) and therefore f(x) is continuous at x = 0.

Now $Rf'(0)=\lim_{h\to 0}\dfrac{f(0+h)-f(0)}{h}=\lim_{h\to 0}\dfrac{f(h)-f(0)}{h}$

$$=\lim_{h\to 0}\frac{(1+\sin h)-(1+\sin 0)}{h}=\lim_{h\to 0}\frac{\sin h}{h}=1;$$

and $Lf'(0)=\lim_{h\to 0}\dfrac{f(0-h)-f(0)}{-h}=\lim_{h\to 0}\dfrac{f(-h)-f(0)}{-h}$

$$=\lim_{h\to 0}\frac{1-(1+\sin 0)}{-h}=\lim_{h\to 0}\frac{0}{-h}=\lim_{h\to 0} 0=0.$$

Since Rf '(0) ≠ Lf '(0), f(x) is not differentiable at x = 0.

(ii) *Continuity and differentiability of f(x) at x = π/2.* We have

$$f\left(\frac{\pi}{2}\right)=2+\left(\frac{\pi}{2}-\frac{\pi}{2}\right)^2=2;$$

$$f\left(\frac{\pi}{2}+0\right)=\lim_{h\to 0} f\left(\frac{\pi}{2}+h\right)=\lim_{h\to 0}\left[2+\frac{\pi}{2}\left\{\left(\frac{\pi}{2}+h\right)-\frac{\pi}{2}\right\}^2\right]$$

$$=\lim_{h\to 0}\left(2+h^2\right)=2;$$

and $f\left(\frac{\pi}{2}-0\right)=\lim_{h\to 0} f\left(\frac{\pi}{2}-h\right)=\lim_{h\to 0}\left[1+\sin\left(\frac{\pi}{2}-h\right)\right]$

$$=\lim_{h\to 0}(1+\cos h)=1+1=2.$$

Thus, $f\left(\frac{\pi}{2}+0\right)=f\left(\frac{\pi}{2}-0\right)=f\left(\frac{\pi}{2}\right)$

and therefore f(x) is continuous at $x=\frac{\pi}{2}$.

Now $Rf'\left(\frac{\pi}{2}\right)=\lim_{h\to 0}\frac{f(\pi/2+h)-f(\phi/2)}{h}$

$$=\lim_{h\to 0}\frac{\left[2+\{\pi/2+h-\pi/2\}\right]-\left[2+(\pi/2-\pi/2)^2\right]}{h}$$

$$=\lim_{h\to 0}\frac{2+h^2-2}{h}=\lim_{h\to 0} h=0;$$

and $Lf'\left(\frac{\pi}{2}\right)=\lim_{h\to 0}\frac{f(\pi/2-h)-f(\pi/2)}{-h}$

$$=\lim_{h\to 0}\frac{1+\sin(\pi/2-h)-2}{-h}$$

$$=\lim_{h\to 0}\frac{-1+\cos h}{-h}=\lim_{h\to 0}\frac{1-\cos h}{h}=\lim_{h\to 0}\frac{2\sin^2(h/2)}{h}$$

$$=\lim_{h\to 0}\left[\frac{\sin h/2}{h/2}\sin h/2\right]=1\times 0=0.$$

Thus, Rf '(0) = Lf '(0) and so f(x) is differentiable at x = π/2.

Example 31:

A function f(x) is defined as follows:

f(x) = 1 + x if x ≤ 2 and f(x) = 5 − x if x ≥ 2.

Is the function continuous at x = 2?

Solution:

We have f(2) = 1 + 2 or 5 – 2 = 3;

$f(2+0) = \lim_{h\to 0} f(2+h)$, where h is +ive and sufficiently small

$= \lim_{h\to 0} [5-(2+h)]$, [$\because$ 2 + h > 2 and f(x) = 5 – x if x > 2]

$= \lim_{h\to 0} (3-h) = 3$

and $f(2-0) = \lim_{h\to 0} f(2-h)$, where h is +ive and sufficiently small

$= \lim_{h\to 0} [1+(2-h)]$, [$\because$ 2 – h < 2 and f(x) = 1 + x if x < 2]

$= \lim_{h\to 0} (2-h) = 3$

Since f(2 + 0) = f(2 – 0) = f(2), the function f(x) is continuous at x = 2.

Example 32:

If f(x) = x² sin(1/x) for x ' 0 and f(0) = 0, show that f(x) is continuous and differentiable at x = 0.

Solution:

(i) *To test f(x) for continuity at x = 0.* We have f(0) = 0;

$$f(0+0) = \lim_{h\to 0} f(0+h) = \lim_{h\to 0} f(h) = \lim_{h\to 0} h^2 \sin\frac{1}{h} = 0;$$

and $f(0-0) = \lim_{h\to 0} f(0-h) = \lim_{h\to 0} f(-h)$

$$= \lim_{h\to 0} (-h)^2 \sin(-1/h)$$

$$= \lim_{h\to 0} h^2 \sin\frac{1}{h} = 0.$$

Now f(0 + 0) = f(0 – 0) = f(0) implies that f(x) is continuous at x = 0.

(ii) *To test f(x) for differentiability at x = 0.* We have

$$Rf'(0) = \lim_{h\to 0} \frac{f(0+h)-f(0)}{h} = \lim_{h\to 0} \frac{f(-h)-f(0)}{-h}$$

$$= \lim_{h\to 0} \frac{h^2 \sin(1/h) - 0}{h} = \lim_{h\to 0} h \sin\frac{1}{h} = 0.$$

Again $Lf'(0) = \lim_{h\to 0} \frac{f(0-h)-f(0)}{-h} = \lim_{h\to 0} \frac{f(-h)-f(0)}{-h}$

$$= \lim_{h\to 0} \frac{(-h)^2 \sin(-1/h) - 0}{-h} = \lim_{h\to 0} \frac{-h^2 \sin(1/h)}{-h}$$

$$= \lim_{h\to 0} h \sin\frac{1}{h} = 0.$$

Now, Rf (0) = Lf '(0) implies that f(x) is differentiable at x = 0. The derivative of f(x) at x = 0 has the value zero.

Example 33:

Examine the following curve for continuity and differentiability:

$y = x^2$ for $x \le 0$, $y = 1$ for $0 < x < 1$, $y = 1/x$ for $x > 1$.

Solution:

Let y = f(x). We need to test f(x) for continuity and differentiability at the points x = 0 and 1. It is obviously continuous and differentiable at all other points.

At x = 0. We have f(0) = 0^2 = 0; f(0 + 0) = $\lim_{h\to 0} f(0+h)$ $= \lim_{h\to 0} f(h) = \lim_{h\to 0} 1 = 1$. Since f(0 + 0) ≠ f(0), the function f(x) is not continuous at x = 0. Consequently it is also not differentiable at x = 0.

At x = 1. The function f(x) is not defined at x = 1. Therefore it is discontinuous as well as non-differentiable at x = 1.

Example 34:

Give an example to show that a continuous function need not be differentiable.

Solution:

Here we shall give one more such example. Consider the function f(x) defined as follows:

f(x) = x sin (1/x) for x ≠ 0, f(0) = 0.

As already proved in part (b) this function f(x) is continuous at x = 0. Now we shall show that the function f(x) is not differentiable at x = 0. We have

$$Rf'(0) = \lim_{h\to 0} \frac{f(0+h) - f(0)}{h} = \lim_{h\to 0} \frac{f(h) - f(0)}{h}$$

$$= \lim_{h\to 0} \frac{h \sin(1/h) - 0}{h}$$

$= \lim_{h \to 0} \sin \frac{1}{h}$, which does not exist.

Similarly, Lf (0) does not exist. Hence f(x) is not differentiable at x = 0.

Example 35:

Examine the following curve for continuity and differentiability at the points $x = \pm 1$:

$$y = x - 1 \text{ for } x \geq 1,\ y = \frac{3}{2} + x \text{ for } x \leq -1,$$
$$y = 1 + x + x^2 + x^3 + \ldots \infty \text{ for } -1 < x < 1.$$

Solution:

Obviously $y = \frac{1}{1-x}$ for $-1 < x < 1$. Let y = f(x).

(i) *At* $x = 1$. We have f(1) = 1 – 1 = 0;

$$f(1+0) = \lim_{h \to 0} f(1+h) = \lim_{h \to 0} (1+h-1) = 0;$$

and $f(1-0) = \lim_{h \to 0} f(1-h) = \lim_{h \to 0} \frac{1}{1-(1-h)} = \lim_{h \to 0} \frac{1}{h} = \infty.$

Since f(1 + x) ' f(1 – 0), the function f(x) is not continuous at x = 1. Consequently f(x) is also not differentiable at x = 1.

(ii) *At* $x = -1$. We have $f(-1) = \frac{3}{2} - 1 = \frac{1}{2}$;

$$f(-1+0) = \lim_{h \to 0} f(-1+h) = \lim_{h \to 0} \frac{1}{1-(-1+h)}$$

$$= \lim_{h \to 0} \frac{1}{2-h} = \frac{1}{2};$$

and $f(-1-0) = \lim_{h \to 0} f(-1-h) = \lim_{h \to 0} \left[\frac{3}{2} + (-1-h)\right]$

$$= \lim_{h \to 0} \left(\frac{1}{2} - h\right) = \frac{1}{2}.$$

Since f(– 1 + 0) = f(– 1 – 0) = f(– 1), the function f(x) is continuous at x = – 1.

Now $$Rf'(-) = \lim_{h \to 0} \frac{f(-1+h) - f(-1)}{h}$$

$$= \lim_{h \to 0} \frac{\frac{1}{1-(-1+h)} - \left(\frac{3}{2} - 1\right)}{h} = \lim_{h \to 0} \frac{\frac{1}{2-h} - \frac{1}{2}}{h}$$

$$= \lim_{h\to 0} \frac{2-2+h}{2h(2-h)} = \lim_{h\to 0} \frac{1}{2(2-h)} = \frac{1}{4}.$$

Again $Lf'(-1) = \lim_{h\to 0} \frac{f(-1-h)-f(-1)}{-h}$

$$= \lim_{h\to 0} \frac{\left[\frac{3}{2}+(-1-h)\right]-\left(\frac{3}{2}-1\right)}{-h}$$

$$= \lim_{h\to 0} \frac{\frac{1}{2}-h-\frac{1}{2}}{-h} = \lim_{h\to 0} 1 = 1.$$

Since $Rf'(-1) \neq Lf'(-1)$, the function f(x) is not differentiable at x = – 1.

Example 36:

If $f(x) = \dfrac{xe^{1/x}}{1+e^{1/x}}$ *for* $x \neq 0$ *and* $f(0) = 0$, *show that f(x) is continuous at x = 0, but f '(0) does not exist.*

Solution:

Here f(0) = 0. Also right hand limit *i.e.*,

R.H.L. $= f(0+0) = \lim_{h\to 0} f(0+h) = \lim_{h\to 0} f(h)$

$$= \lim_{h\to 0} \frac{he^{1/e}}{1+e^{1/h}} = \lim_{h\to 0} \frac{h}{e^{-1/h}+1} \text{ (Note)} = \frac{0}{0+1} = 0,$$

and L.H.L. $= f(0-0) = \lim_{h\to 0} f(0-h) = \lim_{h\to 0} f(-h)$

$$= \lim_{h\to 0} \left[\frac{-he^{1/h}}{1+e^{-1/h}}\right] = \frac{0}{1+0} = 0$$

Since f(0 + 0) = f(0 – 0) = f(0), the function is continuous at x = 0.

Now we have to the derivatives of f(x) at x = 0.

We have,

$$Rf'(0) = \lim_{h\to 0} \frac{f(0+h)-f(0)}{h} = \lim_{h\to 0} \frac{f(h)-f(0)}{h}$$

$$= \lim_{h\to 0} \frac{\left(\frac{he^{1/h}}{1+e^{1/h}}\right)}{h} = \lim_{h\to 0} \frac{e^{1/h}}{1+e^{1/h}} = \lim_{h\to 0} \frac{1}{e^{1/h}+1}$$

$$= \frac{1}{0+1} = 0$$

and $Lf'(0) = \lim_{h \to 0} \frac{f(0-h)-f(0)}{-h} = \lim_{h \to 0} \frac{f(-h)-f(0)}{-h}$

$$= \lim_{h \to 0} \frac{\frac{-he^{-1/h}}{1+e^{-1/h}} - 0}{-h} = \lim_{h \to 0} \frac{e^{-1/h}}{1+e^{-1/h}} = \frac{0}{1+0} = 0\cdot$$

Since $Rf'(0) \neq Lf'(0)$, the derivative of f(x) at x = 0 does not exist.

Example 37:

Define the limit of a function. Discuss the existence of the limit of the function $f(x) = 1$, if $x < 1$; $f(x) = 2 - x$, if $1 < x < 2$; $f(x) = 2$, if $x \geq 2$ at $x = 1$ and $x = 2$.

Solution:

For definition of limit (see definition)

R.H.L. At x = 1,

i.e., $f(1 + 0) = \lim_{h \to 0} f(1 + h)$,

where h is +ive and sufficiently small

$$= \lim_{h \to 0} [2 - (1 + h) = \lim_{h \to 0} (1 - h) = 1;$$

L.H.L. At x = 1,

i.e., $f(1 - 0) = \lim_{h \to 0} f(1 - h) = \lim_{h \to 0} (1) = 1$

since R.H.L. = L.H.L. = 1,

therefore $= \lim_{x \to 1} f(x)$ exists and is equal to 1.

R.H.L At x = 2,

i.e., $f(2 + 0) = \lim_{h \to 0} f(2 + h) = \lim_{h \to 0} (2) = 2;$

L.H.L. At x = 2,

i.e., $f(2 - 0) = \lim_{h \to 0} (2 - h) = \lim_{h \to 0} [2 - (2 - h)]$

$$= \lim_{h \to 0} h = 0.$$

$\because$ left hand limit ≠ right hand limit,

$\therefore$ $f = \lim_{x \to 2} f(x)$ does not exist.

Example 38:

Prove that $\lim_{h\to 0}(1 + x)^{1/x} = e.$

Solution:

Let$f(x) = (1 + x)^{1/x}$.

We have R.H.L.= $f(0 + 0) = \lim_{h\to 0} f(0 + h) = \lim_{h\to 0} f(h) = \lim_{h\to 0}(1 + h)^{1/h}$

$$= \lim_{h\to 0}\left[1+\frac{1}{h}.h + \frac{\frac{1}{h}\left(\frac{1}{h}-1\right)}{1.2}h^2 + \frac{\frac{1}{h}\left(\frac{1}{h}-1\right)\left(\frac{1}{h}-2\right)}{1.2.3}h^3 + ...\right]$$

$$= \lim_{h\to 0}\left[1+\frac{1}{1!} + \frac{1.(1-h)}{2!} + \frac{1.(1-h)(1-2h)}{3!} + ...\right]$$

$$= 1+\frac{1}{1!} + \frac{1}{2!} + \frac{1}{3!} + ...\infty = e.$$

We have, R.H.L. $f(0 - 0) = \lim_{h\to 0} f(0 - h) = \lim_{h\to 0} f(-h)$

$$= \lim_{h\to 0} f(1 - h)^{-1/h} = e.$$

Since both $f(0 + 0)$ and $f(0 - 0)$ exist and are equal to e, therefore $\lim_{x\to 0}(1 + x)^{1/x} = e$.

Example 39:

Evaluate the following limits if they exist: $\lim_{x\to 2}\frac{x^2-4}{x-2}$.

Solution:

Let $f(x) = \frac{x^2-4}{x-2} = \frac{(x-2)(x+2)}{x-2}$

R.H.L.x = 2, $f(2 + 0) = \lim_{h\to 0} f(2 + h)$

$$= \lim_{h\to 0}\frac{(2+h-2)(2+h+2)}{2+h-2} = \lim_{h\to 0}\frac{h(h+4)}{h}$$

$$= \lim_{h\to 0}(h + 4) = 4.$$

L.H.L. x = 2, *i.e.*, $f(2 - 0) = \lim_{h\to 0} f(2 - h)$

$$= \lim_{h\to 0}\frac{(2-h-2)(2-h+2)}{2-h-2} = \lim_{h\to 0}\frac{-h(-h+4)}{-h}$$

$= \lim_{h\to 0}(-h + 4) = 4.$

Since both f(2 + 0) f = f(2 – 0), therefore $\lim_{x\to 2} f(x)$ exists and is equal to 4.

Example 40:

Evaluate the limits: $\lim_{x\to 0}\frac{1+3x^2}{x}$.

Solution:

We have $\lim_{x\to 0}\frac{1+3x^2}{x}$

Let $f(x) = \frac{1+3x^2}{x}$

We get, R.H.L. *i.e.*, $f(0 + 0) = \lim_{h\to 0} f(0 + h) = \lim_{h\to 0} f(h)$

$$= \lim_{h\to 0}\frac{1+3h^2}{h} = \lim_{h\to 0}\left(\frac{1}{h}+3h\right) = \infty$$

Again, L.H.L. *i.e.*, $f(0 - 0) = \lim_{h\to 0} f(0 - h) = \lim_{h\to 0} f(-h)$

$$= \lim_{h\to 0}\frac{1+3h^2}{-h} = \lim_{h\to 0}\left(-\frac{1}{h}-3h\right) = -\infty$$

R.H.L. ≠ L.H.L

Since f(0 + 0) ≠ f(0 – 0), therefore $\lim_{x\to 0} f(x)$ does not exist.

Example 41:

Show that $\lim_{x\to 2}\frac{|x-2|}{x-2}$ *does not exist.*

Solution:

Let $f(x) = \frac{|x-2|}{(x-2)}$

Here, R.H.L., $f(2 + 0) = \lim_{h\to 0} f(2 + h) = \lim_{h\to 0}\frac{|2+h-2|}{(2+h-2)} = 1$

L.H.L., $f(2 - 0) = \lim_{h\to 0} f(2 - h) = \lim_{h\to 0}\frac{|2-h-2|}{(2-h-2)}$

$$= \lim_{h\to 0}\frac{|-h|}{-h} = \lim_{h\to 0}\frac{h}{-h} = -1.$$

Since both f(2 + 0) and f(2 – 0), therefore $\lim_{x\to 2}\frac{|x-2|}{x-2}$ does not exist.

Example 42:

Evaluate: $\lim_{x\to 1}\frac{x^3-1}{x^2-1}$.

Solution:

We have $\lim_{x\to 1}\frac{x^3-1}{x^2-1} = \lim_{x\to 1}\frac{(x-1)(x^2+x+1)}{(x-1)(x+1)}$

$$\lim_{x\to 1}\frac{x^2+x+1}{x+1} = \frac{3}{2} \text{ Ans.}$$

Example 43:

Evaluate: $\lim_{x\to 2}\frac{x^2+3x+2}{x-2}$

Solution:

Let $f(x) = \frac{x^2+3x+2}{x-2}$

We have, R.H.L. *i.e.*, $f(2 + 0) = \lim_{h\to 0} f(2 + h)$

$$= \lim_{h\to 0}\frac{(2+h)^2+3(2+h)+2}{2+h-2} = \lim_{h\to 0}\frac{12+7h+h^2}{h}$$

$$= \lim_{h\to 0}\left(\frac{12}{h}+7+h\right) = \infty$$

Also, L.H.L. *i.e.*, $f(2 - 0) = \lim_{h\to 0} f(2 - h)$

$$= \lim_{h\to 0}\frac{(2-h)^2+3(2-h)+2}{2-h-2} = \lim_{h\to 0}\frac{12-7h+h^2}{-h}$$

$$= \lim_{h\to 0}\left(-\frac{12}{h}+7-h\right) = -\infty$$

Since $f(2 + 0) \neq f(2 - 0)$, therefore $\lim_{x\to 2} f(x)$ does not exist.

Example 44:

Evaluate: $\lim_{x\to 0}\frac{(1+x)^{1/3}-(1+x)^{1/3}}{x}$

Solution:

We have $\lim\limits_{x\to 0}\dfrac{(1+x)^{1/3}-(1-x)^{1/3}}{x} = \lim\limits_{h\to 0}\dfrac{(1+h)^{1/3}-(1-h)^{1/3}}{h}$

$$= \lim_{h\to 0}\frac{1+\frac{1}{3}h+\ldots-(1-\frac{1}{3}h+\ldots)}{h} = \lim_{h\to 0}\frac{\frac{2}{3}h+\ldots}{h} = \frac{2}{3}.$$

Example 45:

Evaluate: $\lim\limits_{x\to 0} e^{-1/x}$.

Solution:

We have $\lim\limits_{x\to 0} e^{-1/x}$ let $f(x) = e^{1/x}$.

R.H.L. $f(0 + 0) = \lim\limits_{h\to 0} f(0 + h) = \lim\limits_{h\to 0} f(h) = \lim\limits_{h\to 0} e^{-1/h} - \infty$

$$= \lim_{h\to 0}\frac{1}{e^{1/h}} = 0.$$

Again, L.H.L. $f(0 - 0) = \lim\limits_{h\to 0} f(-h) = \lim\limits_{h\to 0} e^{1/h} \quad - \infty$

Since $f(0 + 0) \neq f(0 - 0)$ therefore $\lim\limits_{x\to 0} e^{-1/x}$ does not exist.

Example 46:

Evaluate: $\lim\limits_{x\to 0}\dfrac{1}{1-e^{1/x}}$.

Solution:

We have $\lim\limits_{x\to 0}\dfrac{1}{1-e^{1/x}}$

Let $f(x) = \dfrac{1}{1-e^2x}$

We have $f(0 + 0) = \lim\limits_{h\to 0} f(h) = \lim\limits_{h\to 0}\dfrac{1}{1-e^{1/h}} = 0$

Again $f(0 - 0) = \lim\limits_{h\to 0} f(-h) = \lim\limits_{h\to 0}\dfrac{1}{1-e^{-1/h}}$

$$= \lim_{h\to 0}\frac{1}{1-(1/e^{1/h})} = 1$$

L.H.L $\neq$ R.H.L

$\because f(0 + 0) \neq f(0 - 0) \therefore \lim_{x\to 0} \frac{1}{1-e^{1/x}}$ does not exist.

Example 47:

Evaluate: $\lim_{x\to 0} \frac{\sin x}{x}$

Solution:

Let $\quad f(x) \frac{\sin x}{x}$

We have R.H.L. $= f(0 + 0) = \lim_{h\to 0} f(0 + h) = \lim_{h\to 0} f(h) = \lim_{h\to 0} \frac{\sin h}{h}$

$$= \lim_{h\to 0} \frac{h - \frac{h^3}{3!} + \frac{h^5}{5!} - \dots}{h} = \lim_{h\to 0}\left(1 - \frac{h^2}{3!} + \frac{h^4}{5!} - \dots\right) = 1$$

L.H.L., $= f(0 - 0) = \lim_{h\to 0} f(0- h) = \lim_{h\to 0} f(- h)$

$$= \lim_{h\to 0} \frac{\sin(-h)}{h} = \lim_{h\to 0} \frac{\sin h}{h} = 1.$$

L.H.L. = R.H.L.

Since $f(0 + 0) \neq f(0 - 0) = 1$ therefore $\lim_{x\to 0} \frac{\sin x}{x} = 1.$

Example 48:

Evaluate: $\lim_{x\to\infty} \frac{\sin x}{x}.$

Solution:

Put $x = \frac{1}{y}$. Then $= \lim_{h\to\infty} = \frac{\sin x}{x} = \lim_{y\to 0} y \sin\left(\frac{1}{y}\right)$

Now let $f(y) = y \sin\left(\frac{1}{y}\right)$.

We have R.H.L. $f(0 + 0) = \lim_{h\to 0} f(0 + h) = \lim_{h\to 0} f(h) = \lim_{h\to 0} h \sin\left(\frac{1}{h}\right) = 0$

Since $\sin\left(\frac{1}{h}\right)$ lies between -1 and 1.

Also L.H.L. $f(0 - 0) = \lim_{h\to 0} f(0 - h) = \lim_{h\to 0} f(-h) = \lim_{h\to 0} (-h)$

$$= \lim_{h\to 0} f \sin\left(-\frac{1}{h}\right) = \lim_{h\to 0} h \sin\left(\frac{1}{h}\right) = 0$$

Since both the limits f(0 + 0) and f(0 – 0) exist and are equal to zero, therefore $\lim_{y\to 0} y \sin\left(\frac{1}{y}\right) = 0$, Hence $\lim_{x\to\infty} \frac{\sin x}{x} = 0.$

Example 49:

Evaluate: $\lim_{x\to 0} = \sin\frac{1}{x}$.

Solution:

Let $f(x) = \sin\frac{1}{x}$

We have $f(0 + 0) = \lim_{h\to 0} f(0 + h) = \lim_{h\to 0} f(h) = \lim_{h\to 0} \sin\left(\frac{1}{h}\right)$

As $h \to 0$, the value of $\sin\left(\frac{1}{h}\right)$ oscillates between + 1 and –1, passing through zero and intermediate values an infinite number of times. Thus, there is no definite number A to which $\sin\left(\frac{1}{h}\right)$ tends as h hends to zero. Therefore the right hand limit f(0 + 0) does not exist.

Similarly, the left hand limit f(0 – 0) also does not exist. Hence $\lim_{x\to 0} \sin\frac{1}{x}$ does not exist.

Example 50:

Evaluate: $\lim_{x\to a} = \frac{x^m - a^m}{x - a}$.

Solution:

$$\lim_{x\to a} \frac{x^m - a^m}{x - a}$$

Let $f(x) = \frac{x^m - a^m}{x - a}$

We have R.H.L. $f(a + 0) = \lim_{h\to 0} f(a + h) = \lim_{h\to 0} = \frac{(a-h)^m - a^m}{a + h - a}$

$$= \lim_{h\to 0} \frac{a^m\left[\left(1+\frac{h}{a}\right)^m - 1\right]}{h}$$

$$= \lim_{h\to 0} \frac{a^m}{h}\left[1+m.\frac{h}{a}+\frac{m(m-1)}{2!}\frac{h^2}{a^2}+...-1\right]$$

$$\lim_{h\to 0}\left[\frac{h}{a}+\frac{m(m-1)}{2}\frac{h}{a^2}+...\right] = a^m.\frac{m}{a} = ma^{m-1}$$

L.H.L. = $f(a-0) = \lim_{h\to 0} f(a-h) = \lim_{h\to 0}\frac{(a-h)^m}{a-h-a} = ma^{m-1}$.

Left hand limit = Right hand limit

Thus, $f(a+0) = f(a-0) = ma^{m-1}$

Therefore $\lim_{x\to a} f(x) = ma^{m-1}$.

Example 51:

Evaluate: $\lim_{x\to 0}\frac{1}{x}e^{1/x}$.

Solution:

Let $f(x) = \frac{1}{x}e^{1/x}$

R.H.L. = $f(0+0) = \lim_{h\to 0} f(0+h) = \lim_{h\to 0} f(h) = \lim_{h\to 0}\frac{1}{h}e^{1/h} = \infty$

[Since both and $e^{1/h}$ tend to ∞ as $h\to 0$]

Again we have

L.H.L. = $f(0-0) = \lim_{h\to 0} f(0-h) = \lim_{h\to 0} f(-h) = \lim_{h\to 0} -\frac{1}{h}e^{-1/h}$

$$= \lim_{h\to 0}\frac{-1}{he^{1/h}} = \lim_{h\to 0}\frac{-1}{h\left(1+\frac{1}{h}+\frac{1}{2!}\frac{1}{h^2}+...\right)}$$

$$= \lim_{h\to 0}\frac{-1}{h+1+(1/2h)+...} = 0.$$

L.H.L. $\neq$ R.H.L. Since both the limits $f(0+0)$ and $f(0-0)$ are unequal, therefore $\lim_{x\to 0}\frac{1}{x}e^{1/x}$ does not exit.

Example 52:

Here the right hand limit i.e., $f(0+0) = h\to 0\, f(0-h)$, where h is +ive and sufficiently small

Evaluate: $\lim_{x\to 0}\frac{e^x-1}{x}$.

Solution:

$= \lim_{h \to 0} f(h) = \lim_{h \to 0} h$, *[∵ h > 0 and f(x) = x when x > 0]*

$= 0.$

Again the left hand limit i.e., f(0 − 0) = $= \lim_{h \to 0} f(0-h)$,

where h is +ive and sufficiently small

$= \lim_{h \to 0} f(-h) = \lim_{h \to 0} -(-h)$, *[∵ − h < 0 and f(x) = − x when x < 0]*

$= \lim_{h \to 0} h = 0$.

Example 53:

Since both the limits f(0 + 0) and f(0 − 0) exist and are equal to zero, therefore $\lim_{x \to 0} f(x)$ *exists and is equal to zero.*

Solution:

Let $f(x) = \frac{e^x - 1}{x} = \frac{1 + x + \frac{x^2}{2!} + ... - 1}{x} = \frac{x\left(1 + \frac{x}{2!} + ...\right)}{x}$.

R.H.L. $f(0 + 0) = \lim_{h \to 0} f(0+h) = \lim_{h \to 0} f(h)$

$= \lim_{h \to 0} \frac{h[1 + (h/2!) + ...]}{h} = \lim_{h \to 0} \left(1 + \frac{h}{2!} + ...\right) = 1$.

L.H.L. $f(0 - 0) = \lim_{h \to 0} f(0-h) = \lim_{h \to 0} f(-h)$

$= \lim_{h \to 0} \frac{-h[1 = (h/2!) + ...]}{-h} = 1$.

Example 54:

Thus, f(0 + 0) = f(0 − 0) = 1. Therefore $\lim_{x \to 0}$ *$(e^x - 1)/x = 1$.*

Evaluate: $\lim_{x \to 0} \frac{a^x - 1}{x}$.

Solution:

$\lim_{x \to 0} \frac{a^x - 1}{x}$. Let $f(x) = \frac{a^x - 1}{x}$

$= \frac{1 + x \log a + (x^2/2!)(\log a)^2 + ... - 1}{x}$

Now, $= \dfrac{x\left[\log a + \frac{1}{2}x\,(\log a)^2 + \ldots\right]}{x}$

R.H.L. $= f(0+0) = \lim\limits_{h\to 0} f(h) = \lim\limits_{h\to 0} \dfrac{h\left[\log a + \frac{h}{2}(\log a)^2 + \ldots\right]}{h} = \log a$.

L.H.L. $= f(0-0) = \lim\limits_{h\to 0} f(0-h) = \lim\limits_{h\to 0} f(-h) = \log a$.

Thus, $f(0+0) = f(0-0) = \log a$. Therefore

$\lim\limits_{x\to 0} \dfrac{(a^x - 1)}{x} = \log a$.

Example 55:

Find the right hand and the left hand limits in the following cases and discuss the existence of the limit in each case:

(i) $\lim\limits_{x\to 2} \dfrac{2x^2 - 8}{x-2}$;

(ii) $\lim\limits_{x\to 0} \dfrac{e^{1/x} - 1}{e^{1/x} + 1}$;

(iii) $\lim\limits_{x\to 0} f(x)$, *where* $f(x)$ *is defined as*

$f(x) = x$, *when* $x > 0$

$f(x) = 0$, *when* $x = 0$

$f(x) = -x$, *when* $x < 0$

Solution:

Let $f(x) = \dfrac{2x^2 - 8}{x-2}$.

We have L.H.L. $= f(2+0) = \lim\limits_{h\to 0} f(2+h) = \lim\limits_{h\to 0} \dfrac{2(2+h)^2 - 8}{2+h-2}$

$= \lim\limits_{h\to 0} \dfrac{2(4+4h+h^2) - 8}{h} = \lim\limits_{h\to 0} \dfrac{8h + 2h^2}{h} = \lim\limits_{h\to 0} \dfrac{h(8+2h)}{h}$

$= \lim\limits_{h\to 0} (8 + 2h) = 8.$

Again L.H.L. *i.e.* = $f(2-0)=\lim_{h\to 0} f(2-h)=\lim_{h\to 0}\frac{2(2-h)^2-8}{2-h-2}$

$$=\lim_{h\to 0}\frac{2(4-4h+h^2)}{-h}=\lim_{h\to 0}\frac{-8h+2h^2}{-h}$$

$$=\lim_{h\to 0}\frac{-h(8-2h)}{-h}=\lim_{h\to 0}(8-2h)=8.$$

Since f(2 + 0) = f(2 – 0) = 8, therefore $\lim_{x\to 0}\frac{2x^2-8}{x-2}$ exists and is equal to 8.

(ii) Let f(x) $f(x)=\frac{e^{1/x}-1}{e^{1/x}+1}$

We have R.H.L.

$$f(0+0)=\lim_{h\to 0} f(0+h)=\lim_{h\to 0} f(h)=\lim_{h\to 0}\frac{e^{1/h}-1}{e^{1/h}+1}$$

$$=\lim_{h\to 0}\frac{e^{1/h}\left[1-\left(1/e^{1/h}\right)\right]}{e^{1/h}\left[1+\left(1/e^{1/h}\right)\right]}=\lim_{h\to 0}\frac{1-\left(1/e^{1/h}\right)}{1+\left(1/e^{1/h}\right)}=1.$$

Again L.H.L. = $f(0-0)=\lim_{h\to 0} f(0-h)=\lim_{h\to 0} f(-h)=\lim_{h\to 0}\frac{e^{-1/h}-1}{e^{-1/h}+1}$

$$=\lim_{h\to 0}\frac{\left(1/e^{1/h}\right)-1}{\left(1/e^{1/h}\right)+1}=\frac{0-1}{0+1}=-1.$$

L.H.L. ≠ R.H.L.

Since f(0 + 0) ≠ f(0 – 0), therefore $\lim_{x\to 0}\frac{e^{1/x}-1}{e^{1/x}+1}$ does not exist.

Example 56:

Evaluate: $\lim_{x\to 0}\frac{(1+x)^n-1}{x}$.

Solution:

$\lim_{x\to 0}\frac{(1+x)^n-1}{x}$. Let $f(x)=\frac{(1+x)^n-1}{x}$

R.H.L. f(0 + 0) = $\lim_{x\to a} f(h)=\lim_{x\to a}\frac{(1+h)^n-1}{h}$

$$= \lim_{h\to 0} \frac{1 + nh + \frac{n(n-1)}{2!}h^2 + \ldots - 1}{h}$$

$$= \lim_{h\to 0} \frac{h\left[n + \frac{n(n-1)}{2!}h + \ldots\right]}{h}$$

$$= \lim_{h\to 0}\left[n + \frac{n(n-1)}{2!}h + \ldots\right] = n.$$

$$\text{L.H.L.} = f(0-0) = \lim_{h\to 0} f(-h) = \lim_{h\to 0} \frac{(1-h)^n - 1}{-h}$$

$$= \lim_{h\to 0} \frac{1 + n(-h) + \frac{n(n-1)}{2!}(-h)^2 + \ldots - 1}{-h} = n.$$

R.H.L. = L.H.L.

Thus, f(0 + 0) = f(0 – 0) = n. Therefore, $\lim_{x\to 0} f(x) = n$.

EXERCISES

1. *Evaluate:* $\lim_{x\to 1} \frac{(x-1)\sqrt{2-x}}{x^2-1}$. $\left[\textbf{Ans. } \frac{1}{2}\right]$

2. $\lim_{x\to 1/2} \frac{8x^3-1}{5x^2-5x+1}$. **[Ans. 6]**

3. $\lim_{x\to 1} \frac{x^m-1}{x^n-1}$ (m and n are integers). $\left[\textbf{Ans. } \frac{m}{n}\right]$

4. $\lim_{x\to 0} \frac{\sqrt{1+x^2}-1}{x}$. **[Ans. 0]**

5. $\lim_{x\to 0} \frac{\sqrt{1+x}-1}{x^2}$. **[Ans. 8]**

6. $\lim_{x\to 0} \frac{\sqrt{x-b}-\sqrt{a-b}}{x^2-a^2}$ (a > b). $\left[\textbf{Ans. } \frac{1}{4a\sqrt{a-b}}\right]$

7. $\lim_{x\to 0} \frac{3\sqrt{1+x^2}-4\sqrt{1-2x}}{x+x^2}$. $\left[\textbf{Ans. } \frac{1}{2}\right]$

8. $\lim_{x\to 1} \frac{3\sqrt{7+x^3} - \sqrt{3-x^2}}{x-1}$. $\left[\textbf{Ans. } -\frac{1}{4}\right]$

9. $\lim_{x\to 0} \frac{1\_\sin x - \cos x}{1-\sin x - \cos x}$. **[Ans. – 1]**

10. $\lim_{y\to a} \left[\sin\frac{y-a}{2} . \tan\frac{\pi 4}{2a}\right]$. $\left[\textbf{Ans. } \frac{-a}{n}\right]$

11. Show that x^r, where x is a positive integer, its continuous at x = a.

12. Show that $\frac{1}{x}$ is continuous at x = a, (a ≠ 0).

13. If f(x) = x for x ≤ 1 and f(x) = x^2 for x < 1 show that f is continuous at x = 1 but not derivable at x = 1.

14. Show that f(x) = x|x| is derivable at the origin.

15. Show that the function f(x) = (x – a) sin $\frac{1}{x-a}$.

16. Show that the function f(x) = |x – 1| + |x + 1| is not derivable at x = – 1, 2 and is deriable at every other point.

3

ELEMENTARY FUNCTIONS AND POWER SERIES

SEQUENCES

Recall that a sequence in a set A is a function from N (the set of positive integers) into A. In this section we shall be concerned only with sequences in C (or as a special case in R). By the term 'sequence' we shall mean 'sequence in C' unless otherwise stated. Sequences in R will be referred to as *real sequences.*

Definition 1:

We say that a sequence $< z_n >$ *has the limit* z_0 *written*

$$\lim_{n\to\infty} z_n = z_0$$

if to each $\varepsilon > 0$*, there exists a positive integer* n_0 *such that*

$$| z_n - z_0 | < \varepsilon \text{ for all } n \geq n_0.$$

A sequence which has a limit is said to be convergent. A sequence which does not converge is said to be divergent.

If $\lim_{n\to\infty} z_n = \infty$, we say that the sequence diverges to infinity

It can be seen that the limit of a sequence, if exists, is unique.

Definition 2:

A sequence $< z_n >$ *is said to be a Cauchy (or Fundamental) sequence if to each* $\varepsilon > 0$*, there exists a positive integer no such that*

$$| z_m - z_n | \; \varepsilon \text{ for all } m, n \geq n_0.$$

Theorem:

Every convergent sequence is a Cauchy sequence.

Proof:

Let $< z_n >$ converge to z_0. Then to each $\varepsilon > 0$, there exists n_0 such that

$$| z_n - z_0 | < \varepsilon/2 \text{ for all } n \geq n_0.$$

Hence ifm $\geq n_0$, $n \geq n_0$,

then $$| z_n - z_0 | < \varepsilon/2 \text{ and } | z_n - z_0 | < \varepsilon/2 \quad ...(1)$$

$\therefore$ $$| z_m - z_n | = | z_m - z_0 + z_0 - z_n$$

$$\leq | z_m - z_0 | + | z_0 - z_n | < \varepsilon/2 + \varepsilon/2 = \varepsilon \text{ by (1).}$$

Hence $< z_n >$ is a Cauchy sequency.

Remark:

It can be proved that C is complete. By this we mean that every Cauchy sequence in C is Convergent. Hence we may state :

A sequence in C is convergent if and only if it is a Cauchy sequence.

This is known as Cauchy's criterion for convergence of sequences.

SERIES

An infinite sum of complex numbers of the form

$$z_1 + z_2 + \ ... + z_n + ... \quad ...(1)$$

is called a series of complex numbers and will be denoted by $\sum_1^{\infty} z_n$ or simply by Σz_n. If

$$S_n = z_1 + z_2 + ... + z_n,$$

then s_n is called the nth partial sum of the series (1). Thus associated with each series, we have a sequence $< S_n >$ of partial sums. The series is said to converge if and onty if the corresponding sequence of partial sums is convergent.

Thus Cauchy's criterion for convergence for a series will read:

The series Σz_n converges if and onty if to every $\varepsilon > 0$, there exists a positive integer no such that

$$| z_n | + z_{n+1} + 1 + ... + 2_{n+p} | < \varepsilon$$

for all $n \geq HQ$ and all $p \geq 0$.

In particular, it $p = 0$, we have $| z_n | < \varepsilon$ for all $n \geq$ no. It follows that $\lim_{n\to\infty} z_n = 0$. Hence if the series (1) converges, then its general terms z_n must tend to zero. This condition is only necessary but not sufficient as can be easily seen. If

$$R_n = z_n + z_{n+1} + + \ldots,$$

Then R_n is called the *remainder after n terms.* If S denotes the sum of the series, then

$$S = S_n + R_n$$

The series (1) is said to *converge absolutely* if the series

$$| z_1 | + | z_2 | + \ldots + | z_n | + \ldots$$

formed by absolute values of the terms converges.

It is easy to see that an absolutely convergent series is convergent but not conversely.

SEQUENCES AND SERIES OF FUNCTIONS

Uniform Convergence

Let A be any set and for each positive integer n, let S_n be a function defined on A with valued S_n (x) in C. Consider the sequence $< S_n (x) >$ of complex valued functions each defined on the same set A. If for each x, the sequence $< S_n (x) >$ of constant, terms converges, then we say that the sequence converges *pointwise.* Observe that in this case, the limit S (x) is again a function on A and is defined by

$$S(x) = \lim_{n\to\infty} S_n(x).$$

We call S (x) the *limit function* of the sequence $< S_n (x) >$. In this case, for a fixed x in A and arbitrary $\varepsilon > 0$, there exists (by definition of convergence) a positive integer no such that

$$| S_n (X) - S(X) | < \varepsilon \qquad \ldots(1)$$

for all $n \geq n_0$.

The integer n_0 depends, in general, both on x and e and vary from point to point. For example, if

$$S_n(x) = \frac{x}{n}, \text{ then } S(x) = \lim_{n\to\infty} \frac{x}{n} = 0.$$

Hence in orde.r that, we may have

$$| S_n(x) - S (x) | \left|\frac{x}{n} - 0\right| = \frac{|x|}{n} < \varepsilon$$

for $n \geq n_0$, it is necessary that $n_0 > \frac{|x|}{\varepsilon}$. Such as n_0 exists for every fixed x so that the sequence $< \frac{x}{n} >$ converges pointwise. But the requirement cannot be met simultaneously for all x. If, however, an n_0 exists such that the inequality (1) holds for all $n \geq n_0$ and all x in A, then we say $< S_n(x) >$ *converges uniformly* to S (x) on A. The formal definition is as follows :

Definition:

This sequence $< S_n(x) >$ is said to converge uniformly to S (x) on the set A if to each $\varepsilon > 0$, there exists an $n_0 > 0$ such that

$$| S_n(x) - S(x) | < \varepsilon$$

for all $n \geq n_0$ and all x in A.

Theorem I: (Cauchy's Criterion for uniform convergence).

The sequence $< S_n(x) >$ converges uniformly on A if and only if to each $\varepsilon > 0$, there exists a positive integer n_0 such that

$$| S_n(x) - S_n(x) | < \varepsilon \qquad ...(1)$$

for all m, $n \geq n_0$ and all x in A.

Proof:

The 'only if part: Let the sequence converge uniformly to S (x) on A. Then, given $\varepsilon > 0$, we can find a positive integer n_0, such

that $$| S_n(x) - S(x) | < \frac{1}{2}\varepsilon$$

for all $n \geq n_0$ and all x in A. Hence if $m \geq n_0$ and $n \geq n_0$, then

$$| S_m(x) - S(x) | < \frac{1}{2}\varepsilon$$

and $$| S_n(x) - S(x) | < \frac{1}{2}\varepsilon$$

for all x in A. Hence for all m, $n \geq n_0$ and all x in A, we have

$$| S_m(x) - S(x) = | S_m(x) - S(x) + S(x) - S_n(x) |$$
$$\leq | S_m(x) - S(x) | + | S(x) - S_n(x) |$$
$$< \frac{1}{2}\varepsilon + \frac{1}{2}\varepsilon = \varepsilon$$

The if part : Let the condidon (1) hold. Then the limit function S (x) exists by Cauchy's criterion of ordinary convergence. In the inequality (1), we keep n fixed and let $n \to \infty$ so that

$$\lim_{m \to \infty} S_m(x) = S(x)$$

it then follows that

$$| S(x) - S_n(x) | < \varepsilon$$

for all $n \geq n_0$ and all x in A. Hence the convergence is uniform.

Theorem II: (Cauchy's Criterion for Series)

The series $\sum_{n=1}^{\infty} f_n(x)$ *of functions each defined on the same set A converges uniformly on A if and only if to each ε > 0, there exists a positive integer no such that*

$$| f_n(x) + f_{n+1}(x) + ... + f_{n+p}(x) | < \varepsilon$$

for all $n > n_0$, $p \geq 0$ *and all x in A.*

Proof:

Set $S_n(x) = f_1(x) + f_2(x) + ... + f_n(r)$.

Hence the proof is the same as that of theorem I if we replace the series $\Sigma f_n(x)$ by the sequence $< S_n(x) >$. The limit function of the sequence is called the sum function of the series.

Theorem III: (Weierstrass M-Test)

The series $\Sigma f_n(x)$ *of functions each defined on the same set A converges uniformly on A if (i)* $| f_n(x) | \leq Mn$ *for every positive integer n and every x in A, where Mn is a positive constant independent of x and (ii) the series* ΣM_n *converges.*

Proof:

Since ΣM_n converges, for a given ε > 0, there exists a positive integer n_0 such that

$$M_{n+1} + M_{n+2} + ... M_{n+p} < \varepsilon$$

for all $n > n_0$ and all $p \geq 0$. Then the condition (i) gives

$$| f_{n+1}(x) + f_{n+2}(x) + + f_{n+p}(x)$$

$$\leq | f_{n+1}(x) | + | f_{n+2}(x) | + ... + | f_{n+p}(x) |$$

$$\leq M_{n+1} + m_{n+2} + ... + M_{n+p} < \varepsilon$$

for all $n > n_0, p \geq 0$ and all x in A. Hence the series $\Sigma f_n(x)$ converges uniformly on A.

Note:

The above test gives one of the simplest sufficient conditions for uniform convergence.

Power Series

A series of the form $\sum_{n=0}^{\infty} a_n z^n$ or $\sum_{n=0}^{\infty} a_n (z-a)^n$, whose terms are variable is called a power series where z is a complex variable and a_n, are complex constants.

The second form car be reduced to the first from merely by changing origin. So the consideration of the series of the second form is always reduced to that of the first form

The form $\sum_{n=0}^{\infty} a_n z^n$ being simpler, we have discussion of power series by considering the form $\sum_{n=0}^{\infty} a_n z^n$

Definition of Power Series

A series of the type

$$\sum_{n=0}^{\infty} a_n (z - z_0)^n = a_0 + a_1 (z - z_1) + \dots + a_n (z - z_0)^n + \dots$$

is called the power series where variable z and the constants a_n, z_0 are complex numbers and a_n is independent of z.

As a special case z, a_n, z_0 may be real. But we shall prove various theorems and results for the general case in which these are complex numbers. By a change of variable $z = \xi + z_0$, the above power series reduces to $\sum_{n=0}^{\infty} a_n \xi^n$. Hence it is sufficient to consider the series of the form $\sum_{n=0}^{\infty} a_n z^n$.

Theorem I:

The power series $\Sigma a_n z^n$ either

(i) converges for all values of z,

(ii) converges only for $z = 0$,

(iii) converges for z in some region in the complex plane.

Proof:

It is sufficient to produce an example of each case :

(i) The series $\sum \frac{z^n}{n!}$ converges absolutely for all values of z,

For if $u_n = \frac{z^n}{n!}$ $u_{n+1} = \frac{z^{n+1}}{(n+1)!}$, then

$$\lim_{n\to\infty} \frac{|u_n|}{|u_n + 1|} = \lim_{n\to\infty} \frac{n+1}{|z|} = \infty > 1.$$

Hence by D' Alemberts' ratio test, the series converges absolutely for all values of z.

(ii) The series $\Sigma n!\, z^n$ converges only for z = 0. For we have for $z \neq 0$.

$$\lim_{n \to \infty} n!\, z^n = \infty$$

Thus the terms of the series do not converge to zero for $z \neq 0$ and consequently, the series does not converge for $z \neq 0$, but it converges for z = 0.

(iii) The geometric series $\sum_{n=0}^{\infty} z^n$ converges for $|z| < 1$ and diverges for $|z| \geq 1$.

Theorem II: (Abel's theorem).

If the power series $\sum_{n=0}^{\infty} a_n z^n$ *converges for a particular value 20 of z, then it converges absolutely for all values of z for which* $|z| < |z_0|$.

Proof:

Let $\Sigma a_n z_n$ converge. Then its wth term $a_n z_0^n$ must tend to 0 as $n \to \infty$. So we can find a number M > 0 such that

$$|a_n z_0^n| \leq M$$

for all n. Then

$$|a_n z_0^n| \leq M \left|\frac{z}{z_0}\right|^n$$

Since $|z| < |z_0|$, the geometric series $\left|\frac{z}{z_0}\right|$ converges. It follows by the comparison test that $\Sigma |a_n z^n|$ converges for all values of z for which $|z| < |z_0|$. In other words, $\Sigma a_n z^n$ converges absolutely for all z such that $|z| < |z_0|$.

Absolute Convergence of Power Series $\Sigma a_n z^n$

The power series $\Sigma a_n z^n$ is said to be absolutely convergent if series $\Sigma |a_n z^n|$ is convergent

If the series $\sum_{n=0}^{\infty} a_n z^n$ convergent but the series $\sum_{n=0}^{\infty} |a_n z|^n$ not converge, then the series $\sum_{n=0}^{\infty} a_n z^n$ is called conditionally convergent.

Radius of Convergent of Power Series

Applying Cauchy's not test to the series $\Sigma\ |a_n|\ |z|^n$ we find that $\Sigma\ a_n\ z^n$ is convergent or divergent according as limit of nth root of the nth term is less or greater than unity Thus.

$\Sigma\ |a_n|\ |z|^n$ convergent if $\lim\limits_{n\to\infty} |a_n|^{1/n}\ |z| < |$ *i.e.* if $1/R\ .\ |z| < |$ where $\lim|a_n|^{1/n} = 1/R$ or if $|z| < R$ and divergent if $|z| > R$

Thus, for every power series $\Sigma\ a_x\ z^n$. There exist a non-negative real number R such that for every $|z| < R$ The series is absolutely convergent, and for every $|z| > R$ the series is not convergent.

Such a number R is called the Radius of convergence of the power series $\Sigma\ a_x\ z^n$. For if we draw a circle whose centre is origin and radius equal to R, then for all values of z with in this circle power series $\Sigma\ a_x\ z^n$ is absolutely convergent and for all values of z outside this circle the power series $\Sigma\ a_x\ z^n$ is divergent.

Some Useful Tests for Convergence

The following tests whose proofs are trivial should be recollected

Comparison Test : If $\sum|\sqrt{n}|$ converges and $|u_n|\ \Sigma\ |v_n|$ Then $\Sigma|u_n|$ converges absolutely.

Ratio Test : The series Σu_n converges (absolutely) or diverges according as $\lim\limits_{n\to\infty}\left|\frac{u_{n-1}}{u_n}\right| < 1$ or > 1. If this limit equal to 1 the test fails.

Root Test : (n^{th} root test) the series Σu_n converges (absolutely) or diverge according as $\lim\limits_{n\to\infty}\sqrt[n]{(|u_n|)} < 1$ or > 1

If this limit is equal to 1, the test fails.

Series absolutely convergent : The series Σu_n is convergent (absolutely) the series $|\Sigma u_n|$ is convergent.

Theorem 1:

If the power series $\Sigma a_n x^n$ is such that $a_n \neq 0$ for all n and $\lim\limits_{n\to\infty}\left|\frac{a_{n+1}}{a_n}\right| = \frac{1}{R}$, then $\Sigma a_n x^n$ is convergent (absolutely convergent) for $|x| < R$ and divergent for $|x| > R$..

Proof:

Let $u_n = a_n\ x^n$ so that $u_{n+1} = a_{n+1}\ x^{n+1}$.

$$\therefore \quad \lim_{n\to\infty}\left|\frac{u_{n+1}}{u_n}\right| = \lim_{n\to\infty}\left|\frac{a_{n+1}\,x}{a_n}\right| = \frac{|x|}{R}.$$

By D' Alembert's ratio test, $\Sigma a_n\, x^n$ converges absolutely, if

$$\frac{|x|}{R} < 1 \text{ i.e., } |x| < R.$$

Further $\Sigma a_n\, x^n$ diverges if $|x| > R$. Hence the theorem.

Remark 1:

By Cauchy's second theorem on limits, if $\{a_n\}$ is sequence of positive constants, then

$$\lim_{n\to\infty}(a_n)^{1/n} = \lim_{n\to\infty}\left(\frac{a_{n+1}}{a_n}\right),$$

provided the limit on the R.H.S. exists. It follows that :

If $\lim_{n\to\infty}|a_n|^{1/n} = \frac{1}{R}$, *Then the series $\Sigma a_n\, x^n$ is convergent (absolutely convergent) for $|x| < R$ and divergent for $|x| > R$.*

In view of the above discussion, the *radius of convergence R of a power series $\Sigma a_n\, x^n$ may be determined by the following :*

$$R = \lim_{n\to\infty}\left|\frac{a_n}{a_{n+1}}\right| = 1 \div \lim_{n\to\infty}|a_n|^{1/n}$$

$R = \infty$, when $\lim |a_n|^{1/n} = \infty$.

$R = 0$, when $\lim |a_n|^{1/n} = \infty$.

Remark 2:

Every power series converges absolutely within its interval of convergence.

Theorem 2:

If a power series $\Sigma a_n x^n$ converges for $|x| < R$, then it converges uniformly on $[-R + \varepsilon, R - \varepsilon]$, for each $\varepsilon > 0$.

Proof:

Let $x_0 = R - \varepsilon < R$ so that $\Sigma a_n x_0^{\,n}$ converges absolutely.

For $|x| \le x_0$, $|a_n x^n| \le |a_n|\; x_0^n$.

Since $\Sigma a_n x_0^n$ converges absolutely, therefore, by Weierstrass's M-test, the series $\Sigma a_n x^n$ converges uniformly on

$[-x_0, x_0] = [-R + \varepsilon, R - \varepsilon]$. Hence the theorem.

Ex.:

Show that a power series converges uniformly on any closed and bounded subinterval of its interval of convergence.

Theorem 3:

If a power series $\Sigma a_n x^n$ converges for $x = x_0$, then

(i) *it is absolutely convergent in the interval* $|x| < |x_0|$

(ii) *it is uniformly convergent in the interval* $|x| \le |x_1|$ *where* $|x_1| \le |x_0|$.

Proof:

(i) Since $\Sigma a_n x_0^n$ converges, so $\lim_{n\to\infty} a_n x_0^n = 0$.

Consequently there exists a positive integer m such that

$$|a_n x_0^n = 0| < 1 \ \forall\, n \ge m \text{ or } |a_n| < \frac{1}{|x_0|^n} \ \forall\, n \ge m \qquad \ldots (1)$$

$$\Rightarrow |a_n x^n| = |a_n|\,|x|^n < \frac{|x|^n}{|x_0|^n} \ \forall\, n \ge m, \text{ by (1)}$$

$$\Rightarrow |a_n x^n| < \left\{\frac{|x|}{|x_0|}\right\}^n \ \forall\, n \ge m.$$

The series on the R.H.S. converges for $|x| < |x_0|$ (being a geometric series with common ratio < (1), it follows by the comparison test that $\Sigma |a_n x^n|$ is convergent for $|x| < |x_0|$.

Hence $\Sigma a_n x^n$ is absolutely convergent for $|x| < |x_0|$.

(ii) Let $M_n = \dfrac{|x_1|^n}{|x_0|^n}$. Then ΣM_n converges, since $|x_1| < |x_0|$ (being a geometric series with common ratio <1).

Using (1), we obtain

$$|a_n x^n| = |a_n|\,|x|^n < \frac{|x|^n}{|x_0|^n} \le \frac{|x_1|^n}{|x_0|^n},$$

for $|x| \le |x_1|$ and $n \ge m$

$\therefore |a_n x^n| < M_n \ \forall\, n \ge m$, where ΣM_n converges.

By the Weierstrass M-Test, $\Sigma a_n x^n$ is uniformly convergent in $|x| \le |x_1$.

Note : *If a power series whose radius of convergence is 1, then it converges absolutely in]– 1, 1[and uniformly in [–k, k], |k| < 1.*

Theorem 4:

Two power series $\sum_{n=0}^{\infty} a_n x^n$ *and* $\sum_{n=0}^{\infty} b_n x^n$ *can be multiplied to obtain the power series* $\sum_{n=0}^{\infty} c_n x^n$, *where*

$$c_n = a_0 b_n + a_1 b_{n-1} + a_2 b_{n-2} + \dots + a_n b_0,$$

the result being valid for each x within the common interval of convergence.

The proof of these theorems are omitted.

Some Important Power Series

Consider the following power series :

$$1 + \frac{x}{1!} + \frac{x^2}{2!} + \frac{x^3}{3!} + \dots + \frac{x^n}{n!} + \dots\dots$$

$$1 - \frac{x^2}{2!} + \frac{x^4}{4!} - \dots + (-1)^n \frac{x^{2n}}{(2n)!} + \dots\dots$$

$$x - \frac{x^3}{3!} + \frac{x^5}{5!} - \dots + (-1)^n \frac{x^{2n+1}}{(2n+1)!} + \dots\dots$$

For the first series, $\lim_{n\to\infty} \left|\frac{a_n}{a_{n+1}}\right| = \lim_{n\to\infty} \frac{(n+1)!}{n!} = \lim_{n\to\infty} (n+1) = \infty$.

Thus, the radius of convergence is $R = \infty$ so that the series is everywhere convergent (absolutely and uniformly). Similarly we can verify that the other two power series are also everywhere convergent (absolutely and uniformly). In this section we shall study their exclusive properties and show that the sums of these power series are actually the functions e^x, cos x and sin x respectively.

Theorem 5:

(Abel's Theorem): *If a power series converges at an end point of its interval of convergence, then the power series is uniformly convergent in the interval which includes this end point.*

Remarks:

1. *If a power series with interval of convergence]–R, R[converges at both the end-points – R and R, then the power series is uniformly convergent in [–R, R].*

2. *If a power series converges at the end-point x = R of the interval of convergence]–R, R[, then it is uniformly convergent in]–R, R] or [–R + ε, R], where ε > 0. In particular, the series is uniformly convergent in [0, R].*

Theorem 6:

(Abel's Limit Theorem): *But $\Delta a_n x^n$ be a power series with finite radius of convergence R that r (x) = $\Sigma a_n x^n$, $-R \Delta x < R$. If the series $\Sigma a_n R^n$ converges, be*

$$\lim_{x \to R-} f(x) = \Sigma a_n R^n.$$

Remark 3 : *The case R = 1 is of much practical use :*

Let $\Sigma a_n x^n$ *be a power series with unit radius of convergence such that* $f(x) = \Sigma a_n x^n, -1 \Delta x < 1$. *If the series* $\Sigma a_n x^n$ *converges for x = 1 i.e., if* Σa_n converges, then

$$\lim_{x \to 1-} f(x) = \Sigma a_n.$$

Theorem 7:

Suppose a power series $\Sigma a_n x^n$ converges for $|x| < R$ and that $f(x) = \Sigma a_n x^n$. Then

(i) *f(x) is continuous in]–R, R[.*

(ii) *$\Sigma a_n x^n$ can be integrated term by term on]–R, R[and the integrated series has the same radius of convergence as $\Sigma a_n x^n$.*

(iii) *$\Sigma a_n x^n$ can be differentiated term and term on]–R, [R and $f'(x) = \Sigma n\, a_n x^{n-1}$, $|x| < R$. Further the differentiated series has the same radius of convergence as $\Sigma a_n x^n$.*

Proof:

(i) Since each term of the power series $\Sigma a_n x^n$ is continuous in]–R, R[and the series is uniformly convergent on]–R, R[, so the sum f(x) of the given series is continuous in]–R, R.

(ii) Since each term of $\Sigma a_n x^n$ is continuous in]–R, R[and $\Sigma a_n x^n$ converges uniformly to f(x) in]–R, R[, so $\Sigma a_n x^n$ can be integrated term by termin] –R, R[and the integrated series is $\Sigma \frac{a_n}{n+1} x^{n+1}$. Further

$$\lim_{n \to \infty} \left| \frac{u_n}{u_{n+1}} \right| = \lim_{n \to \infty} \left(\frac{n+2}{n+1} \frac{a_n}{a_{n+1}} \right) = \lim_{n \to \infty} \frac{a_n}{a_{n+1}} = R,$$

which shows that $\Sigma a_n x^n$ and $\Sigma \frac{a_n x^{n+1}}{n+1}$ have the same radius of convergence.

(iii) We know each term of $\Sigma a_n x^n$ is continuous, has continuous derivative in] – R, R[and $\Sigma a_n x^n$ is uniformly convergent in] – R, R[. Thus the series obtained by differentiating the power series $\Sigma a_n x^n$ is $\Sigma n a_n x^{n-1}$. Further

$$\lim_{n\to\infty}\left|\frac{u_n}{u_{n+1}}\right| = \lim_{n\to\infty}\left|\frac{n\,a_n}{(n+1)\,a_{n+1}}\right| = \lim_{n\to\infty}\left|\frac{a_n}{a_{n+1}}\right| = R.$$

Hence the differentiated series $\Sigma n\, a_n\, x^{n-1}$ is also a power series which has the same radius of convergence as $\Sigma\, a_n\, x^n$.

Note : If $f(x) = \Sigma a_n x^n$, *then* $f(x)$ *is called the* **sum function** *of the series.*

Theorem 8:

Define cosine and sine functions as sums of power series. Prove that

(i) S(x + y) = S(x)C(y) + C(x)S(y),

(ii) C(x + y) = C(x)C(y) − S(x)S(y),

where C, S denote cosine and since respectively.

Proof:

The *cosine function* is defined as

$$C(x) = 1 - \frac{x^2}{2!} + \frac{x^4}{4!} - ... + (-1)^n \frac{x^{2n}}{(2n)!} + ... \quad \forall\ x \in \Re \qquad ...(1)$$

The *sine function* is defined as

$$S(x) = x - \frac{x3}{3!} + \frac{x^5}{5!} - ... + (-1)^n \frac{x^{2n+1}}{(2n+1)!} + ... \qquad ...(2)$$

$\forall\ x \in \Re$

These two power series are uniformly convergent $\forall\ x \in \Re$ and consequently, the functions C(x) and S(x) are continuous $\forall\ x \in \Re$.

Differentiating term by term the convergent series (2).

$$S'(x) = 1 - \frac{x^2}{2!} + \frac{x^4}{4!} + ...$$

which gives us the uniformaly convergent series (1),

Thus S(x) is variable, $\forall x \in \Re$ and S'(x) = C(x) ...(3)

SimilarlyC'(x) = −S(x). ...(4)

From (1) and (2); S(0) = 0 and C(0) = 1. ...(5)

Let y be any arbitrary but fixed real number. We write

f(x) = S(x + y) − S(x)C(y) − C(x)S(y), ...(6)

g(x) = C(x + y) − C(x)C(y) + S (x) S (y). ...(7)

Differentiating w.r.t. x, we obtain

f' (x) = C(x + y) − C(x)C(y) + S(x)S(y) = g(x), ...(6)

$g'(x) = -S(x + y) - S(x)C(y) + C(x) S(y) = -f(x).$ ...(7)

[Using (3), (4)]

Now $\frac{d}{dx}[f^2(x) + g^2(x)] = 2f(x) f'(x) + 2g(x) g'(x)$

$= 2f(x) g(x) - 2g(x) f(x) = 0 \quad \forall x$

If follows that $f^2(x) + g^2(z)$ is a constant $\forall x$

$\Rightarrow f^2(x) + g^2(x) = f^2(0) + g^2(0) \quad \forall x$

$= [S(y) - S(0) C(y) - C(0) S(y)]^2$

$+ [C(y) - C(0) C(y) + S(0) S(y)]^2$

$= 0$ [Using (5)],

$\therefore f^2(x) + g^2(x) = 0 \ \forall x \in \Re$ implies the $f(x) = 0$ and $g(x) = 0$.

Hence (6) and (7) yield

$S(x + y) = S(x) C(y) + C(x) S(y)$,

$C(x + y) = C(x) C(y) - C(x) S(y)$.

Cor. 1. $S(-x) = -S(x); C(-x) = C(x) \quad \forall x \in \Re.$

We have $S(-x) = -x - \frac{(-x)^8}{3!} + \frac{(-x)^5}{5!} - \ldots\ldots$

$$= -\left[x - \frac{x^3}{3!} + \frac{x^5}{5!} - \ldots\ldots\right] = -S(x).$$

Similarly we can prove the second part.

Cor. 2. $S(x - y) = S(x) C(y) - C(x) S(y)$,

$C(x - y) = C(x) C(y) + S(x) S(y)$.

Replacing y by –y in (i) and (ii)

$S(x-y) = S(x) C(-y) + C(x) S(-y)$,

$C(x-y) = C(x) C(-y) - S(x) S(-y)$.

The desired results follow by Cor. 1.

Cor. 3. $C^2(x) + S^2(x) = 1$ or $\cos^2 x + \sin^2 x = 1 \quad \forall x \in \Re.$

We have $1 = C(0) = C(x - x)$

$= C(x) C(-x) - S(x) S(-x)$

$= C^2(x) + S^2(x)$, by Cor. 1.

Hence $\cos^2 x + \sin^2 x = 1 \ \forall x \in \Re$.

Cor. 4. $| C(x) \leq 1, | S(x) | \leq 1, \quad \forall x \in \Re.$

OR

$$| \cos x | \leq 1, | \sin x | \leq 1 : \forall x \in \mathfrak{R}.$$

This follows by Cor. 3.

Cor. 5. *sin 2x = 2 sin x cos x, cos 2x = cos²x – sin² x.*

Replacing y by x in (i) and (ii) of Theorem 8, we obtain

$S(2x) = 2S(x)\, C(x),\ C(2x) = C^2(x) - S^2(x)$

Hence the results follow.

Remark:

It may be noted that the above properties of C(x) and S(x) are similar to those of the trigonometric functions cos x and sin x respectively which the students do at the elementary, stage. Thus we have

$C(x) \equiv \cos x$ *and* $S(x) \equiv \sin x.$

Theorem 9:

Let f be a non-zero function continuous on R^+ *such that* $f(xy) = f(x) + f(y)\ \forall\ x, y > 0.$ ...(1)

Show that $f(x)\ \log_a x,\ x \in \mathfrak{R}^+\ (a > 0,\ a \neq 1).$

Proof:

For $x > 0$, let us take $t = \log_e x \Leftrightarrow x = e^t,\ t \in \mathfrak{R}.$ ...(2)

Let $g(t) = f(e^t)\ \forall\ t \in \mathfrak{R}$. Then g is continuous on $\mathfrak{R}$ and

$g(t + s) = f(e^{t+s}) = f(e^t e^3) = f(e^t) + f(e^s)$ by (1)

or $g(t + s) = g(t) + g(s).$

Here $t, s \in \mathfrak{R}$. $g(t) = ct,\ \forall\ t \in \mathfrak{R}$, c being a constant.

Thus $f(x) = c \log_e x\ \forall x \in \mathfrak{R}^+$, where $c \neq 0$ as f is non-zero.

Let $a = e^{1/e}$. Then $f(x) = \log_a x\ \forall\ x \in \mathfrak{R}^+\ (a > 0,\ a \neq 1).$

Ex.:

See the exponential function as the sum of a power series and determine its range. Hence define the logarithmic function and deduce that it is continuous.

[**Hint.** It can be verified that the exponential function $E : R \to R^+$ is strictly increasing on R *i.e.*, E is one-one and onto. Thus E has inverse function, say $L : R^+ \to R$. L is called the *logarithmic function*, defined as

$$E\{L(y)\} = y\ (y > 0) \text{ or } L\{E(x)\} = x\ (x \in R).$$

In other words, E (x) = y ⇒ I. (y) = x or $e^x = y \Rightarrow \log_e y = x$.

Since the function E is differentiable, so its inverse function L is false differentiable and hence continuous.

Theorem 10:

Define exponential function E(x) as the sum of power series. Show that the domain is the set of all real number Prove that

E (x + y) = E (x) E (y) for all x, y ∈ ℜ.

If e denotes E(1), prove that E (x) = e^2 for all real x.

Proof:

The exponential function E(x) is defined as the sum of the power series

$$E(x) = 1 + \frac{x}{1!} + \frac{x^2}{2!} + ... + \frac{x^n}{n!} + ... \quad ...(1)$$

We have $R = \lim_{n\to\infty} \left|\frac{a_n}{a_{n+1}}\right| = \lim_{n\to\infty} \frac{(n+1)!}{n!} = \lim_{n\to\infty} (n+1) = \infty$.

Thus, the radius of convergence of the above power series is R = ∞ that the power series is everywhere convergent *i.e.*, E(x) is defined ∀ x ∈ ℜ. This shows that the domain of the exponential function is ℜ.

It is clear that the function E(x), defined by (1), is continuous and has derivatives of all orders, for each x ∈ ℜ.

Differentiating (1), we get

E'(x) = E(x) and so E'(x) = E(x), E'(x) = E(x) etc.

In fact $E^{(n)}$ (x) = E(x) ∀ n ∈ N.

By Taylor's Theorem, for all real values t and x

$$E(t) = E(x) + \frac{E'(x)}{1!}(t-x) + \frac{E''(x)}{2!}(t-x)^2 + ...$$

$$\text{or } E(t) = E(x) + \frac{E(x)}{1!}(t-x) + \frac{E(x)}{2!}(t-x)^2 + ...$$

Replacing t by x + y, we get

$$E(x+y) = E(x)\left\{1 + \frac{y}{1!} + \frac{y^2}{2!} + ...\right\} = E(x)E(y)$$

Thus, E (x + y) = E(x) E (y) ∀ x, y ∈ ℜ. ...(2)

From (1), $E(1) = 1 + \frac{1}{1!} + \frac{1}{2!} + ... + \frac{1}{3!} + ...$

The above series on the right converges to a number which lies between 2 and 3.

We denote this number by e so that E(1) = e.

The property (2) can be extended as

$E(x_1 + x_2 + ... + x_n) = E(x_1) E(x_2)...E(x_n)$ ...(3)

for any positive integer n and $\forall x \in \Re$.

Taking $x_1 = x_2 = ... = x_n = x$ in (3), we obtain

$$E(nx) = \{E(x)\}^n \ \forall x \in \Re, \forall n \in N. \quad ...(4)$$

For x = 1, we obtain

$$E(n) = e^n \ \forall n \in N \qquad (\because E(1) = e) \quad ...(5)$$

Taking x = m/n (m and n being positive integers) in (4),

$E(m) = \{E(m/n)\}^n$ or $e^m = \{E(m/n)\}^n$, by (5)

$\therefore E(m/n) = (e^m)^{1/n} = e^{m/n}$.

Thus, $E(q) = e^n$ for all positive rationals q. ...(6)

Let x be any *positive irrational* number. Then there always exists a sequence $\{x_n\}$ of positive rational numbers such that $x_n \to x$.

Using (6), $E(x_n) = e^{xn}$ $\forall n \in N$.

Since $x_n \to x$ as $n \to \infty$ and E is a continuous function $\forall x \in \Re$, therefore

$E(x) = e^n$ for all positive irrationals. ...(7)

From (6) and (7), we conclude that

$E(x) = e^x$ for all positive reals. ...(8)

Taking y = – x in (2), we get

$E(0) = E(x)E(-x)$ or $1 = E(x) E(-x)$ $(x \geq 0)$

$[\because E(0) = 1$, by (1)].

or $E(-x) = \dfrac{1}{E(x)} = \dfrac{1}{e^x} = e^{-x}$, using (8)

Hence, $E(x) = e^x \quad \forall x \in \Re$.

Theorem 11:

Let f be a continuous function on $\Re$ *such that*

$f(x + y) = f(x) + f(y) \ \forall x, y \in \Re$. ...(1)

Show that $f(x) = e^x$ *for some constant c and* $\forall x \in \Re$.

Proof:

Putting y = x in (1), f(2x) = 2 f(x).

In fact f(nx) = nf(x) $\forall$ x $\in \mathfrak{R}$, $\forall$ n $\in$ N.

Replacing x by x/n, we get

f(x) = nf(x/n) or f(x/n) = (1/n) = (1/n) f(x) $\forall$ x $\in \mathfrak{R}$.

For any integers p and p (q > 0), it follows that

$$f\left(\frac{p}{q}x\right) = \frac{p}{q} f(x). \ \forall x \in \mathfrak{R}.$$

Thus, f(rx) = r f(x), for any rational number r. ...(2)

Let us write f(1) = c. Taking x = 1 in (2), we get

f(r) = cr, for every rational number r. ...(3)

Let α be any irrational number. Then there exists a sequence $\{r_n\}$ of rational numbers such that $r_n \to a$

$\Rightarrow f(r_n) \to f(a)$, continuity of f

$\Rightarrow f(a) = \lim f(r_n) = \lim cr_n = c \lim r_n = ca$, using (3).

Hence f(x) = cx $\forall$ x $\in \mathfrak{R}$.

Theorem 12:

Define cos x as a power series and determine its domain. Prove that there exists a least positive number π such that $\cos\left(\frac{1}{2}\pi\right) = 0$.

Proof:

cos x is defined as the sum of the power series

$$1 - \frac{x^2}{2!} + \frac{x^4}{4!} - \ldots + (-1)^n \frac{x^{2n}}{(2n)!} + \ldots..$$

Its radius of convergence is

$$R = \lim_{n\to\infty} \left|\frac{a_n}{a_{n+1}}\right| = \lim_{n\to\infty} \left|\frac{(2n+2)!}{(2n+1)!}\right| = \lim_{n\to\infty} (2n+2) = \infty.$$

Thus, this power series is convergent for $\forall$ x $\in \mathfrak{R}$ and so the domain of cos x is $\mathfrak{R}$.

$$\cos x = 1 - \frac{x^2}{2!} + \frac{x^4}{4!} - \frac{x^6}{6!} + \frac{x^8}{8!} + \ldots\ldots\ldots \quad \forall x \in \mathfrak{R} \qquad ...(1)$$

$\therefore$ cos 0 = 1 > 0 and

$$\cos 2 = 1 - \frac{2^2}{2!} + \frac{2^4}{4!} - \frac{2^6}{6!} + \frac{2^8}{8!} + \ldots\ldots\ldots$$

$$= 1 - \frac{2^2}{2!}\left(1 - \frac{2^2}{3.4}\right) - \frac{2^6}{6!}\left(1 - \frac{2^2}{7.8}\right) - \ldots\ldots..$$

Since the brackets are all positive, therefore

$$\cos 2 < 1 - \frac{2^2}{2!}\left(1 - \frac{2^2}{3.4}\right) = -\frac{1}{3} \text{ and so } \cos 2 < 0.$$

Thus, we see that cos x is a continuous function in the closed interval [0, 2], where cos 0 and cos 2 are of opposite signs. By Intermediate value theorem, there exists at least one number $\alpha \in]0, 2[$ such that $\cos \alpha = 0$. We now proceed to show that α is unique.

Let, if possible, $\beta \in]0, 2[$ satisfy $\cos \beta = 0$ so that

$\cos \alpha = \cos \beta = 0,\ 0 < \alpha, \beta < 2.$

By Rolle's theorem, there exists some number λ, $\alpha < \lambda < b$, such that $-\sin \lambda = 0$.

$\therefore\ \sin \lambda = 0,\ 0 < \lambda < 2.$ ...(2)

By definition,

$$\sin x = x - \frac{x^3}{3!} + \frac{x^5}{5!} - \frac{x^7}{7!} + \ldots\ldots \quad \forall\, x \in \Re$$

$$\therefore \quad \sin \lambda = \frac{\lambda}{1!}\left(1 - \frac{\lambda^2}{2.3}\right) + \frac{\lambda^5}{5!}\left(1 - \frac{\lambda^2}{6.7}\right) + \ldots\ldots > 0, \text{ for } 0 < \lambda < 2.$$

This contradicts (2).

Thus, there exists one and only one that of the equation cos x = 0 lying between 0 and 2. *i.e.*, $\cos \alpha = 0,\ 0 < \alpha < 2$.

We denote α as $\frac{1}{2}\pi$. Hence $\frac{1}{2}\pi$ is the *least positive root* of the equation $\cos x = 0$ *i.e.*, $\cos \frac{1}{2}\pi = 0$.

Also, therefore, we have $\cos x > 0$ when $0 \le x < \frac{1}{2}\pi$.

Theorem 13:

Let f be a non-zero continuous function on $\Re$ such that

$f(x + y) = f(x)\, f(y)\ \forall\ x, y \in \Re.$ ...(1)

Show that $f(x) = e^{cx}$, for some constant $c \neq 0$.

Proof:

It is given that $f(x) \neq 0\ \forall\ x \in \Re$. From (1)

$$f(x) = f\left(\frac{1}{2}x\right) f\left(\frac{1}{2}x\right) \text{ or } f(x) = \left\{f\left(\frac{1}{2}x\right)\right\}^2 > 0\ \forall\ x \in \Re.$$

Let $g(x) = \log_e f(x) \; \forall \; x \in \mathfrak{R}$. Then by (1),

$$g(x + y) = g(x) + g(y) \; \forall \; x, y \in \mathfrak{R}. \qquad ...(2)$$

Now g, being the composition of two continuous functions f(x) and $\log_e x$, is itself continuous on R and g satisfies (2).

It follows that

$g(x) = cx \; \forall \; x \in \mathfrak{R}$, c being a constant

$\Rightarrow \log_e f(x) = cx$

$\Rightarrow f(x) = e^{cx} \; \forall \; x \in \mathfrak{R}$.

SOLVED EXAMPLES

Example 1:

Find the radius of convergence of $\sum_{n=1}^{\infty} nx^{n-1}$.

Solution:

Here $\lim_{n\to\infty} \left|\frac{a_n}{a_{n+1}}\right| = \lim_{n\to\infty} \frac{n}{n+1} = 1$.

Hence the radius of convergence = 1.

Ex:

Find the radius of convergence of the series

$$x + \frac{x^2}{2^2} + \frac{2!}{3^3} x^2 + \frac{3!}{4^6} x^6 + ...$$

Solution :

$$a_n = \frac{(n-1)!}{n^n}, \; a_{n+1} = \frac{n!}{(n+1)^{n+1}}$$

$$\therefore \; R = \lim_{n\to\infty} \left|\frac{a_n}{a_{n+1}}\right| = \lim_{n\to\infty} \frac{(n-1)!}{n!} \frac{(n+1)^{n+1}}{n^n}$$

$$= \lim_{n\to\infty} \left(\frac{n+1}{n}\right)^{n+1} = \lim_{n\to\infty} \left(1+\frac{1}{n}\right)^n \left(1+\frac{1}{n}\right) = e.$$

Hence the radius of convergence = e.

Example 2:

Show that the series

$$1 + \frac{x}{2} + \frac{x^2}{3} + \frac{x^3}{4} + ...$$

is uniformly convergent in [–1, k], 0 < k < 1.

Solution:

We have

$$\lim_{n\to\infty}\left|\frac{a_n}{a_{n+1}}\right| = \lim_{n\to\infty}\left(\frac{n+1}{n}\right) = \lim_{n\to\infty}\left(1+\frac{1}{n}\right) = 1.$$

The radius of convergence is R = 1 and so the given series is uniformly convergent in]–1, 1[.

For x = 1, given series $\sum\frac{1}{n}$, which is divergent.

However for x = 1, given series becomes $1-\frac{1}{2}+\frac{1}{3}+\frac{1}{4}+.......$, which is convergent by Leibnitz's Test. Hence by Abel's Theorem, given power series is uniformly convergent in [–1, 1[or [–1, k], where 0 < k < 1.

Example 3:

Show that

(i) $\log(1-x) = -x - \frac{x^2}{2} - \frac{x^3}{3} - ...., -1 \le x < 1.$

(ii) $\log 2 = 1 - \frac{1}{2} + \frac{1}{3} - \frac{1}{4} + ...$

(iii) $\frac{1}{2}[\log(1-x)]^2 = \frac{x^2}{2} + \left(1+\frac{1}{2}\right)\frac{x^3}{3} + \left(1+\frac{1}{2}+\frac{1}{3}\right)\frac{x^4}{4} + ..., -1 < x < 1.$

Solution:

(i) We know that

$(1-x)^{-1} = 1 + x + x^2 + x^3 + ..., |x| < 1.$ ...(1)

Its radius of convergence is 1. So the above power series converges absolutely for | x | < 1 and uniformly for [– k, k\, | k | < 1. The integrated series is also convergent absolutely for | x | < 1 and uniformly for [–k, k], | k | < 1,

Integrating, we get

$$-\log(1-x) = x + \frac{x^2}{2} - \frac{x^3}{3} + ... + c$$

Putting x = 0, we get c = 0.

$$\therefore \log(1-x) = -x - \frac{x^2}{2} - \frac{x^3}{3} - ......, -1 < x < 1.$$

By Leibnitz Test, the power series on the R.H. S. converges at x = –1. So by Abel's Theorem.

$$\log(1-x) = -x - \frac{x^2}{2} - \frac{x^3}{3} - \ldots\ldots, \; -1 < x < 1. \qquad \ldots(2)$$

(ii) At x = –1, by Abel's Limit Theorem

$$\log 2 = \lim_{x \to -1-} \log(1-x) = 1 - \frac{1}{2} + \frac{1}{3} - \frac{1}{4} + \ldots\ldots$$

(iii) both the series given on the R.H.S. of (1) and (2) are absolutely convergent in]–1, 1[, so their Cauchy's product will converge to $(1-x)^{-1} \log(1-x)$. Thus

$$(1-x)^{-1}\log(1-x) = -\left[x + \left(1+\frac{1}{2}\right)x^2 + \left(1+\frac{1}{2}+\frac{1}{2}\right)x^2 + \ldots\ldots\right], \quad -1 < x < 1$$

Integrating, we get

$$\frac{1}{2}[\log(1-x)]^2 = \frac{x^2}{2} + \left(1+\frac{1}{2}\right)x^3 + \left(1+\frac{1}{2}+\frac{1}{3}\right)\frac{x^4}{4} + \ldots\ldots \quad -1 < x < 1,$$

where the constant of integration vanishes.

Since the series on the right converge at x = –1, so by Abel's theorem, the above expansion is valid for – 1 < x < 1.

Example 4:

Find the radius of convergence and the exact interval of convergence of the following power series :

(i) $\sum \frac{(n+1)}{(n+2)(n+3)} x^{n},$

(ii) $\sum \frac{(n!)^2 x^{2n}}{(2n)!}.$

Solution:

(i) $a_n = \frac{(n+1)}{(n+2)(n+3)}, \; a_{n+1} = \frac{(n+2)}{(n+3)(n+4)}$

$$\therefore \; R = \lim_{n \to \infty} \left|\frac{a_n}{a_{n+1}}\right| = \frac{(n+1)(n+4)}{!\,(n+2)^2} = 1.$$

Thus, the given series converges for | x | < 1 and diverges for | x | > 1. We now check at the end points x = 1, – 1.

For x = 1, the nth term of the series is

$$u_n = \frac{(n+1)}{(n+2)(n+3)} \sim \frac{n}{n^2} = \frac{1}{n}, \text{ which diverges.}$$

However, for x = – 1, the given series is an alternating series for which $u_{n+1} < u_n \; \forall$ n and $\lim_{n\to\infty} u_n = 0$. Thus, by Leibnitz's test, the series converges for x = –1. Hence the interval of convergence is [–1, 1[.

(ii) We have $a_n = \dfrac{(n!)^2}{(2n)!}$, $a_{n+1} = \dfrac{[(n+1)!]^2}{(2n+2)!}$.

$$\text{Then } \frac{a_n}{a_{n+1}} = \frac{(n!)^2}{\{(n+1)!\}^2}\frac{(2n+2)!}{(2n)!} = \frac{(2n+2)(2n+1)}{(n+1)^2}$$

$$R = \lim_{n\to\infty}\left|\frac{a_n}{a_{n+1}}\right| = \lim_{n\to\infty}\frac{\left(2+\frac{2}{n}\right)\left(2+\frac{1}{n}\right)}{(1+1/n)^2} = 4.$$

It follows that the given series converges for | x | < 4 diverges for | x | > 4. Hence the interval of convergence is]–4,.4[.

Example 5:

Show that the series $\Sigma x^n/n^2$ is uniformly convergent in [–1, 1].

Solution:

We have $a_n = \dfrac{1}{n^2}$, $a_{n+1} = \dfrac{1}{(n+1)^2}$ so that

$$\lim_{n\to\infty}\left|\frac{a_n}{a_{n+1}}\right| = \lim_{n\to\infty}\frac{(n+1)^2}{n^2} = \lim_{n\to\infty}\left(1+\frac{1}{n}\right) = 1$$

The radius of convergence is R = 1 and so the given series is uniformly convergent in]–1, 1[.

For x = 1, given series is $\sum \frac{1}{n^2}$, which is convergent.

For x = –1, given series becomes

$$-1 + \frac{1}{2^2} - \frac{1}{3^2} + \frac{1}{4^2} - \ldots\ldots$$

This is an alternating series for which $u_{n+1} \le u_n \; \forall$ n and

$$\lim_{n\to\infty} u_n = \lim_{n\to\infty}\frac{1}{n^2} = 0.$$

So by Leibnitz's Test, the series to convergent or x = –1. Hence by Abel's Theorem, given power series is uniformly convergent in [–1, 1].

Example 6:

Show that

$$\frac{1}{2}[\log(1+x)]^2 = \frac{x^2}{2} - \frac{x^3}{3}\left(1+\frac{1}{2}\right) + \frac{x^4}{4}\left(1+\frac{1}{2}+\frac{1}{3}\right) + ..., -1 < x < 1.$$

Solution:

By the above example,

$$\log(1+x) = x - \frac{x^2}{2} + \frac{x^3}{3} + \frac{x^4}{4} + ..., -1<x<1.$$

and $(1 + x)^{-1} = 1 - x + x^2 - x^3 + x^4 - ......, -1 < x < 1.$

Both the series are absolutely convergent in]–1, 1[, ($\because$ R = 1), so their Cauchy's product will converge to $(1 + x)^{-1} \log (1 + x)$. Thus

$$(1 + x)^{-1} \log (1 + x) = x - x^2 (1 + ½) + x^3 (1 + ½ + ½) - .....,$$
$$-1 < x < 1$$

Integrating, we get

$$\frac{1}{2}[\log(1+x)]^2 = \frac{x^2}{2} - \frac{x^3}{3}\left(1+\frac{1}{2}\right) + \frac{x^4}{4}\left(1+\frac{1}{2}+\frac{1}{3}\right) - ...., -1<x<1$$

where the constant of integration vanishes.

Since the series on the right converges at x = 1, so by Abel's theorem the above expansion is valid for $-1 < x \leq 1$.

Example 7:

Prove that

$$\int_0^x \frac{dt}{1+t^n} = x - \frac{x^{n+1}}{n+1} + \frac{x^{(2n+1)}}{2n+1} - ...., - < x < 1, n > 0.$$

Solution:

For n > 0, we have

$$(1 + t^n)^{-1} = 1 - t^n + t^{2n} - t^{2n} + ...$$

It is clear that the series on the right has its radius of convergence R = 1.

This series can be integrated term by term on]–1, 1[and the integrated series will also have the radius of convergence as unity. Thus

$$\int_0^x \frac{dt}{1+t^n} = x - \frac{x^{n+1}}{n+1} + \frac{x^{(2n+1)}}{2n+1} - ...., - < x < 1. \quad ....(1)$$

At x = 1, the series on the right is convergent, by Leibnitz's test.

Hence, (1) is true for $-1 < x \leq 1$.

Example 8:

Show that

$$\log(1+x) = x - \frac{x^2}{2} + \frac{x^3}{3} - \frac{x^4}{4} + \ldots\ldots, -1 < x \leq 1$$

and deduce that

$$\log 2 = 1 - \frac{1}{2} + \frac{1}{3} - \frac{1}{4} + \ldots\ldots$$

Solution:

We know

$$(1 + x)^{-1} = 1 - x + x^2 - x^3 + \ldots\ldots\ldots, \quad -1 < x < 1. \qquad \ldots(1)$$

Its radius of convergence is $R = 1$.

Thus the power series is absolutely convergent for $|x| < 1$ and uniformly convergent for $[-k, k]$, $|k| < 1$.

The integrated series is also convergent absolutely in $]-1, 1[$ and uniformly in $[-k, k]$, $|k| < 1$.

Integrating (1), we get

$$\log(1+x) = c + x - \frac{x^2}{2} + \frac{x^3}{3} - \frac{x^4}{4} + \ldots\ldots, 1 < x < 1.$$

Putting $x = 0$ gives $c = 0$. This

$$\log(1+x) = x - \frac{x^2}{2} + \frac{x^3}{3} - \frac{x^4}{4} + \ldots\ldots, 1 < x < 1.$$

The series on the R.H.S. is convergent for $x = 1$ (by Leibnitz's test). Hence by Abel's theorem,

$$\log(1+x) = x - \frac{x^2}{2} + \frac{x^3}{3} - \frac{x^4}{4} + \ldots\ldots, 1 < x < 1.$$

At $x = 1$, by Abel's limit theorem, we get

$$\log 2 = \lim_{x \to 1-} \log(1+x) = 1 - \frac{1}{2} + \frac{1}{3} - \frac{1}{4} + \ldots\ldots$$

Example 9:

Show that

(i) $\tan^{-1} x = x - \dfrac{x^3}{3} + \dfrac{x^5}{5} \dfrac{x^7}{7} + \ldots\ldots\ldots, -1 < x \leq 1$

(ii) $\dfrac{\pi}{4} = 1 - \dfrac{1}{3} + \dfrac{1}{5} - \dfrac{1}{7} + \ldots\ldots$

(iii) $\frac{1}{2}(\tan^{-1} x)^2 = \frac{x^2}{2} - \frac{x^4}{4}\left(1+\frac{1}{3}\right)$

$$+\frac{x^6}{6}\left(1+\frac{1}{3}+\frac{1}{5}\right)+\ldots\ldots\ldots, -1 < x \le 1.$$

Solution:

We know

$$(1 + x^2)^{-1} = 1 - x^2 + x^4 - x^6 + \ldots\ldots, \quad |x| \le 1. \qquad \ldots(1)$$

Radius of convergence is

$$R = \lim_{n\to\infty}\left|\frac{a_n}{a_{n+1}}\right| = 1.$$

Thus the series is convergent absolutely for all x such that $|x| < 1$, and is uniformly convergent in $[-k, k]$, $|k| < 1$.

The integrated series is also convergent absolutely in $]-1, 1[$ and uniformly in $[-k, k]$, $|k| < 1$.

Integrating (1), we get

$$\tan^{-1} x = \left(x - \frac{x^3}{3} + \frac{x^5}{5} - \frac{x^7}{7} + \ldots\ldots\right) + C, \quad |x| < 1.$$

where C is constant of integration.

Putting x = 0, we get C = 0 and so

$$\tan^{-1} x = x - \frac{x^3}{3} + \frac{x^5}{5} - \frac{x^7}{7} + \ldots\ldots, \quad |x| < 1.$$

Now the series

$x - \frac{x^3}{3} + \frac{x^5}{5} - \frac{x^7}{7} + \ldots\ldots$ is convergent at $x = \pm 1$.

$\left[\because\right.$ for $x = 1$, $1 - \frac{1}{3} + \frac{1}{5} - \frac{1}{7} \ldots\ldots$ is an alternating series which converges, by Leibnitz's test, Similarly it is convergent for $\left. x = -1\right]$.

By Abel's Theorem, it is uniformly convergent in $[-1, 1]$.

Hence, $\tan^{-1} x = x - \frac{x^3}{3} + \frac{x^5}{5} - \frac{x^7}{7} + \ldots, -1 < x \le 1.$

(ii) Putting x = 1, by Abel's Limit Theorem,

$$\frac{\pi}{4} = \tan^{-1} 1 = \lim_{x\to 1-0} \tan^{-1} x = 1 - \frac{1}{3} + \frac{1}{5} - \frac{1}{7} + \ldots\ldots$$

(iii) We have

$$\tan^{-1} x = x - \frac{x^3}{3} + \frac{x^5}{5} - \frac{x^7}{7} + \ldots, -1 < x \le 1.$$

and $(1 + x^2)^{-1} \tan^{-1} x = x - x^2 + x^4 - x^6 + \ldots\ldots, 1 < x < 1.$

By part (i), both the series are absolutely convergent in]–1, 1[, so they can be multiplied and their Cauchy's product will be equal, to

$$(1 + x^2)^{-1} \tan^{-1} x = x - \left(1 + \frac{1}{3}\right)x^2 + \left(1 + \frac{1}{3} + \frac{1}{5}\right)x^2 \quad -1 < x < 1.$$

Integrating, we get

$$\frac{1}{2}(\tan^{-1} x)^2 = \frac{x^2}{2} - \frac{x^4}{4}\left(1 + \frac{1}{3}\right) + \frac{x^6}{6}\left(1 + \frac{1}{3} + \frac{1}{5}\right) - \ldots\ldots,$$

$$-1 < x < 1$$

Here the constant of integration vanishes on taking $x = 0$.

By Leibnitz's Test, the series on the R.H.S. converges for $x = 1$. Hence the above expansion is valid for $-1 < x < 1$.

Example 10:

Find the radius of convergence of the series

$$\frac{1}{2}x + \frac{1.3}{2.5}x^2 + \frac{1.3.5}{2.5.8}x^2 + \ldots\ldots$$

Solution:

$$R = \lim_{n\to\infty}\left|\frac{a_n}{a_{n+1}}\right|$$

$$= \lim_{n\to\infty} \frac{1.3.5\ldots..(2n-1)}{2.5.8\ldots..(3n-1)}, \frac{2.5.8\ldots\ldots(3n-1)(3n+2)}{1.3.5\ldots..(2n-1)(2n+1)}$$

$$= \lim_{n\to\infty} \frac{3n+2}{2n+1} = \frac{3}{2}.$$

Example 11:

Show that

$$\sin^{-1} x = x + \frac{1}{2}\frac{x^3}{3} + \frac{1.3}{2.4}\frac{x^5}{5} + \frac{1.3.5}{2.4.6}\frac{x^7}{7} + \ldots\ldots, 1<x<1.$$

Deduce that

$$\frac{\pi}{2} = 1 + \frac{1}{2}.\frac{1}{3} + \frac{1.3}{2.4}.\frac{1}{5} + \frac{1.3.5}{2.4.6}.\frac{1}{7} + \ldots\ldots$$

Solution:

We know that

$$\frac{1}{\sqrt{1-x^2}} = (1-x^2)^{-1/2}$$

$$= 1 + \frac{1}{2}x^2 + \frac{1.3}{2.4}x^4 + \frac{1.3.5}{2.4.6}x^6 + ..., |x| < 1.$$

The series on the R.H.S. is a power series with radius of convergence 1 and so it is absolutely convergent in]–1, 1[and uniformly convergent for [–k, k], | k | < 1. The integrated series is also convergent in]–1, 1[and uniformly convergent for [–k, k], | k | < 1. Integrating, we get

$$\sin^{-1} x = c + x + \frac{1}{2}.\frac{x^3}{3} + \frac{1.3}{2.4}.\frac{x^5}{5} + \frac{1.3.5}{2.4.6}.\frac{x^7}{7} + ..., |x| < 1$$

Putting x = 0, we get c = 0.

$$\therefore \sin^{-1} x + \frac{1}{2}.\frac{x^3}{3} + \frac{1.3}{2.4}.\frac{x^5}{5} + \frac{1.3.5}{2.4.6}.\frac{x^7}{7} + ..., -1 < x < 1 \quad ...(1)$$

For x = 1, the nth term of the series of the R.H.S. of (1) is

$$u_n = \frac{1.3.5...........(2n-1)}{2.4.6.........2n(2n+1)}.$$

$$u_{n+1} = \frac{1.3.5...........(2n+1)}{2.4.6.........(2n+2)(2n+3)}.$$

$$\therefore \frac{u_n}{u_{n+1}} = \frac{(2n+2)(2n+3)}{(2n+1)^2}. \; n\left(\frac{u_n}{u_{n+1}} - 1\right) = \frac{6n^2+5}{(2n+1)^2}$$

$$\lim_{n\to\infty} n\left(\frac{u_n}{u_{n+1}} - 1\right) = \frac{3}{2} > 1.$$

So by Raabe's Test, the series is convergent for x = 1. Hence

$$\sin^{-1} x = x + \frac{1}{2}.\frac{x^3}{3} + \frac{1.3}{2.4}\frac{x^5}{5} + \frac{1.3.5}{2.4.6}\frac{x^7}{7} + ..., - < x < 1.$$

(ii) At x = 1, by Abel's Limit Theorem

$$\frac{\pi}{2} = \lim_{x\to 1-} \sin^{-1} x = 1 + \frac{1}{2}.\frac{1}{3} + \frac{1.3}{2.4}.\frac{1}{5} + \frac{1.3.5}{2.4.6}\frac{1}{7} + ...$$

Example 12:

Prove that the power series

$$1 + \frac{a.b}{1.c}x + \frac{a(a+1)\,b(b+1)}{1.2c\,(c+1)}x^2 + ...$$

has unit radius of convergence.

Solution:

$$a_n = \frac{a(a+1)\,.....(a+n-1)\; b(b+1)\,.....(b+n-1)}{1.2......(n+1)\; c(c+1)......(c+n-1)}$$

(omitting the first term)

$$a_{n+1} = \frac{a(a+1)\,.....(a+n)\; b(b+1)\,.....(b+n)}{1.2......(n+1)\; c(c+1)......(c+n)}$$

$$R = \lim_{n\to\infty}\left|\frac{a_n}{a_{n+1}}\right| = \lim_{n\to\infty}\frac{(n+1)\,(c+n)}{(a+n)\,(b+n)}$$

$$= \lim_{n\to\infty}\frac{(1+1/n)\,(1+c/n)}{(1+a/n)(1+b/n)} = 1.$$

Example 13:

Find the domain of convergence of the series

(i) $\sum \frac{x^n}{n^2}$,

(ii) $\sum \frac{(-1)^n (x-1)^n}{2^n (3n-1)}$.

Solution:

(i) $a_n = \frac{1}{n^3}$, $a_{n+1} = \frac{1}{(n+1)}$ so that

$$\lim_{n\to\infty}\frac{a_n}{a_{n+1}} = \lim_{n\to\infty}\left(\frac{n+1}{n}\right)^3 = 1. \text{ Thus } R = 1.$$

For $x = 2$, the given series is $\sum\frac{(-1)^{n+1}}{n}$, which is convergent by Leibnitz's Test. Hence the exact interval of convergence is]0, 2].

(iii) The given power series is about the point $x = -2$.

$$\lim_{n\to\infty}\left|\frac{a_n}{a_{n+1}}\right| = \lim_{n\to\infty}\frac{n!}{n^n}\,\frac{(n+1)^{n+1}}{(n+1)!} = \lim_{n\to\infty}\left(\frac{n+1}{n}\right)^n$$

$$= \lim_{n\to\infty}\left(1+\frac{1}{n}\right)^n = e.$$

$\therefore R = e$ and the interval of convergence is $]-2-e,\ -2+e[$.

Example 14:

Show that the following series

$$x+\frac{1}{2}\frac{x^2}{3}+\frac{1.3}{2.4}\frac{x^5}{5}+\frac{1.3.5}{2.4.6}\frac{x^7}{7}+......$$

is uniformly convergent in [–1, 1].

Solution:

Ignoring the first term, we have

$$a_n=\frac{1.3.5......(2n-1)}{2.4.6.....2n\,(2n+1)},\ a_{n+1}=\frac{1.3.5.....(2n-1)\,(2n+1)}{2.4.6......2n(2n+2)\,(2n+3)}$$

$$\therefore\ \lim_{n\to\infty}\frac{a_n}{a_{n+1}}=\lim_{n\to\infty}\frac{(2n+2)\,(2n+3)}{(2n+1)^2}=1.$$

Since the radius of convergence is R = 1, given power series is uniformly convergent in]–1, 1[. For x = 1, we see that the D'Alembert's Ratio Test fails. Now

$$\lim_{n\to\infty}\left(\frac{a_n}{a_{n+1}}-1\right)=\lim_{n\to\infty}\frac{n(6n+5)}{(2n+1)^2}=\frac{6}{4}>1.$$

By Raabe's Test, the series is convergent for x = 1.

Again for x = – 1, the series is convergent.

($\therefore\ \Sigma\, a_n$ is convergent $\Rightarrow -\Sigma\, a_n$ is convergent).

Hence, the given power series is uniformly convergent in [–1, 1] (Abel's Theorem).

4

ANALYTIC FUNCTIONS

COMPLEX DIFFERENTIATION

Curves in the Argand Plane

A curve is usually thought of as a particular kind of geometrical configuration but for the needs of complex function theory, it is important to consider a curve as having an additional structure, viz., a specific parametric representation.

We know that the equations of the type x = x (t) and y = y (t) give the parametric representation of a curve in the plane.

Using complex variable, the above equations can be given by a single equation

$z = z(t) = x(t) + iy(t)$ where $z = x + iy$.

Definitions:

(i) *A curve Γ in the Argand plane is a continuous complex valued function z (t) of a real variable defined on a real interval $\alpha \leq t \leq \beta$ where $\alpha < \beta$. We call $z(\alpha)$ and $z(\beta)$ the end points of Γ, $z(\alpha)$ being the initial point and $z(\beta)$ the terminal point of Γ. If $z(\alpha) = z(\beta)$, r is called a closed curve.*

(ii) *A curve Γ is called a Jordan arc or a simple curve if there exists some parametric representation*

$$z = z(t) = x(t) + iy(t),\ \alpha \leq t \leq \beta$$

such that $t_1 \neq t_2$ implies $z(t_1) \neq (z)(t_2)$, that is, z (t) is one-one.

(iii) *A closed curve Γ is called simple if there exists a parametric represenation $z = z(t) = x(t) + iy(t)$, $\alpha \leq t \leq \beta$ such that $t_1 < t_2$ and $z(t_1) = z(t_2)$ imply $t_1 = \alpha$ and $t_2 = \beta$.*

We usually refer to such curves as *simple closed Jordan curves.*

Roughly speaking, a closed curve is simple if no two points of it conicide except the end points. For example, the curve Γ_1 defined by $z(t) = t^2, -1 \le t \le 1$ is closed but not simple. It is closed since $z(-1) = z(1)$. It is not simple since $-\frac{1}{2} < \frac{1}{2}$ and $z\left(-\frac{1}{2}\right) = z\left(\frac{1}{2}\right) = \frac{1}{4}$ but $-\frac{1}{2} \neq \alpha$ and $\frac{1}{2} \neq \beta$. (Note that here $\alpha = -1$ and $\beta = 1$). As another example, the circle

$$z = \cos t + i \sin t, \ 0 \le t \le 2\pi,$$

is a simple closed Jordan curve since the values of $z(t)$ coincide only at the end points $t = 0$ and $t = 2\pi$.

The Jordan curve theorem: It states' that a simple closed Jordan curve divides the Argand plane into two open domains which have the curve as common boundary.

On of these domains is bounded and is called the *interior* domain. The other is unbounded and is called the *exterior*. For example, the circle $|z| = r$, divides the Argand plane into two open domains defined by $|z| < r$ which is the interior and $|z| > r$ which is the exterior. The circle $|z| = r$ is the common boundary of the two domains.

FUNCTION OF A COMPLEX VARIABLE

Definition: *If a rule or set of rules be given by means of which it is possible to find one or more complex numbers w for every value of z in a certain domain D, we say that w is a function of z defined on the domain D and write*

$$w = f(z).$$

Since $z = x + iy$, $f(z)$ will be of the form $u + iv$ where u and v are functions of two real variables x and y.

We may then write

$$w = u(x, y) + iv(x, y).$$

Single valued and multiple valued functions: w is said to be single valued or multiple valued function ofz according as for a given value of z there correspond one or more than one values of w.

LIMITS AND CONTINUITY

Limit of a function: Let $w = f(z)$ be any function of z defined in a bounded and closed domain D. We say that f(z) tends to the limit I as z tends to a along any path in D, if to each positive arbitrary number ε, however small, there corresponds a positive number 6 such that $|f(z) - l| < \varepsilon$, for all points z of D for which

$$0 < | z - a | < \delta.$$

We write $\lim_{z \to a} f(z) = l.$

Thus above definition means that there exists a *deleted neighbourhood* of the point z = a in which | f(z) – *l* | can be made as small as we please.

Continuity: A function w = f(z) defined in the bounded closed domain D, is said to be continuous at a point z = a of D, if, given any positive number ε, we can find a positive number δ, such that | f(z) – f(a) | < ε for all points z of D for which

$$0 \leq | z - a | < \delta.$$

It follows from the above definition and the definition and the definition of limit that f(z) will be continuous at z = a if

$$\lim_{z \to a} f(z) = f(a)$$

Again a function f(z) is said to be continuous in a domain D if it is continuous at every point of D.

Continuity in terms of real and imaginary parts of f(z): It can be easily shown that if

$$f(z) = u(x, y) + iv\,(x, y).$$

is a continuous function of z, then u(x, y) and v (x, y) are separately continuous functions of x,y and conversely if u (x, y) and v (x, y) are continuous functions of x, y then f(z) is a continuous function of z.

Also if lim f(z) = *l*, then lim $f(\overline{z}) = \overline{l}$.

Uniform continuity: A function f(z) is said to be *uniformly continuous in the Domain D* if for a given ε > 0, it is possible to find a number δ > 0 depending upon ε only such that the inequality $| f(z_1) - f(z_2) | < \varepsilon$ holds for every pair of points z_1, z_2 of the domain D for which

$$| z_1 - z_2 | < < \delta.$$

It should be noted that continuity at every point of an open domain D does not necessarily imply uniform continuity in D. If however, the function f(z) is continuous at every point of a closed and bounded (*i.e.* compact) domain D, then it is uniformly continuous in D.

DIFFERENTIABILITY

Let w = f(z) be a function of z defined in a domain D. Then f(z) is said to be differentiable at z = a if the increment ratio

$$\frac{\Delta w}{\Delta z} = \frac{f(a + \Delta z) - f(a)}{\Delta z}$$

tends to a unique finite limit as z tends to a (*i.e.* as Δz tends to zero) along any path of the domain D, and this unique limit is called the *derivative* of f(z) at z = a and is denoted by f' (a).

$$\text{Thus } f'(a) = \lim_{\Delta z \to 0} \frac{f(a + \Delta z) - f(a)}{\Delta z} \text{ if the limit exists.}$$

$$\text{Equivalently we write } f'(a) = \lim_{z \to 0} \frac{f(z) - f(a)}{z - a}$$

If we get different values of this limit as $z \to a$ from different points of D, *i.e. if the limit depends upon amp* Δz, we say that the derivative of f(z) at z = a does not exist and the function f(z) is said to be *non-differentiable* at z = a.

Hence in order to prove non-differentiability of f(z), we should try different paths for Δz. Convenient paths for Δz are along real and imaginary axes *i.e.* by taking Δz either *wholly real or wholly imaginary.*

Just as in the case of real variable, we also have in the case of complex variable the theorem which states.

Theorem I:

Continuity is a necessary but not a sufficient condition for the existence of a finite derivative.

Proof:

From the identity,

$$f(a + \Delta z) - f(a) = \Delta z. [f(a + \Delta z) - f(a)]/\Delta z$$

we obtain $\lim_{\Delta z \to 0} [f(a + \Delta z) - f(a)] = 0f'(a) = 0$

or $$\lim_{z \to 0} [f(z) - f(a)] = 0$$

that is, $\lim_{z \to 0} f(z) = f(a)$

It follows that f(z) is continuous at z = a.

Rule of differentiation: We have defined the derivative of a complex function in precisely the same manner as the corresponding notion in the case of a function of a single real variable.

The definition depends upon the rational operations of arithmetic and the notion of a limit, both of which remain unchanged when we go over from the real domain to the complex domain.

Consequently, all the rules of differential calculus remain the same when applied to complex functions. Thus the following rules hold :

MULTIPLE VALUED FUNCTIONS; BRANCHES

While defining analytic functions, we have seen that an analytic function must be *one-valued or uniform*. There are, however, a large number of functions which are many-valued e.g. $\tan^{-1}z$, $\log z, z^n$ (n not an integer). To explain the idea of many valuedness, we consider the simple case of the function $z^{1/2}$.

Let $$w = z^{1/2}.$$

Putting $z = r(\cos\theta + i\sin\theta)$, where r is fixed and θ lies between 0 and 2π, we see that two obvious values of w are given by $w_1 = |\sqrt{r}|\, e^{(1/2)i\theta}$ and $w_2 = |\sqrt{r}\, e^{i(1/2)(\theta+\pi)} = -|\sqrt{r}|\, e^{(1/2)i\theta}$, and called the two *branches* of the two-valued function w.

A branch F of a multiple valued function f if any single-valued function which is analytic in some domain at each point of which F(z) is one of the values of f(z).

Branch-Cut or Cross-cut: By making a narrow slit, extending from the origin to infinity along the positive real axis, we see that each of the branches wi and w2 is a one-valued function in the z-plane if we distinguish between the values of the function at points on the upper and lower edges of the cut.

If OA = a, the value of w_1 at A (θ = 0) is $|\sqrt{a}|$ and the value of w_1 at B (θ = 2π) is $-|\sqrt{a}|$. Now on account of the cut, a complete circuit about the origin is not passible.

Hence if we start with a value of z belonging to the branch w_1, we can never change over to the branch w_2. Thus w_1 (and similarly w_2) is a one-valued function on the cut plane.

The part of the real axis from x = 0 to x = ∞, is called *branch-cut* or *cross-cut* for the branch w_1. Cross-cut is a boundary so introduced that the corresponding branch is single-valued and regular throughout the cut plane. It is conventional to choose the positive real axis as the branch-cut. We might, if we like, take the negative real axis, or more generally, any simple curve connecting the point z = 0 and z = ∞.

In general, if w = f(z) is the mathematical solution of a wellposed physical problem and w is many-valued, only one of its branches has a physical meaning. Hence complete turns around a branch point must be forbidden to ensure a one-one correspondence between z and w. This is obtained by drawing a line on the z-plane forbidden z to cross it. Such a line is called a cross-cut or branch-cut.

Branch point: If z describes a circle of radius r about the origin, $\omega_1 = |r|\, e^{(1/2)\theta i}$ varies continuously, its value at θ = 0 being $|\sqrt{r}|$ and the final value of w_1 is $|\sqrt{r}|\, e^{(1/2)2\pi i} = -|\sqrt{r}| = w_2$ at θ = 2π.

Hence the function w_1 is apparently discontinuous along the positive real axis since the value just above and just below the real axis differ in sign and are not zero except at the origin itself. If, however, z describes a circle round the origin a second time, the values of w_1 continue those of wz and at the end of second round, we have $w_2 = w_1$ along the positive real axis.

We now distinguish the point $z = 0$ from all other points. We see that if z describes a circle about any point a and the origin lies outside this circle, then arg z is not increased by 2π but returns to its initial value. Hence the values of w_1 and w_2 are exchanged only when z turns *about the origin.*

On accout of this fact, the point $z = 0$ is called a branch-point of the function $w = \sqrt{z}$ and as we have already stated, w_1 and w_2 are called its two branches.

Definition: If a point is such that some of the branches of a many-valued function interchange as the independent variable describes a closed path about it, then it is called a *branch-point.*

The banch-points of a function are always to be found among those points for which two or more of the values of the function become equal. This common value of the various branches of the function may be finite or infinite.

ANALYTIC FUNCTION

Let f(z) be a single valued function defined in a domain D. Then f(z) is said to be analytic at a point z_0 of D if it is differentiable not only at z_0 but also in some neighbourhood of z_0.

A single valued function which is differentiable at each point of a domain D is said to be analytic in the domain D.

A function, which is analytic, is also called a *Holomorphic function.*

If a function f(z) is analytic in every neighbourhood of a point z_0 except at z_0 itself, z_0 is called an *isolated singularity* of f(z).

A function f(z) defined in a domain D is said to have *removable singularity* at a point z_0 of D if f(z) is not analytic at z_0 but can be made analytic by simply assigning a suitable value to f(z) at the point z_0.

A function f(z) is said to be ***regular*** at a point z_0 if it is analytic in some deleted neighbourhood of z_0 and has a removable singularity at z_0. Some authors use the term regular as a synonym for analytic.

THE NECESSARY AND SUFFICIENT CONDITIONS FOR F(Z) TO BE ANALYTIC

(a) The Necessary Condition for f(z) to be Analytic.

Theorem 1:

If a function $f(z) = u(x, y) + iv(x, y)$ is differentiable at any point $z = x + iy$, the partial derivatives u_x, v_x, u_y, v_y should exist and satisfy the equations $u_x = v_y$, $u_y = -v_x$.

Proof:

We have

$$w = f(z) = u(x, y) + iv(x, y) \quad ...(1)$$

andz $= x + iy$, $\Delta z = \Delta x + i\Delta y$,

Since the function is differentiable at any point z, therefore the limit given by

$\lim\limits_{\Delta z \to 0} \frac{\Delta f}{\Delta z} = \lim\limits_{\Delta z \to 0} \frac{f(z + \Delta z) - f(z)}{\Delta z}$ must exist uniquely as $Dz \to 0$ along any path we choose.

Using relations (1) the above limit can be written as

$$\lim_{\Delta z \to 0}\left[\frac{u(x + \Delta x, y + dy) - u(x, y)}{\Delta x + i\Delta y} + i\frac{v(x + \Delta x, y + \Delta y) - v(x, y)}{\Delta x + i\Delta y}\right] \quad ...(2)$$

Taking $\Delta z \to 0$ along real exist, we get $\Delta y = 0$. In this case the limit given by (2) becomes

$$\lim_{\Delta x \to 0}\left[\frac{u(x + \Delta x, y) - u(x, y)}{\Delta x} + i\frac{v(x + \Delta x, y) - v(x, y)}{\Delta x}\right]$$

$= \frac{\partial u}{\partial x} + i\frac{\partial v}{\partial x}$, since f(z) is differentiable therefore the partial derivatives $\frac{\partial u}{\partial x}, \frac{\partial v}{\partial x}$ must also exist

$$= u_x + iv_x. \quad ...(3)$$

Again taking $Dz \to 0$ along imaginary axis, we get $\Delta x = 0$. In this case the limit given in (2) becomes

$$\lim_{\Delta y \to 0}\left[\frac{u(x, y + \Delta y) - u(x, y)}{i\Delta y} + i\frac{v(x, y + \Delta y) - v(x, y)}{i\Delta y}\right]$$

$= \frac{1}{i}\frac{\partial u}{\partial y} + \frac{\partial v}{\partial y}$, since f(z) is differentiable, therefore $\frac{\partial u}{\partial y}, \frac{\partial v}{\partial y}$ also exist

$$= -iu_y + v_y \equiv v_y \quad iu_y. \quad ...(4)$$

Since the limit given by $\lim_{\Delta z \to 0} \frac{\Delta f}{\Delta z}$ is unique, therefore equating real and imaginary parts of (3) and (4), we get

$$u_x = v_y, \ v_x = -u_y.$$

These two equations are known as *Cauchy-Riemann Partial Differential Equations.*

(b) Sufficient Condition for f(z) to be Analytic.

Theorem 2:

The single valued continuous function f(z) is analytic in a domain D if the four partial derivatives u_x, v_x, u_y, v_y exist, are continuous and satisfy Cauchy-Riemann equations at each point of D.

Proof:

We have $w = f(z) = u(x, y) + iv(x, y)$.

Now, $u = u(x, y)$, so that $u + \Delta u = u(x + \Delta x, y + \Delta y)$.

$\therefore \quad \Delta u = u(x + \Delta x, y + \Delta y) - u(x, y)$

$= u(x + \Delta x, y + \Delta y) - u(x + \Delta x, y) + u(x + \Delta x, y) - u(x, y)$

$= \Delta y \, u_y(x + \Delta x, y + \theta_1 \Delta y) + \Delta x \, u_x(x + \theta_2 \Delta x, y)$, ...(1)

where $0 < \theta_1 < 1$, $0 < \theta_2 < 1$, by the Mean Value Theorem.

Since u_x and u_y are continuous in the given domain D, therefore by the definition of uniform continuity, we have

$$|u_x(x + \theta_2 \Delta x, y) - u_x(x, y)| < \varepsilon, \quad ...(2)$$

and $|u_y(x + \Delta x, y + \theta_1 \Delta y) - u_y(x, y)| < \varepsilon$

provided $|\Delta x| < \delta$ and $|\Delta y| < \delta$.

Let $u_y(x + \Delta x, y + \theta_1 \Delta y) - u_y(x, y) = \alpha_1$

and $u_x(x + \theta_2 \Delta x, y) - u_x(x, y) = \beta_1$.

Then from (2), we have $|\alpha_1| < \varepsilon_1$, $|\beta_1| < \varepsilon_1$.

Putting these values in (1), we get

$$\Delta u = \{\alpha_1 + u_y(x, y)\} \Delta y + \{\beta_1 + u_x(x, y)\} \Delta x.$$

Proceeding in the same way, we shall get

$\Delta v = \{\alpha_2 + v_y(x, y)\} \Delta y + \{\beta_2 + v_x(x, y)\} \Delta x$, where $|\alpha_2| < \varepsilon_2$, $|\beta_2| < \varepsilon_2$.

Now, $\frac{\Delta f}{\Delta z} = \frac{\partial u + i\Delta v}{\partial x + i\Delta y}$

$$= \frac{\left(u_y \Delta y + u_x \Delta x + \alpha_1 \Delta y + \beta_1 \Delta x\right) + i\left(v_y \Delta y + v_x \Delta x + \alpha_2 \Delta y + \beta_2 \Delta x\right)}{\Delta x + i\Delta y}$$

$$= \frac{-v_x \Delta y + u_x \Delta x + iu_x \Delta y + \alpha_1 \Delta x + \alpha_1 \Delta y + \beta_1 \Delta x + i\alpha_2 \Delta y + i\beta_2 \Delta x}{\Delta x + i\Delta y}$$

$[\because\ u_x = v_y,\ v_x = -u_y]$

$$= \frac{\left(u_x + iv_x\right)\left(\Delta x + i\Delta y\right) + \alpha_1 \Delta y + \beta_1 \Delta x + i\alpha_2 \Delta y + i\beta_2 \Delta x}{\Delta x + i\Delta y}$$

$$= u_x + iv_x + \frac{\left(\alpha_1 + i\alpha_2\right)\Delta y}{\Delta x + i\Delta y} + \frac{\left(\beta_1 + i\beta_2\right)\Delta x}{\Delta x + i\Delta y}$$

or $$\left|\frac{\Delta f}{\Delta z} - \left(u_x + iv_x\right)\right| = \left|\frac{\left(\alpha_1 + i\alpha_2\right)\Delta y}{\Delta x + i\Delta y} + \frac{\left(\beta_1 + i\beta_2\right)\Delta x}{\Delta x + i\Delta y}\right|$$

$$\leq \frac{\left|\alpha_1 + i\alpha_2\right|\left|\Delta y\right|}{\left|\Delta x + i\Delta y\right|} + \frac{\left|\beta_1 + i\beta_2\right|\left|\Delta x\right|}{\left|\Delta x + i\Delta y\right|}$$

$$\leq |\alpha_1| + |\alpha_2| + |\beta_1| + |\beta_2|$$

$[\because\ |\Delta x| \leq |\Delta x + i\Delta y| \text{ and } |\Delta y| \leq |\Delta x + i\Delta y|]$

$$\therefore \qquad \left|\frac{\Delta f}{\Delta z} - \left(u_x + iv_x\right)\right| \leq 2\varepsilon_1 + 2\varepsilon_2 .$$

Hence, $u_x + iv_x = \lim_{\Delta z \to 0} \frac{\Delta f}{\Delta z} = f'(z)$.

Note : (i) $|f'(z)|^2 = |u_x|^2 + |v_x|^2$

$= u_x^2 + v_x^2 = u_x v_y - v_x u_y$, using Cauchy-Riemann Equations

$$= \frac{\partial(u, v)}{\partial(x, y)}.$$

(ii) Statement of Lagrange's Mean Value Theorem :

If f(x) is defined and continuous in $a \leq x \leq a + h$, differentiable in $a < x < a + h$, then there exists a point $c = a + \theta h$, $(0 < \theta < 1)$ in] a, a + h [such that

$f(a + h) - f(a) = hf'(a - qh)$.

(iii) We have $w = f(z) = u + iv$, where $z = x + iy$.

In the above theorem we get the result

$$f'(z) = u_x + iv_x$$

or $$\frac{dw}{dz} = \frac{\partial u}{\partial x} + i\frac{\partial v}{\partial x}$$

or $$\frac{dw}{dz} = \frac{\partial}{\partial x}(u + iv) \quad \text{or} \quad \frac{dw}{dz} = \frac{\partial w}{\partial x}.$$

ORTHOGONAL SYSTEM

Two facilities of curves are said to form an orthogonal system if they intersect at right angles at each of their points of intersection.

Theorem:

If $f(z) = u + iv$ be an analytic function of $z = x + iy$, prove that the families of curves $u = c_1$, $v = c_2$ are orthogonal to each other, where c_1 and c_2 are parameters.

Proof:

It is given that $f(z) = u + iv$ is an analytic function therefore we have

$$u_x = v_y,\ v_x = -u_y. \qquad ...(1)$$

The given systems are

$$u(x, y) = c_1, \qquad ...(2)$$

$$v(x, y) = c_2. \qquad ...(3)$$

Let m_1 and m_2 be the slopes of curves (2) and (3) respectively.

From(2) $$\frac{dy}{dx} = -\frac{\partial u/\partial x}{\partial u/\partial y} = m_1.$$

From(3) $$\frac{dy}{dx} = -\frac{\partial u/\partial x}{\partial u/\partial y} = m_2.$$

Now $$m_1 m_2 - \left(-\frac{\partial u/\partial x}{\partial u/\partial y}\right) \times \left(-\frac{\partial v/\partial x}{\partial v/\partial y}\right)$$

$$= -1, \text{ from (1)}.$$

Hence the systems $u = c_1$ and $v = c_2$ are orthogonal to each other.

HARMONIC FUNCTION

Any function of x and y possessing continuous partial derivatives of the first and second orders and satisfying Laplace's equation is called a harmonic function.

Theorem:

Let f(z) = u + iv is an analytic function, u and v are both harmonic functions.

Proof:

Let f(z) = u + iv be an analytic function. Then it satisfies Cauchy-Riemann equations.

$$\therefore \frac{\partial u}{\partial x} = \frac{\partial v}{\partial y} \text{ and } \frac{\partial u}{\partial y} = -\frac{\partial v}{\partial x} \quad \text{...(1)}$$

Since u and v are the real and imaginary parts of an analytic function therefore partial derivatives of u and v of all orders exist and are continuous functions of x and y.

From (1), we have

$$\frac{\partial^2 u}{\partial x^2} = \frac{\partial^2 v}{\partial x\, \partial y} \text{ and } \frac{\partial^2 u}{\partial y^2} = -\frac{\partial^2 v}{\partial y\, \partial x}.$$

$$\therefore \quad \frac{\partial^2 u}{\partial x^2} + \frac{\partial^2 u}{\partial y^2} = 0.$$

Similarly, $\frac{\partial^2 v}{\partial x^2} + \frac{\partial^2 v}{\partial y^2} = 0$.

Therefore, the functions u and v satisfy the Laplace's equation

$$\frac{\partial^2 \phi}{\partial x^2} + \frac{\partial^2 \phi}{\partial y^2} = 0.$$

Hence, u and v are harmonic functions.

Note: If f(z) = u + iv is analytic then u and v are both harmonic functions. Such functions u and v are called *Conjugate Harmonic Functions* or simply *Conjugate Functions.*

DETERMINATION OF THE CONJUGATE FUNCTION

If f(z) = u + iv is an analytic function, u and v are called conjugate functions. Being given one of these say, u (x, y), to determine the other v(x, y).

We have $dv = \frac{\partial v}{\partial x}dx + \frac{\partial v}{\partial y}dy$, since v is a function of x and y

or $dv = -\frac{\partial u}{\partial y}dx + \frac{\partial u}{\partial x}dy$, ...(1)

by Cauchy-Riemann Equations.

The equation (1) is of the form dv = Mdx + Ndy,

where $M = -\frac{\partial u}{\partial y}$, $N = \frac{\partial u}{\partial x}$.

Now $\frac{\partial M}{\partial y} = -\frac{\partial^2 u}{\partial y^2}$ and $\frac{\partial N}{\partial x} = \frac{\partial^2 u}{\partial x^2}$.

Since f(z) is an analytic function therefore u is a harmonic function *i.e.*, it satisfies Laplace's Equation.

$$\therefore \frac{\partial^2 u}{\partial x^2} + \frac{\partial^2 u}{\partial y^2} = 0 \text{ or } \frac{\partial^2 u}{\partial x^2} = -\frac{\partial^2 u}{\partial y^2} \text{ so that } \frac{\partial M}{\partial y} = \frac{\partial N}{\partial x}.$$

The equation (1) satisfies the condition of exact differential equation. Therefore v can be determined by integrating (1).

METHODS OF CONSTRUCTING A REGULAR FUNCTION

Mine-Thomson's Method : We have f(z) = u(x, y) + iv(x, y) and z = x + iy.

Then $x = \frac{1}{2}(z + \bar{z})$, $y = \frac{1}{2i}(z - \bar{z})$.

We can write

$$f(z) = u\left[\frac{1}{2}(z + \bar{z}), \frac{1}{2i}(z - \bar{z})\right] + iv\left[\frac{1}{2}(z + \bar{z}), \frac{1}{2i}(z - \bar{z})\right]. \quad \text{...(1)}$$

This relation can be regarded a formal identity into two independent variables z and $\bar{z}$. Putting z = $\bar{z}$ in (1), we get

$$f(z) = u(z, 0) + iv(z, 0).$$

We have $f'(z) = \frac{\partial f}{\partial x} = u_x + iv_x$

$= u_x - iu_y$, by Cauchy-Riemann Equations.

Let $u_x = \phi_1(x, y)$, $u_y = \phi_2(x, y)$.

Then $f'(z) = \phi_1(x, y) - i\phi_2(x, y)$

$= \phi_1(z, 0) - i\,\phi_2(z, 0)$.

Integrating we get

$$f(z) = f(z) = \int \phi_1(z, 0)\, dz - i \int \phi_2(z, 0)\, dz + c,$$

where c is constant of integration.

Similarly if v is given, we have

$$f\,f(z) = \int \psi_1(z, 0)\,dx - i\int \phi_2(z, 0)\,dz + c',$$

where $v_y = \phi_1(x, y),\ v_x = \psi_2(x, y).$

Theorem:

If the real part of an analytic function f(z) is a given harmonic function u(x, y), then

$f(z) = 2u(z/2, z/2i) - u(0, 0) + ci$, where c is real.

Proof:

Let $f(z) = f(x + iy) = u(x, y) + iv(x, y)$.

Then $\overline{f(z)} = \overline{f(x+iy)} = u(x, y) + iv(x, y)$

Adding, we get $f(x + iy) + \overline{f(x+iy)} = 2u(x, y)$

Since $\overline{f(z)}$ is a function independent of z, therefore it can be regarded as a function of $\bar{z}$. So we can write

$$\overline{f(z)} = \bar{f}(\bar{z}).$$

We can rewrite relation (1) as

$$u(x, y) = \frac{1}{2}\left[f(x + iy) + \bar{f}(x - iy)\right]. \qquad \text{...(2)}$$

We can regard (2) as a formal identity, therefore, it holds even when x and y are complex. Putting $x = z/2 = z/2i$, we get

$$u(z/2, z/2i) = \frac{1}{2}\left[f\left(\frac{z}{2} + i\frac{z}{2i}\right) + \bar{f}\left(\frac{z}{2} - i\frac{z}{2i}\right)\right] = \frac{1}{2}\left[f(z) + \bar{f}(0)\right].$$

$\therefore f(z) = 2u(z/2, z/2i) - \bar{f}(0)$.

Since f(z) is only determined upto a purely imaginary constant, we may assume that f(0) is real. So we have

$$\bar{f}(0) = u(0, 0).$$

$\therefore \qquad f(z) = 2u(z/2, z/2i) - u(0, 0).$

Adding a purely imaginary constant, we have

$f(z) = 2u(z/2, z/2i) - u(0, 0) + ci$, where c is real.

POLAR FORM OF CAUCHY-RIEMANN EQUATIONS

We have $\qquad x = r\cos\theta,\ y = r\sin\theta.$

$\therefore \qquad x^2 + y^2 = r^2$ ...(1)

and $\theta = \tan^{-1}(y/x)$. ...(2)

and $\theta = \tan^{-1}(y/x)$

Differentiating (1) and (2) partially w.r.t. x and y, we get

$$\frac{\partial r}{\partial x} = \frac{x}{r} = \cos\theta, \frac{\partial r}{\partial y} = \frac{y}{r} = \sin\theta$$

$$\frac{\partial \theta}{\partial r} = \frac{1}{1+(y/x)^2}\left(-\frac{y}{x^2}\right) = -\frac{y}{x^2+y^2} = -\frac{\sin\theta}{r}$$

and $$\frac{\partial \theta}{\partial y} = \frac{1}{1+(y/x)^2}\left(\frac{1}{x}\right) = \frac{x}{x^2+y^2} = \frac{\cos\theta}{r}.$$

Now, $$\frac{\partial u}{\partial x} = \frac{\partial u}{\partial r}\frac{\partial r}{\partial x} + \frac{\partial u}{\partial \theta}\frac{\partial \theta}{\partial x} = \frac{\partial u}{\partial r}\cos\theta + \frac{\partial u}{\partial \theta}\frac{\sin\theta}{r},$$

$$\frac{\partial u}{\partial y} = \frac{\partial u}{\partial r}\frac{\partial r}{\partial y} + \frac{\partial u}{\partial \theta}\frac{\partial \theta}{\partial y} = \frac{\partial u}{\partial r}\sin\theta + \frac{\partial u}{\partial \theta}\frac{\cos\theta}{r},$$

$$\frac{\partial v}{\partial x} = \frac{\partial v}{\partial r}\frac{\partial r}{\partial x} + \frac{\partial v}{\partial \theta}\frac{\partial \theta}{\partial x} = \frac{\partial v}{\partial r}\cos\theta - \frac{\partial v}{\partial \theta}\frac{\sin\theta}{r},$$

and $$\frac{\partial v}{\partial y} = \frac{\partial v}{\partial r}\frac{\partial r}{\partial y} + \frac{\partial v}{\partial \theta}\frac{\partial \theta}{\partial y} = \frac{\partial v}{\partial r}\sin\theta + \frac{\partial v}{\partial \theta}\frac{\cos\theta}{r}.$$

Cauchy-Riemann Equations in cartesian form are

$$\frac{\partial u}{\partial x} = \frac{\partial v}{\partial y} \text{ and } \frac{\partial u}{\partial y} = -\frac{\partial v}{\partial x}.$$

Substituting in these equations from above, we get

$$\frac{\partial u}{\partial r}\cos\theta - \frac{\partial u}{\partial \theta}\frac{\sin\theta}{r} = \frac{\partial v}{\partial r}\sin\theta + \frac{\partial v}{\partial \theta}\cos\theta \qquad ...(3)$$

and $$\frac{\partial u}{\partial r}\sin\theta + \frac{\partial u}{\partial \theta}\frac{\cos\theta}{r} = -\frac{\partial v}{\partial r}\cos\theta + \frac{\partial v}{\partial \theta}\frac{\sin\theta}{r}. \qquad ...(4)$$

Multiplying (3) by $\cos\theta$ and (4) by $\sin\theta$ and adding, we get

$$\frac{\partial u}{\partial r} = \frac{1}{r}\frac{\partial v}{\partial \theta}. \qquad ...(5)$$

Again multiplying (3) by $\sin\theta$ and (4) by $\cos\theta$ and subtracting, we get

$$\frac{1}{r}\frac{\partial u}{\partial \theta} = -\frac{\partial v}{\partial r}. \qquad ...(6)$$

Equations (5) and (6) are the Cauchy-Riemann equations in polar form.

DERIVATIVE OF W = F(Z) IN POLAR FORM

We have $\dfrac{dw}{dz}\ \dfrac{\partial w}{\partial x} = \dfrac{\partial w}{\partial r}\dfrac{\partial r}{\partial x} + \dfrac{\partial w}{\partial \theta}\dfrac{\partial \theta}{\partial x}$

$$= \left(\frac{\partial u}{\partial r} + i\frac{\partial v}{\partial r}\right)\frac{\partial r}{\partial x} + \left(\frac{\partial u}{\partial \theta} + i\frac{\partial v}{\partial \theta}\right)\frac{\partial \theta}{\partial x}$$

$[\because\ w = u + iv]$

$$= \left(\frac{\partial u}{\partial r} + i\frac{\partial v}{\partial r}\right)\cos\theta + \left(\frac{\partial u}{\partial \theta} + i\frac{\partial v}{\partial \theta}\right)\left(-\frac{\sin\theta}{r}\right),$$

$$= \left(\frac{\partial u}{\partial r} + i\frac{\partial v}{\partial r}\right)\cos\theta - \left(-r\frac{\partial v}{\partial r} + ir\frac{\partial u}{\partial r}\right)\frac{\sin\theta}{r}, \text{ from (5) and (6)}$$

$$= \left(\frac{\partial u}{\partial r} + i\frac{\partial v}{\partial r}\right)\cos\theta - i\left(\frac{\partial u}{\partial r} + i\frac{\partial v}{\partial r}\right)\sin\theta$$

$$= \left(\frac{\partial u}{\partial r} + i\frac{\partial v}{\partial r}\right)(\cos\theta - i\sin\theta)$$

$$= \frac{\partial w}{\partial r}e^{-i\theta}.$$

A SUFFICIENT CONDITION FOR CONTINUITY

A sufficient condition that a function f be continuous at (a, b) is that one of the partial derivatives exists and is bounded in a neighbourhood of (a, b) and that the other exists at (a, b).

Let f_x exist and be bounded in a neighbourhood of (a, b) and let $f_y(a, b)$ exist; then for any point (a + h, b + k) of this neighbourhood, we have

$f(a + h, b + k) - f(a, b)$

$= hf_x(a + \theta h, b + k) + k[f_y(a, b) + \eta]$

where $0 < \theta < 1$, and $\eta \to 0$ as $k \to 0$.

Proceeding to limits as $(\eta, k) \to (0, 0)$, since $f_x(a + \theta h, b + k)$ is bounded, we have

$$\lim_{(h,k)\to(0,0)} f(a + h, b + k) = f(a, b)$$

$\Rightarrow$ f is continuous at (a, b).

Note: A sufficient condition that a function be continuous in a *closed region* is that both the partial derivatives exist and are bounded throughout the region.

DIFFERENTIABILITY AT A POINT

Definition: Let $f : D \to R$ be a real-valued function defined on an open set $D \subset R^2$. Then f is said to be *differentiable at a point (a, b)* $\in$ D, if

$$f(a + h, b + k) - f(a, b) = Ah + Bk + \sqrt{h^2 + k^2}\, g(h, k),$$

where A and B are real numbers independent of h and k, and g is a real-valued function such that $\lim_{(h,k)\to(0,0)} g(h, k) = 0$.

Equivalently, f is differentiable at (a, b), if

$$f(a + h, b + k) - f(a, b) = Ah + Bk + h\phi(h, k) + k\phi(h, k),$$

where A and B are real numbers independent of h and K and $\phi(h, k)$, $\phi(h, k) \to 0$ as $(h, k) \to (0, 0)$.

Theorem 1:

If a function $f : D \to R$ is differentiable at (a, b) $\in$ D, then f has partial derivatives f_x and f_y at (a, b).

Proof:

Since f is differentiable at the point (a, b) $\in$ D, so there exist real numbers A and B, and a function g such that

(i) $f(a + h, b + k) - f(a, b) = Ah + Bk + \sqrt{(h^2 + k^2)}g(h, k)$, ...(1)

(ii) A and B are independent of h and k, and

(iii) $\lim_{(h,k)\to(0,0)} g(h, k) = 0$

Putting k = 0 in equation (i) we have

$f(a + h, b) - f(a, b) = Ah + |h|\, g(h, 0)$.

Dividing throughout by h, and taking limits as $h \to 0$, then we have

$$\lim_{h\to 0} \frac{f(a+h, b) - f(a, b)}{h} = \lim_{h\to 0}\left[A + \frac{|h|}{h} g(h,0)\right]$$

$= A + (\pm 1).0 = A$, since $g(h, 0) \to 0$ as $h \to 0$.

$\therefore \quad f_x(a, b) = A.$

Putting h = 0 in (1), we have

$f(a, b + k) - f(a, b) = Bk + |k|\, g(0, k)$.

Dividing throughout by k, and taking limits as $k \to 0$, we have

$$\lim_{k\to 0} \frac{f(a, b + k) - f(a, b)}{k} = B.$$

∴ $f_y(a, b) = B$.

Hence f_x and f_y exist at the point (a, b).

Remark 1:

If may be noted that the constants A, B appearing in the definition of differentiability of f are given by:

$A = f_x(a, b),\ B = f_y(a, b).$

Remark 2:

If either of f_x, f_y does not exists at (a, b), then f is not differentiable at (a, b).

Remark 3:

The converse of the above example is not true as shown in the following example.

Theorem 2:

If a function $f: D \to R$ has continuous partial derivatives f_x and f_y at $(a, b) \in D$, then f is differentiable at (a, b).

Proof:

Since f_x and f_y are continuous at (a, b), so f_x and f_y both exist in a nbd. $N \equiv N((a, b), \delta)$ of (a, b). Let (a + h, b + k) be any point of N. We have

$$f(a + h, b + k) - f(a, b) = [f(a + h, b + k) - f(a + h, b)] + [f(a + h, b) - f(a, b)]. \quad ...(1)$$

We define two functions G and H as given below

$G(y) = f(a + h, y) \quad \forall \quad y \in [b, b + k],$

and $H(x) = f(x, b) \quad \forall \quad x \in [a, a + h].$

Since f_y exists in N, so the function G satisfies both the conditions of Lagrange's Mean Value Theorem in [b, b + k]. Thus there exists a θ_1 $(0 < \theta_1 < 1)$ such that

$G(b + k) - G(b) = kG'(b + \theta_1 k)$

or $f(a + h, b + k) - f(a + h, b) = kf_y(a + h, b + \theta_1 k). \quad ...(2)$

Similarly, since H satisfies both the conditions of Lagrange's mean value theorem in [a, a + h], there exists θ_2 $(0 < \theta_2 < 1)$ such that

$f(a + h, b) - f(a, b) = h\, f_x(a + \theta_2 h, b). \quad ...(3)$

Using (2) and (3) in (1), we have

$f(a + h, b + k) - f(a, b) = hf_x(a + \theta_2 h, b) + kf_y(a + h, b + \theta_1 k)$

$= hf_x(a, b) + kf_y(a, b) + h\,[f_x(a + \theta_2 h, b) - f_x(a, b)]$

$+ k\,[f_y(a + h, b + \theta_1 k) - f_y(a, b)]$

$= hf_x(a, b) + kf_y(a, b) + \sqrt{(h^2 + k^2)}.\ F(h, k),$ ...(4)

where$f(h, k) = h[f_x(a + \theta_2 h, b) - f_x(a, b)]/\sqrt{(h^2 + k^2)}$

$+ k[f_y(a + h, b + \theta_1 k) - f_y(a, b)]/\sqrt{(h^2 + k^2)}.$ ...(5)

Since f_x and f_y are both continuous at (a, b), so

$$\left.\begin{aligned} &\lim_{(h,k)\to(0,0)} f_x(a+\theta_2 h, b) = f_x(a,b), \\ \text{and}\quad &\lim_{(h,k)\to(0,0)} f_y(a+h, b+\theta_1 k) = f_y(a,b), \end{aligned}\right\} \quad ...(6)$$

From (5) and (6), we have

$$\lim_{(h,k)\to(0,0)} F(h, k) = 0, \quad ...(7)$$

since $\left|\dfrac{h}{\sqrt{(h^2+k^2}}\right| \le 1, \left|\dfrac{k}{\sqrt{(h^2+k^2}}\right| \le 1,$

for all values of (h, k), such that $h^2 + k^2 \neq 0$.

From (4) and (7), we get

$f(a + h, b + k) - f(a, b)$

$= h\,f_x(a, b) + k\,f_y(a, b) + \sqrt{(h^2 + k^2)}\,F(h, k),$

where $F(h, k) \to 0$ as $(h, k) \to (0, 0)$.

Hence f is differentiable at (a, b).

Remark 1:

The conditions of the above theorem are sufficient, but are not necessary. If a function f is differentiable at a point (a, b), then f_x, f_y may not be continuous at (a, b) as shown below:

Remark 2:

If a function f is not differentiable at (a, b), then f_x and f_y cannot be continuous at (a, b).

Theorem 3:

If a function $f : D \to R$ is differentiable at a point $(a, b) \in D$, then f is continuous at (a, b).

Proof:

Since f is differentiable at (a, b), so there exist real numbers A and B, and a function g such that

(i) $f(a + h, b + k) - f(a, b) = Ah + Bk + \sqrt{(h^2 + k^2)}\, g(h, k)$, ...(1)

(ii) A and B are independent of h and k, and

(iii) $\lim_{(h,k)\to(0,0)} g(h, k) = 0$.

Since $\lim_{(h,k)\to(0,0)} [Ah + Bk + \sqrt{(h^2 + k^2)}\, g(h, k)] = 0$,

$\therefore \lim_{(h,k)\to(0,0)} [f(a + h, b + k) - f(a, b)] = 0$, by (1)

$\Rightarrow \lim_{(h,k)\to(0,0)} f(a + h, b + k) = f(a, b)$.

Hence f is continuous at (a, b).

Remark:

The converse of the above theorem may not be true. A function may be continuous at a point without being differentiable at that point as shown below.

Theorem 4:

(Young's Theorem): *Let f be a real-valued function defined on an open set $D \subset R^2$ and $(a, b) \in D$. If f_x and f_y are both differentiable at (a, b), then $f_{xy}(a, b) = f_{yx}(a, b)$.*

Proof:

Since f_x and f_y are differentiable at (a, b), it follows that f_x and f_y both exist in a neighbourhood $N \equiv N((a, b), d)$ of (a, b), and that $f_{xx}, f_{yx}, f_{xy}, f_{yy}$ all exist at (a, b). Let $(a + h, b + h) \in N$ and that

$G(y) = f(a + h, y) - f(a, y) \quad \forall \; y \in (b, b + h)$. ...(1)

If $F = G(b + h) - G(b)$, then

$F = [f(a + h, b + h) - f(a, b + h)] - [f(a + h, b) - f(a, b)]$.

Since f_y exists in N, so G is differentiable in [b, b + h]. By Lagrange's Mean Value Theorem, there exists a $\theta \in (0, 1)$ such that

$F = hG'(b + \delta h) = h(a + h, b + \delta h) - f_y(a, b + \delta h)]$, by (1) ...(2)

Since f_y is differentiable at (a, b), therefore

$f_y(a + h, b + \delta h) - f_y(a, b) = Ah + B\theta h + h\delta_1(h, h) + \delta h\, \phi_2(h, h)$, ...(3)

where $\phi_1(h, h) \to 0$, $\phi_2(h, h) \to 0$ as $h \to 0$ and

$A = f_{xy}(a, b)$, $B = f_{yy}(a, b)$. ...(4)

Again, since f_y is differentiable at (a, b), therefore

$f_y(a, b + \delta h) - f_y(a, b) = A.0 + B.\delta h + 0.\phi_3(h, h) + \delta h\phi_4(h, h)$ ...(5)

where $\phi_2(h, h) \to 0$, $\phi_4(h, h) \to 0$ as $h \to 0$.

From equations (2) – (5), we obtain

$F/h^2 = f_{xy}(a, b) + \phi_1(h, h) + \delta\phi_2(h, h) - \delta\phi_4(h, h)$, ...(6)

where $\phi_1, \phi_2, \phi_4 \to 0$ as $h \to 0$.

Similarly if we take $F = H(a + h) - H(a)$, where

$H(x) = f(x, b + h) - f(x, b), \quad \forall\ x \in [a, a + h]$,

we can show that there exists a $\delta' \in (0, 1)$ such that

$F/h^2 = f_{yx}(a, b) + \psi_1(h, h) + \delta'\psi_2(h, h) - \delta'\psi_4(h, h)$, ...(7)

where $\psi_1, \psi_2, \psi_4 \to 0$ as $h \to 0$.

From (6) and (7), we obtain

$$\lim_{h \to 0} F/h^2 = f_{xy}(a, b) = f_{yx}(a, b).$$

Hence $f_{xy}(a, b) = f_{yx}(a, b)$.

Remark:

The conditions of Schwarz's and Young's Theorems are sufficient but they are not necessary conditions. The following example shows that the conditions are not necessary.

SCHWARZ'S AND YOUNG'S THEOREMS

In this section we shall discuss sufficient conditions so that

$f_{xy}(a, b) = f_{yx}(a, b)$.

These sufficient conditions are due to Schwarz and Young.

Theorem 5:

(Schwarz's Theorem): *Let f be a real-valued function defined on an open set $D \subset R^2$ and $(a, b) \in D$. If*

(i) f_x *exists in a neighbourhood of (a, b),*

(ii) f_{xy} *is continuous at (a, b),*

then $f_{yx}(a, b)$ *exists and is equal to* $f_{xy}(a, b)$.

Proof:

The hypotheses of the theorem imply that f_x, f_y and f_{xy} all exist in a neighbourhood $N \equiv N((a, b), \delta)$ of (a, b).

Let $(a + h, b + k) \in N$ and that

$G(y) = f(a + h, y) - f(a, y) \quad \forall \ y \in [b, b + k]$. ...(1)

If $F = G(b + k) - G(b)$, then by (1),

$F = [f(a + h, b + k) - f(a, b + k)] - [f(a + h, b) - f(a, b)]$. ...(2)

Since f_y exists in N, so by (1), G is differentiable in [b, b + k]. By Lagrange's Mean Value Theorem, there exists a $\delta \in (0, 1)$ such that

$F = kG'(b + \delta k) = k[f_y(a + h, b + \delta k) - f_y(a, b + \delta k)]$, by (1)

Again, since f_{xy} exists in N, the function $f_y(x, b + \delta k)$ is differentiable in [a, a + h]. Using Lagrange's Mean Value Theorem, there exists a $\delta' \in (0, 1)$ such that

$F = hk\, f_{xy}(a + \delta' h, b + \delta k)$. ...(3)

From (2) and (3), we obtain

$$\frac{1}{k}\left[\frac{f(a + h, b + k) - f(a, b + k)}{h} - \frac{f(a + h, b) - f(a, b)}{h}\right]$$
$$= f_{xy}(a + \delta' h, b + \delta k).$$

Since f_x exists in N, so on taking the limit as $h \to 0$, we obtain

$$\frac{1}{k}[f_x(a, b + k) - f_x(a, b) = \lim_{h \to 0} f_{xy}(a + \delta' h, b + \delta k).$$

$$\Rightarrow \lim_{k \to 0}[f_x(a, b + k) - f_x(a, b)]/k = \lim_{k \to 0} \lim_{h \to 0} f_{xy}(a + \delta' h, b + \delta k)$$

$\Rightarrow f_{yx}(a, b) = f_{xy}(a, b)$, since f_{xy} is continuous at (a, b).

Hence, $f_{yx}(a, b)$ exists and is equal to $f_{xy}(a, b)$.

Corollary:

If f_{xy} and f_{yx} are both continuous at (a, b), then

$f_{xy}(a, b) = f_{yx}(a, b)$.

Theorem 6:

Taylor's Theorem for a function of two variables.

If f(x, y) is a function of two independent variables x and y which possesses continuous partial derivatives of the nth order in some neighbourhood of a point (a, b), and if (a + h, b + k) is any point of this neighbourhood, then there exists some θ, $0 < \theta < 1$, such that

$$f(a + h, b + k) = f(a, b) + df(a, b) + \frac{1}{2!} d^2 f(a, b) + \ldots$$
$$+ \frac{1}{(n-1)!} d^{n-1} f(a,. b) + \frac{1}{n!} d^n f(a + \theta h, b + \theta k),$$

where $d = \left(h\frac{\partial}{\partial x} + k\frac{\partial}{\partial y}\right), \ldots, d^n = \left(\frac{\partial}{\partial x} + k\frac{\partial}{\partial y}\right)^n.$

Proof:

Let $x = a + ht$, $y = b + kt$, where $0 \le t \le 1$.

$\therefore \frac{dx}{dt} = h$ and $\frac{dy}{dt} = k$.

Now, $f(x, y) = f(a + ht, b + kt) = g(t)$ (say) ...(1)

Thus, g(t) is a function of a single variable t.

Since f possesses continuous partial dervatives of order n, so the function $g^n(t)$ is continuous in [0, 1]. Now

$$g'(t) = \frac{dg}{dt} = \frac{\partial g}{\partial x}\frac{dx}{dt} + \frac{\partial g}{\partial y}\frac{dy}{dt} = h\frac{\partial g}{\partial x} + k\frac{\partial g}{\partial y}$$

$$\therefore \quad g'(t) = \left(h\frac{\partial}{\partial x} + k\frac{\partial}{\partial y}\right)g.$$

Again $g''(t) = \frac{d^2g}{dt^2} = \frac{d}{dt}\left(h\frac{\partial}{\partial x} + k\frac{\partial}{\partial y}\right)g$

$$= \left(h\frac{\partial}{\partial x} + k\frac{\partial}{\partial y}\right)\frac{dg}{dt}.$$

$\therefore \quad g''(t) = \left(h\frac{\partial}{\partial x} + k\frac{\partial}{\partial y}\right)^2 g$ and so on.

Thus $g^k(t) = \left(h\frac{\partial}{\partial x} + k\frac{\partial}{\partial y}\right)^k g = d^k g$ (k = 1, 2, ..., n), ...(2)

where $\quad d = h\frac{\partial}{\partial x} + k\frac{\partial}{\partial y}.$

since $g^n(t)$ is continuous in [0, 1], so by Maclaurin's theorem, there exists a number θ, $0 < \theta < 1$, sucht aht

$$g(t) = g(0) + tg'(0) + \frac{t^2}{2!}g''(0) + \ldots + \frac{t^{n-1}}{(n-1)}g^{n-1}(0) + \frac{1}{n!}g^n(\theta t)$$

Putting t = 1, we get

$$g(1) = g(0) + g'(0) + \frac{1}{2!}g''(0) + \ldots + \frac{1}{(n-1)!}g^{n-1}(0) + \frac{1}{n!}g^n(\theta)$$

$$\left.\begin{aligned} &\text{From (1), } g(1) = f(a+h, b+k),\ g(0) = f(a, b). \\ &\text{From (2), } g^k(0) = \left(h\frac{\partial}{\partial x} + k\frac{\partial}{\partial y}\right)^k g(0) = d^k f(a, b). \end{aligned}\right\} \quad \ldots(4)$$

From (3) and (4), we obtain

$$f(a+h, b+k) = f(a, b) + df(a, b) + \frac{1}{2!}d^2f(a, b) + \ldots.$$

$$+ \frac{1}{(n-1)!}d^{n-1}f(a, b) + \frac{1}{n!}d^n f(a+\theta h, b+\theta k).$$

Remark:

For $t = 1$, we have $x = a + h$, $y = b + k$.

Thus Taylor's Theorem can be restated as :

$$f(x, y) = f(a, b) + \left[(x-a)\frac{\partial}{\partial x} + (y-b)\frac{\partial}{\partial y}\right] f(a, b)$$

$$+ \frac{1}{2}\left[(x-a)\frac{\partial}{\partial x} + (y-b)\frac{\partial}{\partial y}\right]^2 f(a, b) + \ldots.$$

$$+ \frac{1}{(n-1)!}\left[(x-a)\frac{\partial}{\partial x} + (y-b)\frac{\partial}{\partial y}\right]^{n-1} f(a, b) + R_n,$$

Where $R_n = \frac{1}{n!}\left[(x-a)\frac{\partial}{\partial x} + (y-b)\frac{\partial}{\partial y}\right]^n f(a + (x-a)\theta, b + (y-b)\theta)$.

*This is called the **Taylor's expansion** of $f(x, y)$ about the point (a, b) in powers of $x - a$ and $y - b$.*

DIRECTIONAL DERIVATIVES

Let f be a real-valued function defined on an open set $D \subset R^2$ and let $p = (a, b)$ be a point of D. Let $u = (h, k)$ be such that $h^2 + k^2 = 1$. Since D is an open set containing p, so there exists; an open disc $N(p, \delta)$ such that $N(p, \delta) \subset D$ for some $\delta > 0$. Thus for sufficiently small values of t, $(a + ht, b + kt) \in D$.

The directional derivative of f in the direction u at the point p denoted by $d_u f(p)$ or $f_u(p)$, is defined as

$$f_u(p) = \lim_{t\to 0} \frac{f(p + tu) - f(p)}{t},$$

provided the limit exists.

Equivalently,

$$f_u(p) = \lim_{t\to 0} \frac{f(a + ht, b + kt) - f(a, b)}{t}.$$

Remark 1:

If u = (1, 0), then

$$f_u(p) = \lim_{t\to 0} \frac{f(a + t, b) - f(a, b)}{t} = f_x(a, b).$$

Again if u = (0, 1), then

$$f_u(p) = \lim_{t\to 0} \frac{(a, b + t) - f(a, b)}{t} = f_y(a, b).$$

If follows that the partial derivatives are simply the directional derivatives along the axes.

Remark 2:

A function may possess a directional derivative in every direction at a point, but may fail to be continuous at that point as shown in the following example:

SOLVED EXAMPLES

Example 1:

If $f(z) = \dfrac{x^3(y - ix)}{x^6 + y^2}$, *z* $\neq$ *0 and f(0) = 0, show that* $\dfrac{f(z) - f(0)}{z} \to 0$ *as z → 0 along any radius vector but not as z → 0 in any manner.*

Solution:

We have $\dfrac{f(z) - f(0)}{z} = \dfrac{f(z) - 0}{z} = \dfrac{f(z)}{z}$

$$= \frac{x^3y(y - ix)}{(x^6 + y^2)(x + iy)} = \frac{-ix^3y(x + iy)}{(x^6 + y^2)(x + iy)} = -\frac{x^3y}{x^6 + y^2}$$

Let z → 0 along the radius vector y = mx. Then we have

$$\lim_{z\to 0} \frac{f(z) - f(0)}{z} = \lim_{x\to 0} \frac{-ix^3.mx}{x^6 + (mx)^2} = \lim_{x\to 0} \frac{-imx^2}{x^4 + m^2} = 0.$$

Now let $z \to 0$ along $y = x^3$. Then

$$\lim_{z\to 0}\frac{f(z)-f(0)}{z} = \lim_{x\to 0}\frac{-ix^3.x^3}{x^6+(x^3)^2} = -\frac{i}{2} \neq 0.$$

Hence the result.

Example 2:

Show that the function $f(z) = u + iv$,

where $f(z) = \dfrac{x^3(1+i)-y^3(1-i)}{x^2+y^2}$, $z \neq 0$ *and* $f(0) = 0$

is continuous and that Cauchy-Riemann Equations are satisfied at the origin, yet $f'(0)$ does not exist.

Solution:

We have $u = \dfrac{x^3-y^3}{x^2+y^2}$, $v = \dfrac{x^3+y^3}{x^2+y^2}$, $z \neq 0$.

Here u and v are rational functions of x and y with non-zero denominators. Therefore u and v are continuous everywhere when $z \neq 0$.

To test the continuity at $z = 0$, changing u and v to polars by putting $x = r\cos\theta$, $y = r\sin\theta$, we get

$u = r(\cos^3\theta - \sin^3\theta)$, $v = r(\cos^3\theta + \sin^3\theta)$,

each of which tends to 0 as $r \to 0$ whatever may be the value of θ. Also we have $f(0) = 0$.

Since actual and limiting values of u and v are same at origin therefore f(z) is continuous at origin. Hence f(z) is continuous for all values of z.

Now at the origin, we have

$$\frac{\partial u}{\partial x} = \lim_{x\to 0}\frac{u(x,0)-u(0,0)}{x} = \lim_{x\to 0}\frac{x-0}{x} = 1,$$

$$\frac{\partial u}{\partial y} = \lim_{y\to 0}\frac{u(0,y)-u(0,0)}{y} = \lim_{y\to 0}\frac{-y-0}{y} = -1,$$

$$\frac{\partial v}{\partial x} = \lim_{x\to 0}\frac{x-0}{x} = 1 \text{ and } \lim_{y\to 0}\frac{y-0}{y} = 1.$$

Since $\dfrac{\partial u}{\partial x} = \dfrac{\partial v}{\partial y}$ and $\dfrac{\partial u}{\partial y} = -\dfrac{\partial v}{\partial x}$, therefore u and v satisfy Cauchy-Riemann Equations at origin.

We have $f'(0) = \lim_{z \to 0} \frac{f(z) - f(0)}{z}$

$$= \lim_{z \to 0} \frac{(x^3 - y^3) + i(x^3 + y^3)}{(x^2 + y^2)} \cdot \frac{1}{(x + iy)}.$$

Taking z → 0 along y = x, we get

$$f'(0) = \lim_{x \to 0} \frac{i2x^3}{2x^2} \cdot \frac{1}{(x + ix)} = \frac{i}{1+i} = \frac{1}{2}(1 + i).$$

Again taking z → 0 along x-axis, we get

$$f'(0) = \lim_{x \to 0} \frac{x^3 + ix^3}{x^2} \cdot \frac{1}{x} = 1 + i.$$

Since f'(0) has different values along different curves therefore f'(0) is not unique. So f'(0) does not exist.

Example 3:

Show that the function $f(z) = z^n$, where n is a positive integer in an analytic function.

Solution:

We have $f(z) = z^n$.

Now, $f'(z) = \lim_{\Delta z \to 0} \frac{f(z + \Delta z) - f(z)}{\Delta z} = \lim_{\Delta z \to 0} \frac{(z + \Delta z)^n - z^n}{\Delta z}$

$$= \lim_{\Delta z \to 0} \frac{z^n + nz^{n-1}\Delta z + \frac{1}{2}n(n-1)z^{n-2}(\Delta z)^2 + ... + (\Delta z)^n - z^n}{\Delta z}$$

by binomial theorem

$$= \lim_{\Delta z \to 0} \left[nz^{n-1} + \frac{1}{2}n(n-1)z^{n-2}\Delta z + ... + (\Delta z)^{n-1} \right]$$

$= nz^{-1}$, which exists for all finite values of z.

Hence, f(z) is an analytic function.

Example 4:

If $u + v = \frac{2\sin 2x}{e^{2y} + e^{-2y} - 2\cos 2x}$, find the corresponding analytic function $f(z) = u + iv$).

Solution:

We have f(z) = u + iv, if(z) = iu – v.

$\therefore$ $$(1 + i)\, f(z) = u - v + i\,(u + v) = U + iV, \text{ say.}$$

Here $V = u + v = \dfrac{2\sin 2x}{e^{2y} + e^{-2y} - 2\cos 2x} = \dfrac{\sin 2x}{\cosh 2y - \cos 2x}$.

Let $\dfrac{\partial V}{\partial y} = \psi_1(x, y)$ and $\dfrac{\partial V}{\partial x} = \psi_2(x, y)$.

Then $y_1(x, y) = \dfrac{\partial V}{\partial y} = -\dfrac{\sin 2x(2\sinh 2y)}{(\cosh 2y - \cos 2x)^2}$

and $y_2(x, y) = \dfrac{\partial V}{\partial x} = \dfrac{2\cos 2x\,(\cosh 2y - \cos 2x) - 2\sin^2 2x}{(\cosh 2y - \cos 2x)^2}$

$$= \frac{2\cos 2x\cosh 2y - 2}{(\cosh 2y - \cos 2x)^2}$$

$\therefore$ $$y_1(z, 0) = -\frac{\sin 2z(2\sinh 0)}{(\cosh 0 - \cos 2z)^2} = 0$$

and $y_2(z, 0) = \dfrac{2\cos 2z\cosh 0 - 2}{(\cosh 0 - \cos 2z)^2} = \dfrac{2\cos 2z - 2}{(1 - \cos 2z)^2} = \dfrac{-2}{1 - \cos 2z}$

$$= -\operatorname{cosec}^2 z.$$

By Milne's Method, we have

$(1 + i)\, f(z) \int = \int[\psi_1(z, 0) + i\psi_2(z, 0)]\, dz + z$

$$= f(0 - i\operatorname{cosec}^2 z)\, dz + c = i\cot z + c.$$

$\therefore f(z) = \dfrac{i}{1+i}\cot z + \dfrac{c}{1+i} = \dfrac{1}{2}(1 + i)\cot z + d$.

Example 5:

Show that the function $u = x^3 - 3xy^2$ is harmonic and find the corresponding analytic function.

Solution:

We have $u = x^3 - 3xy^2$.

$$\frac{\partial u}{\partial x} = 3x^2 - 3y^2,\ \frac{\partial^2 u}{\partial x^2} = 6x,$$

$$\frac{\partial u}{\partial y} = -6xy \text{ and } \frac{\partial^2 u}{\partial y^2} = -6x.$$

Now $\frac{\partial^2 u}{\partial x^2}+\frac{\partial^2 u}{\partial y^2}=0$, so that u satisfies Laplace's equation.

Also first and second order partial derivatives of u are continuous functions of x and y. Consequently u is a harmonic function.

Now $f'(z)=\frac{\partial u}{\partial x}-i\frac{\partial u}{\partial y}=3x^2-3y^2-i(-6xy)$

$$=3(x^2-y^2+2ixy)=3(x+iy)^2=3z^2.$$

Integrating, $f(z)=z^3+c$.

Example 6:

If $f(z)=u+iv$ is an analytic function of z and

$u-v=\frac{\cos x+\sin x-e^{-y}}{2\cos x-e^{y}-e^{-y}}$, *find f(z) subject to the condition* $f\left(\frac{\pi}{2}\right)=0$.

Solution:

Here $u-v=\frac{\cos x+\sin x-e^{-y}}{2\cos x-e^{y}-e^{-y}}$

$$=\frac{1}{2}\left[1+\frac{2\cos x+2\sin x-2e^{-y}}{2\cos x-e^{y}-e^{-y}}\right]=\frac{1}{2}\left[1+\frac{\sin x+\sinh y}{\cos x-\cosh y}\right].$$

Now $\frac{\partial u}{\partial x}-\frac{\partial v}{\partial x}=\frac{1}{2}\left[\frac{\cos x(\cos x-\cosh y)+(\sin x+\sinh y)\sin x}{(\cos x-\cosh y)^2}\right]$

$$=\frac{1}{2}\left[\frac{1-\cos x\cosh y+\sin x\sinh y}{(\cos x-\cosh y)^2}\right] \quad ...(1)$$

and $\frac{\partial u}{\partial y}-\frac{\partial v}{\partial y}=\frac{1}{2}\left[\frac{\cosh y(\cos x-\cosh y)+\sinh y(\sin x+\sinh y)}{(\cos x-\cosh y)^2}\right]$

$$=\frac{1}{2}\left[\frac{\cosh y\cos x+\sinh y\sin x-1}{(\cos x-\cosh y)^2}\right]$$

or $-\frac{\partial v}{\partial x}-\frac{\partial u}{\partial x}=\frac{1}{2}\left[\frac{\cosh y\cos x+\sinh y\sin x-1}{(\cos x-\cosh y)^2}\right]$, ...(2)

(by Cauchy-Riemann Equations)

Solving (1) and (2), we get

$$\frac{\partial u}{\partial x} = \frac{1}{2}\left[\frac{1-\cos x \cosh y}{(\cos x-\cosh y)^2}\right] = \phi_1(x, y)$$

and $\dfrac{\partial v}{\partial x} = -\dfrac{\sin x \sinh y}{2(\cos x-\cosh y)^2} = \phi_2(x, y)$

$\therefore \quad f'(z) = \dfrac{\partial u}{\partial x} + i\dfrac{\partial v}{\partial x} = \phi_1(z, 0) + i\,\phi_2(z, 0)$

$$= \frac{1}{2}\frac{1-\cos z}{(\cos z-1)^2} = \frac{1}{2(1-\cos z)} = \frac{1}{4}\operatorname{cosec}^2\frac{z}{2}.$$

$\therefore \quad f(z) = \dfrac{1}{4}\displaystyle\int \operatorname{cosec}^2\frac{1}{2}z\,dz + c$

$$= -\frac{1}{2}\cot\frac{1}{2}z + c.$$

At $\quad z = \dfrac{\pi}{2},\ f(z) = 0,$

$\therefore \quad c = f\left(\dfrac{\pi}{2}\right) + \dfrac{1}{2}\cot\dfrac{\pi}{4} = \dfrac{1}{2}$

$\therefore \quad f(z) = \dfrac{1}{2}\left(1-\cot\dfrac{1}{2}z\right).$

Example 7:

Show that the function $u(x, y) = e^x \cos y$ is harmonic. Determine its harmonic conjugate $v(x, y)$ and the analytic function $f(z) = u + iv$.

Solution:

Here $u = e^x \cos y$.

$$\frac{\partial u}{\partial x} = e^x \cos y,\ \frac{\partial u}{\partial y} = -\,e^x \sin y$$

so $\dfrac{\partial u}{\partial x^2} = e^x \cos y$ and $\dfrac{\partial^2 u}{\partial y^2} = -\,e^x \cos y.$

Now $\dfrac{\partial^2 u}{\partial x^2} + \dfrac{\partial^2 u}{\partial y^2} = 0,$ so u satisfies Laplace's Equation.

Also first and second order partial derivatives of u are continuous therefore is a harmonic function.

Since v is the harmonic conjugate of u, therefore

$$dv = \frac{\partial v}{\partial x}dx + \frac{\partial v}{\partial y}dy$$, v is a function of x, y

$$= -\frac{\partial u}{\partial y}dx + \frac{\partial u}{\partial x}dy$$, Cauchy-Riemann Equations

$= e^x \sin y\, dx + e^x \cos y\, dy.$

Integrating $v = e^x = \sin y + c$, where c is a real constant.

$\therefore\ f(z) = u + iv = e^x \cos y + i(e^x \sin y + c).$

$= e^x(\cos y + i \sin y) + ic = e^{x+iy} + d$, where d is a complex constant

$= e^z + d.$

Example 8:

Show that the functions

(i) $u = \frac{1}{2}\log\left(x^2 + y^2\right)$

(ii) $u = \cos x \cosh y$

are harmonic, find their harmonic conjugates.

Solution:

(i) We have $u = \frac{1}{2}\log\left(x^2 + y^2\right).$

$$\frac{\partial u}{\partial x} = \frac{x}{x^2 + y^2}, \quad \frac{\partial^2 u}{\partial x^2} = \frac{y^2 - x^2}{\left(x^2 + y^2\right)^2}$$

$$\frac{\partial u}{\partial y} = \frac{y}{x^2 + y^2} \text{ and } \frac{\partial^2 u}{\partial y^2} = \frac{x^2 - y^2}{\left(x^2 + y^2\right)^2}.$$

All the first and second order partial derivatives of u are continuous functions of x and y.

Also $\frac{\partial^2 u}{\partial x^2} + \frac{\partial^2 u}{\partial y^2} = 0$ *i.e.*, u satisfies Laplace's Equation.

$\therefore$ u is a harmonic function.

Let v be the harmonic conjugate of u.

We have $dv = \frac{\partial v}{\partial x}dx + \frac{\partial v}{\partial y}dy$

$= -\frac{\partial u}{\partial y}dx + \frac{\partial u}{\partial x}dy$, by Cauchy-Riemann Equations

$$= -\frac{x}{x^2+y^2}dx + \frac{x}{x^2+y^2}dy$$

or $$dv = \frac{x\,dy - y\,dx}{x^2+y^2}.$$

Integrating, we get $v = \tan^{-1}\frac{y}{x} + c$, where c is a real constant.

(ii) We have u = cos x cosh y.

$$\frac{\partial u}{\partial x} = -\sin x \cosh y, \quad \frac{\partial^2 u}{\partial x^2} = -\cos x \cosh y$$

$$\frac{\partial u}{\partial y} = \cos x \sinh y \quad \text{and} \quad \frac{\partial^2 u}{\partial y^2} = \cos x \cosh y.$$

All the first and second order partial derivatives of u are continuous functions.

Also $\frac{\partial^2 u}{\partial x^2} + \frac{\partial^2 u}{\partial y^2} = 0$, *i.e.*, satisfies Laplace's equation.

∴ u is a harmonic function.

Let v be the harmonic conjugate of u.

We have $dv = \frac{\partial v}{\partial x}dx + \frac{\partial v}{\partial y}dy$

$= -\frac{\partial u}{\partial y}dx + \frac{\partial u}{\partial x}dy$, by Cauchy-Riemann Equations

$= -\cos x \sinh y\,dx - \sin x \cosh y\,dy$

$= -(\cos x \sinh y\,dx + \sin x \cosh y\,dy)$.

Integrating, $v = -(\sin x \sinh y) + c$, where c is a real constant.

Example 9:

If $u = \frac{\sin 2x}{\cosh 2y + \cos 2x}$, *find the corresponding analytic function* $f(z) = u + iv$.

Solution:

Here $u = \frac{\sin 2x}{\cosh 2y + \cos 2x}$.

Then $$\frac{\partial u}{\partial x} = \frac{2\cos 2x(\cosh 2y + \cos 2x) - \sin 2x(-2\sin 2x)}{(\cosh 2y + \cos 2x)^2}$$

$$= \frac{2 + 2\cos 2x \cosh 2y}{(\cosh 2y + \cos 2x)^2} = \phi_1(x, y).$$

$$\frac{\partial u}{\partial y} = -\frac{2\sin 2x \sinh 2y}{(\cosh 2y + \cos 2x)^2} = \phi_2(x, y).$$

By Milne-Thomson's Method the function f(z) is given by

$$f(z) = \int[\phi_1(z, 0) - i\phi_2(z, 0)]dz + c$$

$$= \int\left[\frac{2 + 2\cos 2z}{(1 + \cos 2z)^2} - i0\right] dz + c$$

$$= \int\frac{2\,dz}{1 + \cos 2z} + c = \int\sec^2 z\,dz + c = \tan z + c.$$

Example 10:

If f(z) = u + iv be an analytic function in a domain D, prove that f(z) is constant in D if any one of the following conditions holds:

(i) *f'(z) vanishes identically in D.*

(ii) *R(f(z)) = u = constant.*

(iii) *I(f(z)) = v = constant.*

(iv) *|f(z)| = constant.*

(v) *arg f(z) = constant.*

Solution:

Since f(z) = u + iv is analytic in D, therefore it satisfies Cauchy-Riemann Equations,

$$\left.\frac{\partial u}{\partial x} = \frac{\partial v}{\partial y}, \frac{\partial u}{\partial y} = -\frac{\partial v}{\partial x}.\right\} \qquad ...(1)$$

(i) We have $f'(z) = \frac{\partial u}{\partial x} + i\frac{\partial u}{\partial x} = \frac{\partial}{\partial y} - i\frac{\partial u}{\partial y}$, from (1).

$\therefore$ if f'(z) = 0, we have

$$\frac{\partial u}{\partial x} + i\frac{\partial v}{\partial x} = 0 \text{ and } \frac{\partial v}{\partial y} - i\frac{\partial u}{\partial y} = 0.$$

$$\therefore \frac{\partial u}{\partial x} = 0, \frac{\partial v}{\partial x} = 0, \frac{\partial v}{\partial y} = 0 \text{ and } \frac{\partial u}{\partial y} = 0.$$

Thus, u and v are constants and consequently f(z) is a constant function.

(ii) R f(z)) = u = constant

$$\Rightarrow \qquad \frac{\partial u}{\partial x} = 0 = \frac{\partial u}{\partial y}.$$

Now $\quad f'(z) = \frac{\partial u}{\partial x} + i\frac{\partial v}{\partial x} = \frac{\partial u}{\partial x} - i\frac{\partial u}{\partial y}$, from (1)

= 0.

∴ f(z) is a constant function.

(iii) I(f(z)) = v = constant $\Rightarrow \frac{\partial u}{\partial x} = 0, \frac{\partial v}{\partial y} = 0$.

Now $f'(z) = \frac{\partial u}{\partial x} + i\frac{\partial v}{\partial x} = \frac{\partial v}{\partial y} + i\frac{\partial v}{\partial x}$, from (1)

∴ f(z) is a constant function.

(iv) |f'(z)| = constant ⇒ $u^2 + v^2$ = constant

$$\Rightarrow u\frac{\partial u}{\partial x} + v\frac{\partial v}{\partial x} = 0 \text{ and } u\frac{\partial u}{\partial y} + v\frac{\partial v}{\partial y} = 0$$

$$\Rightarrow u\frac{\partial u}{\partial x} + v\frac{\partial v}{\partial x} = 0 \text{ and } -u\frac{\partial v}{\partial x} + v\frac{\partial u}{\partial x} = 0$$

$$\Rightarrow \frac{\partial u}{\partial x} = 0 \text{ and } \frac{\partial v}{\partial x} = 0, \text{ provided } u^2 + v^2 \text{ ı } 0.$$

Therefore, if $u^2 + v^2 \neq 0$, u and v are constants and consequently f(z) is constant. If $u^2 + v^2 = 0$ at a single point, it is constantly zero and so f(z) is zero. Hence, in either case f(z) is constant.

(v) Here arg f(z) = $\tan^{-1}\frac{v}{u}$.

arg f(z) = c (constant) ⇒ $\tan^{-1}\frac{v}{u} = c \Rightarrow (v/u) = \tan c$

⇒ u = v cot c ⇒ u = kv, taking cot c = k.

We observe u – kv = 0 unless v is identically zero. But u – kv is the real part of (1 + ik) f, therefore it follows from part (ii) that (1 + ik) f is constant. But (1 + ik) is a constant, therefore f is also a constant.

Example 11:

Show that the function

$$f(z) = \sin x \cosh y + i \cos x \sinh y$$

is continuous as well as analytic everywhere.

Solution:

Let u(x, y) = sin x cosh y, v(x, y) = cos x sinh y. Here u and v both rational functions of x and y having non-zero denominators for all values of x and y, therefore u and v are both continuous everywhere.

Hence f(z) is continuous everywhere.

We have $\frac{\partial u}{\partial x} = \cos x \cosh y, \frac{\partial u}{\partial y} = \sin x \sinh y$

and $\frac{\partial v}{\partial x} = -\sin x \sinh y, \frac{\partial v}{\partial y} = \cos x \cosh y$.

These relations show $\frac{\partial u}{\partial x} = \frac{\partial v}{\partial y}, \frac{\partial v}{\partial x} = -\frac{\partial u}{\partial y}$.

$\therefore$ u and v satisfy Cauchy-Riemann equations.

Example 12:

Show that the function f(z) = $\sqrt{|xy|}$ *is not analytic at origin although the Cauchy-Riemann equations are satisfied at that point.*

Solution:

Let f(z) = u(x, y) + iv(x, y).

Then u(x, y) = $\sqrt{|xy|}$, v(x, y = 0.

At the origin, we have

$$\frac{\partial u}{\partial x} = \lim_{x \to 0} \frac{u(x, 0) - u(0, 0)}{x} = \lim_{x \to 0} \frac{0-0}{x} = 0$$

$$\frac{\partial u}{\partial x} = \lim_{y \to 0} \frac{u(0, y) - u(0, 0)}{y} = \lim_{y \to 0} \frac{0-0}{y} = 0$$

Similarly, $\frac{\partial v}{\partial x} = 0, \frac{\partial v}{\partial y} = 0$.

Hence, Cauchy-Riemann equations are satisfied at origin.

Now, $f'(0) = \lim_{z \to 0} \frac{f(z) - f(0)}{z} = \lim_{z \to 0} \frac{\sqrt{|xy|} - 0}{x + iy}$.

Suppose z → 0 along y = mx, then we have

$$f'(0) = \lim_{z \to 0} \frac{\sqrt{|mx^2|}}{x + i\,mx} = \lim_{z \to 0} \frac{\sqrt{|m|}}{(1 + im)},$$

which is not unique, since it depends on m.

$\therefore$ f'(0) does not exist.

Example 13:

If f(z) is an analytic function of z, prove that

$$\left(\frac{\partial^2}{\partial x^2}+\frac{\partial^2}{\partial y^2}\right)|Rf(z)|^2 = 2|f'(z)|^2.$$

Solution:

Let f(z) = u + iv,

where z = x + iy.

Then Rf(z) = u.

Now $\dfrac{\partial u^2}{\partial x} = 2u\dfrac{\partial u}{\partial x}$

and $\dfrac{\partial^2 u^2}{\partial x^2} = 2\left(\dfrac{\partial u}{\partial x}\right)^2 + 2u\dfrac{\partial^2 u}{\partial x^2}$.

Similarly $\dfrac{\partial^2 u^2}{\partial y^2} = 2\left(\dfrac{\partial u}{\partial y}\right)^2 + 2u\dfrac{\partial^2 u}{\partial x^2}$.

$$\therefore \quad \frac{\partial^2 u^2}{\partial x^2}+\frac{\partial^2 u^2}{\partial y^2} = 2\left[\left\{\left(\frac{\partial u}{\partial x}\right)^2 + \left(\frac{\partial u}{\partial y}\right)\right\}\right] + u\left(\frac{\partial^2 u}{\partial x^2}+\frac{\partial^2 u}{\partial y^2}\right)$$

or

$$\left(\frac{\partial^2}{\partial x^2}+\frac{\partial^2 u^2}{\partial y^2}\right)u^2 = 2\left[\left\{\left(\frac{\partial u}{\partial x}\right)^2 + \left(\frac{\partial u}{\partial y}\right)^2\right\}\right] + 0,$$

since u is a harmonic function

or $$\left(\frac{\partial^2}{\partial x^2}+\frac{\partial^2}{\partial y^2}\right)u^2 = 2\left[\left(\frac{\partial u}{\partial x}\right)^2 + \left(\frac{\partial v}{\partial x}\right)^2\right],$$

using Cauchy-Riemann Equations

or $$\left(\frac{\partial^2}{\partial x^2}+\frac{\partial^2}{\partial y^2}\right)|u|^2 = 2|f'(z)|^2$$

since $$f'(z) = \frac{\partial u}{\partial x} + i\frac{\partial v}{\partial x}.$$

Hence $$\left(\frac{\partial^2}{\partial x^2}+\frac{\partial^2}{\partial y^2}\right)|Rf(z)|^2 = 2|f'(z)|^2.$$

Example 14:

Let $f(x, y) = \dfrac{x^3y}{x^2 + y^2}$, $x^2 + y^2 \neq 0$, $f(0, 0) = 0$.

Prove or disprove $f_{xy}(0, 0) = f_{yx}(0, 0)$

Solution:

$$f_y(0, 0) = \lim_{k\to 0} [f(0, 0 + k) - f(0, 0)]/k$$

$$= \lim_{k\to 0} \frac{0-0}{k} = 0,$$

$$f_y(h, 0) = \lim_{k\to 0} [f(h, 0 + k) - f(h, 0)]/k$$

$$= \lim_{k\to 0} \frac{h^3}{h^2 + k^2} = h,$$

$$\therefore \quad f_{xy}(0, 0) = \lim_{h\to 0} [f_y(0 + h, 0) - f_y(0, 0)]/h$$

$$= \lim_{h\to 0} \frac{h}{h} = 1.$$

Again $$f_x(0, 0) = \lim_{h\to 0} [f(0 + h, 0) - f(0, 0)]/h$$

$$= \lim_{h\to 0} \frac{0-0}{h} = 0,$$

$$f_x(0, k) = \lim_{h\to 0} [f(0 + h, k) = f(0, k)]/h$$

$$= \lim_{h\to 0} \frac{h^2k}{h^2 + k^2} = 0,$$

$$\therefore \quad f_{yx}(0, 0) = \lim_{k\to 0} [f_x(0, 0 + k) - f_x(0, 0)]/k$$

$$= \lim_{k\to 0} \frac{0 - 0}{k} = 0.$$

Hence $f_{xy}(0, 0) \neq f_{yx}(0, 0)$.

Example 15:

Show that for the function

$$f(x, y) = \begin{cases} \dfrac{x^2 y^2}{x^2 + y^2}, & (x, y) \neq (0, 0) \\ 0 \quad, & (x, y) = (0, 0) \end{cases}$$

$f_{xy}(0, 0) = f_{yx}(0, 0)$.

Solution:

$$f_y(0, 0) = \lim_{k\to 0} [f(0, 0 + k) - f(0, 0)]/k$$

$$= \lim_{k\to 0} \frac{0-0}{k} = 0,$$

$$f_y(h, 0) = \lim_{k\to 0} [f(h, 0 + k) - f(h, 0)]/k$$

$$= \lim_{k\to 0} \frac{h^2 k}{(h^2 + k^2)} = 0,$$

$\therefore$
$$f_{xy}(0, 0) = \lim_{h\to 0} [f_y(0 + h, 0) - f_y(0, 0)]/h$$

$$= \lim_{h\to 0} \frac{0-0}{h} = 0.$$

Again
$$f_x(0, 0) = \lim_{h\to 0} [f(0 + h, 0) - f(0, 0)]/h$$

$$= \lim_{h\to 0} \frac{0-0}{h} = 0.$$

$$f_x(0, k) = \lim_{h\to 0} [f(0 + h, k) - f(0, k)]/h$$

$$= \lim_{h\to 0} \frac{hk^2}{(h^2 + k^2)} = 0,$$

$\therefore$
$$f_{yx}(0, 0) = \lim_{k\to 0} [f_x(0, 0 + k) - f_x(0, 0)]/k$$

$$= \lim_{k\to 0} \frac{0-0}{k} = 0.$$

Hence $f_{xy}(0, 0) = f_{yx}(0, 0)$.

Example 16:

Show that the function $f : R^2 \to R$ defined by setting

$$f(x, y) = \begin{cases} x \sin(1/x) + \sin(1/y), & \text{when } xy \neq 0 \\ x \sin(1/x) & , \text{ when } x \neq 0, y = 0 \\ y \sin(1/y) & , \text{ when } x = 0, y \neq 0 \\ 0 & , \text{ when } x = y = 0 \end{cases}$$

is continuous but not differentiable at (0, 0).

Solution:

f is continuous at (0, 0).

Now $f_x(0, 0) = \lim_{h\to 0} [f(0 + h, 0) - f(0, 0)]/h$

$$= \lim_{h\to 0} \frac{h \sin(1/h) = 0}{h} = \lim_{h\to 0} \sin\frac{1}{h},$$

which does not exist.

Similarly $f_{yx}(0, 0)$ does not exist. Hence f is not differentiable at (0, 0).

Example 17:

Let $f : R^2 \to R$ be defined by setting

$f(x, y) = xy/\sqrt{(x^2 + y^2)}$, when $(x, y) \neq (0, 0)$, $f(0, 0) = 0$.

Show that f_x and f_y exist at (0, 0) but f is not differentiable at (0, 0). Also show that f is continuous at (0, 0).

Solution:

$$f_x(0, 0) = \lim_{h\to 0} \frac{f(h, 0) - f(0, 0)}{h} = \lim_{h\to 0} \frac{0-0}{h} = 0.$$

$$f_y(0, 0) = \lim_{k\to 0} \frac{f(0, k) - f(0, 0)}{k} = \lim_{k\to 0} \frac{0-0}{k} = 0.$$

Thus, $f_x(0, 0)$ and $f_y(0, 0)$ both exist and are equal to 0.

Let, if possible, f be differentiable at (0, 0). Then

$f(h, k) - f(0, 0) = Ah + Bk + \sqrt{(h^2 + k^2)}\, g(h, k)$, ...(1)

where $\lim_{(h,k)\to(0,0)} g(h, k) \to 0$ ...(2)

and $A = f_x(0, 0) = 0$, $B = f_y(0, 0) = 0$.

From (1), we obtain

$hk/\sqrt{(h^2 + k^2)} - 0 = 0.h + 0.k + \sqrt{(h^2 + k^2)}\, g(h, k)$,

or $g(h, k) = \dfrac{hk}{h^2 + k^2}$.

Taking $k = mh$, we see that

$\lim_{h\to 0} g(h, mh) = \dfrac{m}{1+m^2}$, which depends on m.

Thus, $\lim_{(h,k)\to(0,0)} g(h, k)$ does not exist, which contradicts (2).

Hence f is not differentiable at (0, 0). f is continuous at (0, 0).

Example 18:

Let $f : R^2 \to R$ be the function defined by setting

$f(x, y) = |x| + |y|$, for all $(x, y) \in R^2$.

Show that f is continuous at (0, 0) but is not differentiable at (0, 0).

Solution:

$| f(x, y) - f(0, 0) | = | x | + | y |$.

Let $\varepsilon > 0$ be given.

If we take $\delta = \frac{1}{2}\varepsilon$, then

$| x | < \delta, | y | < \delta \Rightarrow | f(x, y) - f(0, 0) | < \varepsilon$.

Hence f is continuous at (0, 0).

Now we show that f is not differentiable at (0, 0). We have

$$\lim_{h\to 0} \frac{f(h, 0) - f(0, 0)}{h} = \lim_{h\to 0} \frac{|h|}{h},$$

which does not exist. Therefore $f_x(0, 0)$ does not exist. Similarly $f_y(0, 0)$ does not exist.

Hence f is not differentiable at (0, 0).

Example 19:

Find the value of k for which the function f where

$f(x, y) = \{ | x + y | + (x + y)\}^2$

is everywhere differentiable.

Solution:

For $k \le 0$, the given function is not defined if

$$x + y \le 0 \; [\because \text{ then } | x + y | = -(x + y)]$$

For $k > 0$, $f(x, y) = \{2 (x + y)\}^2$, if $x + y > 0$,

$= 0$, if $x + y \le 0$.

Let $0 < k < 1$. Now $f_x(0, 0) = \lim_{h\to 0} [f(h, 0) - f(0, 0)]/h$

or $f_x(0, 0) \lim_{h\to 0} \frac{2^k . h^k}{h} = \lim_{h\to 0} \frac{1}{h^{1-2}}$,

which does not exist.

Similarly, $f_y(0, 0)$ does not exist.

Hence, f cannot be differentiable if $0 < k < 1$.

Suppose $k \ge 1$. In this case

$$f_x(x, y) = f_y(x, y) = \begin{cases} k, 2^k (x+y)^{k-1}, & \text{if } x + y > 0, \\ 0, & \text{if } x + y \le 0. \end{cases}$$

Since f_x and f_y are both continuous at each point $(x, y) \in r^2$, so f is differentiable everywhere is $k \geq 1$.

Example 20:

Investigate the differentiability of the function f where $f(x, y) = (xy)^{1/3}$ at all points $(x, y) \in R^2$.

Solution:

Let $x \neq 0$, $y \neq 0$. Then

$f_x(x, y) = \frac{1}{2}(y^{1/3}/x^{3/2})$, $f_y(x, y) = \frac{1}{3}(x^{1/3}/y^{2/3})$.

Since f_x and f_y are both continuous at each point $(x, y) \neq (0, 0)$, so f is differentiable at each point $(x, y) \neq (0, 0)$.

$$\text{Now, } f_x(0, 0) = \lim_{h \to 0} [f(h, 0) - (f(0, 0)]/h = \lim_{h \to 0} \frac{0 - 0}{h} = 0,$$

$$f_y(0, 0) = \lim_{k \to 0} [f(0, k) - f(0, 0)]/k = 0.$$

Suppose f is differentiable at (0, 0). Then

$$f(h, k) - f(0, 0) = 0h + 0k + \sqrt{h^2 + k^2}\ \phi(h, k),$$

where$\phi(h, k) \to 0$ as $(h, k) \to (0, 0)$. ...(1)

For $h = k \neq 0$, we obtain

$$f(h, h) = \sqrt{2}\, h\, \phi(h, h) \quad \text{or} \quad \phi(h, h) = (hh)^{1/3}/\sqrt{2}h$$

$$\therefore \lim_{h \to 0} \phi(h, h) - = \lim_{h \to 0} \left(\frac{1}{\sqrt{2}h^{1/3}}\right), \text{ which does not exits.}$$

This contradicts (1). Hence f is differentiable at all points (x, y) except (0, 0).

Example 21:

Prove that the function $f(x, y) = \sqrt{|xy|}$ is not differentiable at the point (0, 0), but that f_x and f_y both exist at the origin and have the value 0. Hence deduce that these two partial derivatives are continuous except at the origin.

Solution:

$$f_x(0, 0) = \lim_{h \to 0} \frac{f(h, 0) - f(0, 0)}{h} = \lim_{h \to 0} \frac{0}{h} = 0,$$

$$f_y(0, 0) = \lim_{k \to 0} \frac{f(0, k) - f(0, 0)}{k} = \lim_{k \to 0} \frac{0}{k} = 0.$$

Thus, f_x, f_y both exist at (0, 0).

If the function f is differentiable at (0, 0), then by definition

$$f(h, k) - f(0, 0) = 0h + 0k + \sqrt{h^2 + k^3}\ g(h, k)$$

where $g(h, k) \to 0$ as $(h, k) \to (0, 0)$.

or $| hk |^{1/2} = \sqrt{h^2 + k^2}\ g(h, k)$.

Putting $h = r \sin\theta$, $k = r \sin\theta$ and dividing by r, we get

$| \cos\theta \cos\theta |^{1/2} = g(h, k)$

Now for arbitrary θ, $r \to 0$ implies that $(h, k) \to (0, 0)$.

Taking the limit as $r \to 0$, we get

$| \cos\theta \sin\theta |^{1/2} = 0$, which is impossible for all values of θ.

Hence, the function f is not differentiable at (0, 0), and consequently the partial derivatives f_x, f_y cannot be continuous at (0, 0), for otherwise the function would be differentiable thereat.

Example 22:

Show that the function $f(x, y) = \sqrt{|xy|}$ *is continuous at the origin but is not differentiable thereat.*

[Hint. $| f(x, y) - f(0, 0) | = | \sqrt{|xy|} - 0 | \le | xy |]$

$= | x | | y | < \varepsilon$, if $| x | < \delta$, $| y | < \delta$ $(\delta = \sqrt{\varepsilon} > 0)$]

Hence, f is continuous at the origin.

Example 23:

Show that $f(x, y) = \sqrt{|xy|}$ *is not derivable at (0, 0).*

Solution:

Do yourself.

Example 24:

Show that the function

$$f(x, y) = \begin{cases} x^2y / (x^2 + y^2), & \text{when } x^2 + y^2 \neq 0 \\ 0 & , \text{when } x^2 + y^2 = 0 \end{cases}$$

is continuous but not differentiable at (0, 0).

Solution:

Putting $x = r\cos\theta$, $y = r\sin\theta$; we get

$$|f(x, y) = f(0, 0)| = \left|\frac{r^2\cos^2\theta \,.\, r\sin\theta}{r^2} - 0\right|$$

$$= r\,|\cos\theta|\;\;|\cos\theta|\;\;|\sin\theta| < r = \sqrt{x^2 + y^2}$$

Let $\varepsilon > 0$ be given. Choose $\delta = \varepsilon$. Then

$|f(x, y) - f(0, 0)| < \varepsilon$ if $\sqrt{x^2 + y^2} < \delta$.

Hence, f is continuous at the origin.

Now $f_x(0, 0) = \lim_{h\to 0} [f(h, 0) - f(0, 0)]/h = \lim_{h\to 0} \dfrac{0-0}{h} = 0.$

Similarly $f_y(0, 0) = 0$.

Let, if possible, f be differentiable at (0, 0). Then

$$f(h, k) - f(0, 0) = Ah + Bk + \sqrt{h^2 + k^2}\, g(h, k),$$

where $A = f_x(0, 0)$, $B = f_y(0, 0)$ and $g(h, k) \to 0$ as $(h, k) \to (0, 0)$. ...(1)

$$\therefore \frac{h^2k}{h^2 + k^2} = \sqrt{h^2 + k^2}\, g(h, k) \Rightarrow g(h, k) = \frac{h^2k}{(h^2 + k^2)^{3/2}}.$$

Now $\lim_{h\to 0} g(h, mh) = \dfrac{m}{(1+m^2)^{3/2}}$ $(k = mh)$

$$\therefore \lim_{(h,k)\to(0,0)} g(h, k) = \frac{m}{(1+m^2)^{3/2}}.$$

which depends on m and so the limit does not exist. This contradicts (1). Hence f is not differentiable at (0, 0).

Example 25:

Discuss the continuity and differentiability of the following function at (0, 0):

$$f(x, y) = \begin{cases} xy^2/(x^2+y^2), & (x, y) \neq (0, 0) \\ 0, & (x, y) = (0, 0) \end{cases}$$

[**Hint.** Show that the given function is continuous but not differentiable at (0, 0)].

Example 26:

Let $f : R^2 \to R$ be defined by setting

$f(x, y) = x^2 \sin(1/x) + y^2 \sin(1/y)$, when $xy \neq 0$,

$f(x, 0) = x^2 \sin(1/x)$, when $x \neq 0$,

$f(0, y) = y^2 \sin(1/y)$, when $y \neq 0$, $f(0, 0) = 0$.

Show that (i) f_x and f_y both exist at (0, 0) but are not continuous at (0, 0) ; (ii) f is differentiable at (0, 0).

Solution:

We have

$$f_x(x, y) = 2x \sin(1/x) - \cos(1/x),\ x \neq 0, \quad ...(1)$$

$$f_x(0, y) = 0.$$

Again $f_y(x, y) = 2y \sin(1/y) - \sin(1/y),\ y \neq 0,$

$$f_y(x, 0) = 0.$$

Since $\lim_{x\to 0} \cos(1/x)$ does not exist, so by (1), f_x is not continuous at (0, 0). Similarly f_y is not continuous at (0, 0).

Now $f_x(0, 0) = \lim_{x\to 0} \dfrac{f(h, 0) - f(0, 0)}{h} = \lim_{h\to 0} \dfrac{h^2 \sin(1/h) - 0}{h}$

$$= \lim_{h\to 0} h \sin(1/h) = 0.$$

Similarly $f_y(0, 0) = 0$. Thus, f_x, f_y both exist at (0, 0) but are not continuous at (0, 0).

Now we show that f is differentiable at (0, 0).

We shall verify that

$$f(h, k) - f(0, 0) = Ah + Bk + \sqrt{h^2 + k^2}\ g(h, k) \quad ...(2)$$

where $\lim_{(h, k)\to(0, 0)} g(h,k) = 0$

we know $A = f_x(0, 0) = 0$, $B = f_y(0, 0) = 0$. Also $f(0, 0) = 0$...(3)

From (2) and (3), we obtain

$$h^2 \sin(1/h) + k^2 \sin(1/k) = \sqrt{h^2 + k^2}\ g(h, g)$$

or $g(h, k) = \dfrac{h}{\sqrt{h^2 + k^2}} . h \sin(1/h) + \dfrac{k}{\sqrt{h^2 + k^2}} . k \sin(1/k)$

$\leq h \sin(1/h) + k \sin(1/k)$ $\quad [\because h, k \leq \sqrt{h^2 + k^2}\,]$

$\therefore \lim_{(h,k)\to(0,0)} g(h,k) = 0.$ $\quad [\because \lim_{h\to 0} h \sin(1/h) = 0 = \lim_{k\to 0} k \sin(1/k)]$

Hence f is differentiable at (0, 0).

Example 27:

If $f(x, y) = xy\,(x^2 - y^2)/(x^2 + y^2)$, when $(x, y) \neq (0, 0)$ and $f(0, 0) = 0$, show that $f_{xy}\,(0, 0) \neq f_{yx}\,(0, 0)$.

Solution:

We have

$$f_{xy}(0, 0) = \lim_{h\to 0} \frac{f_y(0+h,0)-f_y(0,0)}{h}$$

Now, $$f_y(0, 0) = \lim_{k\to 0} \frac{f(0, 0 + k)-f(0, 0)}{k} \lim_{k\to 0} \frac{0}{k} = 0,$$

and $$f_y(h, 0) = \lim_{k\to 0} \frac{f(h, 0 + k)-f(h, 0)}{k} \lim_{k\to 0} \frac{hk(h^2 - k^2)}{k(h^2 + k^2)} = h,$$

$$\therefore \quad f_{xy}(0, 0) = \lim_{h\to 0} \frac{h - 0}{h} = 1.$$

Again $$f_{yx}(0, 0) = \lim_{k\to 0} \frac{f_x(0, 0 + k)-f_x(0, 0)}{k}$$

Now, $$f_x(0, 0) = \lim_{h\to 0} \frac{f(0+h,0)-f(0,0)}{h} = 0,$$

and $$f_x(0, k) = \lim_{h\to 0} \frac{f(0+h,k)-f(0,k)}{h}$$

$$= \lim_{h\to 0} \frac{hk(h^2 - k^2)}{h(h^2 + k^2)} = - k.$$

$$\therefore \quad f_{yx}\,(0, 0) = \lim_{k\to 0} \frac{-k-0}{k} = - 1.$$

Thus, $f_{xy}\,(0, 0) \neq f_{yx}\,(0, 0)$.

Example 28:

Let $f(x, y) = 2xy/\sqrt{(x^2 + y^2)}$, if $(x, y) \neq (0, 0)$ and $f(0, 0)$. Show that f_{yx} $(0, 0) \neq f_{xy}\,(0, 0)$.

Solution:

$$f_y(0, 0) = \lim_{k\to 0}\, [f(0, 0 + k) - f(0, 0)]/k = \lim_{k\to 0} \frac{0-0}{k} = 0,$$

$$f_y(h, 0) = \lim_{k\to 0}\, [f(h, 0 + k) - f(h, 0)]/k = \lim_{k\to 0} \frac{2h-0}{\sqrt{h^2 + k^2}}$$

$$= \frac{2h}{|h|} = \pm 2.$$

$$\therefore f_{xy}(0, 0) = \lim_{h\to 0} [f_y(0 + h, 0) - \phi(0, 0)]/h = \lim_{h\to 0} \left(\pm \frac{2}{4}\right),$$

which does not exist.

$$f_x(0, 0) = \lim_{h\to 0} [f(0 + h, 0) - f(0, 0]/h = \lim_{h\to 0} \frac{0 - 0}{h} = 0,$$

$$f_x(0, k) = \lim_{h\to 0} [f(0 + h, 0) - f(0, k)]/h = \lim_{h\to 0} \frac{k}{\sqrt{h^2 + k^2}} = \pm 2,$$

$$\therefore f_{yx}(0, 0) = \lim_{k\to 0} [f_x(0, 0 + k) - f_x(0, 0)]/h = \lim_{k\to 0} \left(\pm \frac{2}{k}\right),$$

which does not exist.

Thus $f_{xy}(0, 0) \neq f_{yx}(0, 0)$.

Example 29:

Examine the equality of $f_{xy}(0, 0)$ and $f_{yx}(0, 0)$ if

$$f(x, y) = \sqrt{(x^2 + y^2)} \sin 2\phi,$$

where $f(0, 0) = 0$ *and* $\phi = \tan^{-1}(y/x)$.

Solution:

Clearly $x = 0 \Rightarrow \phi = \pm \frac{1}{2}\pi$ and $y = 0 \Rightarrow \phi = 0$.

$\therefore f(x, y) = 0$, if $xy = 0$

For $xy \neq 0$, $\sin 2\phi = \dfrac{2\tan\phi}{1 + \tan^2\phi} = \dfrac{2y/x}{1+(y^2/x^2)} = \dfrac{2xy}{x^2+y^2}$.

$$\therefore \qquad f(x, y) = \begin{cases} \dfrac{2xy}{\sqrt{x^2+y^2}}, & \text{if } xy \neq 0 \\ 0, & \text{if } xy = 0 \end{cases}$$

By Example 33, it follows that

$$f_{xy}(0, 0) \neq f_{yx}(0, 0).$$

Example 30:

Prove or disprove : $f_{xy}(0, 0) = f_{yx}(0, 0)$, where

$$f(x, y) = \frac{(x^2y + xy^2)\sin(x - y)}{x^2 + y^2}, \quad (x, y) \neq (0, 0)$$

$$f(0, 0) = 0.$$

Solution:

$$f_y(0, 0) = \lim_{k\to 0} [f(0, 0 + k) - f(0, 0)]/k = \lim_{k\to 0} \frac{0 - 0}{k} = 0,$$

$$f_y(h, 0) = \lim_{k\to 0} [f(h, 0 + k) - f(h, 0)]/k$$

$$= \lim_{k\to 0} \frac{[(h^2k + hk^2) \sin (h-k)-0]}{k(h^2 + k^2)}$$

$$= \lim_{k\to 0} \frac{(h^2 + hk) \sin (h-k)}{(h^2 + k^2)} = \sin h.$$

$$\therefore f_{xy}(0, 0) = \lim_{h\to 0} [f_y(0 + h, 0) - f_y(0, 0)]/h = \lim_{h\to 0} \frac{\sin h}{h} = 1.$$

Now $f_x(0, 0) = \lim_{h\to 0} [f(0 + h, 0) - f(0, 0)]/h$

$$= \lim_{h\to 0} \frac{0 - 0}{h} = 0,$$

$$f_x(0, k) = \lim_{h\to 0} [f(0 + h, 0) - k(0, k)]/h$$

$$= \lim_{h\to 0} \frac{(h^2k + hk^2) \sin (h-k)}{h(h^2 + k^2)} = - \sin k.$$

$$\therefore f_{xy}(0, 0) = \lim_{k\to 0} [f_x(0, 0 + k) - f_x (0, 0)]/k$$

$$= \lim_{k\to 0} \left(\frac{-\sin k}{k}\right) = -1$$

Hence $f_{xy}(0, 0) \neq f_{yx}(0, 0)$.

Example 31:

If $f(x, y) = x^2 + y^2) \tan^{-1}(y/x)$, *when* $x \neq 0$

and $f(0, k) = \pi y^2/2$,

Show that $f_{xy}(0, 0) \neq f_{yx}(0, 0)$.

Solution:

$$f_x(0, 0) = \lim_{h\to 0} \frac{f(h, 0) - f(0, 0)}{h} = \lim_{h\to 0} \frac{0 - 0}{h} = 0.$$

$$f_y(0, 0) = \lim_{k\to 0} \frac{f(0, k) - f(0, 0)}{k} = \lim_{k\to 0} \left(\frac{\pi k}{2}\right) = 0.$$

For $k \neq 0$,

$$f_x(0, k) = \lim_{h\to 0} [f(h, k) - f(0, k)]/h$$

$$= \lim_{h \to 0} \frac{(h^2 + k^2)\tan^{-1}(k/h) - \pi k^2/2}{h} \left(\frac{0}{0}\right)$$

$$= \lim_{h \to 0} 2h \tan^{-1}(k/h) + (h^2 + k^2) \cdot \frac{1}{1 + (k^2/h^2)} \left(\frac{-k}{h^2}\right)$$

(by L' Hospital's Rule)

$$= 0\left(\pm \frac{\pi}{2}\right) - k = -k.$$

$\therefore \quad f_{yx}(0, 0) = \lim_{k \to 0} [f_x(0, k) - f_x(0, 0)]/k = \lim_{k \to 0} (-k)/k = -1.$

For $h \neq 0$, $f_y(h, 0) = \lim_{k \to 0} [f(h, k) - f(h, 0)]/k$

$$= \lim_{k \to 0} [(h^2 + k^2)\tan^{-1}(k/h) - 0]/k$$

$$= \lim_{k \to 0} \frac{h^2 + k^2}{h} \frac{\tan^{-1}(k/h)}{(k/h)} = h \cdot 1 = h$$

$\therefore \quad f_{xy}(0, 0) = \lim_{h \to 0} [f_y(h, 0) - f_x(0, 0)]/h = \lim_{h \to 0} h/h = 1.$

Hence $f_{xy}(0, 0) \neq f_{yx}(0, 0)$.

Example 32:

If $f(x, y) = (x^2 + y^2) \tan^{-1}(x/y)$, when $y \neq 0$ and $f(x, 0) = \pi x^2/2$, show that $f_{yx}(0, 0) \neq f_{xy}(0, 0)$.

Solution:

Do your self.

Example 33:

Let

$$f(x, y) = \begin{cases} x^2y^2/(x^2 + y^2), & \text{if } (x, y) \neq (0, 0), \\ 0 \quad , & \text{if } (x, y) = (0, 0) \end{cases}$$

Show that $f_{xy}(0, 0) = f_{yx}(0, 0)$, but the conditions of Schwarz's and Young's Theorems are not satisfied.

Solution:

$f_{xy}(0, 0) = f_{yx}(0, 0)$, we have

For $(x, y) \neq (0, 0)$, we have

$f_x(x, y) = [(x^2 + y^2)(2xy^2) - x^2y^2(2x)]/(x^2 + y^2)^2$

$\Rightarrow \quad f_x(x, y) = 2xy^4/(x^2 + y^2)^2 \quad$ ...(1)

$\therefore \quad f_{yx}(x, y) = 8xy^3 (x^2 + y^2)^{-2} - (4y)(2xy^4)(x^2 + y^2)^{-3}$

$\Rightarrow \quad f_{yx}(x, y) = 8x^3y^3/(x^2 + y^2)^3.$

Similarly, for $(x, y) \neq (0, 0)$,

$$f_y(x, y) = 2x^4y/(x^2 + y^2)^2,$$

and $f_{xy}(x, y) = 8x^3y^3/(x^2 + y^2)^3$

Since $\lim\limits_{(x,y)\to(0,0)} \dfrac{x^3y^3}{(x^2+y^2)^3} = \dfrac{m^3}{(1+m^2)^3}$, (along the path $y = mx$),

so $\lim f_{xy}(x, y)$ and $\lim f_{yx}(y, x)$ do not exist.

Hence f_{xy} and f_{yx} cannot be continuous at (0, 0) and consequently the conditions of Schwarz's Theorem are not satisfied.

Now we show that f_x and f_y are not differentiable at (0, 0).

We can verify that $f_{xx}(0, 0) = 0$. $f_{yy}(0, 0) = 0$.

Let, if possible, f_x be differentiable at (0, 0). Then

$f_x(h, k) - f_{x}(0, 0) = h\, f_{xx}(0, 0) + k\, f_{yx}(0, 0) + h\phi(h, k) + k\psi(h, k)$ ..(2)

or$f_x(h, k) = h\phi(h, k) + k\psi(h, k)$,

where$\phi(h, k)$, $\psi(h, k) \to 0$ as $(h, k) \to (0, 0)$

Taking$h = k \neq 0$ in (1) and (2), we get

$$2h.\ h^4/(h^2 + h^2)^2 = h\,\phi(h, h) + h\,\psi(h, h).$$

or $$\frac{1}{2} = \phi(h, h) + \psi(h, h) \Rightarrow \frac{1}{2} = 0 \text{ as } h \to 0.$$

This is impossible. Hence f_x cannot be differentiable at (0, 0).

Similarly, we can show that f_y cannot be differentiable at (0, 0).

Hence, the conditions of Young's theorem are not satisfied.

Example 34:

Let f(x, y) be defined by

$$f(x, y) = \begin{cases} (x^2+y^2)\log(x^2+y^2), & (x, y) \neq (0, 0), \\ 0, & (x, y) = (0, 0). \end{cases}$$

Prove that f_{xy} and f_{yx} are continuous at (0, 0) but $f_{xy}(0, 0) = f_{yx}(0, 0)$.

Solution:

For $x \neq 0$, $y \neq 0$, we have

$$f_x = 2x\log(x^2 + y^2) + \frac{x^2 + y^2}{(x^2 + y^2)} 2x$$

$\therefore \quad f_x = 2x\,[1 + \log (x^3 + y^2)].$

Similarly, $\quad f_y = 2y\,[1 + \log (x^2 + y^2)].$

Also $\quad f_{xy} = \dfrac{4xy}{(x^2+y^2)} \quad \forall \; (x, y) \neq (0, 0)$

Now, $\quad f_x(0, 0) = \lim\limits_{h\to 0} [f(0 + h, 0) - f(0, 0)/h = \lim\limits_{h\to 0} \dfrac{h^2 \log h^2}{h}$

$$= \lim_{h\to 0} 2h \log h = 2 \lim_{h\to 0} \frac{\log h}{1/h} \left(\frac{\infty}{\infty}\right)$$

$$= 2 \lim_{h\to 0} \frac{-h^2}{h} = 0. \text{ Similarly } f_y(0, 0) = 0.$$

Now, $\quad f_x(0, k) = \lim\limits_{h\to 0} [f(0 + h, k) - f(0, k)]/h$

$$= \lim_{h\to 0} \frac{(h^2 + k^2) \log (h^2 + k^2) - k^2 \log k^2}{h} \left(\frac{0}{0}\right)$$

$$= \lim_{h\to 0} 2h \log (h^2 + k^2) + 2h = 0 \text{ (L' Hospital's Rule)}$$

$\therefore \quad f_{yx}(0, 0) = \lim\limits_{k\to 0} [f_x(0, 0 + k) - f_x(0, 0)]/k$

$$= \lim_{k\to 0} \frac{0 - 0}{k} = 0$$

Similarly, we can show that $f_{xy}\,(0, 0) = 0.$

Thus, $f_{xy}(0, 0) = f_{yx}(0, 0)$

Now, $\quad = \lim\limits_{(x,y)\to(0,0)} f_{xy} = \lim\limits_{(x,y)\to(0,0)} \dfrac{4xy}{x^2+y^2}$

$$= \lim_{x\to 0} \frac{4mx^2}{x^2(1+m^2)}, \text{ along the path } y = mx$$

$\therefore \quad \lim\limits_{(x,y)\to(0,0)} f_{xy} = \dfrac{4m}{1 + m^2},$

and so $\lim\limits_{(x,y)\to(0,0)} f_{xy}$ does not exist.

Similarly, $\lim\limits_{(x,y)\to(0,0)} f_{yx}$ does not exist.

Hence, f_{yx} and f_z are not continuous at (0, 0).

Example 35:

If $f(x, y) = x^2 \tan^{-1} (y/x) - y^2 \tan^{-1} (x/y)$, when $x \neq 0$, $y \neq 0$ and $f(x, y) = 0$, otherwise; show that $f_{xy}\,(0, 0) \neq f_{yx}\,(0, 0)$

Solution:

We have

$$f_x(0, 0) = \lim_{h\to 0} [f(h, 0) - f(0, 0)]/h \lim_{h\to 0} (0-0)/h = 0$$

and $$f_y(0, 0) = \lim_{k\to 0} [f(0, k) - f(0, 0)]/k \lim_{k\to 0} (0-0)/k = 0$$

For $k \neq 0$, we have

$$f_x(0, k) = \lim_{h\to 0} [f(h, k) - f(0, k)]/h = \lim_{h\to 0} f(h, k)/h$$

$$= \lim_{h\to 0} [h^2 \tan^{-1}(k/h) - k^2 \tan^{-1}(h/k)]/h$$

$$= \lim_{h\to 0} [h \tan^{-1}\left(\frac{k}{h}\right) - \frac{k^2}{h} \tan^{-1}\left(\frac{h}{k}\right)$$

$$= 0\left(\pm\frac{\pi}{2}\right) - k^2 \lim_{h\to 0} \frac{\tan^{-1}(h/k)}{h} \quad (\text{as } k > 0, k < 0)$$

$$= -k^2 \lim_{h\to 0} \frac{k^2}{h^2 + k^2}\left(\frac{1}{k}\right) 1$$

(By L'Hospital Rule)

$$= (-k^2)(1/k) = -k.$$

$$\therefore \quad fyx(0, 0) = \lim_{k\to 0} [f_x(0, k) - f_x(0, 0)]/k = \lim_{k\to 0} (-k)/k = -1$$

For $h \neq 0$, $$f_y(h, 0) = \lim_{k\to 0} [f_a(h, k) - f(h, 0)]/k$$

$$= \lim_{k\to 0} [h^2 \tan^{-1}(k/h) - k^2 \tan^{-1}(h/k)/k$$

$$= \lim_{k\to 0} \left[h.\frac{\tan^{-1}(k/h)}{k/h} - k \tan^{-1}(h/k)\right]$$

$$= h \,.\, 1 - 0(\pm \pi/2) = h.$$

$$\therefore \quad f_{xy}(0, 0) = \lim_{h\to 0} [f_y(h, 0) - f_y(0, 0)]/h = \lim_{h\to 0} h/h = 1$$

Hence $fxy(0, 0) \neq f_{yx}(0, 0)$

Example 36:

Let $f(x, y) = (xy^5 - x^2y^3)/(x^2 + xy^2 + y^4)$ when $(x, y) \neq (0, 0)$ and $f(0, 0) = 0$. Show that $f_{xy}(0, 0) \neq f_{xy}(0, 0)$.

Solution:

$$f_y(0, 0) = \lim_{h\to 0} [f(h, 0) - f(0, 0)]/h = 0$$

and $f_y(0, 0) = \lim_{k\to 0} [f(0, k) - f(0, 0)]/k = 0$

For $k \neq 0$, $f_x(0, k) = \lim_{h\to 0} [f(h, k) - f(0, k)]/h = \lim_{h\to 0} f(h, k)/h$

$$= \lim_{h\to 0} [hk^5 - h^2k^3]/h(h^2 + hk^2 + k^4) = k$$

$$= \lim_{h\to 0} \frac{k^3(k^2 - h)}{h^2 + hk^2 + k^4}$$

$$= \lim_{h\to 0} \frac{k^3(k^6 - h^3)}{(h^2 + hk^2 + k^2)} = k$$

$$[\because (k^6 - h^3) = (k^2 - h)(k^4 + k^2h + h^2)]$$

$\therefore \quad f_{yx}(0, 0) \lim_{k\to 0} [f_x(0, k) - f_x(0, 0)]/k = \lim_{k\to 0} (k - 0)/k = 1$

For $h \neq 0$, $f_x(h, 0) = \lim_{k\to 0} [f(h, k) - f(h, 0)]/k = \lim_{k\to 0} f(h, k)/k$

$$= \lim_{k\to 0} (hk^3 - h^2k^2)/k(h^2 + hk^2 + k^4)$$

$$= \lim_{k\to 0} \frac{hk^2(k^6 - h^3)}{(h^2 + hk^2 + k^4)^2} = 0$$

$\therefore f_{xy}(0, 0) = \lim_{h\to 0} [f_y(h, 0) - f_y(0, 0)]/h\ (h, k)/h = \lim_{h\to 0} (0, 0)/h = 0$

Hence $f_{yx}(0, 0) \neq f_{xy}(0, 0)$.

Example 37:

Let f be the function defined by setting

$$f(x,y) = \begin{cases} \dfrac{x^2 + y^2}{x - y}, & \text{if } x \neq y \\ 0, & \text{if } x = y \end{cases}$$

Show that f possesses a directional derivative in every direction at (0, 0) but is not continuous at (0, 0).

Solution:

Let $u = (\cos\theta, \sin\theta)$. Then

$$\frac{f(0 + tu) - f(0)}{t} = t^2 \left(\frac{\cos^2\theta + \sin^2\theta}{\cos\theta - \sin\theta}\right)$$

At $t \to 0$, we obtain

$f_u(0) = 0$, if $\cos\theta \neq \sin\theta$.

Thus, the given function has a directional derivative in every direction at (0, 0). f is not continuous (0, 0).

Example 38:

Let f be the function defined by setting

$$f(x, y) = \begin{cases} \dfrac{xy}{x^2+y^2}, & \text{if } (x, y) \neq (0, 0) \\ 0, & \text{if } (x, y) = (0, 0). \end{cases}$$

Show that f possesses a directional derivative in every direction at (0, 0) but is not continuous at (0, 0).

Also show that f is not differentiable at (0, 0).

Solution:

Let u = (cos θ, sin θ). Now

$$\frac{f(0 + tu) - f(0)}{t} = \frac{f(t\cos\theta, t\sin\theta) - f(0, 0)}{t}$$

$$= \cos\theta \sin\theta, \ t \neq 0$$

At $t \to 0$, we see that $fu(0) = \cos\theta \sin\theta$.

Thus, the given function has a directional derivative in every direction at (0, 0).

$$\text{Now} \lim_{x\to 0} f(x, mx) = \frac{m}{1 + m^2}.$$

which is different for different values of m.

Thus $\displaystyle\lim_{(x,y)\to(0,0)} \frac{xy}{x^2 + y^2}$ does not exist and so the given function is not continuous at (0, 0).

Let, if possible, f be differentiable at (0, 0). Then f is continuous at (0, 0), which is a contradiction. Hence f is not differentiable at (0, 0).

Example 39:

Prove that the first four terms of the Maclaurin Expansion of e^{ax} cos by are

$$1 + ax + \frac{1}{2!}(a^2x^2 - b^2y^2) + \frac{1}{3!}(a^3x^3 - 3ab^2xy^2).$$

Solution:

Let $f(x, y) = e^{ax} \cos by$; a = b = 0; $f(0, 0) = 1$

$\therefore \ f_x(x, y) = ae^{ax} \cos by \quad \Rightarrow f_x(0, 0) = a$

$$f_y(x, y) = -be^{ax} \sin by \quad \Rightarrow \quad f_y(0, 0) = 0$$
$$f_{xx}(x, y) = a^2e^{ax} \cos by \quad \Rightarrow \quad f_{xx}(0, 0) = a^2$$
$$f_{yy}(x, y) = -b^2e^{ax} \cos by \quad \Rightarrow \quad f_{yy}(0, 0) = -b^2$$
$$f_{xy}(x, y) = -abe^{ax} \sin by \quad \Rightarrow \quad f_{xy}(0, 0) = 0$$
$$f_{xxx}(x, y) = a^2e^{ax} \cos by \quad \Rightarrow \quad f_{xxx}(0, 0) = a^3$$
$$f_{yyy}(x, y) = -b^3e^{ax} \sin by \quad \Rightarrow \quad f_{yyy}(0, 0) = 0$$
$$f_{xxy}(x, y) = a^2be^{ax} \sin by \quad \Rightarrow \quad f_{xxy}(0, 0) = 0$$
$$f_{xyy}(x, y) = -ab^2e^{ax} \cos by \quad \Rightarrow \quad f_{xyy}(0, 0) = -ab^2.$$

By Taylor's expansion,

$$f(x, y) = f(0, 0) + \left(x\frac{\partial}{\partial x} + y\frac{\partial}{\partial y}\right) f(0, 0)$$
$$+ \frac{1}{2!}\left(x\frac{\partial}{\partial x} + y\frac{\partial}{\partial y}\right)^2 f(0, 0) + \frac{1}{3!}\left(x\frac{\partial}{\partial x} + y\frac{\partial}{\partial y}\right)^3 f(0, 0).$$

Hence $e^{ax} \cos by = 1 + ax + \frac{1}{2!}(a^2x^2 - b^2y^2) + \frac{1}{3!}(a^3x^3 - 3ab^2xy^2).$

Example 40:

Expand $x^2y + 3y - 2$ in powers of $x - 1$ and $y + 2$.

Solution:

We take $a = 1$, $b = -2$.

Let $f(x, y) = x^2y + 3y - 2 \Rightarrow f(1, -2) = -10,$

$$f_x(x, y) = 2xy \quad \Rightarrow f_x(1, -2) = -4,$$
$$f_y(x, y) = x^2 + 3 \quad \Rightarrow f_y(1, -2) = 4,$$
$$f_{xx}(x, y) = 2y \quad \Rightarrow f_{xx}(1, -2) = -4,$$
$$f_{xy}(x, y) = 2x \quad \Rightarrow f_{xy}(1, -2) = 2,$$
$$f_{yy}(x, y) = 0 \quad \Rightarrow f_{yy}(1, -2) = 0,$$
$$f_{xxx}(x, y) = 0 = f_{yyy}(x, y),\ f_{yxx}(1, -2) = 2 = f_{xxy}(1, -2).$$

All higher derivatives are zero.

By Taylor's Theorem,

$$f(x, y) = f(a, b) + [(x - a) f_x(a, b) + (y - b) f_y(a, b)]$$
$$+ \frac{1}{2!}[(x - a)^2 f_{xx}(a, b) + 2(x - a)(y - b) f_{xy}(a, b)$$
$$+ (y - b)^2 f_{yy}(a, b)] + \dots$$

$$\therefore x^2y + 3y - 2 = -10 - 4(x-1) + 4(y+2) + \frac{1}{2}[-4(x-1)^2 + 4(x-1)(y+2) + 0] + \frac{1}{3!}3(x-1)^2(y+2)(2) + 0$$

Hence $x^2y + 3y - 2 = -10 - 4(x-1)$
$$+ 4(y+2) - 2(x-1)^2 + 2(x-1)(y+2) + (x-1)^2(y+2).$$

Example 41:

Expand $x^4 + x^2y^2 - y^4$ about the point (1, 1) upto the terms of the second degree.

Solution:

Let $f(x, y) = x^4 + x^2y^2 - y^4$; $a = b = 1$; $f(1, 1) = 1$

$f_x(x, y) = 4x^2 + 2xy^2 \Rightarrow f_x(1, 1) = 6,$

$f_y(x, y) = 2x^2y - 4y^2 \Rightarrow f_y(1, 1) = -2$

$f_{xx}(x, y) = 12x^2 - 2y^2 \Rightarrow f_{xx}(1, 1) = 14,$

$f_{yy}(x, y) = 2x^2 - 12y^2 \Rightarrow f_{yy}(1, 1) = -10,$

$f_{xy}(x, y) = 2xy \Rightarrow f_{xy}(1, 1) = 4.$

By Taylor's Thoerem

$$f(x, y) = f(1, 1) + \left[\left\{(x-1)\frac{\partial}{\partial x} + (y-1)\frac{\partial}{\partial y}\right\} f(x, y)\right]_{(1,1)} + \frac{1}{2!}\left[\left\{(x-1)\frac{\partial}{\partial x} + (y-1)\frac{\partial}{\partial y}\right\}^2 f(x, y)\right]_{(1,1)} + \ldots..$$

or $x^6 + x^2y^2 - y^4 = 1 + 6(x-1) - 2(y-1)$
$$+ ½[14(x-1)^2 - 10(y-1)^2 + (8(x-1)(y-1)] + \ldots.$$

Example 42:

Show that for $0 < \theta < 1$,

$\sin x \sin y = xy - \frac{1}{6}[(x^3 + 3xy^2)\cos\theta x \sin\theta y + (y^3 + 3x^2y)\sin\theta x \cos\theta y]$.

Solution:

Let $f(x, y) = \sin x \sin y$. Then $f(0, 0) = 0$.

$f_x(x, y) = \cos x \sin y \Rightarrow f_x(0, 0) = 0,$

$f_y(x, y) = \sin x \sin y \Rightarrow f_y(0, 0) = 0,$

$f_{xx}(x, y) = \sin x \sin y \quad \Rightarrow \quad f_{xx}(0, 0) = 0,$

$f_{yy}(x, y) = -\sin x \sin y \;\Rightarrow\; f_{yy}(0, 0) = 0,$

$f_{xy}(x, y) = \cos x \cos y \;\Rightarrow\; f_{xy}(0, 0) = 1,$

$f_{xxx}(x, y) = -\cos x \sin y,\ f_{yyy}(x, y) = -\sin x \cos y,$

$f_{xxy} = -\sin x \cos y,\ f_{xyy} = -\cos x \sin y.$

Now $\left[\left(x\dfrac{\partial}{\partial x} + y\dfrac{\partial}{\partial y}\right) f(x, y)\right]_{(0,0)} = x.0 + y.0 = 0,$

$$\left[\left(x\frac{\partial}{\partial x} + y\frac{\partial}{\partial y}\right)^2 f(x, y)\right]_{(0,0)}$$

$$= \left[\left(x^2\frac{\partial^2}{\partial x^2} + 2xy\frac{\partial^2}{\partial x \partial y} + y^2\frac{\partial^2}{\partial y^2}\right) f(x, y)\right]_{(0,0)} = 2xy,$$

Also $\left[\left(x\dfrac{\partial}{\partial x} + y\dfrac{\partial}{\partial y}\right)^2 f(x, y)\right]_{(\theta x, \theta y)}$

$$= \left[\left(x^3\frac{\partial^3}{\partial x^3} + 3x^2y\frac{\partial^3}{\partial x^3 \partial y} + 3xy^2\frac{\partial^3}{\partial x \partial y^2} + y^3\frac{\partial^3}{\partial y^3}\right) f(x, y)\right]_{(\theta x, \theta y)}$$

$= [(-x^3 - 3xy^2) \cos x \sin y + (-y^3 - 3x^2y) \sin x \cos]\ y(\theta x, \theta y)$

$= -[(x^3 + 3xy^2) \cos (\theta x) \sin (\theta y) + (y^3 + 3x^2y) \sin (\theta x) \cos (\theta y)].$

Putting these values in

$$f(x, y) = f(0, 0) + \left(x\frac{\partial}{\partial y} + y\frac{\partial}{\partial y}\right) f(0, 0) + \frac{1}{2!}\left(x\frac{\partial}{\partial x} + y\frac{\partial}{\partial y}\right)^2 f(0, 0)$$

$$+ \frac{1}{3!}\left(x\frac{\partial}{\partial x} + y\frac{\partial}{\partial y}\right)^3 f(\theta x, \theta y),$$ we get the desired result.

Example 43:

Find the expansion of the polynomial $x^2 + 2x^2y + y^2$ at (1, 1) upto 2nd degree only.

Solution:

Let $f(x, y) = x^3 + 2x^2y + y^3$; $a = b = 1$; $f(a, b) = 4$

$f_x(x, y) = 3x^2 + 4xy \Rightarrow f_x(1, 1) = 7,$

$f_y(x, y) = 2x^2 + 3y^2 \Rightarrow f_y(1, 1) = 5,$

$f_{xx}(x, y) = 6x + 4y \quad \Rightarrow f_{xx}(1, 1) = 10,$

$f_{xy}(x, y) = 4x \quad \Rightarrow f_{xy}(1, 1) = 4,$

$f_{yy}(x, y) = 6y \quad \Rightarrow f_{xy}(1, 1) = 6,$

By Taylor's Theorem,

$$f(x, y) = f(1, 1) + \left[\left\{(x-1)\frac{\partial}{\partial x} + (y-1)\frac{\partial}{\partial y}\right\} f(x, y)\right]_{(1,1)}$$

$$+ \frac{1}{2!}\left[\left\{(x-1)\frac{\partial}{\partial y} + (y-1)\frac{\partial}{\partial y}\right\}^2 f(x, y)\right]_{(1,1)} + \ldots\ldots$$

$$x^3 + 2x^2y + y^3 = 4 + [7(x-1) + 5(y-1)]$$

$$+ \frac{1}{2}[10(x-1)^2 + 6(y-1)^2 + 8(x-1)(y-1)] + \ldots..$$

Example 44:

Prove that

$$\log(x - y) = x - (y + 1) - \frac{1}{2}x^2 + x(y + 1) - \frac{1}{2}(y + 1)^2$$

$$+ \frac{[x-(y+1)]^2}{3[\theta x + 1 - \theta(y+1)^2]}, 0 < \theta < 1.$$

Solution:

Let $f(x, y) = \log(x - y)$; $a = 0$, $b = -1$, $f(a, b) = 0$.

$$\therefore f_x(x, y) = \frac{1}{x-y} \quad \Rightarrow f_x(0, -1) = 1,$$

$$f_y(x, y) = -\frac{1}{x-y} \quad \Rightarrow f_y(0, -1) = -1,$$

$$f_{xx}(x, y) = -\frac{1}{(x-y)^2} \quad \Rightarrow f_{xx}(0, -1) = -1,$$

$$f_{yy}(x, y) = -\frac{1}{(x-y)^2} \quad \Rightarrow f_{yy}(0, -1) = -1,$$

$$f_{xy}(x, y) = \frac{1}{(x-y)^2} \quad \Rightarrow f_{xy}(0, -1) = 1,$$

$$f_{xxx} = \frac{2}{(x-y)^3},\ f_{xxy} = -\frac{2}{(x-y)^3},\ f_{xyy} = \frac{2}{(x-y)^3},$$

$$f_{yyy} = -\frac{2}{(x-y)^3}.$$

We have

$$\left[\left\{x\frac{\partial}{\partial x}+(y+1)\frac{\partial}{\partial y}\right\}f(x,y)\right]_{(0,-1)}=x-(y+1);$$

$$\left[\left\{x\frac{\partial}{\partial x}+(y+1)\frac{\partial}{\partial y}\right\}^2 f(x,y)\right]_{(0,-1)}\quad (xy+1)^2(-1)+2x(y+1).1$$

$$\left\{x\frac{\partial}{\partial x}+(y+1)\frac{\partial}{\partial y}\right\}^2 (0+(x-0)\theta,-1+(y+1)\theta,$$

$$=\frac{2x^3+3x^2(y+1)(-2)+3x(y+1)^2(2)+(y+1)^2(-2)}{(x-y)^3\,[x=\theta x,\ y=-1+(y+1)\theta}$$

$$=\frac{2\{x-(y+1)\}^3}{[\theta x+1-\theta(y+1)]^3}.$$

Putting these values in the Taylor's expansion

$$f(x,y)=f(0,-1)+\left[\left\{x\frac{\partial}{\partial x}+(y+1)\frac{\partial}{\partial y}\right\}f(x,y)\right]_{(0,-1)}$$

$$+\frac{1}{2!}\left[\left\{x\frac{\partial}{\partial x}+(y+1)\frac{\partial}{\partial y}\right\}^2 f(x,y)\right]_{(0,-1)}$$

$$+\frac{1}{3!}\left[\left\{x\frac{\partial}{\partial x}+(y+1)\frac{\partial}{\partial y}\right\}^2 f(\theta x,-1+(y+1)\theta)\right],$$

we get the required result.

Example 45:

Prove that

$$y^x=1+2(y-1)+(x-2)(y-1)+(y-1)^2+\ldots\ldots$$

Solution:

Let $f(x, y) = y^x$ and $a = 2$, $b = 1$. Then $f(a, b) = 1$.

$f_x(x,y)=y^x\log y \Rightarrow f_x(2,1)=0,$

$f_y(x,y)=xy^{x-1} \Rightarrow f_y(2,1)=2,$

$f_{xx}(x,y)=y^x(\log y)^2 \Rightarrow f_{xx}(2,1)=0,$

$f_{yy}(x,y)=x(x-1)\,y^{x-2} \Rightarrow f_{yy}(2,1)=2,$

$f_{xy}(x,y)=y^{x-1}+xy^{x-1}\log y \Rightarrow f_{xy}(2,1)=1.$

By Taylor's expansion,

$$f(x, y) = f(a, b) + \left[(x-a)\frac{\partial}{\partial x} + (y-b)\frac{\partial}{\partial y}\right] f(a, b)$$

$$+ \frac{1}{2!}\left[(x-a)\frac{\partial}{\partial x} + (y-b)\frac{\partial}{\partial y}\right]^2 f(a, b) + \ldots$$

or $$y^x = 1 + [(x-2).0 + (y-1).2] + \frac{1}{2!}[(x-2)^2 f_{xx}(2, 1)$$

$$+ 2(x-2)(y-1) f_{xy}(2, 1) + (y-1)^2 f_{yy'}(2, 1)] + \ldots\ldots$$

$$= 1 + 2(y-1) + \frac{1}{2}[0 + 2(x-2)(y-1).1 + (y-1)^3.2] + \ldots.$$

Hence, $y^x = 1 + 2(y-1) + (x-2)(y-1) + (y-1)^2 + \ldots.$

Example 46:

Prove that the function

$f(x, y) = x^2 - 2xy + y^2 + x^4 + y^4$

has a minima at the origin.

Solution:

$f_x = 2x - 2y + 4x^3$, $f_y = -2x + 2y + 4y^3$

$f_{xx} = 2 + 12x^3$, $f_{xy} = -2$, $f_{yy} = 2 + 12y^2$.

At the origin, $AC - B^2 = f_{xx} f_{yy} - (f_{xy})^2 = 4 - 4 = 0$.

Thus, it is a *doubtful* case and so requires further investigation. We have

$f(x, y) = (x - y)^2 + x^4 + y^4$. Also $f(0, 0) = 0$.

Clearly $f(x, y) > f(0, 0)$ for all values of (x, y) in a deleted nbd of $(0, 0)$. Hence the given function has a minimum at the origin.

Example 47:

Find the maxima and minima of the function

$f(x, y) = x^2 + y^2 - 3x - 12y + 20.$

Solution:

We have

$f_x = 3x^2 - 3$, $f_y = 3y^2 - 12$, $f_{xx} = 6x$, $f_{yy} = 6y$, $f_{xy} = 0$.

To determine the critical points, we solve

$f_x = 0, f_y = 0 \Rightarrow 3x^2 - 3 = 0, 3y^2 - 12 = 0$

$\Rightarrow x = \pm 1, y = \pm 2$. Hence the critical points are

(1, 2), (1 – 2), (–1, 2), (–1, –2).

At (1, 2), $A = f_{xx} = 6 > 0$.

$$AC - B^2 = f_{xx} \cdot f_{yy} - (f_{xy})^2 = 6 \times 12 - 0 = 72 > 0.$$

Thus f has minimum at (1, 2).

At (1, –2), $AC - B^2 = 6 \times -12 - 0 < 0$

Thus, f has neither maximum nor minimum at (1, – 2).

At (–1, 2), $AC - B^2 = -6 \times -12 - 0 < 0$.

Thus, f has neither maximum nor minimum at (–1, 2)

At (–1, –2), $A = -6 < 0$,

$$AC - B^2 = (-6)(-12) - 0 > 0.$$

Thus, f has maximum at (–1, –2).

Example 48:

Discuss the nature of the critical values of

$f(x, y) = x^3 + y^3 - 3x - 12y + 20 = 0.$

Solution:

Do yourself.

Example 49:

Show that the function

$f(x, y) = (x - y)^2 + x^3 - y^3 + x^5$

has neither a maximum nor a minimum at the origin.

Solution:

We have

$f_x = 2(x - y) + 3x^2 + 5x^4$, $f_y = -2(x - y) - 3y^2$,

$f_{xx} = 2 + 6x + 20x^3$, $f_{xy} = -2$, $f_{yy} = 2 - 6y$.

At (0, 0), $f_x = 0$, $f_y = 0$, $f_{xx} = 2$, $f_{xy} = -2$, $f_{yy} = 2$, so that

$f_{xx} f_{yy} - (f_{xy})^2 = 0.$

Thus, it is a doubtful case. We have $f(0, 0) = 0$.

The given function can be rewritten as

$f(x, y) = (x - y)^2 + (x - y)(x^2 + xy + y^2) + x^5.$

For points along the line $y = x$, we have

$$f(x, y) = x^5.$$

Since the power of x is odd here, so in every neighbourhood of (0, 0), there are points at which f(x, y) is positive and there are points at which f(x, y) is negative. [e.g., (ε, ε), (−ε, −ε) where ε > 0].

Hence, f(0, 0) is neither a maximum nor a minimum value.

Example 50:

Discuss the nature of the critical values of

$$f(x, y) = e^x \sin y.$$

Solution:

$$f_x = e^x \sin y,\ f_y = e^x \cos y,\ f_{xx} = e^x \sin y,$$

$$f_{xy} = e^x \cos y,\ f_{yy} = -e^x \sin y.$$

The critical values are given by solving

$$f_x = 0,\ f_y = 0 \Rightarrow f_x - f_y = 0$$

$$\Rightarrow e^x(\sin y - \cos y) = \Rightarrow \sin y = \cos y \ (\because e^x \neq 0\ \forall\ x)$$

Thus, $(x, \frac{1}{4}\pi)$ is a critical point, where $x \in R$ is arbitrary.

We know that $e^x > 0\ \forall\ x \in R$.

$$\text{At } y = \tfrac{1}{4}\pi,\ A = f_{xx} = \frac{1}{\sqrt{2}} e^x > 0 \quad \forall\ x \in R.$$

$$AC - B^2 = f_{xx} f_{yy} - (f_{xy})^2 = e^{zn}\left[\frac{1}{\sqrt{2}}\left(-\frac{1}{\sqrt{2}}\right) - \left(\frac{1}{\sqrt{2}}\right)^2\right]$$

$$= -e^{zn} < 0.$$

Hence, the given function is neither maximum nor minimum at the critical points $\left(x, \frac{1}{4}\pi\right)$, $x \in R$.

Example 51:

Show that $f(x, y) = y^2 + x^2y + x^4$, has a minimum at (0, 0).

Solution:

We have $f_x = 2xy + 4x^3$, $f_y = 2y + x^2$, $f_{xx} = 2y + 12x^2$, $f_{xy} = 2x$, $f_{yy} = 2$.

At (0, 0); $f_x = 0$, $f_y = 0$, $f_{xx} = 0$, $f_{xy} = 0$, $f_{yy} = 2$.

Thus, at the origin $f_{xx} f_{xy} - (f_{xy})^2 = 0$, so that it is a *doubtful* case and requires further investigation. The given function can be rewritten as

$$f(x, y) = (y + \tfrac{1}{2}x^2)^2 + \tfrac{3}{4}x^4 \text{. Also } f(0, 0) = 0.$$

$\therefore f(x, y) - f(0, 0) = (y + \frac{1}{2}x^2)^2 + \frac{3}{4}x^4 > 0,$

for all (x, y) in a deleted nbd of (0, 0).

Hence, f has a minimum at (0, 0).

Example 52:

Show that the function $(y - x)^4 + (x - 2)^4$ has a minimum at (2, 2).

Solution:

Let $f(x, y) = (y - x)^4 + (x - 2)^4$. Then

$$f_x = -4(y - x)^3 + 4(x - 2)^2,\ f_y = 4(y - x)^3,\ f_{yy} = 12(y - x)^2,$$
$$f_{xx} = 12(y - x)^2 + 12(x - 2)^2,\ f_{xy} = -12(y - x)^2.$$

At (2, 2); $f_x = 0$, $f_y = 0$, $f_{xx} = 0$, $f_{yy} = 0$, $f_{xy} = 0$.

$\therefore\quad f_{xx} f_{yy} - (f_{xy})^2 = 0.$

Thus, it is a doubtful case and requires further investigation. We have $f(2, 2) = 0$.

Now, $f(x, y) - f(2, 2) = (y - x)^4 + (x - 2)^4 > 0$ *i.e.*, $f(x, y) < f(2, 2)$ for all values of (x, y) in a deleted nbd. of (2, 2). Hence the given function has a minimum at (2, 2).

Example 53:

Find all the maxima and minima of the function given by

$f(x, y) = x^3 + y^3 - 63(x + y) + 12xy.$

Solution:

We have

$f_x(x, y) = 3x^2 - 63 + 12y,\ \ f_y(x, y) = 3y^2 - 63 + 12x;$

$f_{xx}(x, y) = 6x,\ f_{xy}(x, y) = 12,\ f_{yy}(x, y) = 6y.$

The critical points of f are given by $f_x = 0$, $f_y = 0$.

Thus, $\quad f_x(x, y) = 3x^3 - 63 + 12y = 0$

$$f_x(x, y) - f_y(x, y) = 3(x^2 - y^2) + 12(y - x) = 0$$

or $$x^2 - 21 + 4y = 0,\ (y - x)(4 - y - x) = 0$$

$$\therefore \begin{cases} x^2 - 21 + 4x = 0 \text{ (if } y = x) \\ (x + 7)(x - 3) = 0 \end{cases} \text{and} \begin{cases} x^2 - 21 + 4y = 0, \\ 4 - y - x = 0. \end{cases}$$

Solving these, the four critical points are

(–7, –7), (3, 3), (5, –1), (–1, 5).

At (–7, –7),

$A = f_{xx} = -42 < 0$ and $AC - B^2 = f_{xx} f_{yy} - (f_{xy})^2 = 1620 > 0$

so that the function is maximum at (–7, –7).

At (3, 3),

$A = f_{xx} = 18 > 0$ and $AC - B^2 = f_{xx} f_{yy} - (f_{xy})^2 = 180 > 0$,

so that the function is minimum at (3, 3).

At each of the other points (5, –1) and (–1, 5),

$AC - B^2 = f_{xx} f_{yy} - (f_{xy})^2 = -324 < 0$

so that the function is neither a maximum nor a minimum.

Example 54:

Find the maxima and minima of

$f(x, y) = x^4 + y^4 = 2(x - y)^2.$

Solution:

$f_x = 4x^3 - 4(x - y)$, $f_y = 4y^2 + 4(x - y)$,

$f_{xx} = 12x^2 - 4$, $f_{yy} = 12y^2 - 4$, $f_{xy} = 4$,

For critical points, $f_x = 0$ and $f_y = 0$

$\Rightarrow \quad f_x - f_y = 0 \quad \Rightarrow \quad 4(x^3 - y^3) - 8(x - y) = 0$

$\Rightarrow 4(x - y)(x^2 + y^2 + xy - 2) = 0$

Similarly, $f_x + f_y = 0 \quad \Rightarrow \quad 4(x^3 + y^2) = 0$

$\Rightarrow \quad (x + y)(x^2 - xy + y^2 = 0).$

Taking $x = y$ in $f_x = 0$ and $f_y = 0$, we see that (0, 0) is a critical point for f(x, y).

Taking $y = -x$ in $f_x = 0$ and $f_y = 0$, we see that

$$4x^3 - 8x = 0 \text{ and } 4y^3 - 8y = 0$$

$\Rightarrow \quad x(x^2 - 2) = 0$ and $y(y^2 - 2) = 0$

or $\quad x = \pm\sqrt{2}$, $y = \pm\sqrt{2}$.

Thus $(\sqrt{2}, -\sqrt{2})$, $(-\sqrt{2}, \sqrt{2})$ are the other critical points for f(x, y).

$$\text{At } (\sqrt{2}, -\sqrt{2}),\ A = f_{xx} = 20 > 0$$

And$AC - BC_2 = 20 \times 20 - 4 > 0$

Thus, f has a minimum at $(\sqrt{2}, -\sqrt{2})$.

At $(\sqrt{2}, -\sqrt{2})$, A $f_{xx} = 20 > 0$ and $AC - B^2 > 0$ and so f also has a minimum at $(\sqrt{2}, \sqrt{2})$.

At (0, 0), $AC - B^2 = 0$. So it is a doubtful case which needs further investigation. We see that f(0, 0) = 0.

Since f(x, y) – f(0, 0) does not keep the same sign near the origin, so the given function has neither a maximum nor a minimum at the origin.

Example 55:

Show that of all triangles inscribed in a circle, the ones with maximum area are equilateral.

Solution:

Let ABC be a triangle inscribed in a circle of radius r. Let $\angle A = x$, $\angle B = y$, $\angle C = z$ so that $x + y + z = \pi$. If S denotes the area of ΔABC, then $S = \frac{1}{2}ab \sin z$, where a, b denote the lengths of the sides containing the angle z. We have

$$S = +\tfrac{1}{2}(2r \sin x)(2r \sin y) \sin z$$

or $\dfrac{S}{2r^2} = \sin x \sin y \sin (x + y)$, since $z = p - (x + y)$.

To maximize S, we shall maximize

$$f(x, y) = \sin x \sin y \sin (x + y)$$

f(x, y) has a maximum at $x = y = \frac{1}{3}\pi$.

Thus, $z = \pi - (x + y) \Rightarrow z = \frac{1}{3}\pi$. Hence ΔABC is equilateral.

Example 56:

Show that the function

$f(x, y) = \sin x \sin y \sin (x + y)$

has a maximum at $(\frac{1}{3}\pi, \frac{1}{3}\pi)$ in the interval $(0, \pi)$.

Solution:

$$f(x, y) = \sin x \sin y \sin (x + y).$$

$\therefore \quad f_x = \{\cos x \sin (x + y) + \sin x \cos (x + y)\} \sin y$

or $\quad f_x = \sin (2x + y) \sin y. \qquad ...(1)$

Now, $\quad f_y = \{\cos yu \sin (x + y) + \sin y \cos (x + y)\} \sin x$

or $\quad f_y = \sin (x + 2y) \sin x. \qquad ...(2)$

Again, $f_{xx} = 2 \cos (2x + y) \sin y$, $f_{yy} = 2 \cos (x + 2y) \sin x$,

$\quad f_{xy} = \sin (2x + y) \cos y + \sin y \cos (2x + y)$

or $\quad f_{xy} = \sin (2x + 2y)$.

Now, $f_x = f_y = 0 \Rightarrow \sin(2x + y) = 0 = \sin(x + 2y)$.

($\because \sin x \neq 0, \sin y \neq 0$ for $0 < x, y < \pi$)

Thus, $2x + y = \pi,\ x + 2y = \pi$ ...(3)

($\because 2x + y = 0 = x + 2y \Rightarrow x + y = 0$

$\Rightarrow \sin(x + y) = 0 \Rightarrow f(x, y) = 0$.)

From (3), we get $x = y = \frac{1}{3}\pi$.

Now, $A = f_{xx}\left(\frac{1}{3}\pi, \frac{1}{3}\pi\right) = 2\cos\pi\sin\frac{1}{3}\pi = -\sqrt{3}$,

$B = f_{xy}\left(\frac{1}{3}\pi, \frac{1}{3}\pi\right) = \sin(4\pi/3) = -\tfrac{1}{2}\sqrt{3}$,

$C = f_{yy}\left(\frac{1}{3}\pi, \frac{1}{3}\pi\right) = 2\cos\pi\sin\frac{1}{3}\pi = -\sqrt{3}$.

$\therefore \quad AC - B^2 = 9/4 > 0$ and $A < 0$.

Hence, f(x, y) has a maximum at $\left(\frac{1}{3}\pi, \frac{1}{3}\pi\right)$.

MAXIMA AND MINIMA OF FUNCTIONS OF TWO VARIABLES

Definition 1:

A function f(x, y) is said to have a *maxima* at a point (a, b) if there exists a nbd. N of (a, b) such that

$$f(a + h, b + k) < f(a, b) \quad \forall\ (a + h, b + k) \in N \sim \{(a, b)\}.$$

The set $N \sim \{(a, b)\}$ is called a *deleted nbd.* of (a, b).

Definition 2:

A function f(x, y) is said to have a *minimum* a point (a, b) if there exists a nbd. N of (a, b) such that

$$f(a + h, b + k) < f(a, b)\ \forall\ (a + h, b + k) \in N \sim \{(a, b)\}.$$

Definition 3:

A function f(x, y) is said to have an *extremum* at a point (a, b) if it has either a maximum or minimum at (a, b).

Theorem 1:

If a function f(x, y) has an extremum at any point (a, b) of the domain of f and if f admits of partial derivatives f_x and f_y at (a, b), then

$f_x(a, b) = 0$ *and* $f_y(a, b) = 0$.

Proof:

Suppose f(x, y) has a maximum at (a, b). Then the function f(x, b) of a single variable x must have a maximum at x = a and so

$f_x(x, b) = 0$ when $x = a$ *i.e.*, $f_x(a, b) = 0$.

Again the function $f(a, y)$ of a single variable y must have a maximum at $y = b$ and so

$f_y(a, y) = 0$ when $y = b$ *i.e.*, $f_x(a, b) = 0$.

Exactly similar is the case when f has a minimum at (a, b).

Remark:

The conditions of the above theorem are only necessary but are not sufficient.

Let $f(x, y) = x^2 - y^2$. Then

$f_x(0, 0) = 0$, $f_y(0, 0) = 0$. Also $f(0, 0) = 0$.

Let N be any nbd. of (0, 0). Let $\varepsilon > 0$.

We take two points of N as A $(\frac{1}{2}\varepsilon, 0)$ and B $(0, \frac{1}{2}\varepsilon)$.

At the point A, $f(\frac{1}{2}\varepsilon, 0) = \frac{1}{4}\varepsilon^2 - 0 = \frac{1}{4}\varepsilon^2$.

At the point B, $f(0, \frac{1}{2}\varepsilon) = 0 - \frac{1}{4}\varepsilon^2 = -\frac{1}{4}\varepsilon^2$.

Thus, $f(\frac{1}{2}\varepsilon, 0) - f(0, 0) = \frac{1}{4}\varepsilon^2 - 0 = \frac{1}{4}\varepsilon^2 > 0$,

$$f(0, \tfrac{1}{2}\varepsilon) - f(0, 0) = -\tfrac{1}{4}\varepsilon^2 - 0 = -\tfrac{1}{4}\varepsilon^2 < 0$$

or $$f(\tfrac{1}{2}\varepsilon, 0) > f(0, 0) \text{ and } f(0, \tfrac{1}{2}\varepsilon) < f(0, 0),$$

where $(\frac{1}{2}\varepsilon, 0), (0, \frac{1}{2}\varepsilon) \in N$.

Hence the given function is neither maximum nor minimum at (0, 0).

Definition 4:

A point (a, b) is said to be a *critical point* for a function f(x, y) if f_x and f_y both exist at (a, b) and

$f_x(a, b) = 0$, $f_y(a, b) = 0$.

If (a, b) is a critical point for a function f(x, y), then f(a, b) is called a *stationary value* of f.

Remark:

If f has an extremum at (a, b), then (a, b) is a cretical point but not conversely.

Theorem 2:

Let $f_x(a, b) = 0, f_y(a, b) = 0;$

and $f_{xx}(a, b) = A, f_{xy}(a, b) = B, f_{yy}(a, b) = C$. *Then*

(i) f has minimum at (a, b), if $AC - B^2 > 0$, $A > 0$,

(ii) f has maximum at (a, b), if $AC - B^2 > 0$, $A < 0$,

(iii) f has neither maximum value nor minimum value at (a, b), if $AC - B^2 < 0$.

(In this case, the point (a, b) is called a saddle point.)

(iv) f may or may not have an extremum at (a, b) if $AC - B^2 = 0$.

(The case (iv) is often called the doubtful case, which needs further investigation.)

MAXIMA AND MINIMA SUBJECT TO CONSTRAINTS

First we discuss the method of finding the maxima and minima of a function of three variables.

EXTREME POINTS OF A FUNCTION OF THREE VARIABLES

The extreme point of a function f(x, y, z) of three independent variables x, y, z can be determined by the following:

Rule:

If $df(a, b, c) = f_x\, dx + f_y\, dy + f_z\, dz,$

$$d^2f(a, b, c) = f_{xx}(dx)^2 + f_{yy}(dy)^2 + f_{zz}(dz)^2 + 2f_{xy}\, dx\, dy + f_{yz}\, dy\, dz + 2f_{xz}\, dz\, dx, \text{ then}$$

(i) f(x, y, z) has a ***maximum*** *at a point (a, b, c) if*

$$df = 0 \ (i.e., f_x = f_y = f_z = 0) \text{ and } d^2 f > 0.$$

(ii) f(x, y, z) has a ***minimum*** *at a point (a, b, c) if*

$$df = 0 \ (i.e., f_x = f_y = f_z = 0) \text{ and } d^2f > 0.$$

LAGRANGE'S METHOD OF UNDETERMINED MULTIPLIERS

Suppose we have to find the stationary points of a function f(x, y, z) = 0 subject to the conditions (constraints).

$$\phi_1(x, y, z) = 0 \quad \text{and } \phi_2(x, y, z) = 0. \qquad ...(1)$$

The stationary points of the given function f are given by determining the stationary points of the function F, where

$$F(x, y, z) = f + \lambda_1 \phi_1 + \lambda_2 \phi_2.$$

and considering the variables x, y, z as independent variables. The constants λ_1 and λ_2 are known as *Lagrange's Undetermined Multipliers.*

The stationary points of the function F are given by

$dF = F_x\,dx + F_y\,dy + F_z\,dz = 0$ (*i.e.*, $F_x = F_y = F_z = 0$). ...(2)

The equations (1) and (2) help us to determine the undertermined multipliers λ_1 and λ_2 as well as the extreme points of the given function f(x, y, z).

We shall illustrate the Lagrange's method of undetermined multipliers with the help of examples.

SOLVED EXAMPLES

Example 1:

Find the shortest distance from the origin to the hyperbola

$x^2 + 8xy + 7y^2 = 225,\ z = 0.$

Solution:

We have to find the minimum value of $x^2 + y^2$ (the square of the distance from the origin to any point in the xy-plane) subject to the constraint $x^2 + 8xy + 7y^2 = 225$.

Consider the function

$$F = x^2 + y^2\ \lambda(x^2 + 8xy + 7y^2 - 225). \qquad ...(1)$$

Now, $F_x = (2x + 2x\lambda + 8y\lambda),\ F_y = (2y + 8x\lambda + 14y\lambda)$

$$\left.\begin{aligned} F_x &= 0 \Rightarrow (1+\lambda)\,x + 4\lambda y = 0 \\ F_y &= 0 \Rightarrow 4\lambda x + (1+7\lambda)y = 0 \end{aligned}\right\} \quad \because \lambda = 1; -\frac{1}{9}.$$

Putting, $\lambda = 1,\ x = -2y$ in $x^2 + 8xy + 7y^2 = 225$, we get

$y^2 = -45$. This is impossible

Putting, $\lambda = -\frac{1}{9},\ y = 2x$ in $x^2 + 8xy + 7y^2 = 225$, we get

$$x^2 = 5,\ y^2 = 20, \text{ and so } x^2 + y^2 = 25.$$

Now, $A = F_{xx} = 2(1 + \lambda),\ B = F_{xy} = 8\lambda,\ C = F_{yy} = 2\,(1 + 7\lambda).$

At $\lambda = -1/9,\ A = 16/9 > 0,\ C = 4/9,\ B = -8/9.$

$\therefore\ AC - B^2 = 0$. Putting $\lambda = -1/9$ in (1), we get

$F = \frac{2}{9}(2x - y)^2 + 25 > 0$ for all values of (x, y).

Hence the function $x^2 + y^2$ has a minimum value 25.

Example 2:

Show that the maximum and minimum values of r^2, where

$r^2 = a^2x^2 + b^2y^2 + c^2z^2,$ ...(1)

$x^2 + y^2 + z^2 = 1$ *and* $lx + my + nz = 0$ ...(2)

are given by the equation

$$\frac{l^2}{a^2 - r^2} + \frac{m^2}{b^2 - r^2} + \frac{n^2}{c^2 - r^2} = 0.$$

Solution:

Let us consider the function

$F = (a^2x^2 + b^2y^2 + c^2z^2) + \lambda_1 (x^2 + y^2 + z^2 - 1) + \lambda_2 (lx + my + nz)$

$\therefore \qquad dF = F_a\, dx + f_y\, d_y + F_z\, dz,$

where$F_x = 2a^2x + 2\lambda_1 x + \lambda_z l,$

$F_y = 2b^2y + 2\lambda_1 y + \lambda_2 m,$

$F_z = 2c^2z + 2\lambda_1 z + \lambda_2 n.$

At stationary points.

$F_x = F_z = F_2 = 0.$

$\therefore \qquad xF_x + yF_z + zF_2 = 0$ given us

$2(a^2x^2 + b^2y^2 + c^2z^2) + 2\lambda_1 (x^2 + y^2 + z^2) + \lambda_2 \ (lx + my + nz) = 0$

or $\qquad 2r^2 + 2\lambda_1 = 0$

or $\qquad \lambda_1 = -r^2$, using (1) and (2)

Putting $\lambda_1 = - r^2$ in $F_x = 0$, we obtain

$2(a^2 - r^2) x + \lambda_2 l = 0$ or $x = - \lambda_2 l /2 (a^2 = r^2)$ etc.

$$\therefore \qquad x = \frac{-\lambda_2 l}{2(a^2 - r^2)},\ y = \frac{-\lambda_2 m}{(b^2 - r^2)},\ z = \frac{-\lambda_2 n}{(c^2 - r^2)}$$

Substituting these values in $lx + my + nz = 0$, we obtain

$$\frac{l^2}{a^2 - r^2} + \frac{m^2}{b^2 - r^2} + \frac{n^2}{c^2 - r^2} = 0. \qquad (\because \ \lambda_2 \neq 0)$$

Example 3:

Prove that the volume of the greatest rectangular parallelopiped, that can be inscribed in the ellipsoid

$$\frac{x^2}{a^2} + \frac{y^2}{b^2} + \frac{z^2}{c^2} = 1, \text{ is } \frac{8abc}{3\sqrt{3}}$$

Solution:

The volume of a rectangular parallelopiped of sides 2x, 2y, 2z is 2x. 2y. 2z = 8xyz.

We have to find the greates value of 8xyz subject to the condition

$x^2/a^2 + y^2/b^2 + z^2/c^2 = 1, (x > 0, y > 0, z > 0).$ ...(1)

We consider a function F of three independent variables x, y, z;

$$F = 8xyz + \lambda \left(\frac{x^2}{a^2}+\frac{y^2}{b^2}+\frac{z^2}{c^2}=1\right).$$

We know $dF = F_x\, dx + F_v\, dy + F_z\, dz$

or $dF = \left(8yz+\frac{2x\lambda}{a^2}\right) dx + \left(8zx+\frac{2y\lambda}{b^2}\right) dy + \left(8xy+\frac{2z\lambda}{c^2}\right) dz$

For stationary points, $F_y = F_a = F_z = 0$

$$\Rightarrow \quad 8yz+\frac{2x\lambda}{a^2} = 0,\ 8zx+\frac{2y\lambda}{b^2} = 0,\ 8xy+\frac{2zy}{c^2} = 0, \qquad ...(2)$$

Multiplying these by x, y, z respectively and adding, we get

$$24xyz + 2\lambda \left(\frac{x^2}{a^2}+\frac{y^2}{b^2}+\frac{z^2}{c^2}\right) = 0$$

or $\lambda = -12xyz.,$ using (1)

Putting this value of λ in (2), we get $8a^2yz - 24xyz = 0$ etc.

$\therefore\ x = a/\sqrt{3},\ y = b/\sqrt{3},\ z = c/\sqrt{3},$ and so $\lambda = -4\,abc/\sqrt{3}$ ...(3)

Now $d^2F = Fxx\, dx^2 + F_{yy}\, dy^2 + F_{zz}\, dz^2 + 2F_{xy}\, dx\, dy + 2F_{yz}\, dy\, dz + 2F_{zx}\, dz\, dx$

$$= 2\lambda \left(\frac{dx^2}{a^2}+\frac{dy^2}{b^2}+\frac{dz^2}{c^2}\right) + 16z\, dx\, dy + 16x\, dy\, dz + 16y\, dz\, dx$$

Using (3), we get

$$d^2F = -\frac{8abc}{\sqrt{3}}\sum \frac{1}{a^2}dx^2 + \frac{16}{\sqrt{3}}\sum c\, dx\, dy \qquad ...(4)$$

From (1) and (3), we have

$$2x\frac{dx}{a^2} + 2y\frac{dy}{b^2} + 2z\frac{dz}{c^2} = 0$$

or
$$\frac{2}{\sqrt{3}}\left(\frac{dx}{a}+\frac{dy}{b}+\frac{dz}{c}\right) = 0$$

$$\therefore \left(\frac{dx}{a}+\frac{dy}{b}+\frac{dz}{c}\right)^2 = 0$$

$$\Rightarrow \quad \sum \frac{ax^2}{a^2} + 2\sum \frac{dx\, dy}{ab} = 0$$

Multiplying it throughout by abc, we get

$$abc \sum \frac{dx^2}{a^2} = -2\sum c\, dx\, dy \quad ...(5)$$

From (4) and (5), we obtain

$$\therefore \quad d^2F = -\frac{16}{\sqrt{3}} abc \sum \frac{dx^2}{a^2} < 0.$$

Hence $\left(\frac{a}{\sqrt{3}}, \frac{b}{\sqrt{3}}, \frac{c}{\sqrt{3}}\right)$ is a point of maxima and the maximum value of 8xyz is $\frac{8abc}{3\sqrt{3}}$.

Example 4:

Find the maximum and minimum radii vectors of the section of the surface,

$$(x^2 + y^2 + z^2)^2 = a^2x^2 + b^2y^2 + c^2z^2 \quad ...(1)$$

by the plane $lx + my + nz = 0$. ...(2)

Solution:

We have to find the stationary values of $r^2 = x^2 + y^2 + z^2$ subject to the conditions (1) and (2). Let us consider the function

$$F = (x^2 + y^2 + z^2) + \lambda_2 \{(x^2 + y^2 + z^2)^2 - (a^2x^2 + b^2y^2 + c^2z^2)\} + \lambda_2 (lx + mx + nz)$$

$\therefore dF = F_x dx = F_y dy + F_z dz$, where

$F_x = [2x + \lambda_1 \{4x (x^2 + y^2 + z^2) - 2a^2x\} + \lambda_2 l]$,

$F_y = [2y + \lambda_1 \{4y (x^2 + y^2 + z^2) - 2b^2y\} + \lambda_2 m]$,

$F_z = [2z + \lambda_1 \{4z (x^2 + y^2 + z^2) - 2c^2z\} + \lambda_2 n]$.

At stationary points, $F_x = F_y = F_z = 0$

or $\quad xF_x = yF_y + zF_z = 0$

or $\quad 2(x^2 + y^2 + z^2) + 2\lambda_1 [2(x^2 + y^2 + z^2)^2 - (a^2x^2 + b^2y^2 + c^2z^2)] + \lambda_2 (lx + mx + nz) = 0$

or $\quad (x^2 + y^2 + z^2) + \lambda_1 (x^2 + y^2 + z^2)^2 = 0$; using (1) and (2)

$$\therefore \quad r^2 + \lambda_1 r^4 = 0 \Rightarrow \lambda_1 = -\frac{1}{r^2}$$

Now, $\quad F_x = 0 \Rightarrow 2x - \frac{1}{r^2}(4r^2x - 2a^3x) = -\lambda_2 l.$

$\therefore \quad x = -\dfrac{\lambda_2 l r^2}{2(a^2 - r^2)}$. Similarly $y = -\dfrac{\lambda_2 m r^2}{2(b^2 - r^2)}$, $z = -\dfrac{\lambda_2 n r^2}{2(c^2 - r^2)}$

Substituting these values in lx + my + zx = 0, we get

$$\frac{l^2 r^2}{a^2 - r^2} + \frac{m^2 r^2}{b^2 - r^2} + \frac{n^2 r^2}{c^2 - r^2} = 0$$

Example 5:

Find the maxima and minima of $x^2 + y^2 + z^2 = r^2$ *subject to the conditions* $ax^2 + by^2 + cz^2 = l$ *and* $lx + my + nz = 0$.

$$\left[\textbf{Ans. } \frac{l^2}{ar^2 - 1} + \frac{m^2}{br^2 - 1} + \frac{n^2}{cr^2 - 1} = 0\right]$$

Example 6:

Find the stationary value of $x^2/a^4 + y^2/b^4 + z^2/c^4 = r^2$, when $lx + my + nz = 0$ and $x^2/a^2 + y^2/b^2 + z^2/c^2 = 1$.

$$\left[\textbf{Ans. } \frac{l^2 a^4}{1 - a^2 r^2} + \frac{m^2 b^4}{1 - b^2 r^2} + \frac{n^2 c^4}{1 - a^2 r^2} = 0\right]$$

Example 7:

Show that the length of the axes of the section of the ellipsoid $\dfrac{x^2}{a^2} + \dfrac{y^2}{b^2} + \dfrac{z^2}{c^2} = 1$ *by the plane* $lx + my + nz = 0$ *are the roots of the quadratic in* r^2,

$$\frac{l^2 a^2}{r^2 - a^2} + \frac{m^2 b^2}{r^2 - b^2} + \frac{n^2 c^2}{r^3 - c^2} = 0$$

Solution:

We have to find the stationary values of the function r^2, where $r^2 = x^2 + y^2 + z^2$, subject to the two conditions :

$$\frac{x^2}{a^2} + \frac{y^2}{b^2} + \frac{z^2}{c^2} = 1, \; lx + my + nz = 0 \qquad \text{...(1)}$$

Consider a function F of independent variables x, y, z :

$$F = x^2 + y^2 + z^2 + \lambda_1 \left(\frac{x^2}{a^2} + \frac{y^2}{b^2} + \frac{z^2}{c^2} = 1\right) + 2\lambda_2 (lx + my + nz)$$

Then $dF = F_x\, dx + F_y\, d_y + F_z\, dz$

or $dF = 2\left(x + \dfrac{x\lambda_1}{a^2} + \lambda_2 l\right) dx + 2\left(y + \dfrac{x\lambda_1}{b^2} + \lambda_2 m\right) dy$

$$+ \left(z + \frac{z\lambda_1}{c^2} + \lambda_2 n\right) dz$$

For stationary points, $F_x = F_y = F_z = 0$

$$x + \frac{x}{a^3}\lambda_1 + l\lambda_2 = 0,\ y + \frac{y}{b^2}\lambda_1 + m\lambda_2 = 0,\ z + \frac{z}{c^2}\lambda_1 + n\lambda_2 = 0, \quad ...(2)$$

Multiplying these by x, y, z respectively and adding, we get

$$(x^2 + y^2 + z^2)\lambda_1\left(\frac{x^2}{a^2} + \frac{y^2}{b^2} + \frac{z^2}{c^2}\right) + \lambda^2 (lx + my + nz) = 0$$

or $\quad r^2 + \lambda_1 = 0, \quad$ [using (1)]. $\quad \therefore\ \lambda_1 = r^2.$

Putting $\lambda_1 = r^2$ in (2), $\quad x\left(1 - \frac{r^2}{a^2}\right) + l\lambda_2 = 0$

$$\Rightarrow \quad x = \frac{a^2 l\lambda_2}{r^2 - a^2} \text{etc.}$$

$$\text{Thus } x = \frac{a^2 l\lambda_2}{r^2 - a^2},\ y = \frac{b^2 m\lambda_2}{r^2 - b^2},\ z = \frac{c^2 n\lambda_2}{r^2 - c^2}$$

$$\therefore\ 0 = l_x + m_y + n_z = \lambda_2\left\{\frac{a^2 l^2}{r^2 - a^2} + \frac{b^2 m^2}{r^2 - b^2} + \frac{c^2 n^2}{r^2 - c^2}\right\}$$

Hence, $$\frac{a^2 l^2}{r^2 - a^2} + \frac{b^2 m^2}{r^2 - b^2} + \frac{c^2 n^2}{r^2 - c^2} = 0 \quad (\because\ \lambda_2 \neq 0)$$

Example 8:

Show that the maximum and minimum values of the function $f(x, y) = x^2 + xy + y^2$, when $ax^2 + by^2 = ab$ will be the values of θ given by the equation

$$4(\theta - a)(\theta - b) = ab.$$

Solution:

Let $F = x^2 + xy + y^2 + \lambda(ax^2 + by^2 - ab)$,

$\therefore\ F_x = 2x + y + 2\lambda ax,\ F_y = x + 2y + 2\lambda by.$

At a stationary value, $F_x = F_y = 0$ ...(1)

$\therefore \quad xF_x + yF_y = 0$ gives that

$2(x^2 + xy + y^2) + 2\lambda(ax^2 + by^2) = 0$

or $\quad 2f + 2\lambda ab = 0, \quad$ where $f = x^2 + xy + y^2$.

or $\quad \lambda = -f/ab$. Putting this value of λ in (1).

$2x + y - 2fx/b = 0,\ x + 2y - 2fy/a = 0$

or $\quad 2bx + by = 2fx,\ ax + 2ay = 2fy$

or $\quad 2(b - f)x - by,\ ax = 2(f - a)y$

$$\therefore \quad \frac{2(b-f)}{a} = \frac{-b}{2(f-a)}$$

or $$4(f-b)(f-a) = ab$$

Replacing f by θ, we get

$$4(\theta-a)(\theta-b) = ab$$

where θ gives the maximum and minimum values of f.

Example 9:

If the variables x, y z satisfy the equation

$$\phi(x)\phi(y)\phi(z) = k^2$$

and $\phi(a) = \kappa \neq 0$, $\phi'(a) \neq 0$, *show that the function*

$$f(x) + f(y) + f(z)$$

has a maximum, when $x = y = z = a$, *provided that*

$$f'(a)\left\{\frac{\phi'(a)}{\phi'(a)} - \frac{\phi'(a)}{\phi'(a)}\right\} > f'(a).$$

Solution:

Let $F = f(x) + f(y) + f(z) + \lambda\{\phi(x)\phi(y)\phi(z) - k^2\}$

$\therefore$ $$dF = F_x dx + F_y dy + F_z dz$$

or $$dF = \Sigma\ \{f(x) + \lambda\phi'(x)\phi(y)\phi(z)\}dx.$$

At stationary points.

$$\left.\begin{aligned} f'(x) + \lambda\phi'(x)\phi(y)\phi(z) &= 0, \\ f'(y) + \lambda\phi'(y)\phi(z)\phi(x) &= 0, \end{aligned}\right\}$$

$f'(z) + \lambda\phi'(z)\phi(x)\phi(y) = 0$

Since the function has a maximum at (a, a, a), therefore

$$f'(a) + \lambda\phi'(a)\phi(a)\phi(a) = 0$$

or $$\lambda = -\frac{f'(a)}{\phi'(a)\{\phi(a)\}^2} = \frac{f'(a)}{k^2\phi'(a)} \qquad [\because \phi'(a) \neq 0, \phi(a) = k \neq 0]$$

...(1)

Now, $d^2 F = \Sigma\ F_{xx} dx^2 + 2\ \Sigma\ F_{xy} dxdy$

or $d^2 F = \Sigma\{f''(a) + \lambda\phi''(x)\phi(y)\phi(z)\}\ dx^2 + 2\lambda\Sigma\phi'(x)\phi'(y)\phi(z)\ dx\ dy.$

At the stationary point (a, a, a),

$d^2 F = \{f''(a) + \lambda k^2\phi''(a)\}\ \Sigma dx^2 + zk\ [\phi'(a)]^2\ \Sigma\ dx\ dy\ (\because \phi(a) = k)$ ...(2)

Now, $\phi(x)\phi(y)\phi(z) = k^2 \Rightarrow \Sigma\phi'(x)\phi(y)\phi(z)\ dx = 0$

$\Rightarrow \quad k^2\phi'(a)(dx + dy + dz) = 0$, at $\quad (0, a)$

$\Rightarrow \quad dx + dy + dz = 0 \quad (\because k \neq 0, \phi'(a) \neq 0)$

$\Rightarrow \quad (dx + dy + dz)^2 = 0$

$\Rightarrow \quad 2\Sigma d\ \ y = -\Sigma dx^2. \quad ...(3)$

From (2) and (3), we obtain

$d^2 F = \{f''(a) + \lambda k^2\phi''(a)\} \Sigma dx^2 - \lambda k [\phi'(a)]^2 \Sigma dx^2$

$$= \left[f''(a) - f'(a)\frac{\phi''(a)}{\phi'(a)} + f'(a)\frac{\phi'(a)}{\phi(a)} \right] \sum dx^2, \text{ using (1)}$$

For a maximum value at (a, a, a), we have $d^2F<0$

$$\Rightarrow \quad f''(a) - f'(a)\left\{\frac{\phi''(a)}{\phi'(a)} - \frac{\phi'(a)}{\phi(a)}\right\} < 0$$

$$\Rightarrow \quad f''(a) < f'(a)\left\{\frac{\phi''(a)}{\phi'(a)} - \frac{\phi'(a)}{\phi(a)}\right\}.$$

Hence,

$$f'(a)\left\{\frac{\phi''(a)}{\phi'(a)} - \frac{\phi'(a)}{\phi(a)}\right\} > f''(a).$$

Example 10:

If $lx + my + mz = 1$; l, m, n are positive constants, show that the stationary value of $xy + yz + zx$ is

$[2\,lm + 2mn + 2nl - l^2 - m^2 - n^2]^{-1}$

and this value is maximum when it is positive.

Solution:

Let $F = xy + yz + zx + \lambda\,(lx + my + nz - 1)$. Then

$F_x = y + z + \lambda l$, $F_y = z + x + \lambda m$, $F_z = x + y + \lambda n$.

At a stationary value, $F_x = F_y = F_z = 0$. ...(1)

Now $xF_x = yF_y = zF_z = 0$ gives that

$2\,(xy + yz + zx) + \lambda\,(lx + my + nz) = 0$.

$\therefore \lambda = -2f$, where $f = (xy + yz + zx)$. Putting in (1), we get

$y + z = 2lf$, $z + x = 2mf$, $x + y = 2nf$. ...(2)

Adding these equations, we obtain

$x + y + z = (l + m + n)\,f$. ...(3)

from (2) and (3), we get

$x = (m + n - l)f\ (n + l - m)f,\ z = (l + m - n)f.$

Putting these values of x, y, z in $f = xy + yz + zx$, we get

$f = [(m + n - l)\ (n + l - m)(l + m - n) + (l + m - n)(\ m + n - l)f^2$

$= (2mn + 2nl + 2lm - l^2 - m^2 - n^2)^2.$

Hence, $f = [2lm + 2mn + 2nl - l^2 - m^2 - n^2]^{-1}.$ $(\because f \neq 0)$

We have $F_{xx} = F_{yy} = F_{zz} = 0,\ F_{xy} = F_{yz} = F_{zx} = 1.$

If $\phi = lx + my + nz$, then

$\phi_x = l,\ \phi_y = m, = \phi_z,\ a$

For maximum value of $xy + yz + zx$, we have $d^2F < 0$,

Equivalently, $$\begin{vmatrix} F_{xx} & F_{xy} & F_{xz} & \phi_x \\ F_{yx} & F_{yy} & F_{yz} & \phi_y \\ F_{zx} & F_{zy} & F_{zz} & \phi_z \\ \phi_x & \phi_y & \phi_z & 0 \end{vmatrix} < 0$$

$$\Rightarrow \begin{vmatrix} 0 & 1 & 1 & 1 \\ 1 & 0 & 1 & m \\ 1 & 1 & 0 & n \\ l & m & n & 0 \end{vmatrix} < 0 \Rightarrow [l^2 + m^2 + n^2 - 2mn - 2nl - 2lm] < 0$$
$$\Rightarrow [2mn + 2nl + 2lm - l^2 - m^2 - n^2] > 0$$

Hence $[2mn + 2nl + 2lm - l^2 - m^2 - n^2]^{-1} > 0$

Example 11:

If $1/x + 1/y + 1/z = 1$, show that the stationary value of $a^3x^2 + b^3y^2 + c^3z^2$ is given by

$x = (a + b + c)/a,\ y = (a + b + c)/b,\ z = (a + b + c)/c.$

Solution:

Let $F = (a^3x^2 + b^3y^2 + c^3z^2) + \lambda(1/x + 1/y + 1/z).$

$\therefore Fx = 2a^3x - \lambda(1/x^2),\ F_y = 2b^3y - \lambda(1/y^2),\ Fz = 2c^3z - (1/z^2)$ ...(1)

As a stationary value, $F_x = F_y = F_z = 0.$ ...(2)

$\therefore$ $xF_x = yF_y = zF_z = 0$ gives that

$2(a^3x^2 + b^3y^2 = c^3z^2) - \lambda(1/x + 1/y + 1/z) = 0$

or $2f - \lambda = 0 \Rightarrow \lambda = 2f$, where $f = a^3x^2 + b^3y^2 = c^3z^2.$

From (1) and (2),

$$2a^3x^3 + 2b^3y^3 = c^3z^2 \ (= \lambda)$$

$\therefore$ $\quad ax = by = cz = (k, \text{say}) \qquad \ldots(3)$

$\Rightarrow$ $\quad 1/x = a/k,\ 1/y = b/k,\ 1/z = c/k$

$\Rightarrow$ $\quad 1 = 1/x + 1/y,\ 1/z + 1/k\ (a + b + c)$

$\Rightarrow$ $\quad k = (a + b + c).$

Putting this value of k in (3), we get

$x = (a + b + c)/a,\ y = (a + b + c)/b,\ z = (a + b + c)/c.$

Example 12:

Examine the equation $y^2 + yx^2 + x^3 = 0$ for the existence of a unique solution of the form $y = g(x)$ near the origin, and verify by direct calculation.

Solution:

Let $f(x, y) = y^2 + yx^3 + x^2$. Then $f_y(x, y) = 2y + x^2$.

Since $f_y(0, 0) = 0$, the function f does not satisfy the conditions of the Implicit function theorem and so f may or may not possess a unique solution in any nbd. of (0, 0).

Solving $y^2 + yx^3 + x^2 = 0$ for y, we obtain

$$y = \frac{1}{2}\{-x^3 \pm \sqrt{(x^4 - 4x^2)}\}$$

or

$$y = \frac{1}{2}\ (-x^3 \pm |\,x\,|\,\sqrt{(x^4 - 4)}\}.$$

Now, $\quad |\,x\,| < \sqrt{2} \Rightarrow x^4 - 4 < 0$. Thus

$x^6 - 4x^2 < 0$ for $0 < |\,x\,| < \sqrt{2}$.

So $\quad f(x, y) = 0$ has no solution of $0 < |\,x\,| < \sqrt{2}$.

Hence the equation $f(x, y) = 0$ does not possess a solution by any nbd. of (0, 0).

Example 13:

Examine the equation $x^2 + y^2 - 1 = 0$ for existence of unique solutions at the points ($\pm$ 1, 0) and (0, $\pm$ 1). Also find the solutions whenever they exist.

Solution:

Let $f(x, y) = x^2 + y^2 - 1$ so that $f_y(x, y) = 2y$.

At (0, 1) :

(i) $f(0, 1) = 0$,

(ii) $f_y(0, 1) = 2 \neq 0$,

(iii) obviously f_x, f_y are continuous in a nbd. of (0, 1).

Thus f(x, y) = 0 has a unique solution near (0, 1)

Solving $x^2 + y^2 = 1$, $y = \pm\sqrt{1 - x^2}$. But $y = g_1(x) = \sqrt{1 - x^2}$ in the unique solution, since g(0) = 1.

At (0, –1) : it can similarly be shown that $y = g_2(x) = -\sqrt{1 - x^2}$ is the unique solution, since g(0) = 1.

At (1, 0), we notice that $f_y(1, 0) = 0$. Thus the function f does not satisfy the conditions of Implicit function theorem and so f may or may not possess a unique solution in any nbd. of (0, 0).

Solving $x^2 + y^2 - 1 = 0$, $y = \pm\sqrt{(1 - x^2)}$,

Since neither of the functions $y = \sqrt{(1 - x^2)}$ and $y = -\sqrt{(1 - x^2)}$ is defined for $|x| < 1$, so f(x, y) = 0 does not have any solution in any *nbd.* of (1, 0).

Similarly, it can be shown that f(x, y) = 0 does not have any solution in any nbd. of (–1, 0).

Example 14:

Show that the equation $y^2 - yx^2 - 2x^5 = 0$ has a unique solution $y = g(x)$ near the point (1, –1), and find g'(x) at (1, 1). Verify by direct calculation.

Solution:

Let $f(x, y) = y^2 - yx^2 - 2x^5$

$\therefore f_x(x, y) = -2xy - 10x^4$, $f_y(x, y) = 2y - x^2$. Now

(i) f(1, –1) = 0,

(ii) $f_y(1, -1) = -3 \neq 0$,

(iii) f_x and f_y are continuous for all $(x, y) \in R^2$ and so in a nbd. of (1, –1).

Thus f(x, y) = 0 has a unique solution y = g (x) in some nbd. of (1, –1).

By solving the equation $y^2 - yx^2 - 2x^5 = 0$ for y in terms of x,

$$y = \tfrac{1}{2}\left(x^2 \pm \sqrt{x^4 + 8x^5}\right) = \tfrac{1}{2}x^2\left(1 \pm \sqrt{1 + 8x}\right),\ x > -\tfrac{1}{3}.$$

Out of these two possible solutions,

$y = \frac{1}{2}x^2\left(1 - \sqrt{1+8x}\right) = g(x)$

is the unique solution of f(x, y) = 0 for $x > -\frac{1}{8}$, since g(1) = –1.

Now $g'(x) = -\frac{f_x(x, y)}{f_y(x, y)} = \frac{2xy + 10x^4}{2y - x^2}$.

At (1, –1), g'(x) = –8/3.

Example 15:

Show that the equation 2xy – log xy = 2 determines a unique solution near (1, 1). Find the first derivative of the solution at (1, 1).

Solution:

Let f(x, y) = 2xy – log xy – 2.

$\therefore f_x(x, y) = 2y - (1/x)$, $f_y(x, y) = 2x - (1/y)$. Now

(i) f(1, 1) = 0,

(ii) $f_y(1, 1) = 1 \neq 0$

(iii) Clearly f_x and f_y are continuous in a *nbd.* of (1, 1).

Hence by the Implicit function theorem, f(x, y) = 0 has a unique solution near (1, 1). We have

$$g'(x) = -\frac{f_x}{f_y} = \frac{2y - 1/x}{2x - 1/y} = \frac{y}{x}.$$

At (1, 1); g'(x) = 1.

Example 16:

Show that the equation $x^3 - y^3 - 3xy - y = 0$ has a unique solution y = g(x) near the point (2, 1), and find g'(x).

Solution:

Let $f(x, y) = x^3 - y^2 - 3xy - y$.

$\therefore f_x(x, y) = 3x^3 - 3y$, $f_y(x, y) = -3y^2 - 3x - 1$. Now

(i) $f_x(2, 1) = 0$,

(ii) $f_y(2, 1) = -10 \neq 0$,

(iii) f_x and f_y are continuous for all $(x, y) \in R^2$ and so in a nbd of (2, 1). Hence by the Implicit function theorem, f(x, y) = 0 has a unique solution y = g(x) in some nbd. of (2, 1). We have

$g'(x) = -f_x/f_y = 3(x^2-y)/(3y^2 + 3x + 1)$.

Example 17:

Show that the equation

$ax + by + Ax^2 + Hxy + By^2 = 0 \quad (b \neq 0)$

determines a unique solution near (0, 0). Find the first derivative of the solution at (0, 0).

Solution:

Let $f(x, y) = ax + by + Ax^2 + Hxy + By^2$.

$\therefore$ $f_x(x, y) = a + 2Ax + Hy$, $f_y(x, y) = b + Hx + 2By$. Now

(i) $f(0, 0) = 0$,

(ii) $f_y(0, 0) = b \neq 0$,

(iii) f_x and f_y are obviously continuous in a nbd. of (0, 0). So by the Implicit function theorem, $f(x, y) = 0$ has a unique solution $y = g(x)$ near (0, 0). Now

$$g'(x) = -\frac{f_x}{f_y} = \frac{a + 2Ax + Hy}{b + Hx + 2By}.$$

At (0, 0), $g'(x) = -a/b$.

Example 18:

Show that the equation $x^3 + xy + y^2 - 1 = 0$ determines a unique implicit function in a neighbourhood of (1, 0).

Solution:

Let $f(x, y) = x^3 + xy + y^2 - 1$.

$\therefore$ $f_x = 3x^2 + y$, $f_y = x + 2y$. Now

(i) $f(1, 0) = 0$, (ii) $f_y(1, 0) = 1 \neq 0$,

(iii) f_x and f_y are continuous for all $(x, y) \in R^2$ and so in a nbd. of (1, 0)

Hence by the Implicit function theorem, $f(x, y) = 0$ has a unique solution $y = g(x)$ in some nbd. of (1, 0). Solving $x^3 + xy + y^2 - 1 = 0$ for y in terms of x, we obtain

$y = \frac{1}{2}(-x \pm \sqrt{[x^2 - 4(x^5 - 1)]})$

Out of these two possible solutions,

$y = \frac{1}{2}(-x + \sqrt{[x^2 - 4(x^3 - 1)]}) = g(x)$

is the unique solution of $f(x, y) = 0$, since $g(1) = 0$.

Example 19:

Show that the equation $y^3 + x^3 - 3xy + y = 0$ determines a unique implicit function near the origin satisfying the properties laid down in the implicit function theorem.

Solution:

Let $f(x, y) = y^3 + x^3 - 3xy + y$.

$\therefore$ $f_x = 3x^2 - 3y$, $f_y = 3y^2 - 3x + 1$. Now

(i) $f(0, 0) = 0$, (ii) $f_y(0, 0) = 1 \neq 0$,

(iii) f_x and f_y are continuous for all $(x, y) \in R^2$ and so in a nbd of (0, 0).

Hence by the Implicit Function Theorem, $f(x, y) = 0$ has a unique solution $y = s(x)$ in some nbd. of (0, 0).

Example 20:

Show that the function $f(x, y) = 2x^4 - 3x^2y + y^2$ has neither a maximum nor a minimum at (0, 0).

Solution:

$$f_x(x, y) - 8x^3 - 6xy,\ f_y(x, y) = -3x^2 + 2y.$$

$$\therefore \quad f_x(0, 0) = 0 = f_y(0, 0)$$

$$\text{Now} f_{xx}(x, y) = 24x^2 - 6y = 0, \text{ at } (0, 0)$$

$$f_{xy}(x, y) = -6x = 0, \text{ at } (0, 0)$$

$$f_{yy}(x, y) = 2, \text{ at } (0, 0)$$

At (0, 0), $f_{xx}, f_{yy} - (f_{xy})^2 = 0$.

Thus it is a doubtful case, and so requires further examination.

We have $f(x, y) = (x^2 - y)(2x^2 - y)$, $f(0, 0) = 0$.

$$\therefore \quad f(x, y) - f(0, 0) = (x^2 - y)(2x^2 - y)$$

$$> 0, \text{ for } y < 0 \text{ or } x^2 > y > 0$$

$$< 0, \text{ for } y > x^2 > \tfrac{1}{2}y > 0.$$

We observe that $f(x, y) - f(0, 0)$ does not keep the same sign near the origin. Hence the given function has neither a maximum nor a minimum value at (0, 0).

Example 21:

Investigate the maxima and minima of

$f(x, y) = x^2 + 3xy + y^2 + x^3 + y^2$.

Solution:

$$f_x = 2x + 3y + 3x^2,\ f_y = 3x + 2y + 3y^3,$$
$$f_{xx} = 2 + 6x,\ f_{yy} = 2 + 6y,\ f_{xy} = 3.$$

For critical points, we have $f_x = 0$ and $f_y = 0$

$\Rightarrow$ $f_x - f_y = 0$

$\Rightarrow$ $(y - x) - 3(y^2 - x^2) = 0$

$\Rightarrow$ $(y - x)(1 - 3y - 3x) = 0$

$\Rightarrow$ $x = y$ or $3x + 3y = 1$.

Taking $x = y$ in $f_x = 0$, $f_y = 0$, we obtain

$5x + 3x^2 = 0$

$\Rightarrow$ $x = 0,\ -5/3$.

So two critical points are $(0, 0)$, $(-5/3, -5/3)$.

It can be verified that on solving

$\{3x + 3y = 1, f_x = 0\}$, $(3x + 3y = 1, f_y = 0\}$,

we get imaginary points (and so are discarded).

At $(-5/3, -5/3)$, $A = f_{xx} = -8 < 0$ and

$AC - B^2 = (-8)(-8) - 9 = 55 > 0$.

Hence the given function has a maximum at $(-5/3, -5/3)$.

At $(0, 0)$, $AC - B^2 = 4 - 9 = -5 < 0$.

Hence the given function has neither a maximum nor a minimum at $(0, 0)$.

Example 22:

Show that the function $f(x, y) = x^2 - 3xy^2 + 2y^4$ has neither a maximum nor a minimum value at the origin.

Solution:

$f_x = 2x - 3y^2$, $f_y = -6xy + 8y^2$, $f_{xx} = 2$,

$f_{yy} = -6x + 24y^2$, $f_{xy} = -6y$.

At $(0, 0)$, $AC - B^2 = f_{xx},\quad f_{yy} - (f_{xy})^2 = 0$.

Thus, it is a *doubtful* case and so needs further investigation. We have $f(0, 0) = 0$.

Clearly $f(x, y) = (x - y^2)(x - 2y^2)$

$\therefore \quad f(x, y) - f(0, 0) = (x - y^2)(x - 2y^2)$

$$> 0, \begin{cases} \text{for } y^2 > x \text{ (and so } 2y^2 > x) \\ \text{or} \\ \text{for } y^2 < \frac{1}{2}x \text{ (and so } y^2 < x) \end{cases}$$

$$< 0, \text{ for } \tfrac{1}{2}x < y^2 < x.$$

Thus, we observe that f(x, y) – f(0, 0) does not keep the same sign near the origin and so the given function has neither a maximum nor a minimum value at the origin.

EXERCISES

1. Show that the function f(z) = xy + iy is everywhere continuous but is not analytic.
2. If n is real, show that $r^n(\cos n\theta + i \sin n\theta)$ is analytic except possibly when r = 0 and that its derivative is

   $nr^{n-1}[\cos(n-1)\theta + i \sin(n-1)\theta]$.
3. Show that the function $e^x(\cos y + i \sin y)$ is holomorphic and find its derivative.

   Ans. e^z.
4. If $f(z) = \dfrac{xy^2(x+iy)}{x^2+y^4}$, $z \neq 0$, $f(0) = 0$, prove that

   $\dfrac{f(z)-f(0)}{z} \to 0$ as $z \to 0$ along any radius vector but not as $z \to 0$ in any manner.
5. Examine the nature of the function

   $f(z) = \dfrac{x^2y^5(x+iy)}{x^4+y^{10}}$, $z \neq 0$, $f(0) = 0$ in a region including origin.
6. Prove that $w = |z|^2$ is continuous everywhere but nowhere differentiable except at origin.
7. Show that an analytic function with constant modulus is constant.

   Or

   Show that an analytic function cannot have a constant modulus without reducing to a constant.
8. If $\phi(z)$ and $\phi(z)$ are analytic functions in a domain D, prove that $\phi(z) = \phi(z)$ and $\phi(z)\,\phi(z)$ are also analytic in D. Also prove that $\phi(z)/\phi(z)$

is analytic in D, provided that $\phi(z)$ does not vanish there.

9. For what values of z the function w defined by $z = e—(\cos u + i \sin u)$ where $w = u + iv$ ceases to be analytic?

   Ans. $z = 0$.

10. For what values of z do the function w defined by the following equations cease to be analytic :

    (i) $z = \sinh u \cos v + i \cosh u \sin v$, $w = u + iv$

    (ii) $z = \sin u \cosh v + i \cos u \sinh v$, $w = u + iv$.

    Ans. (i) $z = \pm i$; (ii) $z = \pm 1$.

11. For what values of z, the function w defined by $z = \log \rho + i\phi$ where $w = \rho (\cos \phi + i \sin \phi)$ ceases to be analytic?

    Ans. Analytic in any finite domain.

12. Prove that $u = y^3 - 3x^2y$ is a harmonic function. Determine its harmonic conjugate and find the corresponding analytic function f(z) in terms of z.

    Ans. $v = -3xy^2 + x^3 + c$, where c is a real constant; $f(z) = i(z^3 + c)$.

13. If $u = e^x(x \cos y - y \sin y)$, find the analytic function $u + iv$.

    Ans. $f(z) = u + iv = ze^z + c$.

14. If ϕ and ψ are functions of x and y satisfying Laplace's Equation, show that $s + it$ is analytic, where

    $$s = \frac{\partial \phi}{\partial y} - \frac{\partial \psi}{\partial x} \text{ and } t = \frac{\partial \phi}{\partial x} + \frac{\partial \psi}{\partial y}.$$

15. Show that a harmonic function satisfies the formal differential equation

    $$\frac{\partial^2 u}{\partial z\, \partial \bar{z}} = 0.$$

16. If $u = (x - 1)^3 - 3xy^2 + 3y^2$, determine v so that $u + iv$ is a regular function of $x + iy$.

    Ans. $v = 3x^2y - 6xy + 3y - y^3 + c$, where c is a real constant.

17. Prove that if $u = x^2 - y^2$, $v = -y/(x^2 + y^2)$ both u and v satisfy Laplace's Equation but $u + iv$ is not an analytic function of z.

18. Show that the function

    $u = \sin x \cosh y + 2 \cos x \sinh y + x^2 - y^2 + 4xy$

    satisfies Laplace's equation and find the corresponding analytic function $u + iv$.

Ans. $f(z) = u + iv = \sin z + z^2 - 2i(\sin z + z^2) + c.$

19. Find the analytic function f(z) of which the real part is
$e^{-x}\{(x^2 - y^2)\cos y + 2xy \sin y\}$.

Ans. $f(z) = z^2e^{-z} + c.$

20. Construct the analytic function $f(z) = u + iv$ where
(i) $u = x^3 - 3xy^2 + 3x + 1$
(ii) $u = y^3 - 3x^2y$
(iii) $u = \sin x \cosh y$.

Ans. (i) $f(z) = z^3 + 3z + 1 + ci$;
(ii) $f(z) = i(z^3 + c)$
(iii) $f(z) = \sin z + ci.$

21. Show that $u = x^3 - 3xy^2 + 3x^2 - 3y^2 + 1$ is a harmonic function and find the corresponding analytic function $f(z) = u + iv$.

Ans. $f(z) = z^3 + 3z^2 + 1 + ic.$

22. What is the real component u of the function $f(z) = u + iv = \sinh(e^z)$ and show that u is harmonic everywhere?

Ans. $u = \sinh(e^x \cos y)\cos(e^x \sin y).$

23. If $f(z) = u + iv$ and $u - v = e^x(\cos y - \sin y)$, find f(z) in terms of z.

Ans. $f(z) = e^z + c.$

24. If $u - v = (x - y)(x^2 + 4xy + y^2)$ and $f(z) = u + iv$ is an analytic function of $z = x + iy$, find f(z) in terms of z.

Ans. $f(z) = -iz^3 + c.$

25. If $f(z) = u + iv$ is an analytic function of $z = x + iy$ and
$u - v = \dfrac{e^y - \cos x + \sin x}{\cosh y - \cos x}$, find f(z) subject to the condition
$f\left(\dfrac{\pi}{2}\right) = \dfrac{3-i}{2}$.

Ans. $f(z) = \cot\dfrac{1}{2}z + \dfrac{1}{2}(1-i).$

26. If $f(z) = u + iv$ is an analytic function of $z = x + iy$ and ψ any function of x and y with differential coefficients of the first and second orders, prove that

(i) $\left(\frac{\partial\psi}{\partial x}\right)^2 + \left(\frac{\partial\psi}{\partial y}\right)^2 = \left\{\left(\frac{\partial\psi}{\partial u}\right)^2 + \left(\frac{\partial\psi}{\partial v}\right)^2\right\} |f'(z)|^2$

(ii) $\frac{\partial^2\psi}{\partial x^2} + \frac{\partial^2\psi}{\partial y^2} = \left(\frac{\partial^2\psi}{\partial u^2} + \frac{\partial^2\psi}{\partial v^2}\right) |f'(z)|^2.$

27. If f(z) is a regular function of z, prove that

$$\left(\frac{\partial^2}{\partial x^2} + \frac{\partial^2}{\partial y^2}\right) |f(z)|^2 = 4|f'(z)|^2.$$

28. If w = f(z) is a regular function of z, prove that

$$\left(\frac{\partial^2}{\partial x^2} + \frac{\partial^2}{\partial y^2}\right) \log |f'(z)| = 0.$$

If $|f'(z)|$ is the product of a function of x and a function of y, show that

$f'(z) = \exp(\alpha z^2 + \beta z + \gamma)$,

where α is a real and β, γ are complex constants.

29. If f(z) = u + iv is analytic function of z in any domain, prove that

(i) $\left(\frac{\partial^2}{\partial x^2} + \frac{\partial^2}{\partial y^2}\right) |u|^p = p(p-1)\ |u|^{p-2}|\ f'(z)|^2.$